STRATEGY AND MANAGEMENT OF
INDUSTRIAL BRANDS

This book was first published in France in October 1998, Publi-Union éditions, Paris.
Translated and published with permission of Publi-Union.

STRATEGY AND MANAGEMENT OF
INDUSTRIAL BRANDS

Business to Business
Products and Services

by

PHILIPPE MALAVAL

Toulouse Business School (ESC Toulouse), France

With the collaboration of
Christophe Bénaroya

KLUWER ACADEMIC PUBLISHERS
Boston/Dordrecht/London

Distributors for North, Central and South America:
Kluwer Academic Publishers
101 Philip Drive
Assinippi Park
Telephone (781) 871-6600
Fax (781) 681-9045
E-Mail <kluwer@wkap.com>
Distributors for all other countries:
Kluwer Academic Publishers Group
Post Office Box 17
3300 AH Dordrecht, THE NETHERLANDS
Tel: +31 (0) 78 657 60 00
Fax: +31 (0) 78 657 64 74

E-Mail <services@wkap.nl>

 Electronic Services <http://www.wkap.nl>

Malaval, Philippe.
       [Stratégie et gestion de la marque industrielle. English]
       Strategy and management of industrial brands: business to business products
       and services / by Philippe Malaval with the collaboration of Christophe
Bénaroya.
              p.cm.
       Translation of : Stratégie et gestion de la marque industrielle.
       Inclludes bibliographical references and index.
       ISBN 0-7923-7970-5 (hardback) 1-4020-7753-X (paperback)

       HF5415.1263.M35 2000
       658.8'27—dc21
       00-052179

Permission for books published in Europe: permissions@wkap.nl
Permissions for books published in the United States of America:
permissions@wkap.com
Printed on acid-free paper.
Printed in the United States of America
The Publisher offers discounts on this book for course use and bulk purchases.
For further information, send email to <kluwer@wkap.com> .

Contents

Preface

Branding has an ancient history dating back to when earthenware was first stamped to identify the name of a particular potter, or animals were "branded" to show their belonging to one herd. Over the centuries, with the development of economic exchanges and industrialization, branding has become an essential aspect of marketing and strategy in virtually every market. Today everyone is familiar with hundreds of brands, and every day, we "take possession of" new ones: brands are a constant part of our daily environment. Marketing research has analyzed the development of branding in the 20th century, focusing logically on consumer goods and luxury products where brands play a crucial role, in particular in building links between customers and manufacturers. For customers, brands fulfill multiple functions such as providing a means of identification, memorization, security, guarantee, and symbolic value. For companies, branding improves market share; it is a tool for differentiation, positioning, creating loyalty and financial value, and mobilizing human resources.

The aim of this book is to analyze branding in the business to business context, from both a theoretical and operational point of view. The late development of industrial marketing explains the near absence of research on branding in business to business. With recent changes, industrial companies have shifted from a production focus to a customer focus; this change has been accompanied by the launching of genuine marketing and communication actions. Thus industrial branding is fast developing, attested to by the creation of numerous new industrial brands, their ever greater presence in the media, and the simultaneous growth of advertising budgets. Co-branding operations organized by the supplier associating his own brand with that of his customer make it possible to directly reach the end consumer, thus building awareness and image content.

This book presents the functions, mechanisms, role, and influence of branding in industrial marketing and in the customer-supplier relationship. It highlights the main functions of industrial branding:

• To decrease the actual and perceived risks as seen by the customer company,

• To improve the performance of the customer company, first from a technical point of view, and then from a sales perspective.

Three new concepts are suggested for analyzing business to business brands:

• "Printability",
• "Visibility",
• "Purchaseability" by the end customer.

These concepts involve different brand communication strategies. In fact, the objective of a brand policy is to attract customers and to keep them loyal. This goal can be achieved by making the right choices in terms of printability and visibility.

From a practical point of view, this book analyzes industrial brand management and presents the different brand strategies used. Five categories of business to business brands are suggested:

• Entering goods brands,
• Intermediary equipment goods,
• Equipment goods brands,
• Business to business service brands,
• Industrial distributor brands.

Over 40 case studies are presented on companies which have become leaders in their respective sectors. In addition, the 1,500 business to business brands examined in this book have given rise to different ways of classifying brands. But above all, they have revealed certain major trends:

• The development of the role of performance facilitator,
• The development of partnerships for reducing risk,
• The emergence of industrial distributor brands.

This book aims to answer the main concerns of managers:

• How to create and protect your brand?
• How to manage brands in an international context?
• How to manage entering goods brands, equipment goods brands, and business service brands?

Focusing on business to business brands and on the operational questions that they involve, this book is written for managers and those working in companies in the industrial and service sectors as well as for professors and students at universities, and business and engineering schools. Providing a detailed overview, the book should also be of interest to anyone wanting to know more about brands.

Until now marketing research has devoted little attention to business to business product and service brands. The great diversity in this area has provided a wealth of examples to illustrate different brand policies, techniques, and tools adapted to the industrial context. Whatever their geographic origin, these companies operate in an international context and tend to develop visibility strategies, in particular in North American firms. The enthusiasm with which business people have responded to the idea of this book was extremely stimulating. We would like to thank all those who have graciously provided us with information. In particular:

- ACCOR: Jacques Charbit
- ADECCO: Laurence Blay
- AIR LIQUIDE: Alexandra Rocca, Laurence Martin, Pascal Crépin
- AIRBUS INDUSTRIE: Michel Guérard, Robert Alizar, Philippe Jarry, Claire Labedaix
- ALCATEL: Caroline Mille, Philippe Thobie
- ANDERSEN CONSULTING: Isabelle Fougerol, Valérie Durand, Richard Griffith
- GROUPE BDI (PPB / FEDER BÉTON): Albert Bénaroya, Maurice Dietrich
- GROUPE CAILLAU-SERFLEX: Jean-Rémy Bernède, Pascal Da Silva, Jean-François Malaval
- DU PONT DE NEMOURS: Vania Henry (Lycra), Isabelle de Teba (Tactel)
- EDS: Francis Jubert, Florence Cazeaux, Martine Magadoux
- ÉLAN INFORMATIQUE: Jean-Jacques Rigoni, Pierre Delrat
- ELF ATOCHEM: Béatrice Deloustale, Jean-Baptiste Roques, Mireille Gorse Le Bervet
- FRUEHAUF: Jean-Luc Balitrand
- GÉODIS: Marianne Meurice
- GORE: Édouard Frignet des Préaux, Cécile Masson
- INTEL: Benoît Philippe, Christophe Houet, Noria Touenti
- KIMBERLY-CLARK: Georges Héribert
- LAFARGE: Yves Romestan
- LATÉCOÈRE: François Junca, Jean-Pierre Robert
- LEGRAND: Pierre Aiglon
- MANPOWER: Marie-Claude Deshairs
- MICHELIN: Christine Larsen, Gonzague de Jarnac, Max Arazat
- MICROSOFT: Jean-Christophe Castelain, Marie Dubois
- 3M: Hamid Aït-Ouyahia, Catherine Tomasi
- NOMEN INTERNATIONAL: (Vivendi Case) Marcel Botton, Nadège Liard, Betty Biout
- PINAULT: Philippe Le Goupil, Max Coudert, Pascale Gino
- REXEL: Maurice Bodiggiano
- SAGE: Ghislaine Huertas, Antoine Henry

- SAINT-GOBAIN: Philippe Lacoste, Robert Pistres, Michel Garde, Jean-Paul Laurent, Mme Chasselut
- SODEXHO: Myriam Morati-Masson
- TEKELEC AIRTRONIC: Patrice Marcilhacy, Jean-Yves Gigou, Christian Huleux
- TETRA PAK: Valérie Roques, Élyane Fohlen-Weill, Paul Bousser
- USINOR: Alain Bertrand, Élisabeth Cardeau
- VALEO: Denis Berthu, Bénédicte Mesnard
- VEDIORBIS: Nadine Quertier, Denis Perrot
- XEROX: Matthieu Mollet, Patrick Murciani, Marie-Sophie Leprince
- ZODIAC: Dominique Puig
- With thanks to the companies who have kindly supplied their brand logos: Marie-Claude Bechade (AKZO-NOBEL), Bertrand de Courrèges, Mme Marino and M. Krasnopolsky (BASF), Isabelle Casse (BAYER), Philippe Jacon (BECTON DICKINSON), Alain Delacroix (BOSCH), Blandine Delafon (BOUYGUES), Frédéric Rougier (CANON), Jean-Pierre Robillard (DASSAULT AVIATION), Nathalie Marinic (DHL INTERNATIONAL), Anne-Marie Miguirian (FACOM), Francis Fenwick et Christiane Louvet (FENWICK), Jean-Marc Jiry (GEMPLUS), Marèze Cosseron (HEWLETT-PACKARD), Claude Daché and François Gros (HOECHST), Élisabeth Condemine (ICI), M. Dutertre and Mme Sanzano (JOHN DEERE), Katia Grivot and Cécile Jung (LEXMARK), Carine Bonnet, Mme Maire and Xavier Gaydon (LUCENT TECHNOLOGIES), François Costes (MATRA DATAVISION), Philippe Bonnette and Philippe Soum (MOTOROLA), Francis Weill (NOVARTIS), André de Marco (RHÔNE-POULENC), Thibaut de Monts et Philippe Cadoret (SAGEM), Érick Verstraeten et Charles Noguès (SCHNEIDER), Bertrand Guillet (SIDEL), Éric Michel-Villaz and Valérie Rassel (SIEMENS), Marc Cillaire (SIEMENS AUTOMOTIVE), Pascale Groulaud (SMURFIT), M. Hucher and Jean-Paul Rouot (SNECMA), Alain Hirschfeld (SPOT IMAGE), Vincent de la Vaissière and Isabelle Cholet (SUEZ-LYONNAISE DES EAUX), Jean-Luc Pomier and Carole Caubet (THOMSON-CSF), Jean-Michel Miranda (TOSHIBA), Sophie Tois (UPS).
  I would also like to thank:
- Éric Junca, a lawyer specialized in branding for her careful reading of this book and her advice on legal questions,
- Alain Vernhet, a researcher at the CNRS (National Center for Scientific Research), curator of the museum and the archeological dig at Graufesenque (Millau, Aveyron) for his explanations on the archeology of brands.

And of course Toulouse Business School (ESC Toulouse) for its support and in particular, Hervé Passeron, Andres Atenza, Denis Lacoste, the Marketing Department, Florence Levy and her team of the Documentation Center, and Alexandre Levy.

With final thanks to:
- Alain Mainguy and delegates at the CPA Grand Sud-Ouest,
- Jacques Digout and students in the Marketing and Commercial Communication Masters program,
- My students in the Business to Business Management Option for their remarks and their participation.

Thanks to Marika Seletti for the translating and the editing of the English version and also to the other translators: Kathleen Evans, Adrian Pavely, and Bernie Flannery.

Thanks to Geoffrey Staines of Publi-Union as well as Monika Neumann for authorizing this American edition.

Thanks to Allard Winterink and Carolyn O'Neil for their patience and valuable help.

This book was made possible thanks to the in-depth collaboration and coordination of Christophe Bénaroya. His thoughts and our numerous exchanges allowed me to widen my area of research.

Finally, I would like to thank my parents, my wife Isabelle, and my children, Guilhem, Bertrand, and Robin.

Chapter 1

Development of the Concept of Brands

1. BRANDS: FROM THEIR ORIGINS TO COMPLEXITY

1.1 The origins of brands

One of the first identifiable uses of a brand dates back to the Gallo-Roman period. In particular, during the 1st century AD, brands were used to identify the work of different potters. Earthenware was fired in collective ovens holding large quantities of work; one firing lasted two weeks and around 20 different potters used the same oven at one time, consequently a way had to be found to distinguish the work of different craftsmen to avoid any confusion or disagreements. Archeologists have been able to study the period's economic organization from the signed pottery marked with a stamp printed on the bottom of the container. This stamp signified the work of a particular potter. Usually stamps were in the form of pictograms or the initials of names of potters: these were the first logos in history (Figure 1).

Almost all containers were marked inside: the first names of the producers were Latin (IVCVNDVS, HILARVS, SEVERVS, ALBINVS...), Gallic (ANEXTLATVS, CERVESA, CINTVSMVS, LITVGENVS...) or Greek (CALISTVS, DIOGENVS, MELAINVS...). The emancipated slaves were allowed to have three names (QVINTVS IVLIVS HABITVS, CAIVS IVLIVS SABINVS...).

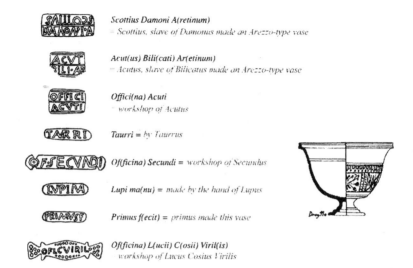

Scottius Damoni A(retinum)
= Scottius, slave of Damonus made an Arezzo-type vase

Acut(us) Bili(cati) Ar(etinum)
= Acutus, slave of Bilicatus made an Arezzo-type vase

Offici(na) Acuti
= workshop of Acutus

Taurri = by Taurrus

Of(ficina) Secundi = workshop of Secundus

Lupi ma(nu) = made by the hand of Lupus

Primus f(ecit) = primus made this vase

Of(ficina) L(ucii) C(osii) Viril(is)
= workshop of Lucus Cosius Virilis

Figure 1. Example of sealed pottery

Etymologically, the French word "marque" (or brand) would seem to come from the German, "marka", meaning sign, while the English, "brand", like the German, "brandt", comes from the hot iron print, "brandon" (firebrand) stamped on the animals in a herd belonging to different owners (from the saxon, "brennen" = burn) (Figure 2). The concepts of *identification* and *differentiation*, going back a long way to the very beginnings of the history of brands, were important, above all, for tradesmen. Concerning this early period, it is not possible to say whether the fabrication brand aimed at end users.

Figure 2. "Brand" or iron stamping

From the 15th to the18th century, freedom of production was limited by manual production methods (small quantities of products) as well as by guild regulations (Cabat, 1989). Many rules were indeed designed to limit competition and production in large quantities (craftsmen were only allowed to have one workshop or to employ a certain number of workmen or apprentices, customs collected at the entrance to cities, etc.). As they were both producers and merchants, craftsmen had to sell their wares near their place of work. The importance of brands in the 18th century is due to guild regulations, which sought to eliminate all competition. The application of the brand was both a sign of respect for production rules and also a way for the guilds to protect their privileges.

From the 17th century to the beginning of the 18th century, the term "manufacturing" still referred to the art of transforming raw material. It was only in the mid-18th century that the "manufactures" (Gobelins royal manufacturers, Tapestries and soap manufacturers, etc.) began to be less of a craft industry, and started producing on a large scale. This was true in particular of the glass and mirror manufacture of Saint-Gobain, created in 1665, by royal edict (Hamon, 1988). With the French Revolution in 1789, the different obstacles to commerce were abolished. Once the freedom of commerce was established, new production and transportation techniques (steam boats, rail, etc.) as well as mechanization began to develop, paving the way for the Industrial Revolution.

In Europe, wide-scale industry gradually began to replace specialized craftsmen owing to manufacturing uniformity and standardization. Division of labor became the norm, with on the one hand, producers handling manufacturing, and on the other, merchants handling distribution: gradually, indirect sales replaced direct sales from the manufacturer to the end customer. With progressive concentration in manufacturing, an independent commercial network developed: merchants distributed the products of manufacturers and producers, who lost the contact they had had with customers when they were craftsmen. Consequently merchants began to guarantee the products that they sold. With changes in industrial production and the transfer of new techniques, the brand began to develop; thus an American, Haviland, established the famous porcelain manufacturing center in Limoges, and William Wilkinson helped to create a canon factory in Indret and the metallurgical factory in Creusot, etc. It was in the 19th century that the modern brand appeared as industrial property (Caron, 1981); from then on the law considered the brand as property to be protected. Its creation was in fact necessary to structure and organize the industrial production market by introducing signs to mark and distinguish products, making them identifiable to consumers.

However, from a wider perspective, brands have developed out of a long history of signs including stamps (sign of ownership of objects or animals), signatures (sign of agreement), seals or flags (sign of union), place signs, icons, portraits, etc. Brands allowed producers to address final customers and, to a certain extent, shifted the producer-distributor balance of power in their favor. At the same time, the 19th century marked an increase in the number of companies created, owing to the establishment of a more clearly defined legal framework. Textiles, mechanical engineering, and chemical companies, which were often organized vertically (from raw materials to finished products), progressively adopted the status of corporations.

With the development of the railroad the need for steel increased, which in turn led to the growth of numerous rail equipment companies. The mechanical engineering industry (industrial equipment, steam engines, locomotives, etc.) in particular, expanded with the growth of companies generally owned by families such as Deere, Mead, Emerson, Rockwell, Duke, Johnson. The chemical industry also developed, particularly in mineral chemical products such as PPG Industries, BASF, Bayer, Monsanto. With the increase in big construction projects, the building industry saw the rise of companies such as Lafarge (1830) and Peter Kiewit (1884).

During the first half of the 20th century, theories and ideas in industrial economy began to appear, coming out of the work of sociologists, economists, and historians. Management sciences were on the rise and new rational systems for the organization of work were set up. After World War I, the reconstruction period was marked by company mergers, a concentration of activities, and the creation of new companies such as the current Alstom which, in 1928, was the fruit of the merger of the rail branch of Thomson and Alsacienne de Constructions Mécaniques, or Rhone Poulenc in the winter of 1928-1929.

The 20th century has seen the development of exchanges and international competition (the US, Germany, France, United Kingdom, etc.). In the years following World War II, the shortages, which had characterized the production economy, disappeared: the new credo was to produce and deliver quickly. Companies began to equip themselves for distribution and supply. New technologies and industries were expanding, in particular in the fields of telecommunications, electricity, and electronics, with companies such as General Electric, Philips, Thomson, IBM, Schneider, and Legrand.

Once society's most basic needs had been satisfied, competition developed and consumers could choose between ever more numerous and sophisticated products and services. Companies began to develop real sales strategies and set up marketing approaches to better respond to the growing complexity of markets: the use of brands and of advertising allowed manufacturers to present their products and services, thus increasing demand. With the growth of advertising expenditures and the extending of brands to other product categories, the number of brands registered increased dramatically.

Modern evolutions in the consumer product commercial network (which began to develop as early as the end of the 19th century with department stores, then popular stores, then supermarkets and hypermarkets, as well as more recently, hard/super discount stores) radically changed the nature of commerce. The manufacturing brand was no longer alone: manufacturer sub-brands, merchant multiple brands and distributor brands, among others, appeared. For industrial products, the change was not as clear: there was no real shift in the balance of power between industrial firms and wholesalers.

1.2   Brand old, brand new

If one looks at the main industrial brands, there is a striking proportion of old, even centennial brands such as Michelin, Du Pont de Nemours, Alcatel, and Siemens, among others. Table 3 a&b presents, in particular, a list of renowned industrial brands still used many decades after their launching.

Table 3a. Classification of some industrial and service brands according to their age

Age	Brands of Industrial Products	Brands of Professional Services
over 150 years	Saint-Gobain (1665), Villeroy & Boch (1748), Du Pont de Nemours (1802), Lafarge (1833), Cooper Industries (1833), Schneider Electric (1836), John Deere (1837), Case (1842), Mead (1846), Siemens (1847)	Bottin (1796), Chase Manhattan (1799), Citicorp (1812), New York Life Insurance (1845), Union Pacific (1848), PriceWaterhouseCoopers (1849), Lehman Brothers (1850)
100 to 150 years	CGE/Vivendi* (1853), Otis (1853), Bethleem Iron (1861), Bayer (1863), Cargill (1865), BASF (1865), Nokia (1865), BFGoodrich (1870), PPG Industries (1883), Peter Kiewit (1884),Johnson NCR (1884), Honeywell (1885), Controls (1885), Bosch (1886), Edison (1886), Michelin (1889), Fluor Corporation (1890), Duke Energy (1890), Emerson Electric (1890), Philips (1891), Crown Cork & Seal (1892), Uniroyal (1892), General Electric (1892), Harris (1895), Zodiac (1896), Becton Dickinson (1897), Alcoa (1898), International Paper (1898), Goodyear (1898), Renault (1898), Sprint (1899), Bethleem Steel (1899)	Metropolitan Life Insurance (1863), JP Morgan (1870) , Prudential Insurance (1874), Merrill Lynch (1885), Ernst&Young (1894)

* See Chapter 8, Creating and Protecting Business to Business Brands

This table shows that brands are not doomed to having short lives, or being quickly replaced. However, along with these very old brands, recent successes such as Yahoo!, Vivendi or Pentium have shown that age is not a prerequisite to making it. A brand can become a "reference" in its product category in less than ten years. Thus in spite of the number of strong, old brands, age is not a necessary condition of brand success (Aaker, 1991).

Table 3b. Classification of some industrial and service brands according to their age

Age	Brands of Industrial Products	Brands of Professional Services
50 to 100 years	Monsanto (1901), TRW (1901), Daimler (1901), 3M (1902), Square D (1902), Ford (1903), Rockwell International (1903), Hamilton Sundstream (1905), General Motors (1908), Reynolds Metals (1913), Carrier (1915), Boeing (1915), Lear (1917), Fruehauf (1918), Citroën (1919), Eaton (1920), Occidental Petroleum (1920), Eastman Chemical (1920), Canon (1922), Raytheon (1922), Textron (1923), Sikorski (1923), Total (1924), IBM (1924), Bull (1925), Caterpillar (1925), Lucent (1925), Pratt and Whitney (1925), ICI (1926), Foster Wheeler (1927), Motorola (1928), Texas Instrument (1930), Baxter (1931), Bridgestone (1931), Owens Corning (1932), Hewlett-Packard (1939), Centex (1950)	First Union (1908), Hertz (1923), UPS (1913), Manpower (1948), Automatic Data Processing (1949)
25 to 50 years	Tetra Pak (1951), Concrete Company (1951), Litton Industries (1953), Thermo Electron (1957), Gore (1958), Tyco International (1960), Halliburton (1962), Sidel (1965), Applied Materials (1967), Daewoo (1967), Intel (1968), AMD (1969), Airbus (1970), Essilor (1972), SAP (1972)	BNP (1966), Sodexho (1966), Sema Group (1958), Cap Gemini (1967), Accor (1967), EDS (1962), DHL (1969), Fedex (1973), Microsoft (1975)
10 to 25 years	Oracle (1977), Solectron (1977), Micron Technology (1978), Sage (1981), Compaq (1982), Sun Microsystems (1982), Elf Atochem (1983), Silicon Graphics (1984), Dell (1984), Cisco (1986), Cyrix (1987), Gemplus (1988)	CSX (1978), Altran (1982), Corporate Express (1985), Unisys (1986/1888), KPMG (1987/1870), Andersen Consulting (1989)
under 10 years	Business Objects (1990), Air Touch (1994), Delphi (1995/1888), Aventis (1999 from the merger of Rhone Poulenc 1929 and Hoechst)	Intershop (1994), Amazon (1995), AltaVista (1995), Wanadoo (1996), Bol (1999)

1.3   The growing sophistication of brand policy

The study of patronymic brands shows an increasing sophistication in brand policy. From the imprint, "ruf", for Rufus, the Gallo-Roman potter, to Saint-Gobain, created in 1665, the scope of brands has progressively extended from the product to diverse media accompanying it such as letter paper or delivery vehicles. If one looks beyond patronymic brands, the sophistication of brand policy is even clearer. Behind the general term, "brand", denominations of a product, of a range, or of different sets of complementary or independent ranges can be distinguished. For example, Lexic equipment boxes from the electricity specialist, Legrand, result from the juxtaposition of different brand levels, all of which need to be defined. Table 4 presents, in an industrial context, the different traditionally defined statuses of brands.

Table 4. The different statuses of brands[1]

Brand Status	Role of the Brand	Example
Product Brand *(Individual Product Brand)*	One name and a specific promise for one product, a brand for each product	Nutrasweet (Monsanto), Lycra, Tactel (DuPont)
Branduit *(branded product)*	(Variant of individual product brand) A product which is identified by its brand	Typon, Cromalin (DuPont), Scotch (3M), Rubafix (Bayer), Pantone, PostScript (Adobe)
Brand-range *(Brand-line)*	A brand for a set of homogeneous products	Scotchgard (3M), Mison (Aga), Altuglass, Aquakeep, Nakan (Elf Atochem, Kevlar, Kapton, Teflon (DuPont), Energy (Michelin)
Umbrella Brand	A brand for a set of heterogeneous products	Siemens, Alcatel, Xerox, Motorola
Guarantee Brand	Linked to several product-lines, caution brand is added to a product name (dual branding)	Air Liquide, Du Pont de Nemours, 3M, Michelin, Schneider, Usinor, Lexmark
Signatures	Original creation signature. The "griffe" territory is not defined by product categories but by a style and a recognized competence	Bertone, Norman Foster, Philippe Starck, Jean Nouvel, Dominique Perrault

The great number of references (products) of industrial manufacturers as well as their different levels of contribution to results, do not always make it possible to justify a brand and a communication by product. The umbrella brand policy (name of the group) is thus more common in industry than product-brand, brand-range or multi-brand policies. However, the status of a given brand is not fixed. It is likely to evolve as a function of the company's product launchings or withdrawals, product-brands progressively becoming brand-ranges.

2. THE EVOLVING STATUS OF BRANDS

A company, depending on its strategic interests, and its desire to modify or confirm its position, can decide to widen a brand's field of application: from product-brand to brand-line, for example.

New brand categories emerge with those which bring additional information and which are juxtaposed to product brands, to specify, for example, a level of equipment. They can thus be considered as "horizontal brands" at the crossroads of different product lines. In the automotive sector, Renault has developed such brands to explain a comparable level of equipment like "Alizée" (air-conditioning, open-roof, etc.) or "Baccara" (leather seats, special interiors, etc.).

An analogy between the brand and the family unit can be made. In the same way that a family is made up of a group of individuals, a brand encompasses a group of products. Like individuals, products have a life cycle. They are born, they evolve, and they disappear. However, like the family, brands tend to live on. A brand thus evolves as a function of its products, its brand policies (product-brand, brand-range, brand-line, etc) and its own image.

The analogy between product-brands and individual family members on the one hand, and the brand-guarantee and the family name on the other, would seem to indicate that the brand, which is more durable, can escape time. However, brand vitality is variable and fragile, as the decline or disappearance of certain brands remind us. There were, for example, over 619 different car brands in France at the beginning of the 20th century as opposed to only three today.

These disappearances or declines can be explained by different variables such as concentration in a sector or technological obsolescence. Thus the brand can disappear because of:

• *Product disappearance*: when the brand is used on one single product category, it disappears at the same time as the product. This is the case, for example, of Lettraset (letter transfer), whose activity has almost completely disappeared with the advent of computers;

• *A decision to suppress it following the buying out or taking over of one company by another*. This decision is often motivated by the desire to add the sales volumes of purchased brands to those of the purchasing company, with the objective of better recouping investments in surveys and communication. This is particularly the case when brands have complementary distribution circuits or zones;

• *Its replacement by a new brand designed and created to be more efficient*. A recent example of this is the company, Imation which, in July 1996, regrouped the computer, medical imagery, graphics, and photographic products activities of 3M. It is also the case of Novartis, born of the merger between Ciba-Geigy and Sandoz in 1997, or Aventis, which is the result of the merger between Rhone Poulenc and Hoechst in 1999.

• *Its replacement in the context of an international standardization strategy*. This is the case of Air Liquide, which rationalized under its label the names of different subsidiaries in the group worldwide. In 1992, unlike its competitor AGA, which uses its name in all markets, Air Liquide[2] included different brands as a result of the many buyouts, which had been made since 1985. Thus Air Liquide was called Oxigeno do Brasil in Brazil, SIO in Italy, Teisan in Japan, etc. Consequently, Air Liquide's image was weakened, the sales force having to justify to international groups belonging to the world leader in industrial gases. Since 1993, the names of subsidiaries have progressively been phased out in favor of Air Liquide, which lost its article, "L", except for the corporate brand, which has kept it. After the purchase of Norton, Saint-Gobain maintained the independence of the Norton brand during a transition phase so as not to shock its employees, customers, and suppliers. Today, the Norton brand is joined with Saint-Gobain with the appearance of the signature, "Saint-Gobain Abrasives" under its logo.

Another example is the British company, Sage, which was created in 1981 in Newcastle and is world leader in management software. In 1997, the company bought two companies, Saari and Sybel, respectively created in 1978 and 1982. Gradually, the brands of these companies have disappeared, first added in fine, grey characters to that of Sage, to be finally "swallowed" by Sage (Figure 5).

Figure 5. Evolution of the brands Saari and Sybel following their purchase by Sage

The highly evolving character of brands, calls for the study, in a more general context, of trends in the development or slowing down of the use of brands.

3.   THE BRAND, A TOOL WITH EVER-WIDENING APPLICATIONS

3.1   The increasing need for symbolic value

In the consumer market sector, research in sociology, in particular, has shown the need of individuals to affirm their position in the social scale through the act of consumption (Maslow, 1943; Sheth, 1974). According to this research, consumers increasingly are looking for symbolic value in the products they choose to acquire. Thus the concept of "normative social beliefs" has been developed. It is suggested that these beliefs influence the consumer in the role that he thinks he is supposed to play: "what we think others think we should do".

This trend is strengthening brands which have been able to create symbolic value meaningful to consumers whose traditional reference points have slowly been weakened. In fact, the decrease in time devoted to work in our society and the lessening of religious or political beliefs have spurred an increased need for consumption and the need to "intensify" how we spend our time (D'Iribarne, 1972). Brands help to answer these needs by giving meaning to what we buy. The branding function is even more important given that "all consumer objects, sooner or later, are endowed with meaning because of a universal, semantical process which makes them lose their material and functional status, transforming them into significant elements"(Barthes, 1985). These observations are much less true of industrial products, sold to business customers. However, whatever the activity sector considered, the brand is one of the ways through which the material substance of a product or service is organized into a meaningful substance with multiple communication levels (product, logotype, packaging, advertising angle, etc.).

3.2   New applications

Increasingly, brands have a more clearly defined, stronger place in industrial markets, just as in consumer markets (McDowell and *al.*, 1997).

3.2.1   The generalization of the use of branding in mass consumer markets

Benefiting from the increased need for symbolic value, brands have begun to play an increasingly important role in the economy, accompanying the ever-more concentrated structuring of consumer markets. Thus products bought without any reference to a brand are generally "non-marketed" products, bought directly from a small producer. This is the case in the building industry where artisans often use a family name rather than a specific brand name. Progressive industrialization, to the detriment of artisanal production, as well as organized commerce have marginalized areas that are still "without brands". Consequently, the consumer is gradually replacing purchases of equipment and everyday consumer goods by branded products.

3.2.2   The increasing use of branding in industrial markets

Industrial markets can essentially be broken down into markets for raw materials, semi-finished products, small and big equipment. For a long time, in these markets, the only brands used have been corporate brands of major groups such as Saint-Gobain, Du Pont de Nemours, Linde, Siemens, etc. Most of them come directly from the name of the company's founder or the geographical place of origin. Today, companies working in business to business marketing, that is to say, selling products or services to other companies, have gradually developed more sophisticated brand policies. Along with the corporate brand used as a brand-guarantee, product-brands have developed, certain of which have benefited from communication policies aimed at the consumer public. Examples of this are brands such as Tetra Pak, Lycra, or Intel, even though their products are not directly purchaseable by consumers. Mass media communication campaigns help to create reference brand status for these brands, in particular, with business target markets. The use of these well-known brands, whether for semi-finished products or equipment, allows the customer-manufacturer or the customer-artisan to indirectly benefit from the image of the industrial "supplier brand".

The growth of brands in the industrial sector can be explained by a combination of several factors:

• The desire to differentiate products and services offered by the company, to give new status to products (components, ingredients, or sub-systems) considered until now as simple raw materials without added value,

• The need to more clearly present the products and services offered, explaining and introducing technology (high technologies, chemistry, etc.),

• The maturity of the end customer, whose field of action, experience and know-how are growing all the time (computers, the building: choice of windows, heating, bathrooms, etc),

• The internationalization of industrial groups, which has meant building a global image (Alcatel, Air Liquide, Lafarge, etc.).

Thus while branding was for a long time traditionally used only in mass consumer markets (Hague and Jackson, 1994), today it is also increasingly important in industrial markets (Egan and *al.*, 1992; Gordon and *al.*, 1993). Branding is in fact a tool with ever-wider applications. However, while the branding concept would seem to be still in the development phase from one perspective, on the consumer market there is a risk of it becoming banal. It is worth presenting the main characteristics of this "trivialization", which could, eventually occur in industrial markets.

3.2.3   The risk of trivialization of brands in consumer markets

While the branding concept is making fast headway in new fields such as business to business marketing, it is interesting to analyze recent trends in the evolution of branding in its original market, the consumer goods market. In fact, in this market, new brand categories have appeared and are constantly developing to the detriment of manufacturing brands: these are distributor and "lowest price" brands.

• The appearance of department stores, then supermarkets (mass distribution outlets), little appreciated by manufacturers, has led these new circuits to create their own brands, by sub-contracting the manufacture of products, which are positioned as close as possible to those of the original manufacturers (Thil and Barroux, 1983). These products are manufactured on a contractual basis after specifications have been defined by the distributor's marketing department. Today distributor brands are better quality and they enjoy higher status. This has been made possible because the distributors' suppliers are offering better product advantages equivalent to those offered by manufacturers. Improvements in quality and thus in the image of distributor brands have generated confidence. The guarantee role, which until now was filled by the manufacturer, is increasingly played by the distributor with his own brand. Distributor brands, have thus been created and then used by distributors who manage them with marketing departments, that are often on a par with those of manufacturers. Nevertheless, distributor brands are limited to their own stores or to the different stores of the controlling group. Thus, unlike manufacturer brands, consumers can not find distributor brands from one group to another. Furthermore, there are different distributor brand policies such as using the name of the group itself (distributor brand), using a distinct brand accompanied by the distributor's name, or creating specific brands for the distributor's products, without mentioning the name of the distributor.

• Unlike distributor brands, first price brands can be found from one distributor to another, even if, sometimes, a specific first price brand is preferred by a distributor and is then called a reserved brand. In general, first price products are sold at lower prices than distributor products (the latter being situated in an intermediary price zone between national brands and first price brands). With the emergence, in the beginning of the nineties, of supermarket super-discounters, the intensity of competition between distributors has increased, thus favoring the development of first price brands in mature product categories, that are of relatively little interest to consumers. First price brands do not benefit from demanding requirements and thus tend to trivialize the product category.

Distributor brands, like first price brands compete with manufacturer brands. The consumer switch, from national manufacturer brands to private and first price brands, points to a decrease in loyalty to manufacturer brands. The consumer sees less and less difference to justify paying the higher price of manufacturer brands. Thus this transfer in consumption, has led to the development of distributor or first price brands to the detriment of manufacturer brands. The brand would seem to be threatened (in particular in food product categories), as its symbolic value is more selectively applied. The trend towards increasing "trivialization" qualifies the positive developments, discussed earlier, for brands in general.

The situation of brands today differs then, depending on whether we are considering consumer markets, luxury products, or business to business (Figure 6).

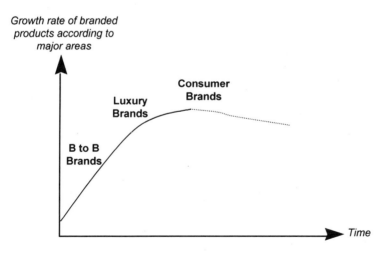

Figure 6. Evolutionary cycle of brands

If an analogy is made with the life cycle of products, brands are not going through the same phase in the main areas of application. While consumer brands are in a mature, or even declining phase, industrial brands, for their part, are fast-expanding, and business service brands are just taking off.

Furthermore, it is possible that the latest changes in the consumer market, which are just beginning to happen in business to business, could in the future, be a factor in the industrial brand sector with, for example, the growth of industrial distributor brands[3].

In spite of certain similarities between industrial and consumer brands, the importance of the brand in terms of buying behavior differs significantly according to whether the purchase is made by an individual consumer or a company. In this context, the main characteristics of the industrial purchase as well as brand influence will be presented.

NOTES

1. Adapted from Botton, M. and Cegarra, J-J., (1990), *Le nom de marque*, Paris, McGraw-Hill.
2. See Chapter 10, Managing the International Brand, Air Liquide: the Global Strategy for a World Leader.
3. See Chapter 15, Industrial Distributor Brands.

REFERENCES

Aaker, D.A., (1991), The power of old brands, in *Managing brand Equity*, New York, Free Press.
Barthes, R., (1985), Sémantique de l'objet, in *L'aventure sémiologique*, Paris, Le Seuil.
Cabat, O., (1989), Archéologie de la marque moderne, in Kapferer, J-N and Thoenig, J-C., *La marque*, Paris, McGraw-Hill.
Caron, F., (1981), *Histoire économique de la France, XIXème et XXème siècles*, Paris, A. Colin.
D'Iribarne, Ph., (1972), La consommation et le bien-être, Approche psycho-socio-économique, *Revue d'Économie Politique*, n°1.
Egan, C., Shipley, D. and Howard, P., (1992), The Importance of Brand Names in Industrial Markets, in *Perspectives on Marketing Management*, vol. n°2, Michael J. Baker, Ed. Wiley, Chichester.
Gordon, G.L., Calantone, R.J. and Di Benedetto, C. A., (1993), Brand Equity in the Business to Business Sector: An Exploratory Study, *Journal of Product and Brand Management*, vol. n°2, n°3, p 4-16.
Hague, P. and Jackson P., (1994), *The Power of Industrial Brands*, Londres, McGraw-Hill.
Hamon, M., (1988), *Du soleil à la terre, Une histoire de Saint-Gobain*, Paris, J-C Lattès.
Maslow H., (1943), A Theory of Human Motivation, *The Psychological Review*, n°50.
McDowell M. S., Doyle, P. and Wong, V., (1997), An Exploration of Branding in Industrial Markets, *Industrial Marketing Management*, vol. n°26, p 433-446.
Sheth, J.N., (1974), *Consumer Behavior: Theory and Application*, Boston, Allyn & Bacon.

Chapter 2

The Role of the Brand in the Industrial Purchase

Since the end of the 1980s, brand management[1] has been of growing interest to companies and has received increasing attention in marketing literature. The research on brand management goes further than brand image and strategy by studying the concepts of brand equity and extension[2]. But the literature essentially deals with consumer product brands, bought by individuals and households for personal use. Industrial brand management involves studying the role of the brand in inter-company trade relationships. This means taking the brand into account when analyzing the buyer's behavior within an industrial context.

1.   THE INDUSTRIAL PURCHASE

A genuine field of research[3], industrial marketing or business to business marketing owes part of its development to the economic importance of industrial markets in developed countries. But, more important than this economic dimension are its remarkable characteristics and in particular, those of industrial demand which have led it to be studied in a more specific way: in fact, the industrial purchase which is considered to be a fundamental (Cova and Salle, 1992) and even a constituent element of industrial marketing research has been the subject of numerous works since the 1960s, notably in terms of modeling industrial buying behavior[4]. Although it is not top of the list of the most popular subjects dealt with by researchers, industrial marketing tends to occupy a growing place (Plank, 1982) in marketing research with the emergence of new research trends on this theme in the 1990s. The industrial purchase is in fact characterized by the interdependence of different factors inherent to industrial markets and constituent of industrial marketing (Malaval, 1996):

*   The nature and diversity of industrial services and products,
*   Restricted number of prospective customers,
*   Concentration of sectors of activity and competition which is often oligopolistic,
*   Heterogeneity of customers concerning activity, size, motivations, financial stakes linked to purchases or geographical location,
*   Customer-supplier relationship which is generally characterized by its duration, often marked by a strong reciprocal involvement and commitment as well as by the active role of the customer,
*   The means of promotion used by companies in the sector: size of the sales team, trade shows and business publications,
*   The existence of a derived demand (especially in the supply chain).

The longevity of customer-supplier relationships results in better rates of loyalty than those found in consumer goods consumption. This is explained by a high level of human investment on the part of both the supplier and the customer (Table 1).

Table 1. Characteristics of 139 customer-supplier relationships [5]

	Semi-finished products	Components	Capital Goods
Customer-Supplier Relationships *(number of years)*	13,5	9,6	11,1
Supplier's Human Investment [*]	8,7	7,1	5,7
Customer's Human Investment [*]	7,2	13,5	14,0

* Average number of persons involved

Long term brand management, i.e. ensuring the durability of the brand, is definitely a characteristic of business to business relationships. In fact, with regard to inter-personal relationships alone, the brand can play a more lasting role in customer-relationships.

1.1   Derived demand

In business to business, the industrial product exists only in relation to the final product into which it is incorporated, to which it is assembled or for whatever production it is used (Bennett, 1988). This concept of derived demand has two main implications for the demand of the industrial product or service.

The first implication is a strong dependence with regard to the derived demand. Within a channel, the manufacturer depends on a customer who, in turn, depends on his customer and so on. This can be defined as a vertical channel of operators ranging from the extraction of raw materials to the manufacturer of an end product. A drop in activity in a given sector has repercussions on all the suppliers concerned. It must be said that this dependence is often aggravated by the fact that industrial companies are often not very diversified.

The second implication relates to the development of a marketing strategy with several levels of intervention. In the business to business context, a supplier has different opportunities to take action, at the level of his own customer, but also at the level of the customer's customer, and so on. Thus suppliers often study their customers' markets and clientele needs; armed with this information, they can provide customers with tailor-made products, as well as useful information about their own market (sales arguments, customer expectations, etc.).

The implications of these specificities have been considerably developed in industrial marketing literature within the framework of analyzing the industrial buyer's behavior. However, the place of the brand in this analysis has been only marginally studied. So as to position the role of the brand in relation to the industrial buy, it is necessary to back up the analysis with contributions from industrial marketing literature on industrial buying behavior, in particular:

- Buying process phases,
- Buying center,
- Buying situations,
- Factors influencing the decision to buy.

These concepts provide a framework of reference within which the role of the brand can be presented.

1.2   Buying process phases and the supplier brand

As a principal area of marketing research (Malhotra, 1988; Machleit and Wilson, 1987), the study of buying behavior is an essential part of marketing, i.e. research on maximum customer satisfaction. Alongside the first research on individual buying behavior[6], industrial marketing researchers have, since the beginning of the 1970s, been investigating the field of industrial buying behavior[7].

One result of this research is that the industrial purchase obviously presents characteristics common to other types of purchase, particularly concerning the buyer's motivation to reduce risk in the purchase decision and purchase rationality.

However, the industrial purchase is clearly distinguished from the individual one because of the industrial context in which it takes place. Secondly, the industrial purchase is fundamentally specific in the sense that it is made for the needs of an organization and managed by individuals. It therefore not only reflects the complexity of the organization but it also conveys the buying behavior of an individual and notably his individual mechanism of solving a deep conflict between his urges and brakes to buy.

The professional purchase cannot therefore be assimilated to the purchase made by the final consumer. Hardly ever spontaneous, it is made by a buyer who is above all a professional buyer, who does not buy for himself but for the company who employs him. Moreover, even if he co-ordinates the procedures, an industrial buyer does not act alone as it is a question of a collective purchase. An industrial buy cannot be made in one go. It is the result of a procedure carried out in different phases. Most authors agree with Robinson, Faris and Wind (1967) who break the purchase down into eight buying phases, which are often concomitant and iterative.

- Anticipation and recognition of need,
- Determination of characteristics and quantities to be bought,
- Detailed description of characteristics and of quantities to be bought,
- Search for and qualification of potential sources,
- Acquisition and analysis of proposals,
- Evaluation of proposals and selection of suppliers,
- Selection of an order routine,
- Feedback on performance evaluation.

The presentation of the main characteristics of these eight phases puts into perspective the potential role of the supplier brand.

1.2.1   Anticipation and recognition of need

This phase consists in the industrial buyer getting information on different needs, whether it is a question of merely renewing existing supplies or of new acquisitions necessary for the company to function properly. The information is generally transmitted by in-house departments, especially production and marketing, each following its own objectives; rationalizing management costs and reducing production costs for the former, seeking final customer satisfaction for the latter. Sometimes the need is made evident by a supplier who brings new ideas from the outside (use of new equipment or new methods) which can contribute to lowering production costs or improving the final product.

Effective recognition of needs depends on a good flow of information not only between the different departments of a company but also between buyers and suppliers. Even in this first phase, the supplier brand can intervene in the purchasing decision process. His reputation, for example, allows the supplier brand to be prescribed or at least mentioned by different in-house departments. The image of the supplier brand is also a potentially important lever of in-house action. To a degree, a strong supplier brand can become almost indispensable and be systematically ordered. It is obvious that an industrial brand must be present at the beginning of this first phase in order to be retained as a potential supplier by the buyer.

1.2.2 Determination of characteristics and of quantities to be bought

This second phase corresponds to listing the different categories of goods to be procured as well as determining the necessary delay in weeks or months for production, after having regrouped the needs of the different services or establishments concerned. Although the aim of this phase is to objectively define the characteristics and the quantities to be bought without referring specifically to a brand, the industrial brand can however play an important indirect role by guiding the purchase definition. For example, when buying equipment, the company which does not know this type of product very well, can orient its purchase pre-definition, consciously or not, by looking to recognized brands on the market.

1.2.3 Detailed description of characteristics and of quantities to be bought

The characteristics of the purchase to be made are defined relative to the expected performances of the final product or service. This means drawing up an extremely detailed specifications sheet. This generally includes not just technical clauses but also commercial ones such as logistics specifications, terms of payment, maintenance conditions and after-sales service. When it is a question of renewing existing products, the operational departments, such as production, are in charge of following up the specifications sheet. However, when it is a question of new products, its elaboration is a lot more complex and requires the collaboration of several departments, notably that of research and development, industrial engineering, quality and maintenance. This stage which continues on from and completes the previous one can offer a strong industrial brand the chance of being chosen as the standard reference in the specifications sheet. Therefore, for example, a company wishing to develop a new product could define its need in microcomputers as "Intel MMX® or equivalent". This reference brand allows potential suppliers to better understand their customer's needs in terms of products and services.

1.2.4   Search for and qualification of potential sources

In order to optimize the search for potential sources, buyers should not stick to suppliers already known to the company just because they work or have already worked for it. Alongside these *in-suppliers*, there are *out-suppliers* and they should be included in the search. Marketing experts recommend widening the search by taking into consideration suppliers using different technologies (Matthyssen and *al.*, 1985; Tarondeau, 1978). In order to draw up a list of companies to consult, buyers not only use available information such as technical directories but also information found in business publications and at trade fairs.

Qualifying potential sources means checking that the supplier is able to fulfill the expressed need. Preliminary interviews allow the buying company to check that the references and achievements of the supplier will allow him to make a proposal while respecting the different restrictions of the specifications sheet.

Therefore, a strong supplier brand, which is easy to identify and find and which is perceived as a market reference is more easily consulted by buyers. Consequently, the brand facilitates the buyers' selection process.

1.2.5   Acquisition and analysis of proposals

It is first of all a question of listing the criteria to be analyzed as a function of the specifications sheet in order to establish a marking grid. Potential suppliers and their propositions are examined closely and are given a mark for each criterion. This "rational" phase of the purchasing decision process can however involve some "irrational" criteria such as the reputation of the supplier brand. For example the excellent reputation of Scotchgard® or Teflon®, can play a very important role in the sofa manufacturer's choice of stain protector.

1.2.6   Evaluation of proposals and selection of suppliers

Following on from the previous phase, the next step is for the buyers, helped by in-house departments, to weigh the different criteria. Moreover, every company has its own criteria of pre-selection. For example, the fact that a supplier works with a particular competitor can be extremely negative. These in-house rules allow the different proposals to be evaluated thoroughly and to carry out a preliminary selection in order to draw up a short list of at least five possible suppliers in general.

It is only after further meetings and interviews with each one that a final choice can be made. This phase therefore allows those supplier brands making the best offers to be retained.

1.2.7 Selection of an order routine

The choice of an order routine depends first of all on the constraints of in-house departments, especially production. For example, if company production is organized in tight flow, the order routine has to be of a just-in-time type. Apart from in-house constraints, the supplier's organization must be taken into account: such as the existence of a local distributor or a nearby hub. The supplier brand hardly ever intervenes as such in this phase; rather it is the services related to the offer, which are of prime importance.

1.2.8 Feedback on performance evaluation

The process is finished only when the product ordered has been received by the company and checked by the department, which will use it. This presumes an inspection phase. The flow of information between the different in-house departments is absolutely necessary if performance is to be evaluated correctly.

The two departments most concerned are production and marketing-sales. In the short run, production is the most apt to react to an anomaly such as the quality and the quantity ordered being different from that received. In the long run, marketing-sales departments can pass on customer judgments: did such-and-such a change lead to an increase in customer satisfaction? A good performance evaluation thus presumes a good flow of information. This allows the buyer to facilitate or even provoke reactions from the different departments which might be used in further negotiations or to question an agreement with a supplier. An appreciated and efficient supplier brand can thus influence the departments carrying out these evaluations either directly by marketing actions targeting the production and marketing departments or else indirectly by actions targeting the final customer.

1.3 Supplier brand influence on the purchasing decision process

In the industrial buying process described here, the role of the brand can be positioned anywhere from the supplier search phase to selection, even at the stage of the performance check. The role of the brand can be seen as twofold:

• On the one hand, it is a question of informing buyers about a supplier and his products or services, so as to be part of the *set evoked* by *buying center* members (see below), and thus to be present right from the pre-negotiation phase,

• On the other hand, it is also a question of influencing the decision thanks to the power of the supplier's image. The brand is involved especially before the buyer has worked with the supplier (i.e. for a new task).

A survey carried out on 200 European buying and marketing managers (Malaval, 1998) in four different industrial sectors (building, textiles, auto parts, packaging) showed precisely how a strong industrial brand can favor its consultation, its short-listing or its final selection. It clearly stands out (95% of the answers on average) that the stronger an industrial brand is, the better chance it has of being consulted and of figuring on the short list (and this no matter what the buying situation is in which the transaction takes place). Likewise, a strong industrial brand has a much better chance of being chosen when it is a totally new task for a company (82.5% of answers on average). When the buying situation deals with goods or services already used by the consumer, supplier brand influence is not as strong.

Supplier brand influence is much stronger at the beginning of the purchasing decision process (recognition of need) than towards the end: the nearer the deal is to being closed, the more a buyer will take into account other aspects than those transmitted by the brand and the more a buyer will try to make an objective decision (Figure 2).

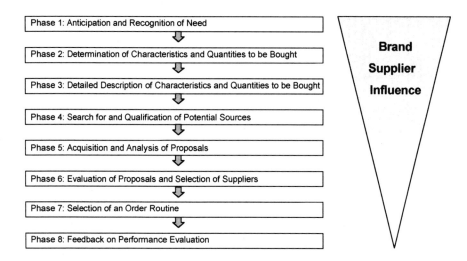

Figure 2. Potential supplier brand influence on the purchasing decision process[8]

The industrial purchase is determined not only by the purchasing process but also by the involvement of a certain number of managers of the buying company whose roles and weight are variable. This specificity needs to be analyzed because of its effects on the role of the brand.

1.4   Influence of the brand on the buying center

The study of the different phases of the purchasing decision process shows the involvement of several internal actors collaborating with buyers (production, marketing, etc.). The industrial purchase is in fact a collective decision made by a variable number of people. It was in the 1970s that the notion of a buying center first appeared (Webster and Wind, 1972a). This groups together operational and functional managers who participate, either formally or informally, directly or indirectly, in the final decision to buy. Contrary to the purchasing department, the buying center is neither a formal nor structured center because its composition changes depending on the size of the project and its technical specificities[9]. Thus the supplier brand must constantly take into consideration both the specific company buyer that he is working with as well as each of the members of the buying center.

1.4.1   The size of the buying center

Taking into account the number and hierarchical position of the managers involved in the purchase envisaged, it is possible to define the buying center according to two dimensions (Mahin, 1991; Mattson, 1988):

• *Lateral dimension* refers to the number of departments concerned by the decision. This mainly depends on the type of purchase, which can be characterized according to the risk perceived by the organization and the size of the budget to be spent. If it is a question of a new task, which can have sizeable consequences on the cost-effectiveness or on the quality of production, then nearly all the departments of the company, from marketing to finance, along with human resources are concerned by it. On the other hand, if it is just a routine purchase, then the buying center will deal with it along with the department requiring it.

• *Vertical dimension* of the buying center is defined by the number of hierarchical levels involved in the decision. Like the previous dimension, this first of all depends on the risk perceived and the budget needed but the number of hierarchical levels involved is also determined by the size of the company. In a large organization, five or six levels of hierarchy can be involved whereas in a small or medium sized company it is rare if more than two levels are involved.

A buying center can also be described according to the amount of direct information exchanged among the different members. It should be noted that the smaller the buying center is, the more information flows easily. The managers who informally make up the buying center are very different insofar as they have had different experiences, different education, different responsibilities and also they differ from each other in respect to the amount of trust they benefit from within the company.

The heterogeneous nature of the buying center is such that its members should be grouped according to their role in relation to the purchase. Industrial marketing research has made it possible to separate the different members of the buying center into four or five sub-groups (depending on whether advisors and influencers are put into the same category), including: deciders, buyers, influencers and users (Webster and Wind, 1972b). The supplier brand has every interest to talk to these different members of the buying center in order to generate an "in-house current" favorable to the brand. This in-house advocacy thus allows the brand to be checked out, then retained and finally to be preferred over others in the final decision to buy.

1.5   Members of the buying center

1.5.1   The deciders

The deciders make the final decision, especially when the other members cannot come to a consensus. It can sometimes be one single person, for example the boss of a small or medium sized company but more often the decider is a group, represented by the board of management, especially in big organizations. The role and importance of the deciders is such that the brand must seduce them.

1.5.2   The buyers

The role of the buyers can be very different depending on whether it is a question of a routine purchase or one involving the buying center. In the first case, the buyers are in charge of the whole procedure from collecting information to performance evaluation. In the second case, the role is mainly to look for the different solutions, which can be found on the market, and to take part in the final selection of the different suppliers competing with each other. Within the buying center, the buyers are the main target of the supplier brand's actions.

1.5.3 The influencers

All those who are neither buyers nor users but who take part either directly or indirectly in the purchase decision can be considered as influencers. This category of members varies the most from one company to another according to the sector observed and to the different kinds of corporate culture. Essentially in-house and external influencers can be distinguished.

In-house influencers are mainly from internal departments such as research and development, maintenance, quality control and marketing. For all of them, it is a question of achieving a defined target. That is why each department has to defend that supplier which it sees as the most efficient from its own perspective. Beyond the rational criteria for making choices used by the different managers, other more irrational motivations can be found: this point will be examined in the next part "main motivations of buyers". The range of external influencers is very wide, including journalists from specialized trade magazines, as well as professionals from other sectors such as architectural firms or engineering offices. It should be noted that certain external influencers are imposed by law such as chartered accountants, auditors in the management field, or architects and surveyors in the construction field.

The supplier brand, who sees both in-house and external influencers as the conveyors of his message (Figure 3), addresses each of the influencers identified by supplying as much useful information as possible and by carrying out specific actions with the aim of being recommended (Farrell and Schroder, 1996; Gilliland and Johnston, 1997).

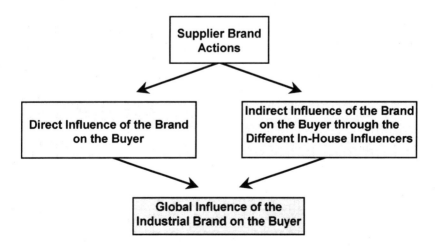

Figure 3. Breakdown of the global influence of the industrial brand on the professional buyer

1.5.4   The users

The weight of the users varies greatly depending on the sector of activity and the corporate culture context: for example in the computer field, where the users are generally highly qualified, it is usual to take their opinion into account: on the other hand, when the users are low-qualified operatives, their opinion is taken into account only from a managerial aspect and depending on the corporate culture and the country. For example, it is common practice to take the user's opinion into consideration in the United States and European countries whereas it is the total opposite in developing countries.

In fact, the study of industrial buying behavior cannot be limited to the study of the buyer's behavior. All the influences, which interact within the buying center, should be taken into account. The analysis of the role of the brand should be carried out not only in relation to whoever is in charge of purchases but also, and ideally, in relation to all those who make up the buying center. Such a study is by definition difficult insofar as the buying center varies in size, depending on the stakes involved, how the company purchases are organized, etc. Another major factor can be added to this complexity: the buying center differs depending on the types of purchases. These types of purchases are more commonly called buying situations.

1.6   The three buying situations

Analyzing the importance of the different buying center members is made more complex by the fact that their influence varies depending on the buying situation. Marketing literature pertinently distinguishes three buying situations: new task, straight rebuy and the modified rebuy (Robinson and *al.*, 1967). Depending on the type of purchase, the buying process phases do not have the same importance and are not followed with the same intensity. It is the same for the buying center, which changes according to the buying situation (Crow and Lindquist, 1985). The influence exerted by the supplier brand on the purchase decision process also varies depending on the phases, on the buying center members, and on the type of situation in which the transaction takes place.

1.6.1   The new task

In this situation the supplier needs to address as many of the buying center members as possible. If the order is new, be it a product, equipment part or a service, there is more uncertainty because of lack of experience. This leads to more interaction between the different departments. The weight of the influencers is predominant since the users and buyers are more inclined to follow their advice. In this type of purchase, suppliers not yet listed stand a better chance. It is also in this type of situation that the company is faced with two alternatives: make or buy? Should the company make the product (or the service) itself or should it buy it from outside?

This new task situation often occurs when the company is launching a new product, which means that its marketing department is strongly involved and thus is an important influencer.

A European multi-sector study carried out on 200 marketing managers and buyers in four different sectors (construction, liquid food packaging, auto parts and textiles) about the influence of the brand as a function of different situations, highlighted several points especially concerning the new task (Malaval, 1998):

- Supplier brand influence on the buying center members is at its strongest in this situation (Table 4),
- Supplier brand influence is perceived as big, even very big on marketing managers, buyers and production managers,
- The brand has rather important influence on research and development managers, general management, and quality control managers,
- Maintenance executives and users consider it as less important.

Table 4. New task situation: level of importance of supplier brand influence as a function of the different members of the buying center

Functions	Rank of Influence Importance
Marketing executives	Very strong
Buyers	Very strong
Production executives	Very strong
R&D executives	Strong
General management	Strong
Quality control executives	Strong
Maintenance executives	Weak
Users	Weak

However, these trends have to be qualified because of the different perceptions of marketing executives and buyers. Marketing executives consider that they are more influenced by the brand than buyers. While buyers consider that brand influence is strongest in respect to their own function, then production, and only in last position, marketing.

1.6.2   The modified rebuy

This situation corresponds to fulfilling an existing need in a modified way; this can be, for example, to reduce cost price or to improve performance. It can be a compulsory modification because of a new regulation. Whatever the case, a potential supplier competing with the current supplier can be at the origin of the suggested modification. This buying situation can result in a change of supplies coming from the same supplier or in a change of supplier. In both cases, the technical departments and the users as well as the marketing department are concerned by the final choice.

Concerning this situation, the study mentioned above on the degree of influence of the brand as a function of the type of buying situation, provides the following useful information (Table 5):

• Supplier brand influence on buying center members is not as strong in this situation as it is for the new task but it is stronger than for the straight rebuy,

• Compared to the previous situation, brand influence is stronger on buyers and weaker on marketing executives. The influence is thus considered as strong on buyers,

• The brand plays a rather significant role for production, marketing, quality control, research and development and general management,

• As in the previous situation, the influence is considered as less strong on maintenance executives and buyers.

Table 5. Modified rebuy situation: level of importance of supplier brand influence as a function of the different members of the buying center

Functions	Rank of Influence Importance
Buyers	Very strong
Production executives	Strong
Marketing executives	Strong
Quality control executives	Strong
R&D executives	Weak
General management	Weak
Maintenance executives	Weak
Users	Weak

1.6.3   The straight rebuy

The most common situation is when there is no change in the need and it is more a question of renewing supplies (small urgent orders...). This is why this situation applies more to the supplies market than to a capital goods market. In this context, the evaluation criteria are thoroughly known by the company and the purchasing department is the main, often the only one to deal with suppliers. The buyer generally contacts his usual supplier which he trusts and with which he has established a good working relationship thanks to past transactions (visits, phone calls, repairs, etc.).

In order to keep a hold of its position, a supplier can go as far as suggesting automatic renewals so as to make the buying procedure easier and also to make it even more difficult for a new competitor to enter their market. The relationship established is therefore comfortable and reassuring: the buyers feel understood. The company is less likely to change suppliers (except in cases of serious letdowns or errors).

Supplier brand influence in straight rebuy situations is thus different from both the modified rebuy and the new task (Table 6). It can be characterized mainly by the following points:

• Supplier brand influence is less strong in the straight rebuy situation than in the previous ones.

• It is however perceived to be stronger on the buyer in this case compared to the modified rebuy situation.

Table 6. Straight rebuy situation: level of importance of supplier brand influence as a function of the different members of the buying center

Functions	Rank of Influence Importance
Buyers	Very strong
Production executives	Strong
Quality control executives	Weak
Maintenance executives	Weak
Users	Weak
Marketing executives	Weak
General management	Weak
R&D executives	Weak

From the analysis of the different buying situations, it can be seen that the higher the level of uncertainty (new task), the more buying center members perceive the influence of the brand to be important. Moving from the new task, to modified rebuy and straight rebuy, the influence of the brand on the buyer gets stronger. Inversely, the influence on the marketing executive gets weaker. For all the situations, the buyer is the member of the buying center who is most subject to brand influence. Brand influence therefore varies according to which type of buying situation is involved. It is seen as weakest for a straight rebuy, stronger for a modified rebuy and is at its strongest for a new task (Figure 7).

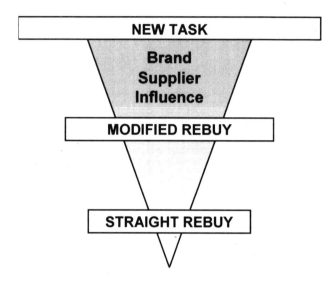

Figure 7. Degree of brand influence depending on buying situation

The analysis of the role of the industrial brand should thus take into account the different dimensions of the industrial purchase, from the purchasing decision process and the buying center to the company's particular buying situation. In fact, these components largely determine the size and constitution of the buying center with which the brand can play a role. Moreover the analysis should take into account the fact that the company's buying behavior is the result of a complex process in which both individuals and interests interact. The buyer, whose role tends to be more and more active, is extremely important to analyze.

1.7   The active role of the customer and the development of purchase marketing

Whatever the situation or the purchasing decision process phase considered, the industrial customer maintains an active role; this characteristic especially distinguishes the industrial buyer's behavior from that of the normal consumer. This active role is seen with the industrial customer's participation in the quality of the product or service sold, from preliminary specifications and design to the use of the good or service.

From the very start of the preliminary design phase, the customer informs the supplier of his needs. But there are very different ways of presenting the company needs, ranging from a brief description of the problem to be solved to the handing over of forty pages of specifications defining main expectations and pointing out technical and financial restrictions. In the latter case, a supplier is better able to define the need, so as to avoid misunderstandings and therefore not waste the potential customer's time.

In the operating phase, the same supplies or capital goods can give very different productivity results depending on the knowledge and skills of the users. Real and perceived performance of the acquired assets therefore depends on how efficient the customer's users are.

But the most active form of this behavior can be observed with the recent development of *purchase marketing*[10]. This concept first appeared at the end of the 1970s, but it was especially applied in the1980s. From the start, purchase marketing was the subject of two different conceptions (Fenneteau, 1992). Presented at the beginning as *reverse marketing* it was a question of applying marketing techniques to suppliers alongside those used with customers (Leenders and Blenkhorn, 1988; Blenkhorn and Banting, 1991): market studies carried out on suppliers, segmentation and typology techniques applied to them and communication actions aimed at them within the framework of supplier conventions, trade-shows and especially reverse trade-shows at which it is the contractors who state their needs and the potential suppliers who visit the stands (Bénaroya, 1997). The second conception consists in being in the supplier's place: "the logic behind this type of marketing consists in appearing attractive as a customer" (Gauchet, 1996).

By analyzing the aims of purchase marketing, it seems that the two conceptions are similar to each other because both are essentially a question of:
- Following different markets in order to target certain suppliers,
- Knowing how to present the company institutionally to suppliers,
- Presenting the company's needs precisely and especially those main expectations not met,
- Making suppliers want to work with the company by underlining the amount of potential activity it can offer, the recognition and prestige that could come from such a collaboration,
- Making it easier for suppliers to draw up their proposals.

Suppliers should know as much as possible about the internal running of the company so as to make their proposals as relevant as possible. The industrial brand of the buying company steps in here: by practicing a type of purchase marketing, by having a purchasing policy, by sending out numerous messages (documents, catalogs, letters, adverts...) to the targeted potential suppliers. Although the strong image of a brand can be used as a reference for suppliers, it can also set a level of requirements in terms of quality of supplies and services which will lead to a partial pre-selection of suppliers. To sum up, purchase marketing essentially consists in optimally maintaining the production asset, giving a competitive edge to the enterprise and presenting a strong proposal to the different in-house departments.

The practice of purchase marketing, and especially its development since the beginning of the 1990s, is the best illustration of the active behavior of industrial customers even before the purchase phase.

Although the analysis of the industrial purchase leads to studying the buying center, buying process and buying situations, it also leads to studying the active role of the customer notably his interaction with suppliers[11]. In recently developed relational models, the relevant analysis unit of the purchase is made up of the customer/supplier couple and no longer just the customer's buying center or just the supplier's selling center. Understanding industrial markets means analyzing not only the customer or the supplier individually but rather the total customer-supplier interaction. In this context, the brand intervenes in the exchange between the customer and the supplier through the image it puts forward and which it procures reciprocally.

The brand partakes of the level of information of the two companies. Moreover, it intervenes in the interaction between the two companies, by being able to influence the power interplay, the "atmosphere" of negotiations in terms of trust, of risk, of dependence and the perception of the counterpart. For example, within the context of a purchase, the customer's brand can, by means of its reputation and image, become a tool to seduce suppliers (reference) or to increase its power of negotiation over them. Thus, the brand plays a dual role in the customer – supplier relationship. With the aid of surveys carried out on the industrial purchase from a personal perspective, it is possible to draw up a diagram integrating the role of the brand in the exchange (Figure 8).

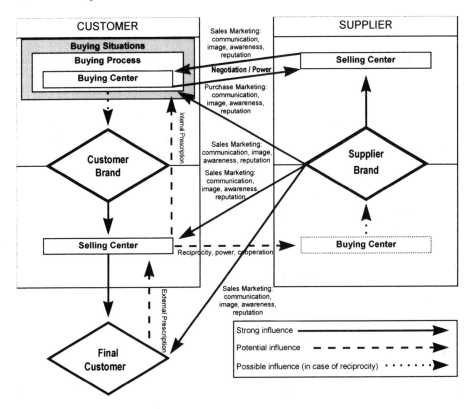

Figure 8. Influence of the brand in customer-supplier interaction[12]

In fact the brand influences the content of the exchanges as well as the atmosphere of the relationship in terms of trust/risk, power/dependence and overall perception of the other company. In addition to these factors, another dimension of the industrial purchase is to be specifically analyzed, that is the motivation of the buyer and of the other members of the buying center.

2.   MAIN MOTIVATION OF BUYERS

All the approaches to the industrial purchase – whether they concern the buying center and its members, the buyer's role as well as the influence which he is subject to, the buying phases, buying situations or the interactions between the organizations – have all contributed to elaborating either partial or global models of industrial buying behavior[13]. Having presented the industrial purchase and in the framework of the study of the brand within the industrial context, it is essential to specify the motivations of the buyer and of the other members of the buying center.

First, the concept of *perceived risk* will be analyzed as it is a particularly crucial aspect in the industrial buyer's decision to buy. Then, the buyer's decision-making criteria will be presented as well as the main motivations of the other members of the buying center.

2.1   Reduction of perceived risk

Different research on the industrial purchase highlight the fact that, as with the individual buyer, the decision-making style of industrial buyers as well as that of the members of the buying center more generally, depends on their behavior faced with risks of uncertainty (Wilson, 1971).

Correlated to the capacity to take risks, likewise the search for information depends on the characteristics of the individuals (Cardozo and Cagley, 1971): age, past experience, level of education, attitude towards innovation. Therefore, the buyer who lacks experience and competence will tend to adopt a particularly cautious behavior.

Innovative behavior is favored by those buyers with a high level of education and competence as well as those with a wide variety of experience (Pras and Tarondeau, 1981). Likewise, the more they are involved in the buying center, have an interest at stake in the buying decision, the more they will participate and exert their influence on the decision process compared to their colleagues. They will also tend to search for more information.

This search for information is notably linked to the tendency to deform information (perception) so that it tends to reinforce beliefs and past experiences (Abelson, 1968). It is necessary to remember that perception is a relational cognitive process through which the individual selects and interprets information. Everyone tends to perceive the information which interests them the most: "all perception is subjective and we very rarely see things as they are but rather the way we want them to be, the way we expect them to be or the way we need them to be" (Runyon and Stewart, 1987; Assael, 1987). This leads to an interaction between the individual's perception and behavior. The search for information is therefore a "tension reducer".

This search for information is explained by the *perceived risk*, which includes two factors (Figure 9):

• Uncertainty as to the outcome of the decision,

• Importance of the consequences linked to making a poor decision.

At the individual level, the perceived risk can in fact have two dimensions:

• One being functional: uncertainty (subjective),

• The other being psychosocial: seriousness of failure.

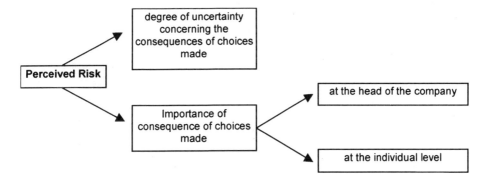

Figure 9. Main components of perceived risk concerning the industrial purchase[14]

From the first studies in the industrial environment, the notion of perceived risk, applied to decision-making for organizational purchasing (Levitt, 1965), has been fundamental to understanding the industrial purchase: perceived risks are the prime-mover of the customer's buying behavior. In fact, the industrial purchase decision-making model "which is the most valid empirically and the richest as to its strategic implications is the one which explains buyers' preferences by the reduction of perceived risk" (Cox, 1967).

Certainly, routine management decisions are often simple, involving a very low level of risk as they correspond to previously encountered problems and for which the decider has adequate experience (Pras and Tarondeau, 1981). However, there are numerous complex, fast-changing situations (changes in regulations, new technologies, internationalization of activities and of competition...) which can increase uncertainty and risk in management's decision-making. These complex situations most often involve contradictory aims, the presence of diverse and divergent information, and the need to reach compromises in the decision-making process. The more uncertainty there is, the higher the perceived risk is, in which case the buyer searches for as much information as possible so as to reduce its importance.

Buyers can thus determine a hierarchized classification of the risks and of the procedures corresponding to the estimated level of risk. For example, if the level of uncertainty is high and if the choice made has substantial consequences, the perceived risk is maximum. In this case, buyers will draw the management's attention to the situation and the buying center will carefully follow each phase of the buying process previously presented.

The perceived risks include both the risks which the buyer himself faces and those which the company faces.

2.1.1   The buyer's risks

These risks can be seen:

• As criticism expressed by the other members of the buying center, for example: looking for an easy solution, continuous relationship with a same supplier, suspected partiality,

• Dissatisfaction, consecutive to the final choice: for example the delayed adoption of a new solution compared to competitors, a disappointing technical performance compared to the supplier's promise, customers less satisfied, higher price to pay than that obtained by a competitor.

It is therefore a question of risks which are both functional (uncertainty as to the supplier's respect of product performance) and psychological (negative reactions of in-house departments). The brand, by means of the image it projects and its reputation can play an important role in making the buyer feel more secure before buying but also afterwards when justifying his decision vis-à-vis the company (Thompson, 1966; Williams, 1983).

2.1.2   The company's risks

These risks are related for example, to the security of the supplies, to the dependence on a supplier or foreign currency fluctuations. Depending on the impact of its purchases, their characteristics, their accessibility and their availability on the market in the short, medium, and long run, the company will be faced with a risk, which is more or less high.

The customer company's risks can be put into three categories (Salle and Silvestre, 1992):

• Risks linked to the nature of the transactions,

• Risks linked to the nature of the relationship between the customer and the supplier,

• Risks linked to the nature of the customer's position on the supply market.

2.1.3   Risks linked to the nature of the transactions

This category includes technical risks, the risks linked to the availability and delivery of the products and services bought, the risks linked to the customers' ability to use the products, and the financial risks generated by the transaction. The risks linked to the nature of the transactions depend on the stakes attached to the type of problem the company has to solve. Several factors have been identified in order to explain the risks linked to transactions such as the level of newness of the transactions for the client, the characteristics of the upstream market, the importance of what is at stake for the customer's activity, and the characteristics of the downstream market. The extent to which the transactions are new for the customer is an important factor when explaining the risks. In fact, the more the characteristics of the purchase are new, the higher the stakes are and the greater the customer's risks are. Risk is maximum for a new task (new strategy, new supplier, new product to launch), less so for a modified rebuy (changes in suppliers' products, delivery, price, technology, organization). Risk is minimum for a straight rebuy (no changes). The higher perceived risk is, the greater the need is felt to reduce it. This is especially true for the new task in which case detailed information is needed (Boyle and *al.*, 1979).

2.1.4 Risks linked to the nature of the customer/supplier relationship

The risks attached to the type of relationship the customer has with the supplier (past dealings, investments) condition the settings for the present and future dealings as well as the company's behavior in the relationship. Can the supplier / does the supplier want to invest in the relationship, follow up on his offer in the medium run (products, services, price, logistics), make changes to his offer without making the customer become too dependent on him? It is mainly a question of two types of risk. First, risk of dependence (durability of this supplier, durability of the relationship with this same supplier, independence in respect to price or supply changes). Secondly, risks due to the level of the suppliers' commitment to the relationship (amount of investment, involvement, availability, will to collaborate, gains in term of innovation and security).

2.1.5 Risks linked to the nature of the customers' position as regards the supply market

The customer should have different supply solutions. Although the supply market undergoes economic changes, which can affect the industrial customer's buying behavior, the structural characteristics of the market exert a much stronger influence. The risks are linked to how stable and homogenous the market is, the suppliers' turnover on the market, and the similarities and differences between suppliers' offers.

For the customer, the nature of the transactions and of the relationship with the supplier as well as the company's position on the upstream market, determine the stakes linked to the purchase i.e. *risks incurred*. These risks incurred correspond to the customers' risks as they are perceived by the supplier. In fact there is a clear difference between perceived risks and incurred risks. This is due to the characteristics of the buying center and to its attitude as regards the risks and stakes involved.

By classifying the customer's risks, it is possible to determine all the risks incurred by the company (Figure 10). These risks are analyzed by the different members of the buying center as a function of their involvement in the purchase and of their position in the hierarchy. The different members turn incurred risks into perceived ones. The latter are more important as they influence the buying center members' behavior and their final decision.

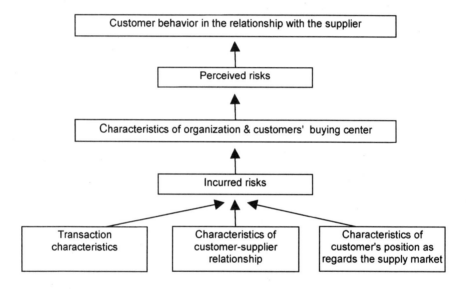

Figure 10. Customer behavior formation[15]

This presentation of the perceived risk concept underlines the fact that the greater uncertainty is, the greater perceived risk is, in which case the buyer searches for as much information as possible so as to reduce this risk. In this case, the brand, because of its reputation and image, can play an important role in making the buyer feel more secure before buying and also afterwards when justifying his decision vis-à-vis his hierarchy. It can thus be seen as a "tension reducer" in so far as it transmits information which will be cognitively processed by the different members of the buying center who will not all be "brand sensitive" to the same extent. Therefore brand influence differs depending on the role and job of each member of the buying center.

In conclusion, it is necessary to insist on the fact that the industrial buyer and the company in general are confronted with a certain number of internal, external, real and/or perceived risks which affect their buying behavior. Risk reduction constitutes one of the essential roles of the buyer who has to fulfill the organization's needs at the same time. The buyer is therefore subject to numerous influences. Guided first of all by objective factors (economic, technical, etc.) the buyer is also influenced by subjective factors (personal motivation, risk reduction, favors). It is therefore important to examine the main criteria used by the buyer when making his choice.

2.2   Decision criteria

Two major characteristics emerge from the study of buying behavior. First, the tendency to reduce the risk surrounding the industrial purchase and second, the rationality of industrial behavior. In fact, the buying process and the industrial buying act are generally qualified as rational when compared to individual consumer behavior. This conception is due to the economic reasoning underlying the purchasing act in industry, notably the search for minimum cost, which can be especially observed in the case of substitutable products. For a long time, research has gone along with the hypothesis that industrial buyers give preference to suppliers according to rational criteria such as:

- Their ability to respect fixed specifications,
- Their possibility of supplying the company at the right time,
- Suggested price (most determining criteria for non-differentiated goods).

However, industrial buying reasoning is not superior to that of individual buying, even if economic and technical considerations are part of the criteria used in decision making. In fact, the buying center's purchasing behavior can seem not so rational. The dominant rationality is not that of positivists but rather that of Simon's *limited rationality*: the actors retain not the best possible solution but the first solution, which offers them a certain level of satisfaction (Simon, 1955).

Moreover, it must be noted that it is often difficult to make the distinction between rational and non-rational criteria as the latter can intervene in the rational decision-making process. In some cases, certain criteria, seen as rational, can correspond to non-rational criteria. For example, as regards the geographical location of the supplier, nearness is both a rational and a non-rational factor. Definitely, it can be a question of "cultural" affinities (same geographical region) but it can also be about getting better service as it can be quicker and cheaper. The investment role of the supplier in the country, normally seen as non-rational can in fact hide hopes of developing reciprocal business dealings with the supplier. The following table gives examples of rational and non-rational criteria (Table 11).

Table 11. Straight rebuy situation: level of influence of a strong supplier brand on the different members of the buying center

Rational	Non-rational
Price	Supplier's prestige & reputation
Terms of delivery	Duration of relationship
Conforming to the norms laid down	Geographical location of supplier
Quality	Supplier's investment role in the country
Accurate estimates and reports of achieved work	Counterpart's education (engineer, university…)
After-sales service	
Nearness of distributor or supplier sales office	
User's physical safety	

The evaluation criteria used by buyers to compare, on the one hand, products and services and on the other, suppliers, have been the subject of a lot of research[16]. However, the small number of studies carried out specifically on the importance of intangible attributes in industrial marketing can be explained by the long-lasting generally accepted idea that the reasoning behind the industrial purchase was uniquely economic (Shaw and *al.*, 1989). Several articles have shown that this is not the only determining factor taken into account in the purchase decision. Some studies show that past experience with the retained supplier is a dominant criterion, as is the supplier's reputation, product quality and deadlines (Cardozo and Cagley, 1971). Other studies, taking up to sixty-five items into account, have been carried out with the aim of analyzing the criteria used (Kisser and *al.*, 1975). Criteria evaluation used by buyers can include:

- Suitability of product as regards needs,
- Supplier's reputation and image (Webster, 1970),
- Reliability of delivery deadlines and terms,
- Supplier's ability to adapt,
- Price and terms of payment,
- Connected services.

Research carried out in the United States and in Great Britain, studied the importance of seventeen factors likely to influence the purchase decision (Lehmann and O'Shaughnessy, 1974):

- Supplier's reputation,
- Terms of payment,
- Ability to adapt,
- Past dealings,
- Technical assistance,
- Trust in representative,

- Flexible as regards the order,
- Information on product reliability,
- Price,
- Technical characteristics,
- Easy to use,
- User's preferences,
- Training possibilities,
- Required training,
- Reliability as regards deadlines,
- Maintenance,
- After-sales service.

The importance of each attribute varies depending on the type of purchase (new, modified, straight). For straight rebuys, reliability as regards deadlines, price, supplier's reputation and past dealings play a major role in the buying decision. In fact, past experience, linked to the learning process, seems to be a determining criterion in this situation (Tomas and *al.*, 1996). Concerning modified rebuys, technical assistance, supplier's ability to adapt, and product reliability are judged as the three very important attributes. Finally, for new tasks decisive criteria include price, reputation, product and service reliability, and supplier's flexibility. Each criterion is not analyzed separately but comparatively. The price of the product alone has little significance (Corey, 1976). What is important is the value of the offer. Among the seventeen criteria used, the supplier's reputation came:

- Second for high risk and high investment purchases,
- Fourth for routine purchases,
- Fifth for purchases requiring a high level of technical complexity,
- Seventh for purchases presenting possible implementation difficulties.

Likewise, this criterion stands out in the following table (see Table 12), which summarizes the result of a study carried out on the textile-clothing sector.

An American study carried out on computer hardware shows that industrial buyers effectively use intangible choice criteria and that these criteria are sometimes more important for the reduction of perceived risk than the objective criteria of product performance. In the intangible criteria, the author notably found the producer's reputation and the affinities with the person in charge of the after-sales service (Shaw and *al.*, 1989). Research carried out on the perceived quality of services to companies reinforces this idea. The analysis of judgment criteria identified thirteen categories of criteria, one of which is called "image factors". This includes the customer's perception of the service provided based on criteria such as reputation, references, know-how, and position compared to competitors. An exploratory study also carried out on the perceived quality of product-service in industry confirms that the supplier's image figures among the top four selection criteria (Table 12). Classifications drawn up by specialized publications or audits done by consulting firms or by specialists can also intervene in the customer's perception of the brand.

Table 12. Examples of selection criteria for supplier's offers[17]

	Criteria often used		Criteria rarely used		Criteria never used	
Supplier's reputation	359	85 %	22	5.2 %	4	1 %
Supplier's ability to adapt	329	78 %	36	8.6 %	6	1.4 %
Financial information on supplier	80	19 %	108	26 %	175	42 %
Product technology	315	75 %	21	5 %	2	0.5 %
Age of product	297	71 %	38	9 %	17	4 %
Level of standardization	276	66 %	17	4 %	2	0.5 %
Differentiation possibilities	243	58 %	25	6 %	13	3 %
Services offered	234	56 %	31	7.4 %	-	-
Respect of delivery deadlines	227	54 %	13	3 %	-	-
Value for money	214	51 %	19	3.8 %	-	-
Terms of payment	209	50 %	14	3.5 %	-	-

These studies confirm how important the influence of intangible elements is on the industrial purchase decision. Among these elements, the perceptual, subjective, and affective dimensions of the brand can be taken into account. Brand evaluation factors are tangible and thus measurable (market share, product life cycle, just-in-time organization, etc.). They are also intangible, therefore depending on a complex cognitive process including a perceptual dimension (reputation, image perceived, quality and reliability, etc.). For example, that is why some small and medium sized industrial firms put forward the image of their country in order to promote their own brand image and increase the reputation of their brand: Italian design, German sturdiness, etc. It is also one of the reasons which leads big international corporations to adopt a global brand[18] thereby giving an image of solidity and perenniality to their public. On the whole, this means that the supplier brand can intervene to varied extents in the formation of the customer's decision to buy.

2.3   Buying center members' motivations

Apart from the buyers themselves, each buying center member has his own evaluation criteria to judge the different products and services offered. These criteria do not depend on rationality alone but can also be emotionally based. The objectives sought by the buyer can in fact be pragmatic such as price, quality, service, and return on investment. But these can be mixed with operational objectives or more personal objectives such as professional security, recognition, social promotion, salary increase, etc.

Criteria evaluation and product perception differ depending on the deciders who in turn differ from each other because of their education, sources and types of information around them, interpretation and retention of relevant information, (perceptual distortion) and the level of satisfaction with previous purchases (Sheth, 1973). Moreover, within the buying center, the more the managers have an interest at stake in the purchase decision, the more they will participate in and exert their influence on the decision-making process, more than their colleagues, and the more they will tend to seek information.

Guided by both collective and personal objectives, the industrial buyer is confronted with a risk of in-house uncertainty in his dealings with the other departments as well as the risk of failing to satisfy them. In fact, once there is a difference of interests within the organization, conflict occurs (Morgan, 1986). So as to solve these conflicts, the brand, as an acceptable medium, can play a role in the different solution strategies, by contributing to the search for mutual satisfaction without changing individual desires (Day and al., 1988).

In this context, the supplier's objective is to go and see several members of the buying center in order to make the final consensus easier during the decision-making. It is thus a question of inciting a channel of internal reccomendation favorable to him within the buying center. The supplier brand, because of the diversity of his potential targets, can, from then on, intervene in the customer's purchasing decision process.

Like buyers, the other members of the buying center can take part in consulting decisions, in supplier short-listing, and selection. It is thus necessary now to examine the other buying center members' motivations, starting with those departments which act as "in-house prescribers" (internal influencers).

2.3.1 Research and development departments

By working with the supplier, this department looks for not only the fulfillment of needs but also at the same time, anything which can improve performance inside the company. This can include information on new developments in projects, recent products or technologies. In order to experiment or test a product technically, the department looks for aid, which can be in the form of a loan or the use of a fully equipped laboratory. It can also expect advice on research methods and other help such as executive training, ranging from visits to target sites to attending research seminars. Finally the Research and Development department can be interested in exclusive territory contracts even if they are only temporary as this can accelerate collaboration with the marketing department.

2.3.2   Industrial engineering department

The first expectation of this department is to improve performance in industrial processes. This can be by working on a project concerning new processes or by projects to improve existing processes. These projects can be materialized by having access to software, notably prototypes and also by specialized training.

2.3.3   Quality department

This department also looks for new means to achieve fixed targets more easily. It can collaborate on implementing or improving quality control procedures. The quality department is always looking for information on future regulations and norms. Personnel training assistance as well as supplier's commitment and guarantees as to the quality of the product are useful in order to materialize quality improvement and to strengthen the relationship with the customer.

2.3.4   Maintenance department

The motivations of this department are also based on improving performance. Their expectations include a need for product maintenance training not only for those in the department but also for the production operatives. Regarding routine work, this department looks for efficient verification and prevention procedures, which are easy to implement, as well as quick action being taken following the detection of a problem.

2.3.5   The users

They look for user-friendly equipment and also for commonality between the different equipment, allowing greater working flexibility and facilitating training and maintenance. Optimization of work conditions is also a requirement, including better security and fewer disadvantages such as reducing the noise level.

2.3.6   Production management

Its expectations are a synthesis of those of the different operational departments as well as of users. It is a question of contributing to improving performance in terms of productivity, quality, maintenance, and work conditions. A loan of equipment for display purposes or for use during a test phase can also satisfy these different expectations in a context of budgetary restrictions.

2.3.7   Marketing department

The marketing department is always looking for information on innovative projects and products and on what is being developed abroad or by its competitors. Always alert, this department can be approached and interested by means of new information.

Among the concerns of the marketing department, we can notably find that new characteristics of a product will meet customer expectations which have not yet been satisfied. Another strong motivation is to obtain exclusive territory contracts even if only temporary which can reinforce the pioneer character of the company brand.

2.3.8   The deciders

Their expectations can be very varied: first of all, it can be a question of finding the best consensus because of the conflicts provoked by the diverse objectives of the different members of the buying center. It can sometimes be a question of getting a status quo with a big supplier so as to avoid or minimize the change cost. The deciders are also motivated by obtaining the best guarantee contract from the supplier and also by reducing the risk incurred by the company. For example, a commitment to take back equipment used for a field test in case of failure is appreciated. The deciders are moreover motivated by obtaining budgetary compensation, which can be in the form of equipment training, or by contributing to joint communication operations.

To conclude on the motivations of the different members of the buying center, we can find one constant, performance facilitation, which each department selfishly evaluates according to its own criteria. As regards irrational motivations, each department and its executives also seek to be more recognized internally by the other executives and notably by the deciders. These unspoken expectations can be detected and used opportunely by the most skilled suppliers. One of the buyer's functions is to support those suppliers' offers which meet the company's main expectations while at the same time conciliating the specific motivations of the department concerned (Dion and *al.*, 1995).

In conclusion, several purchase decision criteria linked to the industrial brand can be retained within the framework of our research. By taking into account the expectations of the different members of the buying center, the following factors can be used to study the supplier brand:

• Ability to innovate,
• Ability to help design and perfect the customer's products,
• Ability to make the users (in the buyer company) accept changes in procedure, in equipment...
• Ability to reach a consensus within the buyer company,
• Ability to improve production by having a high level of maintenance and quality control,
• Ability to help the customer to sell better,
• Ability to commit to a long-term strategy with the customer.

Moreover, it is also necessary to take into account the perceived risks linked to the supplier brand. These principally include:

• Risk of customer depending on the supplier brand,
• Risk of the supplier brand having too much influence on the in-house departments of the buyer company,
• Risk of the supplier brand demanding excessive prices because of the additional cost due to its investments,
• Risk of the supplier brand having an arrogant attitude.

This chapter has described the specific nature of industrial marketing and in particular that of the industrial purchase, through an analysis of the industrial brand. It has been shown that the industrial brand seems to play a role in the buyer company's purchasing process. The supplier must then adapt his brand's advertising and promotional strategy to the realities of the industrial context.

NOTES

1. See Chapter 1, Development of the Concept of Brands.
2. See Chapter 4, The Brand and its Mechanisms and Chapter 5, Brand Functions.
3. Numerous books have been published since the end of 1980s in the US and in Europe: Reeder, R. R., Brierty, E. G. and Reeder, B. H., (1991), *Industrial Marketing*, 2nd ed., Englewood Cliffs, N.J, Prentice Hall; Hutt, M.D and Speh T.W., (1995), *Business Marketing Management*, 5th ed., Orlando, Fla., The Dryden Press; Ford, D., (1997), *Understanding Business Markets: Interactions, Relationships and Networks*, International Marketing and Purchasing Group, London, The Dryden Press; Saporta, B., (1989), *Marketing Industriel*, Paris, Eyrolles; Dayan, A., (1994), *Marketing industriel*, Paris, Vuibert; Mahin, P.W., (1991), *(see references)* Heights; Malaval, Ph., (1996), *Marketing Business to Business*, Paris, Publi-Union...

4. See for instance these books and research: Industrial Marketing Committee Review Board (October 1954), Fundamental Differences Between Industrial and Consumer Marketing, *Journal of Marketing*, n°19; Ozanne, U.B. and Churchill, G.A., (Fall 1968), Adoption Research: Information Sources in Purchasing Decision, *Proceedings of the American Marketing Association*, 352-359; Cardozo, R.N., (1968), Segmenting the Industrial Market, Chicago, *American Marketing Association*; Hillier, (1975), Decision Making in the Corporate Industrial Buying Process, *Industrial Marketing Management*, n°4, 99-106; Sheth, J.N., (1973), A Model of Industrial Buyer Behavior, *Journal of Marketing*, n°37, 50-56, October; Howard, J.A. and Sheth, J., (1969), *The Theory of Buyer Behavior*, New York, John Wiley & Sons; Levitt, Th., (1965), *(see references)*; Robinson, P.J., Faris, C.W. and Wind Y., (1967), *Industrial Buying and Creative Marketing*, Boston, Allyn & Bacon...
5. Sources: Turnbull, P. W. and Valla J-P., (1986), *Strategies for International Industrial Marketing*, Croom Helm.
6. See in particular: Andreasen, A.R., (1965), Attitudes and Consumer Behavior: A Decision Model, in *Research in Marketing*, Preston E. Lee, ed., University of California, Berkeley; Maslow H., (1943), A Theory of Human Motivation, *The Psychological Review*, n°50, p 370-396; Nicosia, F.M., (1966), *Consumer Decision Processes*, Englewood Cliffs, NJ, Prentice Hall; Howard, J.A. and Sheth, J., (1969), *op. cit.*; Engel, J.F., Blackwell R.D. and Kollat, D.T., (1978), *Consumer Behavior*, 3rd ed., Orlando, Fla., The Dryden Press...
7. See in particular: Cardozo, R.N. and Cagley, J.W., (1971), Experimental Study of Industrial Buyer Behavior, *Journal of Marketing Research*, vol. n°8, p 329-334; Moller, K., (1986), Buying Behavior of Industrial Components: Inductive Approach for Descriptive Model Building, in *Research in International Marketing*, Turnbull, P.W. and Paliwoda, S.J., Ed. Croom Held; Bonoma, T.V. and Johnston, W.J., (1978), The Social Psychology of Industrial Buying and Selling, *Industrial Marketing Management*, n°17, p 213-224; Choffray, J-M. and Lilien, G., (1978), Assessing Response to Industrial Marketing Strategy, *Journal of Marketing*, n°42, p 20-31.; Webster, F.E. and Wind Y., (1972), *Organizational Buying Behavior*, Englewood Cliffs, N.J., Prentice-Hall; Corey, E.R., (1976), *(see references)*; Cardozo, R.N., (1983), Modelling Organizational Buying as a Sequence of Decisions, *Industrial Marketing Management*, n°12, p 75-81...
8. Sources: Bénaroya, C., (1998), *working paper*.
9. There is a lot of research upon the organizational buying process: Wilson, J.W., Lilien G.L. and Wilson D.T., (November 1991), Developing and Testing a Contingency Paradigm of Group Choice in Organizational Buying, *Journal of Marketing*, 28, p 452-466; Johnston, W.J. and Spekman, R.E., (1982), Industrial Buying Behavior: A Need for an Integrative Approach, *Journal of Business Research*, June, vol. n°10, p 135-146; Johnston, W.J. and Bonoma, T.V., (1981), The Buying Center: Structure and Interaction Patterns, n°45, p 143-156; McWilliams, R.D., Naumann, E and Scott, S., (1992), Determining Buying Center Size, *Industrial Marketing Management*, n°21, p 43-49; Moriarty, R.T. and Bateson, J.E.G (1982), Exploring Complex Decision Making Units: A New Approach, *Journal of Marketing Research*, n°19, p 182-191...
10. See in particular: Davies, O., (June 1974), The Marketing Approach to Purchasing, *Long Range Planning*, p 2-11; England, W.B. and Leenders M.R., (1975), *Purchasing and Materials Management*, Homewood, Illinois, R.D. Irwin; Kotler, P. and Levy S.J., (1973), Buying is Marketing too!, *Journal of Marketing*, n°37, n°1, p 54-59.
11. See research of IMP, IBB and ISBM groups: selling process and buying process are no more separately analyzed but together according to a relational approach; they are considered as the product of the buyer-seller interaction.
12. Sources: Bénaroya, C., (1998), *working paper*.

13. See the different models developed by: Woodside, A.G. and Vyas, N., (1984), An Inductive Model of Inductive Supplier Choice Processes, *Journal of Marketing*, 48; Moller, K., (1981), Industrial Buying Behavior of Production Materials, Helsinki, *Economics Publications*, n°54B; Campbell, N.C.G., (1985), An Interaction Approach to Organizational Buying Behavior, *Journal of Business Research*, n°13, p 35-48.
14. Sources: Choffray, J-M., (1979), Perception du risque dans l'achat industriel, *Revue Française de Gestion*, n°22, September, p 24-30.
15. Sources: Salle, R. and Silvestre H., (1992), *Vendre à l'industrie: approche stratégique de la relation business to business*, Paris, Liaisons.
16. See for example: Lehmann, D.R. and O'Shaughnessy, J., (1982), Decision Criteria Used in Buying Different Categories of Products, *Journal of Purchasing and Materials Management*, n°18, 9-14; Jackson, R.W., Neidell, L.A. and Lundsford, D.A., (1995), An Empirical Investigation of The Differences in Goods and Services as Perceived by Organizational Buyers, *Industrial Marketing Management*, vol. n°24, n°2, 99-108; Swift, C.S. and Coe, B.J., (1994), Sourcing Preference Scale, *Industrial Marketing Management*, n°23, 171-180...
17. Sources: Excerpts from Juillard-Martin, S., (September 1989), quoted in Dubois, P-L. and Jolibert, A., (1992), *Le marketing, fondements et pratique*, 2nd ed., Paris, Economica.
18. See Chapter 10, Managing the International Brand.

REFERENCES

Abelson, R.P., (1968), *Theories of Cognitive Consistency: A Source Book*, Chicago, Rand McNally.
Assael, H., (1987), *Consumer Behavior and Marketing Action*, Kent, Boston, Ma.
Bénaroya, Ch, (1997), Étude comparée de l'efficacité perçue des outils du marketing achat, *Mémoire de DEA*, Raf, Université de Toulouse I.
Bennett, P. D. (1988), Dictionary of Marketing Terms, *American Marketing Association*, Chicago.
Blenkhorn, D.L. and Banting P.M., (1991), How Reverse Marketing Changes Buyer-Seller Roles, *Industrial Marketing Management*, n°20, p 185-191.
Boyle, P., Woodside, A.G. and Mitchell, P., (1979), Organizations Buying in New Task and Rebuy Situations, *Industrial Marketing Management*, February, p 7-11.
Cardozo, R.N. and Cagley, J. W., (1971), Experimental Study of Industrial Buyer Behavior, *Journal of Marketing Research*, vol. n°8, p 329-334.
Corey, E.R., (1976), *Industrial Marketing, Cases and Concepts*, 2nd ed., Englewood Cliffs, N.J., Prentice-Hall.
Cova, B. and Salle, R. (1992), L'évolution de la modélisation du comportement d'achat industriel: panorama des nouveaux courants de recherche, *Recherche et Applications en Marketing*, vol. n°7, n°2, p 83-106.
Cox, D.F., (1967), *The Influence of Cognitive Needs and Styles in Information Handling in Making Product Evaluation*, Boston, Harvard University.
Crow, L.F. and Lindquist J.D., (1985), Impact of Organizational and Buyer Characteristics on the Buying Center, *Industrial Marketing Management*, n°14, p 49-58.
Day, R.L., Michaels, R.E. and Perdue, B.C., (1988), How Buyers Handle Conflicts, *Industrial Marketing Management*, vol n°17, n°1, p 153-169.
Dion, P., Easterling, D. and Miller, S.J., (1995), What is Really Necessary in Successful Buyer/Seller Relationships?, *Industrial Marketing Management*, vol. n°24.

Farrell, M.A. and Schroder, B., (1996), Influence Strategies in Organizational Buying Decisions, *Industrial Marketing Management*, vol n°25, n°4, p 293-305.

Fenneteau, H., (1992), Les caractéristiques de l'acte d'achat et la logique du marketing amont, *Recherches et Applications en Marketing*, PUF, vol. n°7, n°3.

Gauchet, Y., (1996), *Achat Industriel, Stratégie et Marketing*, Paris, Publi-Union.

Gilliland, D.I. and Johnston, W.J., (1997), Toward a model of Business to Business Marketing Communications Effects, *Industrial Marketing Management*, vol n°26, n°1, p 15-30.

Kisser, G.E., Rao, C.P. and Rao, S.R.G., (1975), Vendor Attribute Evaluations of Buying Center Members Other Than Purchasing Executives, *Industrial Marketing Management*, p 45-74.

Leenders, M. R. and Blenkhorn, D. L., (1988), *Reverse Marketing, The New Buyer Relationship*, New York, The Free Press.

Lehmann, R.D. and O'Shaughnessy, J., (1974), Difference in attribute importance for different industrial products, *Journal of Marketing*, vol. n°38.

Levitt, T., (1965), *Industrial Purchasing Behavior: A Study of Communication Effects*, Boston: Division of Research, Graduate School of Business Administration, Harvard University.

Machleit, K. and T.C. Wilson (1987), A Summary of Three Decades of AMA Educators' Proceedings, *AMA Educators' Proceedings*, n°53, p 254-259.

Mahin, P.W., (1991), *Business to Business Marketing*, Needham Heights, Allyn and Bacon.

Malaval, Ph., (1996), Marketing Business to Business, Paris, Publi-Union.

Malaval, Ph., (1998), Exploratory Survey of the Industrial Brand Performance, perceived by the Purchase and Marketing Managers, *The Example of Four Industrial Markets: Building Trade, Liquid Food Packing, Car Engineering and Textile Industry, Thesis for Business Management Doctorate*, Social Sciences University of Toulouse I.

Malhotra, N. K. (1988), Some Observations on the State of Art in Marketing Research, *Journal of the Academy of Marketing Science*, vol. n°16, n°1, p 4-24.

Matthyssen, P. and Faes, W., (1985), OEM Buying Process for New Components: Purchasing and Marketing Implications, *Industrial Marketing Management*, vol. n°14.

Mattson, R.M., (1988), How to Determine the Composition and Influence of a Buying Center, *Industrial Marketing Management*, vol. n°7.

Morgan, G., (1986), *Images of Organization*, Beverly Hills, Californie, Sage Publications

Plank, R.E. (1982), Industrial Marketing Education: Practitioner's Views, *Industrial Marketing Management*, vol. n°11, p 311-315.

Pras, B. and Tarondeau, J-C., (1981), *Comportement de l'acheteur*, Paris, Sirey.

Robinson, P.J., Faris, C.W., and Wind Y., (1967), *Industrial Buying and Creative Marketing*, Boston, Allyn and Bacon, Inc.

Runyon, K.E. and Stewart D., (1987), *Consumer Behavior*, 3rd ed., Columbus, Ohio, Merrill Publishing Company.

Salle, R. and Silvestre H., (1992), *Vendre à l'industrie: approche stratégique de la relation business to business*, Paris, Liaisons.

Shaw, J., Giglierano, J. and Kallis, J., (1989), Marketing Complex Technical Products: The Importance of Intangible Attributes, *Industrial Marketing Management*, vol. n°18, p 45-53.

Sheth, J.N., (1973), A Model of Industrial Buyer Behavior, *Journal of Marketing*, n°37, p 50-56, October.

Simon, H.A., (1955), A Behavioural Model of Rational Choice, *Quarterly Journal of Economics*, vol. n°69, n°1, February, p 99-118.

Tarondeau, J-C., (1978), *L'acte d'achat et la politique d'approvisionnement*, Paris, Éditions d'Organisation.

Thompson, D.L., (1966), Industrial Advertising and the Purchasing Agent, *Journal of Purchasing*, n°2, p 5-16.

Tomas, G., Hult M. and Nichols E.L., (1996), The Organizational Buyer Behavior Learrning Organization, *Industrial Marketing Management,* vol. n°25, n°3, p 197-209.

Webster, F.E. and Wind Y., (1972a), *Organizational Buying Behavior,* Englewood Cliffs, N.J., Prentice-Hall.

Webster, F.E. and Wind, Y., (1972b), A General Model of Organizational Buying Behavior, *Journal of Marketing,* vol. n°36.

Webster, F.E., (1970), Informal Communication in Industrial Markets, *Journal of Marketing Research,* n°7, p 186-189.

Williams, J.D., (1983), Industrial Publicity: One of the Best Promotional Tools, *Industrial Marketing Management.*

Wilson, D.T., (1971), Industrial Buyer's Decision-Making Styles, *Journal of Marketing,* vol. n°8, p 433-436.

Chapter 3

The Characteristics of Business to Business Communication

Companies have many ways of promoting their brands particularly among other businesses. In view of the nature of inter-company relations, specific tools can be used apart from those applicable to consumer markets. However, first a communication policy coherent with the marketing strategy of the company must be defined.

After defining objectives, budgets and targets, then the most effective tools for promoting the company brands can be chosen. Once these have been introduced, the methods used to evaluate a brand and the functions attributed to that brand for the supplier company and for the customer company will be examined.

Any company, by its very existence, diffuses a certain number of messages and information to external and in-house targets. The organized and carefully thought out channeling of these messages is the very basis of marketing communication and its development. Communication policy is based on defining communication objectives, selecting targets, establishing a budget and controlling measures. The development of this policy makes it possible, in particular, to define the role and the place of the brand within the company.

1.   COMMUNICATION POLICY

The communication policy consists of four phases, the "four I's" (Szapiro, 1988):

- The *Identification Policy*: covers all the distinctive aspects of the company using graphic, visual, written and sound media: logos, initials, brand names, signature, climate, atmosphere...
- The *Integration Policy* brings together in-house and external populations. It concerns all long-term communication activities. For example:
    - Participation in clubs and professional associations,
    - Training centers,
    - Conventions, symposiums and lobbying,
    - Publishing of external newspapers,
    - Use of direct marketing, information retrieval, electronic catalogs, documents, Internet sites,
    - Trade shows,
    - Public relations, corporate advertising, one-off events: anniversaries, shareholder meetings, sponsoring...
- The *Incitement and Influence Policy*, which aims to stimulate the target by a push - pull strategy. The push strategy consists of approaching the target using a sales force, which relies on video or IT presentations, overheads, slides, PC's, technical documents, complete kits, direct marketing, and trade magazines. The pull strategy involves attracting the target using new services, such as direct multimedia marketing or special events.
- The *Investigation Policy* consists mainly of listening to customers, surveys, pre- and post- tests, and communication audits. Impact, image, identification and recognition scores, all make it possible to judge, modify, adapt, and create an efficient, global communication policy.

The very coherence of a coherent communication policy is based on company objectives and how resources and means are taken into account. Managing communication policy means fixing objectives, choosing the right promotional mix (media, media vehicles) and defining the company's key values. In its widest sense, managing communication strategy is essential to the brand, which relies on every type of communication, from the sales force, to distributed material and advertising campaigns, to company vehicles on which there is the company logo or slogan, etc.

1.1   Communication objectives

The communication policy must be in step with the marketing strategy and the overall company strategy: constraints and financial objectives of production, supply, logistics, market share, the competition, distribution channels, suppliers, company culture, etc.

Generally speaking, the objectives of business to business communication are close to those of mass-market communication. The objective is to develop the renown of the company, its expertise, and its products, to improve exposure through better identification, to optimize its attraction, to encourage preference and finally to increase the desire to buy, thus increasing actual purchasing. There are numerous objectives starting with improving the company image (strength, rapidity, quality, ecology, and technological edge) to supporting the sales force and its actions, as well as providing information on products and services (new products, new applications). It is also a question of keeping new customers loyal, reassuring customers and prospective customers with the company renown, image and references, and eventually getting to the often inaccessible people in charge who influence purchasing. In short, the aim of communication is to make selling easier, not to sell.

Even though most communication does not focus on the brand itself, the latter needs to be integrated and optimized in any action undertaken (respecting the corporate identity code, guaranteeing the quality of anything conveying the image, etc.).

For the company, specifically defining communication objectives calls for the development of a communication strategy which can generate synergies and reinforce the impact of anything the company wishes to undertake. These objectives concern targets and market segments where the brand needs to be promoted, the level of anticipated awareness, and the choice of brands to be promoted.

The communication strategy gives a detailed account of the communication actions indicating targets, objectives, sales arguments, the copy strategy to favor, the operations schedule as well as the ways of checking and evaluating the efficiency of the measures carried out as a function of objectives, and finally the sales communication budget. The communication budget determines the choice of media and vehicles, but it also determines the opportunities in terms of brand management (creation of new brands, support of brands in trouble, brand extensions, etc.).

1.2 Choosing targets and establishing the budget

The communication policy must be a strategic continuum, with high points to mark special events, such as exhibitions and launches, so as to bolster the image of the company, the brand and to be ever present for the different targets: customers, prospective customers, distributors, influencers, suppliers, shareholders, customers' clients, etc.

The heterogeneous nature of the target populations calls for a highly specialized communication strategy. Communication actions must be aimed at several population levels in order to gain support for the sale. In-house and external influencers, deciders, buyers, users and opinion-makers all need to be addressed. In other words, targets with different motivations and interests. The company is linked to a far-reaching economic environment; any information diffused (deliberately or not) is picked up by customers or prospective customers, but also by suppliers, shareholders, personnel, financial institutions, administrative bodies, competitors, the job market, the media and the general public, etc (Figure 1).

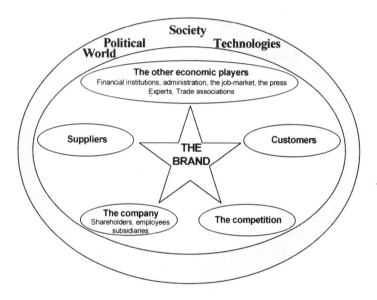

Figure 1. Relationship between the brand and the environment[1]

To reach the company's targets, messages and the use of selected media must be carefully chosen. The purchasing decision is made by a select group, the members of the buying center, each of whom has different backgrounds and responsibilities; as such, they need to be informed using different communication channels in order to catalyze overall support for the purchase. As business to business communication budgets are relatively limited compared to those allotted to everyday consumer goods, companies are looking for maximum impact: messages delivered to the very nerve center of the targets, a rebound media policy in order to reach the prospective customer through several successive channels. The number and the type of targets covered by the communication strategy require using the best adapted and the most efficient communication tools.

1.3 Evaluating measures

It is essential to evaluate and check the effect of any measures taken: before and after studies make it possible to analyze developments resulting from the overall marketing means used (launching of new products, communication, price cuts....). The cost of measures taken must be paralleled by results obtained. By analyzing results, corrective action can be taken, and new directions can be suggested for subsequent measures. However it is of the utmost importance to retain communication unity and coherence, not only regarding the marketing strategy and the company's general objectives, but also with regard to measures taken in the past. In this way, it is possible to keep track of the continuity of image building: public relations, technical documents, company logos, and sales aids.

The company and the brand image depend on it. Communication plays an important role in industry in terms of (Malaval, 1996; Reeder and *al.*, 1991; Levitt, 1966; Webster, 1968):
- Strengthening awareness,
- Presenting and explaining the products and services offered,
- Memorizing the brand,
- Introducing sales representatives,
- Justifying and legitimizing the company,
- Generally improving sales efficiency,
- Reminding and follow-up (reassuring the customer that he has made the right choice).

Depending on the objectives set, targets established, budgets allocated and tools used (push or pull measures), different types of communication are possible. Communication is not just advertising, above all, in business to business: while two thirds of business transactions are between business professionals, business to business advertising represents only a quarter of investment in publicity (Mahin, 1991; Hutt and Speh, 1995).

2. DIFFERENT KINDS OF COMMUNICATION

2.1 Corporate communication

Corporate communication covers all in-house and external communication measures centered on the company and taken with the aim of developing its awareness, and improving and maintaining its image vis à vis the different target populations.

The objective of corporate communication is therefore to:

- Showcase the different areas of expertise and activities of the company,
- Reach the different targets.

In other words, it is a question of presenting and explaining the overall activity of the company, while specifying the different fields of expertise and action. For instance, Du Pont de Nemours chose in particular economic magazines to publicize its various areas of know-how and excellence in chemicals, fibers, life sciences, and polymers.

This type of communication is also used by foreign companies whose full range of activities are still relatively little known nationally such as the Korean conglomerates Hyundai, Ssangyong, Samsung, and Daewoo. Thus corporate communication makes it possible to reach different targets such as opinion makers, institutions, general management, young graduates, personnel, the general public, financial circles, etc. In France, the Saint-Gobain privatization campaign in 1986 made it possible, in particular, to familiarize the financial world with the company's expertise. Institutional communication covers measures which aim to build and strengthen identity, technical credibility, image, short and long-term awareness. It is used to reinforce personnel sense of belonging and motivation (in particular of the sales team), starting with the principle that a known and recognized brand reassures customers and partners. Corporate communication, which expresses the identity of the company, must reflect this: "it must say what it is, what it can do, and what it does" (Garbett, 1981). This type of communication is being developed in business to business. Sponsorship, philanthropy, prestigious publications, exhibitions, factory visits, and corporate advertising are just some aspects of corporate communication. But it is largely widely disseminated media that are most often used, especially business publications. These corporate operations can be associated with public relations and press relations. Participation in big conferences, sports, humanitarian and cultural events (the Olympic Games, the Soccer World Cup, painting retrospectives...) strengthen the image of companies by channeling positive ideas such as durability, confidence, and quality. The big investment that these events call for lends considerable prestige to a brand.

2.2   Brand communication

This kind of communication focuses on a company brand without any specific or technical reference to the products marketed under this brand. Brand communication meets up with corporate communication when the name of the company is also the name of the brand. The aim of this type of communication, which is often used when the group has several brands, is to strengthen the impact of the brand by increasing awareness, improving image, and developing the capacity to modify buying behavior. The targets are varied: general management, financial management, technical specialists, buyers, users, journalists, suppliers and clients' customers. The point is to demonstrate the expertise of the brand using different communication tools and techniques: advertising media, horizontal press, vertical press, economic press, public relations, sponsoring, direct marketing, etc (Figure 2).

Figure 2. Example of brand communication: Tactel[R] by Du Pont de Nemours

2.3   Product communication

The aim of this communication strategy, which focuses on the product or the service, is to support and promote sales. Designed to reach buyers, users, technicians, design offices, as much as distributors and journalists, it can be mainly sales or information oriented (*persuasive or informative communication*). Product communication thus has the double objective of informing and convincing.

- *Informative communication* is meant to:
- Inform the market of the existence of a new product,
- Suggest new applications,

- Publicize a price change,
- Explain how the product functions,
- Describe the services offered,
- Reduce the fears of the buyer.
• *Persuasive communication* makes it possible to:
- Create brand preference,
- Modify market perception of the product's attributes,
- Encourage or strengthen loyalty, stimulate an immediate purchase,
- Facilitate an interview with a sales representative.

Thus product communication is generally used for the launching of a new product or to help products or services which have reached maturity or are in the declining stage of their life cycle. All types of communication can be used, but those with a strong commercial emphasis such as the sales force, technical documentation, show-rooms, trade shows, direct marketing, and promotional sales, are particularly effective. Sales advertising makes it possible to promote sales by featuring a special offer. It reaches a large audience at relatively low cost. Certain media, such as tracts and mailings, are feasible for low budgets, while the press, the radio or television require a comparatively high investment. Classified ads are an effective, inexpensive means of disseminating information concerning a sale, a service, or an event.

2.4   Collective communication

Financed and organized by all or most of the companies in an industrial sector through a trade association, federation or employers' federation, collective communication aims to promote an activity sector or a generic product without referring to any brands. The goal is to institutionalize the product among professional influencers, users and the general public, using mass media, the horizontal and vertical press, public relations, and press relations.

Collective advertising, by promoting the whole industry/activity, generic product, or all of the companies in a given sector, contributes to regulating competition. In addition, it can increase interest in a material such as aluminium, steel, wood, cardboard, leather, plastic, wool or glass. This was the case for the ad campaign on steel which highlighted the material's advantages in terms of easy recycling, thus benefiting all of the actors in the steel industry: manufacturers, packagers, recyclers, etc.

2.5   In-house communication

In-house communication is aimed at targets within the company, the main objective being to increase the personnel's sense of belonging, but also to better channel the messages given out by personnel. Indeed in-house communication reaches beyond the company to address partners and external targets either directly, by exporting in-house communication, or indirectly through the personnel acting as a vehicle for the company's communication. Thus in-house communication plays a very important role in external communication by reinforcing the corporate image of the company and lending credibility to information transmitted to outside contacts (the feeling of having access to confidential, non-sales oriented information). Big firms don't hesitate to segment their internal targets, producing several in-house publications depending on whether they are aimed at the sales team, management, or personnel in general (Figure 3).

Figure 3. Example of an in-house magazine: Motorola

In-house communication that mobilizes people, bringing them together, has a double function:

• To provide information on new products, new markets, new communication campaigns, events (shows or other...),

• To involve, by providing information on the sales performance of different departments, different activities, and different regions. The communication can also involve testimonies through a description of the performance of a particular manager, and especially of the method used to achieve this performance. Communication also lets people know about the media effect of certain measures taken by the company and its partners.

Thus in-house communication expresses the personality of the company. The brand, which is usually associated with the external image, is also a tool to develop loyalty and internal motivation. Developing interactive information, emotional ties and a multi-direction, constant flow of information can strengthen this sense of belonging. By making personnel aware of the challenges faced by the company and involving them in the life of the company, in-house communication fosters team spirit, strengthens cohesion, and helps to build trust. On a human level, it favors relationships based on reciprocity.

In order to reach these objectives, in-house communication relies on different media:

- Company handbook,
- Company audiovisual aids (in-house video magazine or radio tapes),
- Videoconferences and teleconferences,
- In-house newspaper,
- Personnel letter,
- In-house posting,
- Meetings, conferences,
- Telephone magazine,
- Internal electronic messaging, internal computer network, Intranets,
- Participation in trade shows,
- Presentations,
- Training,
- Expression and motivation seminars, trips,
- In-the-field contacts,
- Participation in cultural or sporting events.

Furthermore, the brand image is also expressed internally through the physical makeup of the company, the aesthetics of its architecture, interior decoration and design (cleanliness, lighting, overall harmony, etc.), the appearance of buildings and company premises (signs, shelves, safety equipment, upkeep of lawns, etc.), cars and production materials, working clothes etc.

3.   TARGETED COMMUNICATION

By improving brand awareness and image, communication "pre-sells" the company to different targets thus making the job of the sales department easier. The sale begins long before the first meeting with the sales representative takes place; it starts with recognition of products, services, and the company offering them. In other words, communication is the first step to customer relations.

While the buyer considers the reputation of the company (awareness, know-how, references...) when choosing suppliers, he also takes into account the recommendations of experts, articles in the press, testimonies, and information picked up at events (shows, conferences, colloquiums). Thus the communication strategy used by the supplier brand should:

• Reach all those involved in the buying process: from the prospective customer to influencers to filters and users,

• Provide support at each step of the process leading to the purchase: from discovery of the company, its activities, and its products, to the buying decision.

3.1   Key accounts

Considering the generally limited number of potential customers, the technical complexity of products and services offered, and the human relations' side of business to business, companies are developing targeted approaches in sales and communication. This means first setting up a specialized sales team, but also developing a targeted communication strategy based on the activity sector, the customer category, and key accounts.

This targeted approach allows companies to more efficiently respond to potential customers by providing them with technical information, detailed sales arguments, as well as examples of applications that are perfectly adapted to their activity and to their needs. The most efficient communication strategy is one that is tailor made to key accounts, taking into account:

• The diversity of people involved, each of whom has very different roles, motivations, training and information levels within the customer company,

• The particular buying phase of the customer company, from anticipation and recognition of a need, to information feedback and performance evaluation, etc.

• The customer company's specific buying situations (new task, modified rebuy, straight rebuy).

A highly personalized inter-individual relationship needs to be set up in order to target different members of the buying center.

3.2   Members of the buying center

In companies, the purchasing decision is made as a group by a highly heterogeneous, varied number of people in charge. Each of them has:
- Different experience in their present or previous companies,
- A different level of training,
- Different responsibilities.

In addition, the level of responsibility they hold in their company depends on seniority, professional background, and performance. Finally, they are likely to be under conflicting pressure from different suppliers. Consequently, the buying center, which varies depending on the buying situation and the importance of the project and its technical specifications, requires a highly customized approach from the supplier brand. This means:
- Targeting different decision-makers, after having evaluated their respective input in the final decision,
- Winning each manager over with individualized arguments adapted to their main respective motivations,
- Making sure that there is coherence between the arguments presented to the different managers.

The information disseminated by the brand depends, within the buying center, on the different functions of the members. The following table suggests an example of messages targeted as a function of the responsibilities of the buying center members (Table 4).

Table 4. Targeted communication according to buying center members

Functions	Messages
Production director	- compatibility with existing tool - productivity - operating conditions
Quality director	- quality of finished product - production process
Head of research and development	- gain from integrating product in future developments - helping to find new applications
Marketing director	- product advantages which can be highlighted - influencer in terms of production
Sales director	- himself an influencer on marketing - will facilitate sale of the final product
Head of maintenance	- the new equipment is easy to deal with and his job will not be made more difficult

Functions	Messages
Purchasing director	- respecting procedures as much as possible, by making information available to him early on (ex. purchase marketing)
Financial director	- showing him that he stands to win, in spite of a higher price, thanks to the possible final sale price and/or the quantities sold

Depending on the objectives of the communication policy and the budget, companies must use specialized communication tools to reach each target in a direct and personalized way.

4. USE OF SPECIALIZED MEDIA

In business to business, communication strategy draws on a wide range of tools, from sales documents, such as company brochures, catalogs and technical documents, to sales promotions, public relations, and sponsoring. Certain tools are specific to business to business, such as trade shows or trade magazines. Other tools come from the consumer market, but their relative importance in the communication mix is very different.

Before introducing them, it should be remembered that each of the communication tools has, to varying degrees, both a sales and informative function: from those which make it possible to transmit the message using information and presentation messages, to those which develop sales through demonstrations leading to negotiations and the signing of contracts. The brand, which is contained in and expressed by each of the possible tools, brings together the communication, symbolizing and standing for company values. It is a transversal factor of communication and can be seen in each communication action such as:
- The launching of new products and services,
- Participation in an important event for the sector,
- The announcement of a new industrial site,
- The acquisition of distribution or production units,
- Perfecting of new procedures,
- Registration of patents,
- The launching of a communication campaign,
- Presence at a highly publicized event,
- Presentation of company results,
- Recruitment of partners and distributors.

The brand is thus situated at the center of Figure 5, which schematically situates the main communication tools and brand media according to their principal function, either information or sales.

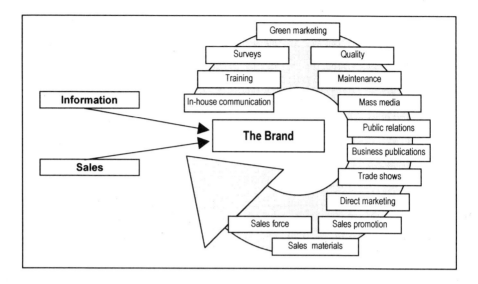

Figure 5. The brand and the double function of communication tools: sales and information[2]

When choosing communication tools the "source effect" or in other words, the credibility and legitimacy of the medium used, in terms of expertise, confidence, and popularity, must be taken into consideration. It is extremely important to make sure that the message is as efficient as possible and coherent both in its own terms, with the company's communication strategy, and especially with the targets aimed at.

However, while there is a great diversity of tools used, certain among them have a major role such as:

- The sales force,
- Trade shows,
- Trade magazines,
- Sales materials,
- Promotional techniques,
- Public relations and lobbying.

4.1   The sales force

A company's most important communication channel is its sales force owing to the technical complexity of products and negotiating procedures. It is through communication that the sales force begins to establish customer relations. The high cost of personal selling means that companies need to provide effective backup to the sales force by adopting the right communication strategy. The company must build up its awareness, its image, and its presentation of services or products offered, so as to pave the way for the sales force, making their job as productive as possible.

From the very first meeting, the sales manager establishes a double communication, one that is both inter-individual and corporate. In other words, beyond the relationship between two people, there is an exchange between two companies building a link. Communicating about the products and activities of the company is easier when there is already strong brand awareness. When the sales representative presents his name and that of the company, he stands to benefit from the good image of the company. The opposite is also true, if the sales representative is impolite or always late, he makes the company and the brand itself look bad. The sales force "is" the company and its brands in the eyes of the customer. The objective of different marketing methods is thus to improve company image, but also to overcome any bad impressions which have already been made. Long-term brand management means guaranteeing the lifetime of the brand beyond inter-personal relationships, which can be effective, but which are difficult to control and often risky.

In addition to the sales force, company employees, suppliers, but also the families and colleagues of the members of buying centers of customers, can all, to a certain extent, be considered inter-individual media, acting as channels for the company. An individual can be a potentially powerful spokesperson for the brand in so far as his personal credibility reinforces that of the brand that he is talking about. Taken in its widest meaning, inter-individual media is, however, difficult for the company to control and can be a potential risk. However, the company's other communication tools make it possible to seduce and influence individuals, thus reducing the uncertainty factor.

Apart from the sales force, the two main communication and sales tools in the industrial context are trade shows and trade magazines.

4.2   Trade shows

Trade shows bring together supply and demand in one place, where it is possible to get market information directly from exhibitors and visitors, and where buyers can look, compare, and order (Banting and Blenkhorn, 1974). They provide a unique opportunity to discover on the spot, the latest developments of interest in the industry.

Trade shows[3] are considered to be a means of:
- Making sales,
- Maintaining the company image for customers,
- Breaking into a new market,
- Changing customer and potential-customer preferences,

- Developing contacts with new distributors and improving the company image with current distributors,
- Establishing contacts and an image with new and prospective customers,
- Testing a new concept or idea,
- Introducing a new product line, and introducing it to a wide public,
- Presenting normally non-transportable, bulky equipment,
- Resolving technical problems,
- Finding new ideas and applications,
- Presenting and developing sales arguments to a relatively large and involved public,
- Motivating and leading the sales force,
- Countering the participation of competitors,
- Recruiting personnel,
- Rapidly, easily, and inexpensively getting information,
- Keeping an eye on the competition (strategy, new products…),
- Developing corporate image (trade magazines present…),
- Strengthening partnerships,
- Meeting professional organizations, official and public institutions, and the press,
- Finding out about other industrial events in the country and abroad,
- Allowing customers and prospective customers to get hands-on experience with the products,
- Prospecting new customers and enriching the sales force's prospective customer file,
- Improving the company image and taking advantage of a "free public",
- Quickly breaking into a foreign market and making contacts at a low cost.

For companies, trade shows are often a big part of the marketing communication budget used to back up sales (Bonoma, 1983). However, the share of the overall marketing communication budget devoted to trade shows varies a great deal, as does the frequency of annual participation in events, depending on the activity sector, the country considered, and the company size. Apart from the sales force and distributors, trade shows sometimes are the only sales marketing tool used by companies, helping to make over 10% of their turnover. It is easier and less expensive for the company to make a sale that has already been started at a show (number of necessary contacts, etc.).

The objectives for participating in a show, when they are defined, are mainly commercial (Lilien, 1983; Tanner and Chonko, 1995). Trade shows, essential for doing international business (O'Hara and *al.*, 1993), are a crucial part of the sales strategy of companies for making contacts, finding new markets, and improving their image. They provide an opportunity to create or improve brand image: over 75% of visitors to a company stand remember having stopped at the stand more than 8 to 10 weeks after the show. Trade visitors, retailers, influencers, users, and decision-makers are key targets of company communication policy. Most visitors (80%) have an important role in their company's buying center, are well informed, and have the power to make decisions (Johnston, 1981). The company needs to have experienced sales people working at the stand, along with sales technicians, and other technically qualified personnel (Hotch, 1991). In addition to the team, the quality of the stand (surface area, originality, cleanliness, comfort, reception, etc.) also benefits the brand. Participation in a show must therefore be carefully planned and prepared so that the stand serves the brand as effectively as possible.

Besides regional, national, and international shows, there are now events organized at customer or supplier firms, exhibition areas at conventions and conferences, and other one-off events. Participation in reverse trade shows is a way to develop brand awareness with potential suppliers.

4.3   The trade press

The trade press includes those publications, which deal with a specialized field and have a mainly professional readership. For these readers, the trade press is a serious, pertinent, and practical professional tool. It includes magazines, newspapers, journals, specialized directories, and confidential letters, among others.

A European study[4] shows that the trade press is the first tool that decision-makers think of when they want to communicate with other professionals (66.8% compared with 17.9% for direct marketing, 6.3% for shows, 1% for the economic press). The trade press dominates in advertising investment for trade communication (41.6% compared with 32% for shows, 19.5% for direct marketing, and 6.9% for the other types of press). The trade press is most often used for product advertising (65.3% as against 34.7% for image advertising) (Figure 6).

In general, there are two types of trade press:

• *Horizontal titles*, or general technical or trade publications, read by people from all different sectors. These are a good way of reaching a wide range of diverse technicians at different levels of the company. *Plant Engineering, Business Week, Advertising Age* are directed at a specific task, technology or function, whatever the industry.

• *Vertical titles*, or specialized trade publications, which only interest the particular members of a sector, i.e. the chemical or the building industries. For example, *Coal Age, Iron Age, Glass Industry, Aerospace Engineering*,

Flight Daily News, Chemical Week, respectively target people working in steel industry, glass, aerospace and aeronautics, and pharmaceuticals.

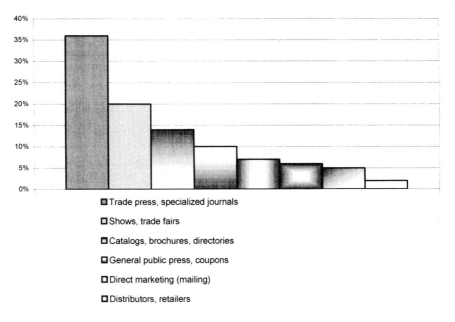

Figure 6. Division of the communication-marketing budget in industry[5]

Companies use trade publications for their communication, with editorial advertising, technical articles, ads, insert ads, etc. In general, they put ads in targeted professional media (directories, specialized trade magazines). Only companies which have international markets or are looking to break into one use more widely disseminated media (national press, etc.).

4.4   Sales documents

Business documentation includes all the company's sales materials from leaflets and brochures, data sheets, technical and business specification sheets, catalogs and guides right up to price lists, tariff schedules and of course CD ROMs. Each of these documents, presenting services and products, must optimize the brand, keeping in mind the visual identity and overall graphics which have been chosen; the contents and layout of these documents must convey the company image. Indeed, they often represent the very first contact between the company and its prospective customers or targets.

The company brochure is the first business and informative document from the company. Care must be taken with it just as much as with all the identifying media, including the company paper and business cards. It conveys the company image and sells its services, know-how, experience, and culture. Most initial business contacts rely on such documents and sometimes even initiate them. After having given out the brochure at an exhibition for example, the company can be contacted by people who have only read this presentation document. Companies pay great attention to documents featuring business references, which serve as commercial and moral guarantees for the company. Even if small and medium sized businesses are more likely to attach great importance to their business references, the larger groups do not hold back on citing their main customers as a proof and recognition of their competence, know-how, and experience. Industrial buyers often demand such guarantees from their suppliers.

Catalogs are the principal means of communication in industrial companies. Here you have a real guide including order forms, designed to provide the potential buyer with clear choices. Catalogs and technical documents are a sort of company display window, giving technical details of the product or service (photographs, technical plans, dimensions, sizes, colors, options, building advice, illustrations of products being used...).

For companies like Pass & Seymour, Square D or Norton, catalogs are key professional communication tools, which often become "bibles" within their respective sectors (electrical equipment, building sector). They are real tools, which are actually used and needed by professionals.

Even if paper is still the main medium in use, today, there are numerous catalogs on CD-ROM (or DVD-ROM), or on company websites. Brochures often accompany the general document, which is sometimes published in several languages (Figure 7).

Figure 7. The Boeing CD-ROM Sea-Launch

Technical documents are absolutely essential sales back-up for any complex or technologically specific product. Destined to be used by professionals, they must be precise and complete without being too detailed, otherwise they will be unusable, incomprehensible and run the risk of making the recipient feel that he or she is incompetent. Above all, these data sheets must be practical, useful and capable of answering most technical questions concerning characteristics, specifications, norms, procedures, special points, etc.

4.5   Promotional techniques

Contrary to advertising, which acts on motivations and has a long-term effect, promotional techniques work more on behavior and have a short-term effect. We are talking here about a group of stimulation techniques destined mainly for industrial customers and prospective customers (samples, bonuses, etc.) but which can also be used by distributors and the sales force (discounts, help with publicity, etc.). As a complementary back-up to advertising or in conjunction with direct marketing actions, promotion gives a more direct, concrete, immediate, ephemeral, exceptional and unusual character to the proceedings: it underlines some special advantage about the product offered. Although promotions are often directed at sales, their very mechanism and the techniques used can just as easily play a part in the building of the brand image. In fact, promotions can very well become part of an actual long-term program, rather than being simple one-off tactics. And even in the latter case, promotions must not be isolated from all the other operations, nor kept apart from company marketing strategy. It is a question of keeping an eye on the coherence between possible promotions and other operations aimed at communication. They must comply with the positioning requirements and the overall graphics laid down by the communications department. Even if sales promotion has an obviously commercial vocation, it is also a tool to be used in communication strategy. Here the company must opt for promotional techniques which will tend to increase its commercial efficiency without at the same time affecting its image.

Among the most frequently used promotional techniques in the industrial sector are:

- *Samples* (materials, spare parts, components, etc.) and *free trials* (equipment, machine tools, vehicles, etc.). A variation of this consists of offering an optional extra, free for a certain period of time. Contrary to supermarket samples, which are all standard, business to business samples are very often tailor made. Some makers offer their customers a symbolic sample, a memory jogging souvenir. This is true for Rox, who give customers a sample of their multi-diameter module (a sort of strippable cable sheathing) used especially for cable and pipe runs in industrial and building applications. The sample gives a good demonstration of how the product works because the customer can strip back the various layers for himself. In the same way, samples of Skyflex®, a material developed by Gore from the famous Gore-Tex® (Polytetrafluoroethylene), are given to aircraft builders in an effort to reinforce product familiarity (texture, resistance, etc.).

- *Payment of advertising*: this is participating in the customer's or distributor's publicity budget. The microprocessor company, Intel, uses this method in its clever and original "Intel Inside® " campaign. Payment of the advertising, from 10 to almost 50% of the campaign costs is made according to how much mention of Intel there is in the customer's message.
- *Games and competitions*: these allow the creation of mobilizing events for the customers, distributors or the sales force.
- *Presents*: small useful objects – calendars, key-rings, diaries – and all other company presents are part of communication. The giving of the object enlivens the handing over of documents as much for regular customers as for prospective ones. This object bears details about the company and possibly a short advertising message. The presence of certain big industrial brand names on advertising objects is designed to keep the name at the forefront, and at the same time, give pleasure to those who receive them and show them off. The objective is for the brand to be better identified and therefore better appreciated. These presents also have an emotional and "at play" dimension to them. They will never be the factor which sets an order going, but they can help to build a good relationship: their effectiveness stems largely from the way they are offered. Above all, they must not be seen as a purchasing constraint. The 3M Post-It® brand produces publicity objects in this way by printing the customer's logo on each leaf of its pads. The customer can then offer these publicity pads to his own clients and by so doing, give a daily reminder in their offices of his brand name. Post-It® has even gone to the extent of making pads of paper in the shape of the customer's logo. There are two categories of small advertising material:
  - The first, which accounts for most of the volume, is made up of small practical, mainly office work objects: writing materials, from throwaway pens to the top of the range, folio-cubes, Post-It®, rulers, calculators, diaries, calendars, etc.
  - The second category covers those objects with no direct link to the company's activities such as advertising clothing, T-shirts, windbreakers, track suits, umbrellas, caps, stickers, watches or smart

cards given to customers, prospective customers, contractors, and distributors. The smaller and more discrete the brand, the more they are appreciated, which goes against all the rules of good advertising.

- The *creation of traffic*: this consists of drawing in customers to a given place for a special show where the brand is present (show rooms, conventions, suppliers, temporary exhibitions, industrial stores, traveling demonstration vans...).

All these promotional techniques establish a relationship between the brand and in-house or outside targets and provide the opportunity of closing the gap between them. Sales promotion mainly includes the following media (see Table 8).

Table 8. Promotional aids classified by producer preference[6]

The most commonly used media by suppliers with industrial customers	Less commonly used media by suppliers with industrial customers	The least often used media by suppliers with industrial customers
Specialized catalogs	Advertising materials	Market studies
Trade fairs and shows	(printer's proofs)	Mobile advertising
Technical aids	New models, giveaways	Information letters for
Product training	Display stands	distributors
Sales and applications	Signs, posters	Information letters for
training	Demonstrators	end-users
Advertising inserts	Visual and audiovisual sales	Samples
Price lists	aids	
	Advertising cooperation	
	programs	

Direct marketing, also mainly considered as a marketing sales tool, covers all the individual and interactive direct communication means which have been designed to trigger an immediate reaction in the people targeted. Direct marketing uses a database, which makes it possible to establish specialized and personal relationships between the company and its potential customers. So as not to hurt the company image, up-to-date data bases need to be used: incorrect targeting is not well looked upon by the managers of customer companies who can base their opinion of the company and its products or services on just such a mistake (wasteful, inefficient, and irrelevant measures). Direct marketing involves all promotional and communication techniques which trigger an immediate response by providing the population targeted with the means to directly transmit an answer to the company. There are many tools, from mail-order sales, mailing, bus-mailing, telesales, fax, and the Internet, to television, and ads in magazines or newspapers with highly specialized readerships. Other tools are also used (Shapiro and Wyman, 1981), such as package inserts, mail ads, take-one ads, posters, catalogs, samples, television, audio or video cassettes, the radio, diskettes, CD-ROMs, and interactive terminals (Figure 9).

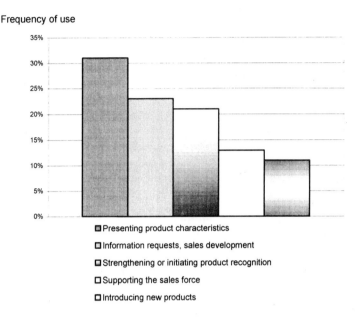

Frequency of use

□ Presenting product characteristics
□ Information requests, sales development
□ Strengthening or initiating product recognition
□ Supporting the sales force
□ Introducing new products

Figure 9. Applications of direct marketing in industrial marketing[7]

4.6   Public relations and lobbying

Public relations covers company communication taking the form of a dialogue with the different groups concerned: customers, prospective customers, partners likely to hold back or encourage the company's activities, and any other related group.

Public relations can have varied in-house or external targets. Such as:
- Institutional and governmental bodies,
- Socio-economic and socio-cultural groups, such as trade unions or the medical profession,
- The stock market, financial circles, shareholders and potential shareholders,
- Trade groups,
- Personnel and personnel representatives,
- Current and potential suppliers, competitors and distributors,

- Trade and general public media (specialized publications), national and international, press, radio, television, press agencies...
- Influencers, experts.

Public relations, which rank high on the credibility scale, are a powerful tool of expression and dissemination. As such, they are very successful at breaking down resistance, and are one of the information sources used by industrial customers to make the purchasing decision. The objectives of public relations can be varied: to increase brand awareness, to explain what the company does and make sure that this activity is understood and accepted, to obtain backing or support for a distribution operation, or to establish a partnership. Public relations require careful follow-up to control their effect on brand image. In general, the goal is to establish a relationship based on trust and understanding with the target population, providing objective information concerning the company's activities. This should be done without any propaganda or commercial advertising, in accordance with the principle of the "free use" of the media. It is less a question of selling, than of obtaining valuable moral support to facilitate the activity of the company. For greater synergy, public relations are often linked to other communication operations like direct marketing.

As with mass marketing, public relations uses the press, in particular, for the launching of new products or company events (press kits, press releases, specialized documents, press conferences, interviews, press trips, editorial advertising, technical articles, seminars, annual reports, the Internet, CD ROMs, etc.) Press relations are used as much by small and medium-sized companies as by big groups because of their cost-effectiveness and impact, the fact that they are easy to set up, and involve very specific targets (press spin-offs, number of articles, lines, media audience, frequency of the appearance of the company name or operations. The French subsidiary of Du Pont de Nemours, world leader in chemicals, launched a press relations operation with the aim of strengthening the innovative image of the group, which spends over 1.2 billion dollars on research and development every year. The company had two surveys made; one concerned inventions in general, and involved a representative panel of public opinion. The other concerned the company's inventions and was aimed at company customers. A press kit was established to present the inventions chosen by the public (the television, the computer, and heart transplants), with a piece on the Du Pont technology necessary for their functioning. Over 300 press kits were released. The magazine, *Les Echos Industries*, which was a priority target because of its readership (deciders), had 4 editorial pages citing Du Pont de Nemours. The eve of publication, 400 customers, journalists, and partners were invited by Du Pont de Nemours to the Cité des Sciences de la Villette to a preview of an exhibit on different Du Pont innovations such as Nylon or

Teflon®. The results of the study were also presented. *France Soir* newspaper, *France Info*, the leading information radio, and *LCI*, the leading French language TV news, also publicized the survey.

Another example is given by the manufacturing company Pechiney, which brought together 15 European industrial firms such as BSN Emballage, Elf Atochem, Solvay, SCA, and others, in the "Pack-EE" (Packaging and Environment in Europe program). The aim of this group was to join in research on optimizing waste from packaging. After obtaining the Eureka label, the program needed a communication strategy that would target the press, industrial users, and governmental administrations. Lead by Pechiney, a press conference was organized at the Maison de la Chimie (Center for Chemistry) in Paris; European researcher, and 200 participants, including 60 journalists from all over Europe, attended. A press kit was produced, which involved the translation of scientific papers and their simplification so as to be understood by a non-specialist public. For a relatively low total budget, the operation successfully optimized the companies' corporate brands in relation to the three defined targets.

The brand can also be promoted using sponsoring or corporate philanthropy. This gives industrial firms a corporate image which can reach a wide range of populations. For the company, sponsoring means supporting an event or an individual, in association with the company name or one of its brands. This commercially oriented, event-based communication strategy has short-term effects (sales objectives, awareness, image). Corporate philanthropy is another form of event-based communication. However, it aims at attaining long-term social approval and recognition for the firm and its corporate name. In comparison to sponsoring, greater discretion is exercised surrounding the event. From organizing conventions, conferences, and seminars, to holding open-door days, publishing art books, or restoring great paintings, all of these measures aim to optimize the company image and strengthen its awareness with respect to target populations, in particular, the general public. To control the brand image, the company which participates in or organizes an event, must first specifically structure any actions within the framework of the communication policy. This generally means setting specific participation objectives, ensuring the coherence of actions, and devoting the necessary budget. Then the results of the operation can be measured.

Lobbying aims to obtain from the authorities the decisions which will make it possible for the company to develop its activity, launch new products, thanks to the adoption of favorable norms, or benefit from government aid. For pressure groups, this means a communication strategy aimed at very specific targets capable of influencing market operating rules. Over 40% of industrial companies use lobbying with the authorities:

administrations, the government, the parliament, ministries, international organizations.

Lobbying can involve direct methods: one-to-one, personal interviews, publications of white papers, invitations to politicians to visit factories, sending of useful information such as company newspapers, technical files, the organization of conventions or symposiums to which well known people have been invited. There are also indirect methods: the press, third party testimonies, dis-information, etc.

4.7   Other business to business communication tools

To promote their brands suppliers can selectively use all of the communication tools discussed so far. Continuing along the same lines and in synergy with them, industrial companies have also developed different types of marketing methods focusing on the products or services they offer. For example, by providing training to customers and potential customers, as well as influencers, the company can strengthen the image of its corporate brand as well as the image of the brands of products presented, as long as the training does not turn into propaganda. Logistics or maintenance services developed by the company can also help to improve the image of its brands (products and corporate), as do instigating a veritable green marketing policy (investments, verifiable measures and results).

Other factors are involved in strengthening the company image, such as setting up a design policy for the products themselves, their packaging and overwrap, the company environment (work clothes, vehicles, premises, letter paper, production sites, production material and tools, truck fleet). Particular care should be taken to ensure that all of the channels for promoting the company brand are well-kept and attractive (maintenance of signs, replacement of old discolored stickers, cleaning and upkeep of vehicles). If not, the image projected will be the opposite of what is desired. The brand image can be reflected using all kinds of communication media and all forms of expression:

- Symbols and logos (themes, styles, types, etc.),
- The choice of media used (written and audiovisual),
- Atmospheres (buildings, cars, agencies, furniture, materials),
- Events.

Big companies often feature their slogans, logos, or graphics on all of the media used for in-house and external communication (public relations, press relations, interpersonal relations, trade fairs and shows, sales documents, mail and mailing, magazines and newspapers, materials, vehicles, etc.). In addition to the content of the message released, the form is paramount; this is true whether the message appears in the press (choice of format, title, texts, pictures, colors), on the radio (recording quality, choice of words, rhythm, voice) or on TV (which has the additional language of gestures and attitudes).

The following drawing (Figure 10) represents the main communication tools described as a function of their commercial role and their capacity to vehicle the brand image:

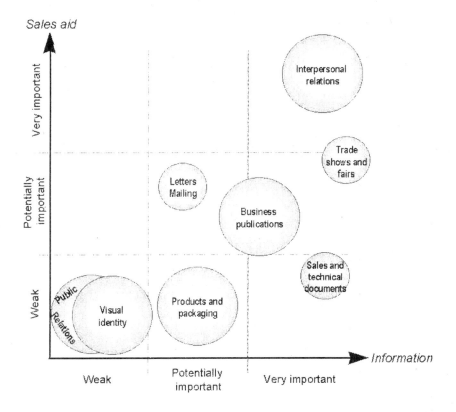

The volume of the circles represents the relative importance of the tools in constructing the brand as a function of their sales and informative roles.

Figure 10. Level of importance of communication tools in constructing the brand[8]

5. USING THE MASS MEDIA

In business to business, use of the mass media is quite limited. Sometimes, for special events, big companies aim their communication at a wider public, beyond the strictly professional world. This is true for corporate campaigns based on ecological themes, the need to increase awareness, present innovations, or communicate changes in the group, and that target all populations.

In particular, companies in the building, electronics, and chemical industries, in the nineties, developed their mass-market communication policy to promote their brands (Figure 11).

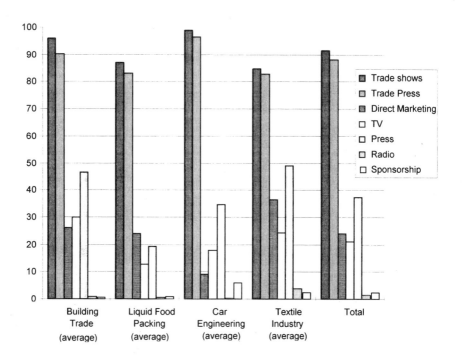

Figure 11. The use of media in four main business sectors[9]

Besides the technical sales arguments that are normally disseminated to direct customers, the company must get involved at the level of the general pubic to strengthen the actions of the company. Support from end-users makes it easier to convince industrial customers. The brand is a key factor in the capital goods industry, as much as it is in the consumer goods sector. Thus Nutrasweet® sweetener, (Monsanto), Teflon® surface coating, (DuPont), Lycra® textile fibers, (DuPont) or the Intel microprocessor have all become benchmarks.

Television and film can both be useful tools for valorizing the company brand. However, these media, with their long reservation times and high cost, are used mostly for the corporate communication of powerful "multimarket" industrial groups, such as General Electric, 3M, Fluor Corporation, Motorola, Owens Corning, Du Pont de Nemours, Dow

Chemical, PPG Industries, Monsanto, Air Products, Alcoa as well as for strong brands such as Gore-Tex®, Intel Pentium®, etc. The Sympatex® membrane, for example, sponsored the weather forecast of Canal Plus (TV Channel).

The particular status of trade service brands often pushes them to opt for mass-market communication. Their services are often mixed, so that they have to address both the general public and professionals, as is the case for banks, temp agencies, insurance, transport, and delivery. Furthermore, their professional clientele is often spread out and heterogeneous (small businesses, artisans, small and medium sized companies, local regional authorities, etc.) so mass market media like television are quite useful.

The radio, which is inexpensive, allows effective local selection. Its flexibility, the rapid effects obtained, and the short reservation times, make it a local communication media often adapted to the announcement of one-off events. For example, sponsorship on a particular radio may increase brand awareness with both the general public and deciders.

6.   THE INTEL COMMUNICATION STRATEGY

At the end of 1991, Intel, world leader in microprocessors, decided to concentrate its energies on microprocessors, after having spent years developing "OEM" (Original Equipment Manufacturer) products, services, and activities for parts manufacturers. The plan was to create ever higher performance computer tools that were more communicative, "transportable", natural, and less expensive. This meant speeding up market acceptance of new technologies: in other words, increasing turnover to be able to maintain the necessary level of investment (research and development budget).

Intel decided to go directly to microprocessor end-users to explain the importance of IT, establish an authenticity label to simplify the choice of the buyer, and to make it easier to commercialize Intel product brands. While Intel had already made a name for itself with its professional clientele, it was almost unknown by the general public: this was no little challenge. How to develop a communication strategy about microprocessors that were not only unseen by most users, but that were also technically complex, and a priori, not particularly attractive, in terms of design, to the general public? The initial step of the first mass-market advertising campaign was to explain to users the key role of the microprocessor in terms of computer performance and user-friendliness. The challenge was to make PC buyers think in terms of technology, as brands such as Gore-Tex®, Teflon®, or Nutrasweet® had, to a certain extent, succeeded in doing. This step was in fact initiated in 1989, with the first Red X mass advertising campaign, which aimed to convince users to switch from 286 to 386 SX technology (Figure 12).

The market continued to perceive the i386 as the top of the range and the 286 as the standard for office use, which created a marketing positioning problem for the i486. Then Windows appeared and the market changed over to 32 bits. Intel couldn't wait. A spectacular and controversial advertising campaign was launched: the "X red" campaign. There was a risk of "killing" the 286 without successfully pushing the 386. The campaign was seen as highly provocative in the IT community. However, people en masse chose the SX version 386 entry level range.

Figure 12. Press and display advertising

Then, in 1991, Intel launched its long-term communication program, "Intel Inside® ". The main goal was to create a visual identity for Intel, a logo that would be as powerfully evocative as the Lacoste crocodile or Adidas's three stripes. The campaign projected a high technology, high performance image, as well as security (reliability and software compatibility). Intel advised PC buyers to check carefully for the logo, the only guarantee of quality.

Using the logo, Intel Inside®, was proposed to PC makers to indicate that their systems integrated a veritable Intel processor and not an imitation: in 1991, 342 makers adopted the Intel Inside® logo, which appeared in 3,000 advertising pages taken out by the very same makers; above all, the logo appeared on the PC itself (increased visibility). The advertising pressure on consumers pushed makers to adopt the Intel Inside® logo in their own ads; what's more, Intel, agreed to pay for part of the cost (25-50%) of the makers' ad space if it included the Intel Inside® logo. Intel used a pull strategy, which aimed to increase brand awareness, beyond computer makers, in downstream markets so as to offset price pressure, as well as pressure from computer makers. By going around the direct customer, and communicating directly with the end consumer, the end market can thus be developed. The Intel brand appeared in ads, and on the machines and packaging of makers, including up to 2,700 appearances a month in the American and European press (Figure 13). The television commercial presenting the new 486 processor took viewers on a spectacular voyage inside a PC (it was directed by the ILM Company, Industrial Light &Magic, George Lucas).

Figure 13. Advertisement promoting the "Intel Inside®" label

In 1993, Intel began a television advertising campaign with, in January/February, the "software library" commercial, explaining Intel Inside®, and in September/October, a commercial highlighting the power of i486 DX2. On March 22, 1993, Intel launched the Pentium processor, which has 3.1 million transistors and 112 million instructions per second power. The Pentium processor is five times more powerful than the standard Intel 486 and 300 times faster than the 8088 processor equipping the first IBM PC's. The commercial features Pentium processors flying inside a PC, giving life to a new generation of multimedia software. The commercials finish with the words "for your next computer, ask for Intel Inside®". It cost over 100 million dollars to launch Intel Inside®, and 150 million to launch Pentium®.

Since 1993, the name of the Pentium® processor has been incorporated into the Intel Inside® logo, thus making a new logo which combines the reliable image of the Intel brand with the MMX® technology developed for the Pentium® brand. Since then, Intel has associated its Intel Inside® logo with each launching of a new product. Intel has created a sound identity by systematically associating its logo during TV commercials with an original 5 note melody (on its own commercials as well as those of makers using or citing the brand). To seduce children, Intel gave a more playful flavor to its commercials with the BunnyPeople characters (Figure 14).

Figure 14. Example of a visual with the "BunnyPeople Characters"

These characters, which first appeared in 1997, are dressed in colorful, fluorescent industrial suits representing Intel engineers and technicians wearing protective clothing. Through these characters at work, Intel aims to promote the reliability and advanced technology of its latest processors, by presenting the designers as technological heroes of the future, rather than basing its communication on the product alone. The characters in colorful outfits, dancing to disco hits such as "Staying alive" or "Play that Funky Music", project a "fun" image, likely to seduce Web surfers; what's more, they seem to be having fun while working. They can be seen as a reference to the white room teams, who, since 1973, have worn bunny suits. The brand awareness went from 20% in 1992, to 80% in 1996 among private buyers, and reached 90% in the professional market. Close to 1,500 PC makers use the Intel Inside® logo, which according to the *American magazine*, *Advertising Age*, has been seen 500 billion times. Eloquent testimony to the success of the Intel brand, in 1997, it was considered to be the number eight brand worldwide in terms of value: 13.27 billion dollars (Willman, 1997).

In the latest campaign, the BunnyPeople Characters invent the Pentium II processor as well as a streamlined vehicle (van designed by the TransFX company, originator of the Batmobile), thanks to which the men in the fluorescent suits can travel all over the world presenting the impressive quality 3D graphics of the new PCs built around this processor. The campaign uses Internet as an advertising channel: besides advertising banners, a promotional contest, called "Around the World", asks users to find clues in seven different sites, the winner getting a PC equipped with a Pentium II processor. A press and radio campaign has been launched to complement the television campaign, so as to create an emotional association between the company and the product. The press campaign emphasizes the symbol "II" in Roman numbers, used in the processor's name (Figure 15).

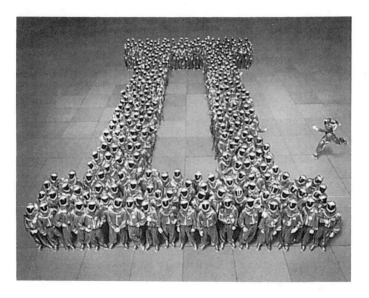

Figure 15. Advertisement for the Pentium II Intel microprocessor

NOTES

1. Bénaroya, C., (1998), *working paper*.
2. Adapted from Malaval, (1996), *Marketing Business to Business*, Paris, Publi-Union.
3. See *Trade Show Bureau* editions (1984), Research Report, East Orleans, Massachusetts.
4. Survey realized by IPSOS-Média in April 1995, for the Trade Press Union.
5. Sources: *McGraw-Hill Research*, LAP report 8015.7 in Mahin, P.W., (1991), p 337.
6. Sources: Hardy, K.G. and Grath A.J., (1988), *Marketing Channel Management, Strategic Planning and Tactics*, Glenview, Illinois, Scott, Foresman and Co., p 611.
7. Sources: Sims and Brown (1979), Increasing the Role of Direct Mail Marketing in Industrial Marketing Strategy, *Industrial Marketing Management*, November, p 295.
8. Bénaroya, C., (1998), *working paper*.
9. Sources: Malaval, Ph., (1998), Exploratory Survey of the Industrial Brand Performance, perceived by the Purchase and Marketing Managers, *The Example of Four Industrial Markets: Building Trade, Liquid Food Packing, Car Engineering and Textile Industry, Thesis for Business Management Doctorate*, Social Sciences University of Toulouse I.
10. Courtesy, Intel Corporation, © 1998 Intel Corporation. Pentium, MMX, BunnyPeople, Intel and Intel Inside logos are trademarks of Intel Corporation.

REFERENCES

Banting, P.M. and Blenkhorn D.L., (1974), The Role of Industrial Trade Shows, *Industrial Marketing Management*, n°3, p 285-295.
Bonoma, T.V., (1983), Get More Out of Your Trade Shows, *Harvard Business Review*, n°61, January-February, p 75-83.
Garbett, T., (1981), *Corporate Advertising: the What, the Why and the How*, New York, McGraw-Hill.
Hotch, M.J., (1991), Improving Your Sales Success at Trade Shows, *Business Marketing*, n°76, n°11, p 26-28.
Hutt, M.D. and Speh, T.W., (1995), *Business Marketing Management, A Strategic View of Industrial and Organizational Markets*, 5th ed., Orlando, Flo., The Dryden Press.
Johnston, W.J., (1981), *Patterns in Industrial Buying Behavior*, New York, Praeger.
Levitt, Th., (1966), Communications and Industrial Selling, *Journal of Marketing*, n°31.
Lilien, G.L., (February 1983), A Descriptive Model of the Trade Show Budgeting Decision Process, *Industrial Marketing Management*, n°12, p 25-29.
Mahin, P.W., (1991), *Business-to-Business Marketing*, Boston, N. Heights, Allyn & Bacon.
Malaval, P., (1996), *Marketing Business to Business*, Paris, Publi-Union.
O'Hara, B., Palumbo F. and Herbig P., (August 1993), Industrial Trade Show Abroad, *Industrial Marketing Management*, n°22, p 233-237.
Reeder, R.R., Brierty, E.G. and Reeder, B.G., (1991), *Industrial Marketing*, Prentice-Hall.
Shapiro, B. and Wyman, J., (1981), New Ways to Reach Your Customers, *Harvard Business Review*, n°59, July-August, p 106.
Szapiro, G., (1988), *Les 10 Principes de la Communication Industrielle*, Paris, Ed. Organisation.
Tanner, J.F. and Chonko L.B., (1995), Trade Show Objectives, Management, and Staffing Practices, *Industrial Marketing Management*, n°24, p 257-264.
Webster, F.E., (1968), On the Applicability of Communication Theory to Industrial Markets, *Journal of Advertising Research*, n°5, p 426-428.
Willman, J., (1997), The Global Company, *Financial Times*, 17th October.

Chapter 4

The Brand and its Mechanisms

Today, brands are of increasing concern to business professionals, as well as being the subject of numerous surveys and research. Most of the time, brands are analyzed in terms of the consumer market, in other words, from the perspective of the end-user rather than the professional purchaser. Many concepts (brand equity, brand associations, etc.) and tools for measuring brand performance have indeed contributed to understanding their main operating mechanisms, without, however, focusing on the specific context of industrial markets.

In particular, the concept of brand equity, which appeared in the eighties, conveys the complex functioning of the brand and provides a general analytical framework. It can be defined as "the associations and behaviors of the brand's customers, its distribution channels, and the company to which it belongs, which allow branded products to generate greater volume or bigger margins than they would normally be able to do without the brand name, and which gives them a strong, sustained advantage, setting them apart from their competitors"(MSI, 1990). Brand equity embodies the value of the relationships between the products and services offered by the company, its targets, and, in particular, its customers (awareness, image, loyalty, negotiation terms, etc.). To analyze the brand equity of suppliers, the lessons drawn from the consumer market need to be adapted and examined in light of industrial practices.

Indeed, the brand's operating mode in this specific context needs to be understood. This requires studying how the brand works in relation to customers; in other words, measuring brand performance insofar as customers are concerned. To measure brand performance from this point of view, two approaches are generally used:

- The *behavioral approach*, consists of observing customer buying behavior. The actual observation of customer buying behavior would seem to be the most accurate method, as this measures facts and not declarations. Adapted to the study of consumer brands, this approach is almost impossible to apply to industrial brands. The confidential nature of transactions, the almost total absence of panel information, and the specialized nature of the buying process (phases, situations, and buying center), all make it very difficult to directly gather information on behavior. While the behavioral approach is not really adapted to measuring brand equity in a business to business context, it can nevertheless be taken into consideration as a complement to the perceptual approach.

• The *perceptual approach*, measures customer perception of the brand, particularly in terms of attention, awareness, and image. Indeed, individual behavior, attitudes, and opinions, are not controlled by reason alone; they are also the result of emotional reactions. An individual opinion is the result of a combination of elements and factors, and not only of a rational process.

Applied to the brand, this concept of individual opinion leads to analyzing the duality of brand content: to study how the brand functions, both its objective (information that it transmits) and subjective dimension (beliefs that it suggests) need to be considered. To make a name for itself and to be convincing, a brand uses logical proofs (*logos*), but also as support, psychological proof (*pathos*) to be persuasive. This is because information, on the one hand, and opinion, on the other, are two interdependent variables. That is why the more an individual is interested in a subject (subjective dimension), the more information he seeks to obtain (objective dimension). This is particularly true of the professional buyer, who is generally highly informed and looking for maximum information on the different possible supply sources or solutions, in order to reduce the perceived risk associated with, for example, a new purchase. While this process is rational, since it consists in finding the best possible solution to needs expressed by his company, it also involves certain aspects of non-rational decisions. Psychologically speaking, it involves trying to diminish or eliminate the individual's state of tension in order to reach an inner balance.

Today, in industry as well, the brand can arouse and maintain a desire such that the buyer tries to fulfill it by acquiring the proposed product. Insofar as the purchasing decision involves both a concrete and an abstract component, the brand must provide an answer to this duality; this answer lies in the products offered, which correspond to rational expectations, and the "communication", which is linked to more symbolic expectations. In fact, the "qualitative" content of the brand seems to be as important as the description of the products that it guarantees. The rational and non-rational dimensions are found in highly variable proportions in different industrial brands. It is thus possible to measure brand performance from the customer perspective using a perceptual approach. To study how the brand functions, the different mechanisms on which its performance is based must be considered: brand awareness, attention, image, and associations, and the loyalty that these generate.

1. BRAND AWARENESS AND ATTENTION

1.1 Different brand awareness levels

Brand or company awareness can be defined as an individual's level of knowledge of the company or brand in question. This is a key concept, since it is through knowledge of the brand name that a customer asks for one brand or another. The different levels of awareness have been identified (Aaker, 1991):

• The maximum awareness level is reached when the brand is present in the mind of the buyer (or of any other buying center member) who refers to it even outside of the purchase of the products or services concerned. The highest degree of brand recall is *top of mind*, corresponding to the brand mentioned first by the buying center member questioned. This awareness level often corresponds to the case where the brand evaluated is already a company supplier, and where, therefore, thanks to acquired experience, it is better known: quality of services, product reliability, available range. As soon as interest in the supplier brand increases, the information level of the customer company increases. A company that is already a customer is hungry for information about the supplier brand, even more so than a potential customer.

• The second awareness level is when the brand is known. The corresponding measure is *brand recall*. When the buying center member is questioned about a product category, he spontaneously refers to the brand, but among other competing brands. This type of awareness corresponds again to a relatively high level of knowledge of the company. There is however a certain difference between the overall knowledge of the company and its activity, and the less complete, indirect knowledge of its product portfolio, its range, and prices. Thus some information is distorted because the evaluation does not come from direct experience of the company, but rather from pre-evaluations, in terms of quality, service, expertise, competence, and products offered. A positive or negative pre-conception is likely to influence the attitude of the customer company towards the supplier brand.

• The third level is when the brand is recognized. The buying center member, when questioned, does not refer directly to the brand, but if he is reminded, he is capable of describing the product categories concerned. The corresponding measure is called *brand recognition*. Brand recall and recognition are always linked, but in a non-linear, variable way, depending on the product (Laurent and *al.,* 1987). Brand recognition corresponds to often limited knowledge of the brand or the company. This knowledge has different sources, from company sales visits, information picked up at trade shows or in business publications, to information passed on by friends, colleagues, or customers. At this stage, there is not enough information to incite a customer company to buy. However, the name of the company can already evoke certain images and suggest certain values (country of origin, activity sector, etc.).

• Finally, there is the case where the brand is *not known* by its potential customers, which corresponds to a zero level of awareness. The brand does not benefit from any awareness and doesn't evoke anything for buying center members.

1.2   Awareness, a quantitative tool for evaluating the brand

Awareness is a multiple tool for the company, making licensing, or forming joint ventures easier (the partner company benefits from brand awareness). In general, it strengthens the brand's credibility and legitimacy. The well-known brand evokes durability and reliability. A familiar part of the everyday environment, the brand becomes a point of reference for people, contributing to the development of their preferences (by limiting the range of other possible choices). Awareness is useful insofar as it shortens and simplifies the choice process (Hoyer and Brown, 1990). Buyers appreciate brands, in particular for helping to make buying easier; the brand awareness level thus helps to justify their choice (or non-choice) to in-house managers.

This is one of the reasons why communication policies often aim to increase or maintain brand awareness. The latter provides a fixed point or an "anchor" for the other aspects of the image transmitted by the company's communication policy or stemming from product or product category characteristics (Aaker, 1991). The theory of memory has shown that the elements referring to the brand, are indeed, stored (Wyer and Srull, 1989). The diversity of this information, as well as the strength of the links between its different aspects, correspond to associations (Ratcliff and MacKoon, 1988). These associations, linked in memory to a brand, can only be re-memorized if the brand has reached a high enough awareness level (Park and *al.,* 1989). Brand awareness, which is difficult to establish, needs to be maintained and supported in light of the influence of other brands and their market positions. In fact, the brand hits a memory saturation threshold. A strong supplier brand limits the memorization of other brands. The psychological phenomenon of memory saturation leads to powerful entrance barriers, thus giving a big advantage to the most well known brand. A brand's striking aspects can thus inhibit the memorization of other brands (Alba and Chattopadhyay, 1986).

Using the *evoked set* concept (Howard and Sheth, 1969), certain measures relating to memorization can be examined. An evoked set refers to the set of brands or products re-found, "remembered", by the individual and considered by him during the buying process. The more the individual is exposed to a certain number of brands in a product category, the more he is able to remember these brands, and at the same time, the less he is able to remember other brands in the same category. This can be compared to a system of *"inter-communicating vessels"*, with regard to an individual's memorization capacity. A brand that invests heavily in advertising can encourage the progressive forgetting of a brand that does not maintain its presence from an advertising perspective. Consequently, measuring awareness makes it possible to evaluate the quantitative memorization performance of a brand or a campaign.

1.3　Attention: adapting to the industrial context

While awareness measures the level of knowledge of a brand, attention measures the existence and importance of the information relating to the brand stored in the memory. *Attention* can be broken down into two components, *re-memorization* and *recognition* (Alba and *al.*, 1991). *Re-memorization* is measured by brand recall, and in particular, by measuring *top of mind*, while *recognition* is measured using *brand recognition*. The ability to spontaneously remember brands (brand name recall) is much lower than the ability to recognize brands (brand recognition). These two measures are obtained by questioning buyers about the brands that they know in the product category.

However, in research carried out in the consumer market, these measurements show their first limitations, since consumers can memorize a brand using other indicators besides the product category, for example using other brands. For the study of industrial brands, these measurements can be used to compare the attention performance obtained by competing brands, but limitations again show up, such as:

• On the one hand, the main players in a professional market quickly obtain high scores in brand recognition, even in brand recall, with professional customers. This is logical as it is part of the responsibilities of a professional buyer to know the main suppliers capable of meeting the needs of the company. Given the limited number of potential customer companies for any one company, the latter is not addressing millions of consumers but, in general, tens or hundreds of potential customers. With this in mind, the means used to reach this target, and above all to inform, can be very effective. Professional buyers thus have a very high level of information. They are not consumers, who from time to time buy several products out of a large number of categories, but rather, specialized buyers choosing their suppliers for a small number of product or service categories.

• On the other hand, increasingly, a professional buyer can and must look for other potential suppliers, offering them a new partnership in its application, using technology or a manufacturing process that the company has already perfected. Some examples of this are aircraft constructors "recruiting" a supplier from automotive parts manufacturers, and visa versa. The development of *purchase marketing*[1] has consequently extended the range of potential suppliers considered by a professional buyer.

These limitations result from an essential characteristic of the industrial customer who, unlike in the consumer market context, actively seeks to know his potential suppliers. That is why it would seem that measurements of supplier brand awareness in industrial customers are not very significant, even if they express the advantage of a known brand over its competitors. A study carried out on 30 brands in four different industrial sectors thus showed that all the brands studied had a considerable awareness level among professionals in the sectors considered (from 95-100%). On the other hand, supplier brand awareness with the general public is much less discriminating: the same study reveals a very wide range in industrial brand awareness with the general public (from 0-100%). Certain brands communicate directly to end consumers. To strengthen its reference status with professional customers the company can exploit this brand awareness. Strong brand awareness among professionals or consumers is not however enough to optimize the brand. The evocation still needs to be positive and the image projected by the brand must be better than competing brands.

2.   THE ROLE OF INNOVATION IN BRAND IMAGE

2.1   Image, a qualitative tool for evaluating the brand

To understand the "advertising efficiency" of the brand, its qualitative content, as well as the associations accompanying it, need to be analyzed. Image specifically measures the quality of the ties established between different kinds of information stored in the brand, in other words, the quality of associations linked to this brand. *Brand image* results mainly from the positioning chosen and the communication policy created by the marketing department, as much in qualitative as quantitative terms. The overall image is an expression of the perceptions and feelings of individuals with regard to the company. A positive or negative image depends on incomplete and biased information (however, it is perceived as complete and objective by the buyer) and is likely to influence the buying decision.

While the use of awareness as a tool for measuring brand performance needs to be adapted to the industrial context, image analysis, is for its part, directly operational in industrial marketing. In fact, the different approaches to the image content of a consumer brand can be adapted to industrial brands by substituting the professional buyer for the end-user.

If we consider the ten dimensions suggested by Aaker for defining brand image, it can be seen that they correspond to the concerns of a professional buyer:
- product attributes,
- consumer-benefits, which here become customer-benefits,
- relative prices,
- place, time/situation, and types of uses,
- buyers and consumers, who in this context become buyers and users,
- stars and personalities associated with the brand, corresponding to the experts and influencers who support the brand communication,
- the brand personality,
- intangible characteristics such as the nationality of the supplier, the personality of managers, the corporate culture, etc.,
- the product or service category concerned,
- competitors.

While buyers have a rational approach, they also recognize that they are often sensitive to image such as the supposed permanence of the supplier, his professionalism, a classification in a trade magazine, expertise in a particular sector, his nationality, quality and reliability of the products or services offered. The "brand image" effect can be felt, in particular, for purchasing or resale operations of used material, licensing, and joint-venture agreements (exchange value).

Other simpler breakdowns of brand image need even less adaptation. *Perceived brand image* is obtained by asking the customer what distinguishes the brand from other competing brands. Another method is to ask the managers concerned to describe the types of companies that are supposed to be customers of the brand and its competitors. Brand image can also be analyzed by distinguishing the image of competing brands, users, the product, and the manufacturer. The latter approaches can be directly applied to the analysis of an industrial brand.

However, brand image depends mainly on its quality as perceived by industrial customers (Chernatony and McDonald, 1992), in other words, its capacity to supply the characteristics that the customer wants. To improve perceived quality, marketing departments ask the research and development people for product improvements so as to get closer to their ideal product. Innovation and the design of new products (functions, exterior and interior design, product maintenance, etc.), cannot be disassociated from the image: they provide its content.

2.2   Innovation objectives

In fact, the first innovation objective is to improve quality as it is perceived by customers. Starting with existing product brands and competing brands, an in-depth satisfaction survey will reveal different improvement directions. The possibilities for improvement take the form of projects that the marketing department suggests to research and development. The solutions proposed by R&D are then tested and validated by the marketing department. The latter verifies that the proposed innovation is seen as an improvement by customers. The perception of the improvement can be viewed in relation to former product brands and/or, what is even better, in relation to competing product brands.

The second objective, related to the first, is to continually set the brand apart from its competitors. Product differentiation is one of the essential elements of a positioning strategy, which in itself is a fundamental brand objective[2].

The consumer's perception of innovation depends upon the improvements made to existing products; but it can also result from the brand entering a new category of products (Schmalensee, 1992) and, in particular, when it is a pioneer (the first one relative to competitor brands).

2.3   The effect of innovation on the image

Through innovation, the brand can acquire "reference" status in the eyes of customers. In this case, it benefits from a sort of newcomer honeymoon period stemming from the very nature of innovation or from customer education and initiation. The pioneer is protected by its "prototype" image or distinctive character, that is by its representativeness of the product category. In fact, the characteristics of the pioneer are adopted by the market as standards for the new product (Urban, 1986). It is a case of adapting the customer's expected ideal to the characteristics of the pioneer. The customer will then judge other competitors as a function of the pioneer's characteristics. The impact of who comes first in preference forming can be explained in the following way (Figure 1):

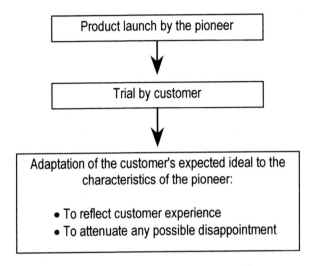

Figure 1. The impact of who comes first in preference forming[3]

The brand which has offered information first, and provided the first customer experience, will obtain stronger loyalty than that of its competitors: "the market pioneer gives the consumer information derived from experience of the product, which in turn rewards the pioneer with a greater market share" (Schmalensee, 1982). For example, when the first automated packaging systems were commercialized, the personnel concerned within the customer company had to learn how they worked and how to maintain them. Less effort will be required if and when new machines are acquired and the company will be more inclined to buy the same brand, or another brand which has adopted the same technical standards, to benefit from the initial learning process.

It is thus more difficult for latecomers to persuade companies to invest in training for their new product than it is for the pioneer. The innovative capacity of the brand and more especially its capacity to introduce itself into a new product category, contributes to improving quality from the customer's standpoint. The communication strategy adopted by the marketing department in support of the sales force, can give rise to the customer's first purchase, thanks in particular to a certain awareness and a positive brand image. This image, maintained by the perceived and proven degree of innovation (number of patents applied for, new products presented, etc.), can result in stronger brand loyalty than for competing brands. To obtain this, quite apart from its awareness and image, the brand must arouse favorable associations and positive recall.

3.   BRAND ASSOCIATIONS

3.1   The mental association process

Although brand equity management has been the subject of a lot of research, books and working papers, none of these looks at the associations linked to the brand in an industrial context. It is however possible to identify the concept of association and its main characteristics, using information from, on the one hand, the consumer market, and practices in the industrial sector on the other (industrial buyer behavior, perceived risk management...).

In order to define the associations, it is possible to compare the brand to the memory process. Studies on memory have shown that only some information is stored in an individual's long-term memory. Information recall, or retention of a new element, sets off an activation process which affects all other related elements. The stronger the links, the stronger the activation. The brand can parallel this process in that:

- It sends out information via all its marketing actions,
- It makes sense, and represents a more or less cohesive packet of knowledge, stored in the memory.

Brand associations can therefore be defined as "anything linked in the memory to the brand" (Aaker, 1991). In the broadest sense, associations are comprised of:

- Concrete elements such as products or services, which are " branded " along with their attributes and the product categories they are attached to,
- More abstract elements such as those expressed in the company's and competitors' various communication measures.

Defined like this, there is no distinction between one industrial brand and another. Whether we are talking about programmable water-jet cutters or electrical engineering, the industrial buyer will associate a brand with its products as well as any information he has been able to gather about it, ranging from the technology used, down to the nationality of the supplier and his address. The associations can be defined in terms of uniqueness, strength, cohesion, and favorability.

3.2 The characteristics of associations

3.2.1 The uniqueness of associations

An association is unique when it is not shared with competing brands. This is obviously a way of reinforcing the difference between itself and competitors, and this measure is independent of the company's activities and the type of customer, general public or professional. Brand strategies like those followed by Du Pont de Nemours and its brand, Lycra®, are indeed formulated to encourage unique associations thereby differentiating itself as much as possible from other elastane fibers. The existence of associations which are unique to the brand are a factor in the latter's success.

3.2.2 Association strength

Some associations are more strongly linked to a brand than others. It all depends on the relevance of the company's choices regarding the mix, communication campaigns, and arguments emphasized. The degree of strength is very important since customer confidence and brand credibility depend on it.

Even if association strength has been developed above all for the consumer market, it can easily be applied to professional brands. For example in the highly competitive domain of veinotonic medicines, the fact of having one brand promoted by a well-known specialist who uses and prescribes it from the outset in a large hospital renowned for the speciality, will produce a stronger association for the brand and from there, greater credibility in the eyes of the medical profession.

3.2.3 Association cohesion

Cohesion, contrary to dilution, must be about clarity and convergence between associations in terms of content and meaning. Cohesion between associations will therefore reinforce their strength simply because the customers, seeing no ambiguity or contradictions between the different bits of information projected, will be more likely to have confidence in the particular brand.

An example of strong cohesion can be found with Tetra Pak, which tries to capitalize on messages linked to preservation of the contents of its packaging as much as preservation of the environment, both for the general public and for various professional targets.

3.2.4   The favorability of associations

Favorability is very close to association strength. It has been developed especially in work on brand extensions (Broniarczyk and Alba, 1994), where the concept is a determining factor in the decision to extend. No company wants to trigger an association with one of its brands which will be unfavorable. Indeed, an association can turn out to be less favorable than another for the same brand, or an association linked to a competing brand. This is the result of poor choices when making up the marketing mix and setting up various marketing campaigns.

When associations are favorable, when there is strong awareness and a good image, the supplier brand can reinforce customer loyalty. This loyalty is in itself another tool for measuring brand performance.

4.   LOYALTY

4.1   The objectives of loyalty

To win over new customers is generally more expensive than to maintain the existing customer pool. In fact, for a prospective customer to become a real customer of the brand, the latter must catalyze a first sale, which will often involve important sales backup (repeated visits from the sales force, etc.), promotions such as special displays, or reimbursement offers. This expense can be decreased after the first purchase, assuming that the customer has been satisfied by the experience. Marketing expenses to trigger the first sale are recouped in direct proportion to customer loyalty.

Apart from this first objective of optimizing sales expenses, the second objective linked to loyalty is to reinforce the brand's position relative to distributors. When the end customer is loyal to a distributor brand, that same distributor risks losing some of his customers if he de-lists the brand.

Brand loyalty also means greater confidence, favoring cooperation between the customer and the supplier brand. Increased loyalty allows the two companies to exchange information, to develop specific projects together, and to confidentially test new products coming from the supplier.

Thus loyalty can be defined as a favorable attitude towards a brand resulting in repeated purchasing of that brand over time. It is a behavioral variable. On the other hand, brand sensitivity is one of the major characteristics of the buyer showing the importance of the brand in the decision making and purchasing process (Kapferer and Laurent, 1992).

Loyal customers react less to offers from competing brands. Consequently, having a loyal customer base allows the company to avoid making snap decisions such as price cuts. There is room to move to set up a modification of the product offered, something which takes more time. Product modification is a long-term solution, often better accepted by the customer especially in the case of innovations.

4.2   The different levels of loyalty

There are different levels of customer loyalty, from "militant" to "indifferent":

• The most loyal level is the "one-brand customer" who is so attached to the brand that he promotes its merits around him. Although infrequent, due to the care needed when buying supplies, this sort of person is sometimes encountered in industry especially when the product is an innovative one.

• The "emotionally loyal" customer is irrationally attached to the brand far beyond the interest he thinks accrues from it. This situation can be found in particular when purchases are made on the basis of length of relationship, i.e. when the supplier is an ex-employee of the customer company there is an attachment, or when buying focuses deliberately on local, regional or national products.

• The third level is the "calculating" customer. When he is satisfied, the latter looks at the risk involved in brand switching. His attachment is thus rationally interested. This type of loyalty is frequent in industry, where it is often difficult to dislodge an in-supplier who is actually involved in his customer's activity. Loyalty can in fact be reinforced by the frequency and depth of contacts between the supplier brand and the customer company.

• The fourth level is the "conservative" customer. This is the "habit" buyer. He has no reason to change if he's not dissatisfied. Brand loyalty facilitates a consensus within the customer company's purchasing department and thus plays a role in reducing internal conflicts. This situation is frequent in industry particularly for miscellaneous goods. In this situation, it is necessary to make sure that brand loyalty is not just on the surface, with the customer actually much more attached to one or other employee of the supplier brand (the salesman or delivery person). The inter-personal relationship takes precedence over the relationship with the brand itself and becomes a weak point for the supplier brand. The affective relationships developed between the customer and the sales person are sometimes such that the customer company values them over the supplier brand itself. If the supplier brand salesperson moves or is moved to another job, the customer will remain loyal not to the brand he represented but to the individual. Loyalty must be built on the brand not on the individual; there must be a solid base, which the customer can count on regardless of changes in the organization or supplier personnel.

• The last level is the customer who is indifferent to the brand. By definition, he is not loyal because for him price is the determining factor. This situation is very common in industry, particularly concerning non-generic products or for offers which do not include useful, and thus much appreciated services. What must be stressed is that the customer company buying policy is to look for reliable suppliers with whom solid relationships can be built, based on the company's particular needs (production cycles, delivery times, adjustment of production tooling, range of customer's competitors, etc.). For the customer company, price is not the determining factor; the purchase is included directly or indirectly into the actual production, thus bringing other criteria into play such as: quality, respect of norms, reliability, and delivery times, ability to react in an emergency, technical expertise, etc.).

In industry, the loyalty of a company to its different suppliers is especially strong: a supplier who has given satisfaction for 5, 10, or 20 years is difficult to shift. The customer company gets to know the supplier brand, and is used to working with its particular methods and culture. Trust becomes mutual when the two companies come to an agreement and work together. Loyalty is in fact the result of constant investment in the customer (awareness, image, and quality of the products) (Figure 2).

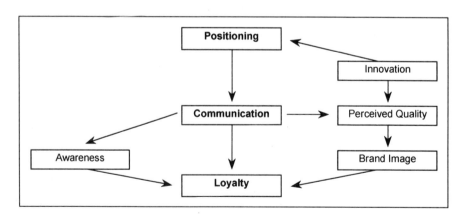

Figure 2. Diagram showing how the brand functions[4]

Actions to build awareness, image, and associations, are useless if they are not part of a larger plan: brand management. Brand management consists of giving life to the brand, from its birth through to its development and evolution (birth of related brands, brand extensions, brand suppressions, etc.). The different measures for evaluating a brand can give a picture of the brand with its strengths and weaknesses. Quality surveys can be carried out with the main members of the company purchasing departments, distributors, partners, and end customers. Perception diagrams can also supply useful information by situating the brand relative to its particular attributes, to other brands, as well as to other previous surveys. These brand management tools identify areas where improvement is possible, as well as the brand's strong points. Thanks to regular brand evaluation, corrective action can be decided, as much for awareness as for image content. Brand management can therefore cover different dimensions. It can be about:

- Creating a brand in order to generate more turnover or control profit/loss margins,
- Reinforcing a brand by consolidating its awareness and image abroad, for example,
- Protecting and defending the brand in the face of competition,
- Spreading out the brand, which means widening applications and activities into new product categories or services using the established brand,
- Eliminating the brand in order to create a new one and thus favor the main brand, or the strongest one in the portfolio, or making equity out of a brand which has been purchased,
- Giving new life to a brand in one particular market segment, for some category of products or services, in order to re-exploit the ever present brand awareness, even though the brand itself has in fact disappeared.

NOTES

1. See Chapter 2, The Role of the Brand in the Industrial Purchase.
2. See Chapter 5, Brand Functions.
3. Sources: Cassan, Ch, (1993), La mesure de l'effet de l'ordre d'entrée sur la performance des marques: un état de l'art, *Recherche et Applications en Marketing*, vol. n°8, n°2, p 45-61.
4. Sources: adapted from Aaker, D.A., (1991), *Managing Brand Equity: Capitalizing on the Value of a Brand Name*, New York, Free Press.

REFERENCES

Aaker D. A., (1991), *Managing Brand Equity: Capitalizing on the Value of a Brand Name*, New York, Free Press.

Alba, J. W., et Chattopadhyay, (November 1986), Salience Effects in Brand Recall, *Journal of Marketing Research*, vol. n°23.

Alba, J.W., Hutchinson, J.W. and Lynch, J.G., (1991), Memory and Decision Making, in *Handbook of Consumer Behavior*, Englewood Cliffs, N.J., Prentice Hall, p 1-49.

Broniarczyk, S. and Alba J.W., (1994), The Importance of the Brand in Brand Extension, *Journal of Marketing Research,* vol. 31, 2, p 214-228.

Chernatony, L. (de) and McDonald, M., (1992), *Creating Powerful Brands,* London, Butterworth-Heinemann.

Howard, J.A. and Sheth, J., (1969), *The Theory of Buyer Behavior,* New York, John Wiley & Sons.

Hoyer, W. and Brown, S., (September 1990), Effects of Brand Awareness on Choice for a Common, Repeat-Purchase Product, *Journal of Consumer Research,* vol. n°17, p 141-148.

Kapferer, J-N. and Laurent, G., (1992), *La sensibilité aux marques, Un nouveau concept pour gérer les marques,* Paris, Éditions d'Organisation.

Laurent, G., Kapferer, J-N. and Roussel, F., (1987), Thresholds of Brand Awareness, Developments in *Advertising and Communication Research,* Montreux, ESOMAR Congress, p 677-699.

MSI, (1988-1990), *Research Topics,* Marketing Science Institute.

Park, C.W., Lawson, R. and Milberg, S., (1989), Memory Structure of Brand Names, *Advances in Consumer Research,* vol. n°16, p 726-731.

Ratcliff, G. and MacKoon G., (1988), A Retrieval Theory of Priming in Memory, *Psychological Review,* vol. n°95.

Schmalensee, R., (1982), Product Differentiation Advantages of Pioneering Brands, *The American Economic Review,* vol. n°72.

Urban, G.L., Carter, Th., Gaskin, S. and Mucha, Z., (June 1986), Market Share Rewards to Pioneering Brands: An Empirical Analysis and Strategic Implications, *Management Science,* vol. n°32, n°6, p 645-659.

Wyer, R. S. and Srull T. V., (1989), Person and Memory Judgment, *Psychological Review,* vol. n°96, p 58-83.

Chapter 5

Brand Functions

In the United States, virtually anything can be registered as a trade mark or service mark with the Patent and Trademark Office. The statutory definition of trade mark in the Trade Mark Act of 1946, as amended (the Lanham Act) includes "any word, name, symbol, or device, or any combination thereof". Courts have interpreted this language very broadly allowing protection for the overall look of a product, including its size, shape, color or color combinations, texture, even perfumes and graphics (Cantor and Chestek, 2000). Thus, a manufacturer's brand name, trade or service mark is "a graphic sign meant to distinguish the products or services of a physical or moral person". The brand can, therefore, be considered as a distinctive sign, but also as a symbol, a design or a combination of these different elements which identify the product and confer upon it a durable competitive advantage: "A winning brand is a brand that consumers want to buy and distributors want to sell" (Doyle, 1990). Its strength is defined by its equity: the sum of "all the strong and transmissible brand associations, and their capacity to influence behavior" (Leuthesser, 1988).

Having taken the concept of equity into account, the brand can thus be presented as a powerful "summary of information" and as a source of added value (Farquhar, 1990). This value corresponds to the major or minor elements that distinguish it from the rest of its competitors and that give it preference in the eyes of the consumer. It is extremely difficult to give any accurate definition of brand given the interaction between the brand and the elements of the marketing mix. The brand is actually a marketing tool, or a sales and communication support; its influences are numerous and varied. For this reason, we will take a closer look at the main brand functions: for the company and for the buyer.

1.   BRAND FUNCTIONS FOR THE COMPANY

Generally speaking, the functions of the brand for a company in the industrial sector are identical to those of a company in the consumer market. In both cases, the two principal functions assigned to the brand are positioning and capitalization.

The *positioning function* corresponds to the company's need to distinguish itself from its competitors. It is true to say that while the sole function of the brand is to identify the manufacturer of the product (brand = name), it nevertheless unites the different dimensions associated with it: quality, delivery, service, etc. (brand = name + symbols). A product, which already fulfills a specific function for the client, is seen as having added value when it is branded. The product itself is enhanced, as well as its perceived characteristics. Branding allows similar products and services to be differentiated.

The *capitalization function* could be summarized in this way: regular investment made by the company in the brand increases sales, which in turn increases the value of the brand. This is the case of American brands such as IBM, Intel or General Electric, considered as brand value leaders. For this reason, when such a strong brand is sold, the notion of goodwill becomes negotiable., it brings a much higher price than its actual value.

From a managerial point of view, these two global and essential functions of the brand correspond to the different objectives set for it; these can be divided into three main categories:
- *Fundamental objectives*:
- Develop positioning,
- Make the product or service more visible to the clients.
- *Intermediary objectives*:
- Increase penetration rate,
- Increase loyalty,
- Increase product diffusion.
- *Final objectives*:
- Improve market share,
- Augment the financial contribution,
- Mobilize internal human resources.

1.1   Fundamental objectives

1.1.1   Develop positioning

The customer company will accept paying a price higher than the regular market price if the supplier brand proposes an advantage in return (Arnold,

1992). This may be based on the guarantee of a certain quality, of immediate maintenance service, or even a symbolic distinction sought by the company. This could mean having the very latest machine tools from an avant-garde high-tech supplier – the company's clients would be duly informed. In other words, an advantage may be based on a concrete, objective characteristic or on an abstract, subjective one.

The company has to succeed in making the buyer acknowledge the difference between their company's products and the competitors'. Each company makes its own choice as to the position of its brand: a certain product advantage is put forward rather than another, be it positive or negative. The positioning may be defined as the sum of the most visible image traits, that is, those which enable the different targets to situate the product in a particular universe and to distinguish it from the others. It is a simplified, limited, comparative, and distinctive representation (or perception) of the product (Ries and Trout, 1982).

Through positioning, a specific place is allocated to the brand in the minds of the clients, differentiating it from its competitors – providing, of course, that the brand brings "added value" to the product it designates. The product and the brand are two different things. A product, or service, exists in reality; a brand has no tangible physical characteristics. It is a "mental translation", an abstraction of the product or service. Taking this argument to the extreme, we could say that the brand only exists in the imagination of the customer (Kim, 1990), and corresponds to the sum of thoughts, feelings, sensations, and associations it evokes. Brand value lies in the ability to continually influence customer buying behavior, make customers loyal, and encourage them to ask for new products. Customer preference for a particular brand depends on the product's intrinsic characteristics and/or the overall characteristics of the brand (Shocker and *al.*, 1994).

1.1.2   Make the product or service more visible to the client

This is the very first function of the brand. To make products or services offered more visible, the company will use different means: communication, media, easily identifiable visual identity (on packaging, and vehicles, etc).

Through communication and the media

Once brand position has been clearly defined, it needs to be communicated to the chosen target. Whatever the brand in question, the primary role of communication is to transmit such information to buyers, and also to influencers, deciders, and users. Following this, it should seduce the different targets, changing their behavior patterns in such a way as to stimulate and trigger purchase.

Without the use of the chosen brand, the transmission of information and its memorization by the different targets would be diluted and have little effect, it would be lost in the mass of other messages received (McInnis and Jaworski, 1989; Alba and Chattopadhyay, 1986; Laurent and *al.*, 1987). The very fact of the brand's existence and its associations make any communication more efficient by facilitating the transfer of information (McInnis and *al.*,1991). This in turn improves the image and reputation of the brand.

Through easily identifiable signs

Thanks to communication (sales force, advertising, exhibitions and shows), the customer now knows about the product – and wants to buy it. The next task is to facilitate the buying process by making the product as visible and distinguishable as possible. Here, the brand explains, describes, and ranks the different products proposed according to quality and category. It also saves the buyer time and simplifies the transaction by providing comprehensible and accessible " signposts ". A certain coherence in packaging design, company vehicle livery or press advertisements will enable the different targets to more easily recognize products of the same brand. Needless to say, the sign or color-coding chosen should be coherent with the positioning. In this way, the brand assures the double function of *continuity* in space and time.

• In *space*, whether:
- At the point of sale itself, if several products of the same brand are displayed in different places (material wholesaler, electrical goods distributor…),
- From one point of sale to another, within the same geographical area,
- From one distribution circuit to another – for example, from a network of dealers to wholesalers by using mail order,
- From one geographical area to another.
• In *time*, whether:
- For the same product, from one time period to another,
- For a product at the end of its life cycle to a new product of the same brand.

1.2 Intermediary objectives

Whether the product is new or not for the brand, its turnover may be improved by acquiring new customers or by assuring greater brand loyalty from existing ones. A rise in sales may be achieved by expanding the clientele – a higher penetration rate – or by increasing the number of sales per customer. The following diagram (Figure 1) illustrates the means by which sales may be increased (we have chosen to ignore the price variable).

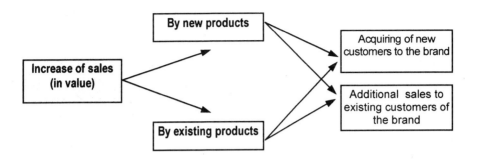

Figure 1. Means by which sales may be increased

1.2.1 Increase penetration rate

This concerns winning new customers. These may be completely new clients for the brand in question or existing clients who also adopt a new product under the same brand name. The increase in penetration rate may be achieved by marketing action focused solely on the brand, solely on the product or a combination of both, with follow-up by the sales force in the field.

1.2.2 Assure greater brand loyalty

This involves consolidating the position already held by the brand and /or the product in the customer company. Investment made by the brand in terms of image and quality aims at producing greater customer satisfaction (Columbo and Morrison, 1989). The greater the customer satisfaction, the higher the likelihood that a new product under that brand will be chosen – whatever the category of product concerned. In an extreme case, the buyer may only accept a certain brand, excluding all competitive offers. This objective, as with the above, is assured by the marketing department and relies heavily on the sales force in terms of customer contact and follow-up.

1.2.3 Widen product diffusion

For branded products to be buyable by the customer company, they must be available in the particular geographical area, in the distribution circuits, and at the points of sale where the customer usually buys. The customer company must be able to procure the products or services proposed for each and everyone of their localities (national or international). Delivery conditions should also be compatible with the company's activity. As a result, one of the intermediary objectives of the brand is to maximize the value availability in order to transform buying intention into purchase.

When a supplier brand is strong, its distribution to wholesalers, dealers, and distributors is facilitated because of the demand generated. The success of the two first objectives mentioned above (penetration and loyalty building) is dependent on this third objective given to the sales force: if the product is insufficiently diffused then it is impossible to build on existing loyalty or win new customers. With a coherent strategy in terms of communication, service, range and packaging, the supplier brand can be distributed appropriately by the different circuits, adapted to the various targets.

1.2.4 Mobilize internal human resources

The supplier brand also has the role of federating and mobilizing the internal resources of the company. It serves as a benchmark and a banner around which the personnel (staff and shareholders) rally, reinforcing cohesion. The brand is a concentrate of the fundamental and distinctive values made visible – on company vehicles, work clothes, or promotional items. Within the company, a well-appreciated brand stimulates a certain warm attachment. This can develop into real pride between colleagues, who may stand up for and defend their brand outside the company, even outside a professional context. A brand that is well liked and supported internally will be better armed against competitors; the worst brand is a brand of which the personnel are ashamed.

A strong in-house attachment to the brand can constitute a useful barrier for the company in the case of takeover. The buying company may be obliged to keep the acquired brand, leaving it a certain autonomy, thus avoiding any disappointment or demotivation on the part of the teams and business partners concerned with it. A strong brand may even become an important communication medium, sales argument, or the basis for the acquiring company's legitimacy.

1.3 The final objectives

1.3.1 Increase market share

Very often, the supplier brand has no way to influence market evolution, all brands considered. Generally speaking, it is impossible to expand the global value of the market, although exceptionally some actions taken collectively by a particular industrial sector – or by a certain supplier brand in a more individual way – influence the market downstream and thus develop the global market. A brand can, however, increase the company's market share, providing the intermediary objectives mentioned above are achieved. Market share thus represents the combined result of the different intermediary objectives. Expressed in volume, then in value, it is finally translated by a financial contribution.

1.3.2   Increase financial contribution

The financial contribution results from the quantitative leverage brought by the brand to the company's communication and promotional efforts, and also from the difference between the acceptable market price and company cost price. By increasing sales, the cost price tends to become more competitive because of the increase in production quantities. Simultaneously, by its perceived value, the brand can support a higher price than an ordinary basic product. The weighted average price may be increased in the case of multiproduct industrial brands by improving the structure of inter-product sales. The objectives of the brand incorporate three financial aspects: the level of sales, the cost price, and the selling price.

Generally speaking, these different brand objectives are almost the same for both the industrial sector and the mass consumer sector. However, it should be added that there seems to be a paradox in these different functions, in particular in the case of the launch of a new range. The brand should simultaneously:

• Attract the attention of clients and inform them of the novelty of the product offered. For this reason, the brand may differentiate itself from existing offers to avoid the possibility of confusing the client who may think that it is simply a revamp;

• And reassure the client by erasing the risks inherent in new products and new technology where reliability is still to be proven. It is for this reason that dual branding is frequently used in the industrial sector. The new product name is juxtaposed with the established and known brand linking the new product to the existing brand; this reassures the client and facilitates purchase.

This apparent paradox can be resolved in studying the functions served by industrial brands for the customer companies. These functions have certain particularities compared to those of the mass consumer sector.

2.   BRAND FUNCTIONS FOR THE CUSTOMER

In the consumer goods sector, brand functions may be defined with reference to the principal types of consumer needs (Park and *al.*, 1986), that is to say:

• Functional needs: those which correspond to solving a concrete problem,

- Symbolic needs: those, which correspond to social role, group belonging or personality identification,
- Use-based needs: corresponding to needs for sensorial pleasure or diversity.

In this context, a *functional brand* aims at fulfilling consumption needs, with no direct link to personality (McWilliam and De Chernatony, 1989). It is defined by the technical characteristics of the product. A symbolic brand allows an individual to be associated with a desired group, or gives a certain self-image. A use-based brand fulfills interior needs of stimulation and diversity: it combines product characteristics and the moment or place of consumption.

This approach seems difficult to apply to the industrial context. Purchases are made to solve a company's particular problem rather than to satisfy use-based or symbolic needs. Basically, the company's needs are functional by nature. However, other dimensions may be added. A company may provide outside catering for its personnel working near difficult building sites; its motivation is to provide meals specially adapted to such hard work (needs based on use). Another company may decide to buy only from suppliers with the ISO 14000 certificate (recognizing respect for the environment), in the aim of using this in its sales argument and communication (symbolic needs). Thus, the different dimensions of need can be found to various degrees and in varying proportions in the industrial market. In both contexts, the brand plays an important role in the customer's choice process.

The supplier brand fulfills several functions. It is through the brand that the buyer becomes aware of the product, identifies it, and memorizes it. By its different associations, the brand plays the major role of "summarizing information". In the industrial sector, the brand fulfills five major functions similar to those noted for the consumer goods market – they differ, however, in their respective level of relative importance:

- The function of identification and indication,
- The function of economizing time and effort,
- The function of reassurance and guarantee,
- The symbolic function,
- The function of variety-seeking amusement.

2.1   The function of identification and indication

The identification function allows the buyer to identify the product or service, distinguishing it more clearly from the many other propositions. It is easier to identify the supplier thanks to the brand signature.

Appropriate color-coding and names selected in the brand's identity code facilitate this. Memorization of the advertising message is influenced by brand communication – defined in its largest sense (from letter heading to company vehicles, and including various other actions such as articles in business publications or presenting a stand at a trade fair). The brand allows the consumer to sort out a particular promotional message from amid the mass. In order to be "heard" by the target, communication must be efficient (Park and *al.*, 1989): this implies constancy in the tone, continuity in the choice of media, and originality in the style of advertising. Efficiency of the brand is complementary to communication strategy efficiency; the latter being indispensable in building brand recognition. In turn, the brand enhances message memorization.

The brand is characterized by its identification function; where potential buyers have seen the product in an advertisement, in business publications or at a fair, the brand helps them to locate the product at a later time. Thus, the time and effort necessary for the buying choice are reduced: known brands are easier to find and acquire.

2.2 The function of economizing time and effort

The function of economizing time and effort derives directly from the memorization process mentioned above. The brand constitutes a practical cognitive tool used to synthesize any information connected with it (slogans, sales arguments, products, values, impressions, etc.). Buyers, like individual consumers, use the brand name to summarize information – for example, product characteristics. Used in an oral form to designate the product, the brand first evokes a name before evoking the product: the brand has its own personality, beyond the confines of the product itself.

The industrial brand carries an even greater amount of information, due to the technical particularities involved in industrial purchasing. The industrial buyer (like the other members of the buying center) needs specific information on the product category and the appropriateness of a given supplier. Through brand associations, the industrial buyer gains time in the transaction: the brand acts as a "summary" of the rational elements related to the product and its delivery, and also of intangible factors such as nationality of origin or the quality of the client-supplier relationship. Thus, the industrial brand can contribute to reducing transaction costs (costs of changing suppliers, information management, supplier prospecting and selection, control and assessment procedures – requiring investment in material as well as time). For the buyer, a strong brand represents an economy in time and in the means used to evaluate the different propositions of other potential suppliers.

2.3   The safety and guarantee function

The brand is also a sign of quality. In signing a product, the brand gives a mark of approval, interpreted by the client as an element of safety – on two different levels (Kapferer and Thoenig, 1992):

• Firstly, the reassurance that the product does come from that particular company, that it has been manufactured with a certain expertise, with certain materials or ingredients...

• Then, the certainty that, in case of defect, there is an identifiable manufacturer to complain to for damages, repairs or replacements.

The safety and guarantee function ensures then that the client is reassured about the qualities of the product and that if there is any grievance after delivery, there is the possibility of recourse. It is for this reason that the notion of tracking ('traceability') has evolved. This involves the possibility of tracking back to the origins of a finished product, of identifying each component or sub-assembly. Should there be any problem in terms of quality, the customer company (the manufacturer of the final product) can rest assured – and reassure its own clients (the final consumers) – that supplier brand responsibility is easily proven. In addition to this, the customer company can explain the advantages of being able to procure the parts or sub-assembly directly from the supplier, and having the competence to replace them. Tracking is the supplier brand's response to the expectations of the industrial customer; it gives reassurance to both parties. And its importance is growing rapidly due to the development of quality control techniques and the customer satisfaction measures with which it is closely linked.

For a certain time now, a particular form of co-branding has also appeared: it is a juxtaposition of the supplier and the finished product brand. This tandem "consumer brand/supplier brand" facilitates the commercialization of the finished product, a building, an article of clothing, TV, stereo, etc. Such products benefit from the technical and technological guarantee of industrial brands and the high degree of quality associated with their production. The customer company benefits from the image and the expertise of the upstream supplier, thus reassuring its own clientele.

In a more general way, the customer company knows that a manufacturer, which signs a product with its own brand, would not take risks where quality was concerned. Any complaint or dissatisfaction, which could be taken up by the media or professional associations, could be highly prejudicial to the reputation of the supplier brand. Whatever the level of information on the different processes used by each company, this notion of quality insurance is widespread in the industrial sector and is crucial due to the specificities of the buying process. It is clear that the behavior of industrial buyers faced with risks, their capacity to cope with incertitude, influence greatly their style of decision. There are many things at stake, bad decisions concern both the company (supplier relations, product availability, financial risks, production quality, sales, production safety, etc.) and the individual (who could be accused of having taken the easy way out, or of having adopted a certain technological solution too late and losing competitive advantage, etc.). Opting for an unknown brand is a serious risk that buyers cannot take: status and internal appreciation of their skills are at stake; in the case of failures, breakdowns or after-sales problems, they will be seen as incompetent buyers. In this case, a known brand can provide a measure of protection against such accusations.

At the moment of the purchasing decision, industrial buyers are confronted with risks they perceive as high. To minimize these risks, they seek as much information as possible, particularly when the purchase is of strategic importance, or when buying a completely new product for the company. In such cases, it is obvious that even if the buyers make an effort to get adequate information, their competence will not be the same as with familiar products. In choosing a brand known and recognized in a specific category, the buyer can rest assured: even if the purchase is not the best, it will not be the worst.

The brand, through its reputation and its image, takes on a dual role: first, of minimizing risk – that is, it reassures the buyer before purchase – and second, of justifying the purchasing decision (or refusal to buy) to hierarchical superiors.

The supplier brand carries a certain amount of information which is also perceived by other members of the buying center, reinforcing reassurance. The brand can convey notions of durability, expertise, professionalism, reliability, quality, etc. It thus contributes to "reducing tension" in the buying center by facilitating consensus around itself. Before the purchase, the supplier brand can act to reassure both the buyer and the members of the buying center; after the purchase, it acts by reducing the perceived risk linked to the decision process. Thus, the industrial brand plays the role of reassuring and justifying purchase on two levels: for the customer company and for the buyers themselves. This is the principal role of the industrial brand.

2.4   The symbolic function

The impact of the symbolic function of the supplier brand is more difficult to estimate in the industrial sector than in the consumer market. However, because of the non-rational nature of certain of the decision criteria in industrial buying, this function may have its importance. Factors such as nationality, environmental protection policy and supplier reputation have their influence: a supplier of electronic components, with a strong image in the military domain, may be chosen by a company whose activity concerns a totally different sector. There are many examples of nationality affecting choice: machine tool sector preference for German suppliers, telecommunications linked to French brands.

The symbolic function is also associated with the image the company wishes to project. The communication of information concerning the purchase of prestigious products – cutting edge technologically or ecologically – illustrates this: Michelin buys a Cray, General Motors buys the latest machine tools robots. In the same way, when a company uses a prestigious auditing firm for its accounts, this may be used to reassure the financial markets. The brand, as a means of communication, also channels identity. For example, in choosing Airbus airplanes, the buying company itself expresses the personality of the airline. The symbolic value of a brand may also be negative: certain production material brands coming from China or some Eastern European countries are connoted with a mediocre or less-than-reliable image. It may happen that an industrial company chooses the brand, which corresponds to – or reflects – its own image. It should be underlined though that in an industrial context this is not the sole function influencing the purchase decision. The symbolic function is of secondary importance compared to rational factors; in the examples given above these would include capacity and power (Cray), or precision (machine tools).

2.5   The function of variety-seeking amusement

This last function appears more clearly in consumer product branding, although it is sometimes applicable to the industrial market. It associates ideas of pleasure, stimulation, and the excitement produced by the plethora of available brands and offers. It also expresses the way in which the company adapts the brand to specific market demands. Examples in the industrial market include Technal and Legrand; they have made particular efforts in bringing a certain "amusing" touch to the designs of products characterized as uniform and serious. Designers such as Bertone have been brought in to work with the Sagane range of Legrand, Starck for Duravit and Nouvel, Wilmotte, Perrault, Foster or Viaplana and Pinon for the Technal stand at the Batimat Fair – this all adds value and a symbolic dimension to the brand.

The traditional functions are also found, to varying degrees, in business-to-business marketing. This is particularly true of the first three: identification, saving time, and reassurance.

The different industrial brand functions can be associated in a model representing their influence – within the buying center – on the composition and motivation of its members, and on the decision process (Figure 2). This influence is in turn dependent on the transaction situation.

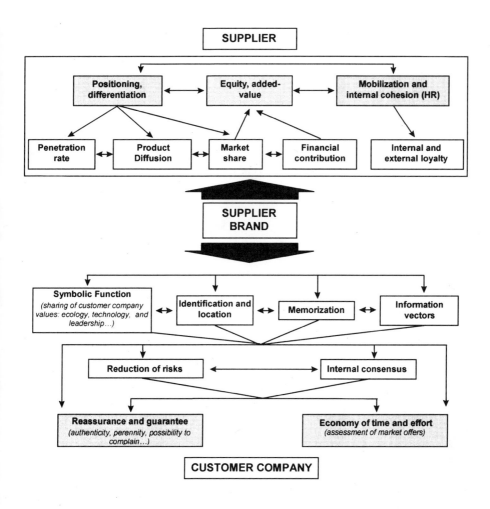

Figure 2. The functions of the supplier brand for the company and for the client[1]

3. THE ROLE OF PERFORMANCE FACILITATOR

The different functions of the industrial brand mentioned above have only a tentative correspondence with those attributed to the brand in the mass consumer market. Because of the specificity of industrial buying, the analysis of the role of industrial brands demands further investigation in order to take into account the expectations of the customer company.

3.1   Analysis of what the customer company expects from the brand

The lack of homogeneity in the industrial market makes it necessary to carry out extensive market studies to analyze the expectations of buying center members. We give the example of one study which contacted two hundred industrial companies in the sectors of building, food and drink packaging, automobile products and textiles (Malaval, 1998). The brands concerned by this study are the following:

• Building sector: Acova, Grohe, Isover, Lafarge, Legrand, Somfy, Technal, Villeroy & Boch,

• Drink packaging sector: Ato, BSN-Emballage, Combibloc, Elopak, Mead-Emballages, PLM, Saint-Gobain, Tetra Pak,

• Automobile products sector: Bertrand Faure, Bosch, Michelin, Siemens, Sommer Allibert, Valeo,

• Textile sector: DMC, Dorlastan, Gore-Tex, Lycra, Rhovyl, Tactel, Tergal, and Woolmark.

The interviews with the heads of purchasing and marketing revealed the main expectations and fears concerning the thirty supplier brands included in the study.

3.1.1   Favorable expectations of the supplier brands

Among the reasons influencing the managers to choose a supplier of a strong brand – reasons which we will name "positive expectations" from here on – we can find:

• The brand's capacity to innovate and encourage innovation within the company,

• Their capacity to assist in the design of company products,

• Their capacity to make changes in processes or materials acceptable to those working with them,

• Their capacity to establish a consensus of decision,

• Their ability to accompany the company in the assurance of quality,

• Their assistance in production and maintenance,

• The commercial weight that these supplier brands represent,

• Their warrantee of durability in the long term.

These positive expectations may be grouped more simply around the four following themes, listed in order of importance:

• The facilitation of production performance,

- The facilitation of innovation performance,
- The facilitation of commercial performance,
- The facilitation of decision making.

Generally speaking, the expectations focus on the technical aspects (production, innovation) and on the commercial aspects of the partnership, the least important being decision making. The relative importance of each varies, however, according to whether the respondent was responsible for buying or marketing. The marketing people expected a commercial partnership, followed by assistance in innovation and production performance. Help in decision making was less important to them than it was to those involved in buying – whose main concern was production (Table 3).

Table 3. Level of importance of expectations in relation to respondent's function

Comparison of Marketer / Purchaser Responses	"Positive" Expectations
Equal level of importance for all respondents	Innovation performance facilitator
Higher level of importance for Purchasers	Decision-making facilitator Production performance facilitator
Higher level of importance for Marketers	Commercial performance facilitator

Comparing responses in relation to sector of activity confirms the trends observed, but with some interesting nuances: the building and textile sectors show the highest expectation of commercial partnership; in the automobile sector, production and innovation expectations dominate (Table 4).

Table 4. Level of importance of expectations in relation to sectors of activity

Positive expectations	Level of importance of expectations in the different sectors
Innovation performance facilitator	General level similar and rather high in the different sectors
Decision-making facilitator	General level similar and rather weak in the different sectors
Production performance facilitator	Particularly high level for the Car Engineering and Building Trade sectors brands
Commercial performance facilitator	Particularly high level for the Building Trade and Textile sectors brands

3.1.2 Fears concerning supplier brands

The studies highlighted the principal risks perceived by the customer companies when choosing a strong supplier brand. Among the possible barriers – which we will call "negative expectations" – the most important have been identified as:

- The risk of excessive prices,
- The risk of dependence on the supplier brand,
- The risk of supplier brand influence on in-base company departments,
- The risk of arrogance from the supplier brand personnel.

The fear of overpricing was by far the principal perceived risk. The studies also showed that the general level of the importance of risks is lower than that of the general level of expectations: in spite of the "threats" they may represent, strong brands are appreciated and often preferred. The responses given by the marketing and buying managers of the customer companies differ however with the type of risk being considered. Globally, the buyers seem more wary of strong brands, and are more afraid of the risks they represent (Table 5).

Table 5. Level of importance of risks in relation to respondent's function

Comparison of Marketer / Purchaser Responses	"Negative" Expectations
General level similar for risk importance	Risk of arrogant attitude from supplier
Higher level of importance for Purchasers	Risk of dependence Risk of excessive prices Too great influence on influencers
Higher level of importance for Marketers	-

Analysis of the different perceived risks, by sector of activity, reveals several interesting elements. For example, it is in the packaging and the textile sectors that the risk of supplier dependence is felt to be the strongest (Table 6).

Table 6. Level of risk importance in relation to sectors of activity

Risks / Negative expectations	Level of risk in the different sectors
Risk of dependence on supplier	Particularly in Packaging and Textile sectors
Risk of too great influence on internal departments	Little importance given for all sectors
Risk of excessive prices	All sectors
Risk of arrogant attitude	Very little importance given, particularly in Car Engineering sector

The answers given by the two hundred respondents allow a better understanding of their expectations and fears concerning supplier brands and provide a clearer definition of the role played – and to be played – by supplier brands in business to business.

3.2   Towards the classification of supplier brands by performance type

The thirty brands concerned may be positioned and mapped using the responses from the two hundred company managers from the four sectors in the study. By plotting the brand scores against the identified expectations (positive and negative), brand performance in relation to these criteria may be measured. Performance is obtained from scores weighted according to the relative importance of expectations in the sector of activity studied. The mapping of these results shows four different brand clusters (Figure 7).

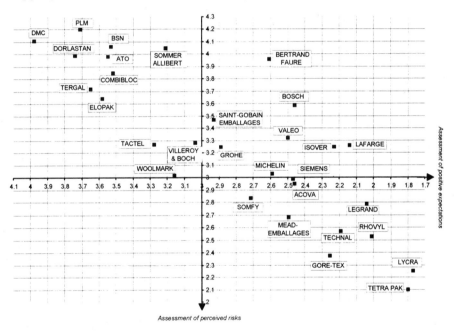

Figure 7. Assessment by company heads of supplier brands: positive expectations against perceived risks

• The top right quadrant shows brands performing doubly well: they received good assessment on positive expectations and are perceived as presenting only slight risks,

• The second quadrant, bottom right, corresponds to those brands which received good evaluations on positive expectations, but which were perceived as presenting a higher level of risk,

• The third quadrant, top left, corresponds to those brands with a relatively low score on positive expectations and a low one also on perceived risks,

• Lastly, the fourth quadrant, bottom left, corresponds to the brands assessed as relatively low on positive expectations with a high level of risks.

If a brand is perceived as a high performer (in fulfilling partnership expectations), then it is also regarded as presenting higher risks; the type of risk perceived depends on the partner company sector. It appears that the more a brand is perceived as an innovation, production or decision-making performance facilitator, then the more it is seen as presenting a risk of dependence – basically for technical reasons. The more a brand is considered as a commercial performance facilitator, the greater chance there is that company heads will perceive the risks of unacceptable influence on deciders, excessive prices, and possible arrogant attitudes.

3.3   Classification of supplier brands by performance type

By reprocessing the results used in the mapping, it is possible to reposition the thirty brands according to their respective performance concerning positive and negative expectations (Figure 8).

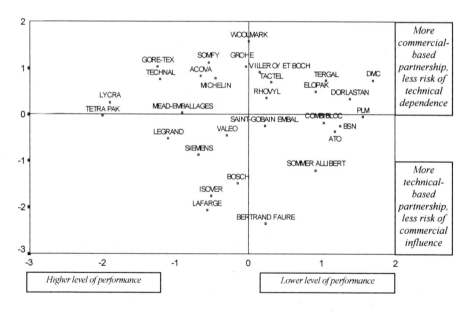

Figure 8. Perception map showing brands positioned by positive and negative expectations

Four clusters of supplier brands can thus be identified (Figure 9):

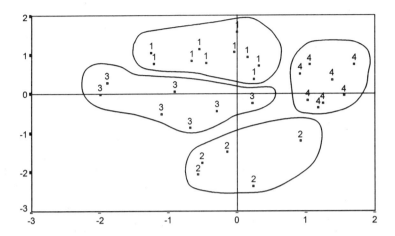

The different levels of partnership:
- Class 1: mainly commercial partners, but with quite high risk
- Class 2: mainly technical partners but, with little risk
- Class 3: high performance partners, but with high risk
- Class 4: lower performance partners, but with low risk

Figure 9. Visualization of the groups

• Class 1 includes mainly commercial partners. In this category we find ten brands: Woolmark, Somfy, Gore-Tex, Technal, Acova, Michelin, Grohe, Villeroy & Bosch, Tactel, and Rhovyl. These brands – as those of class 3 – are not perceived as presenting a risk of arrogant attitude, but more a risk of too great an influence or excessive prices. Compared to those of classes 2 and 3, class 1 brands present significantly less risk of supplier dependence and are perceived less as production performance facilitators, innovation or decision-making facilitators. As those of class 3, class 1 brands are, however, perceived as commercial performance facilitators (the brands in this class receive the best average for the "commercial performance facilitator" variable). This class may, therefore, be characterized essentially by brands perceived as "commercial partners by their clients". Logically, then, they are to be found in the top half of the perception map.

• Class 2 includes mainly technical partners. In relation to the horizontal axis, this class presents a certain symmetry to class 1. It includes the following brands: Bosch, Isover, Lafarge, and Bertrand-Faure. It resembles class 3. The brands in class 2 are perceived as particularly high performers in terms of innovation, production, and decision-making (thus differing from class 1). In terms of commercial performance, the brands in class 2 are perceived as performing less well than classes 1 and 3. Although the brands in this class are seen as presenting a relatively high risk of supplier dependence (as for class 3), by comparison to classes 1 and 3, they present a smaller risk of influence, excessive prices, and arrogant attitude. To summarize, class 2 seems to regroup brands characterized by a strong "technical partnership" and a low risk of commercial influence.

• Class 3 includes partners considered as good performers, but who are also seen as presenting high risks. Seven brands are in this category: Lycra, Tetra Pak, Mead-Emballages, Legrand, Siemens, Valeo, and Saint-Gobain Packaging. These brands obtained the "best" averages for each of the expectation criterion and, like class 2 brands, they were perceived as good performers in terms of innovation, production, and assistance in decision-making. In addition to this, along with class 1 brands, they are recognized as commercial performance facilitators. Brands in class 2 are the real "champions" in terms of positive expectations. However, they are also characterized by the highest level of perceived risk – be it technical risk, risk of too great an influence, excessive prices or arrogant attitude. Class 3 differs from the previous classes in that it receives high scores in both performance and risk criteria.

• Class 4 includes those partners seen as the lowest performers, but who present less risk. The nine brands are: Sommer Allibert, Ato, BSN-Emballage, Combibloc, PLM, Dorlastan, Elopak, Tergal, and DMC. This class is characterized by brands having the lowest appreciation for positive expectations, but also seen as presenting a low level of risk. The scores obtained for the variables are completely different from the three other classes particularly in terms of innovation, decision-making performance facilitator or risk of supplier dependence (Figure 10).

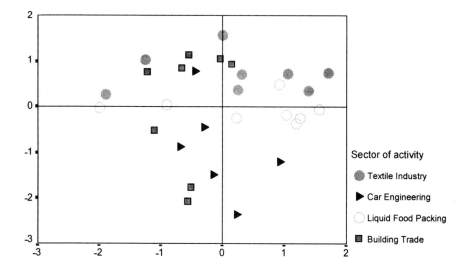

Figure 10. Perception map showing brands characterized by their sector of activity

It is also interesting to see the way these thirty brands are plotted, by sector of activity, on the map (Figure 10). Several remarks can be made:
• The brands in the textile sector can be found along the horizontal axis, but are all characterized by a mostly commercial partnership with their industrial clients,
• The automotive product brands, however, have a more technical partnership with less risk of commercial influence,
• The liquid food packaging brands have a technical partnership, though to a lesser degree than the above sector,
• The building sector obtained high scores for performance. Three were considered as mainly technical partners, however, five others were perceived as more commercial partners.

3.4 The industrial brand and its triple role of performance facilitator

Following the results obtained, other studies were carried out in other sectors of activity[2]. Data analysis brought out three main types of performance assistance. For the supplier brand, this involves facilitating the performance of the customer company from a technical point of view, a commercial point of view, or with its internal running or a combination of the three.

3.4.1 Facilitating technical performance

The word "technical" englobes three possible types of supplier brand/customer partnerships:
• Collaboration between the research and development departments in design and new product launch. Delphi or Valeo are good examples of this: thanks to considerable investment in research and development, these companies have positioned themselves as this particular type of partner in the automotive construction and heavy goods vehicle sectors. In the same way, Intel has contributed to the improvement of computer capacity by working closely with IT companies such as Hewlett-Packard, IBM, Compaq or Toshiba.
• Collaboration between technical departments aims at optimizing the production process by adopting new materials and/or new production methods. The supplier company improves technical performance by facilitating decision-making and consensus among the deciders in the customer company. For example, in the building sector, the prestige of the Lafarge brand contributes to legitimizing the use of certain material-mounting processes on work sites.
• Collaboration between the maintenance department of the supplier company and the production or maintenance department of the customer

company reinforce loyalty. By incorporating the notion of regular investment in equipment maintenance into strategy, a company like Tetra Pak gains the confidence of its industrial customers – which are in turn more likely to stay loyal to their brand and even recommend it.

• Over and above the functional quality of the material, the industrial brand makes tracking possible. In the case of dysfunction or accident for example, the supplier brand can trace back a certain component or spare part to the producer. In the food sector, a policy of tracking ('traceability') enables clients to know the exact origins of ingredients used. Should a problem arise with any particular batch, the exact origin and date of production can be identified.

3.4.2   Facilitating commercial performance

The aim of the supplier brand is to ensure that the customer company product is more easily sold than if it were commercialized under a competing supplier brand. This may be achievd by the juxtaposition of promises made to the final customer, by a close collaboration in communication campaigns and/or in the distribution channel.

• Image partnership: this implies that the industrial customer benefits from the renown and positive reputation already gained by the supplier brand. The partnership of Gore-Tex® with the shoe manufacturer Aigle can be summed up in this way: "The demand for your products is good, but it will be even better if the Gore-Tex® brand appears on the shoes as well." The Gore-Tex® brand communicates a certain promise to the consumer: a unidirectional waterproofness from the inside to the outside, which lets perspiration pass. By improving the performance of hiking boots for example, the supplier brand stimulates consumer demand. Co-branding thus contributes to both the customer's and the supplier's commercial performance.

• The partnership in the previous example was based on the product. This next partnership concerns working together for communication purposes. A supplier brand may agree to help its customers with the design and financing of their advertising campaigns. This results in the type of co-branding used by the computer company Compaq and "Intel Inside®". As well as adding a promise to the product offer, Intel also finances part of the advertising space in exchange for the prominence of its brand name Intel Pentium III® in Compaq advertising.

• Commercial performance is also facilitated through the sales force, particularly during events such as trade fairs. In the IT sector, it is common for an equipment supplier to allow its distribution partners to share its stand and invite their own customers. Such a strategy creates demand from the final customer, which in turn benefits direct professional customers. Some companies have developed a mass market communication strategy, using a freephone number in the press and on television. The calls are transferred free of charge to the craftsman nearest the caller's locality. In all cases, the craftsman (a direct client of these advertisers) receives an information sheet giving details of the project considered.

3.4.3 Facilitating the operating performance of the customer company

From the supplier's viewpoint, this means improving the running of the customer company without directly acting on technical or commercial performance. By facilitating operating performance, higher productivity may be achieved along with a better working atmosphere and improved customer reception. This type of partnership concerns mainly professional service brands.

• Productivity improvement characterizes computer equipment and software suppliers for example. Through know-how and experience, a partner such as EDS (Electronic Data System) helps to improve its customer's management performance. In human resources, temporary work agencies increase productivity by their ability to call directly on a certain category of personnel according to company needs.

• A better working atmosphere can influence the efficiency of customer company teams. For example, thanks to catering companies like Compass, Sodexho-Marriott[3], the customer company can demonstrate to its personnel the efforts made to assure them comfort during lunch and rest breaks. In addition to improving the working atmosphere, this type of partnership contributes to the operating performance of the customer company.

• Improvement in the quality of receiving clients and visitors to the customer company is developed in the aim of increasing final customer satisfaction. This in turn gives a more positive image of the company, perceived as more efficiently run – and results in higher loyalty. Kimberly-Clark has chosen this positioning. The supplier brand shows the lack of cleanliness in kitchens and toilets in a certain company; the image of the company thus suffers – showing that a partnership with Kimberly-Clark[4] could have avoided this problem.

These analyses of the different functions of the supplier brand allow us to clearly distinguish two main dimensions: the role of reducing incertitude, and the role of facilitating performance.

NOTES

1. Bénaroya, C., (1998), Working paper.
2. Surveys realized in 1997/1998 in the sector of professional services (Business Conseil).

3. See Chapter 10, Managing the International Brand, 1-7 Sodexho-Marriott: Adopting a Worldwide Identity.
4. See Chapter 13, Equipment Goods Brands, 6- Kimberly-Clark: Contribution to the Customers' Image.

REFERENCES

Alba, J.W., and Chattopadhyay, A., (1986), Salience Effects in Brand Recall, *Journal of Marketing Research*, vol. n°22, p 363-369.

Arnold, D., (1992), *The Handbook of Brand Management*, Century Business, London.

Cantor, M.,A. and Chestek, P., S., (2000), Protecting product design in the US, in Managing Intellectual Property, *Trade Mark Yearbook 2000*, p. 22-24.

Columbo, R.A. and Morrison, D.G., (1989), A Brand Switching Model With Implications for Marketing Strategies, *Marketing Science*, vol. n°8, p 89-99.

Doyle, P., (1990), Building Successful Brands: Strategic Options, *Journal of Consumer Marketing*, vol. n°7, n°2, p 5-19, Spring.

Farquhar P. H., (1990), Managing Brand Equity, *Journal of Advertising Research*, vol n°30, n°4, RC7-RC12, August-September.

Kapferer, J-N. and Thoenig, J-C., (1992), Les consommateurs face à la copie. Étude sur la confusion des marques créées par l'imitation, *Revue Française du Marketing*, n°136, n°1, p 53-68.

Kim, P., (1990), A Perspective on Brands, *Journal of Consumer Marketing*, vol. n°6, n°4, p 63-67, Fall.

Laurent, G., Kapferer, J-N. and Roussel, F., (1987), Thresholds of Brand Awareness, Developments in *Advertising and Communication Research*, Montreux, Congrès ESOMAR, p 677-699.

Leuthesser, L., (1988), Defining, Measuring and Managing Brand Equity, Cambridge, MA, *Marketing Science Institute*, Report n°88-104.

Malaval, Ph., (1998), Exploratory Survey of the Industrial Brand Performance, perceived by the Purchase and Marketing Managers, *The Example of Four Industrial Markets: Building Trade, Liquid Food Packing, Car Engineering and Textile Industry, Thesis for Business Management Doctorate*, Social Sciences University of Toulouse I.

McInnis D., Moorman, Ch. and Jaworski B., (1991), Enhancing and Measuring Consumer's Motivation, Opportunity and Ability to Process Brand Information From Ads, *Journal of Marketing*, vol. n°55, p 32-53.

McInnis, D. and Jaworski, B., (1989), Information Processing from Advertisements: Toward an Integrative Framework, *Journal of Marketing*, vol. n°53, p1-23.

McWilliam, G. and De Chernatony, L., (1989), Representational Brands and Functional Brands: the Strategic Implications of the Difference, ADMAP, vol. n°25, n°3, p 38-41.

Park, C.W., Jaworski J.B. and McInnis J.D., (1986), Strategic Brand Concept-Image Management, *Journal of Marketing*, vol. n°50, p 135-145.

Park, C.W., Lawson, R. and Milberg, S., (1989), Memory Structure of Brand Names, *Advances in Consumer Research*, vol. n°16, p 726-731.

Ries A. and Trout, J., (1982), *Positioning: the battle for your mind*, New York, Warner.

Shocker, A.D., Srivastava, R.K., Ruekert, R.W., (1994), Challenges and Opportunities Facing Brand Management, *Journal of Marketing Research*, vol. n°31, p 19-158.

Chapter 6

Purchaseability and Visibility of Industrial Brands

Unlike consumer brands, industrial brands are generally not seen or are never purchased by end users. Concerning essentially professional customers, industrial brands can differ greatly depending on "purchaseability" and visibility by end consumers. They are generally unknown by the consumer public, even when they belong to powerful groups. Some brands such as Lycra®, Intel® or Tetra Pak have, however, reached very high awareness rates. These results and the advertising investments dedicated to these brands are surprising, as consumers cannot buy their actual products directly. Brands like Xerox, Grohe, Legrand, Intel® or Gore-Tex® have chosen to advertise on television, while they aim, first of all, at business targets. They are now trying to make themselves known by the consumer public. Whatever their motivations, it seems necessary to explain the different ways an industrial brand can reach the final customer.

1. HOW DO INDUSTRIAL BRANDS REACH THE FINAL CUSTOMER?

The difference between consumer brands and industrial brands is clear enough, except in the areas of office supplies and small do-it-yourself appliances. These products belong to both consumer and business to business markets. In all other cases, an industrial brand has three ways of reaching consumers: product, communication, a change in strategy or a combination of the three factors.

1.1   Industrial brands: reaching consumers through the product

The first low cost way for industrial brands to reach consumers is to be identified through the product itself. This type of access can be observed with "entering goods", equipment goods and production goods:

- *Entering Goods*: End users can get the industrial product without knowing it when they buy consumer goods such as beverages or clothes: orange juice can be contained in Tetra Pak packaging and Dim stockings are made of Lycra® fibers.
- *Intermediary Equipment Goods*: End users can "discover" the product, which is a part of the bought or hired car or house. Some good examples are Lucent, Delphi or Visteon car-parts, Michelin or Goodyear tires, Pass & Seymour electrical appliances or Grohe taps for housing.
- *Equipment Goods*: End users can see the industrial brand of equipment goods when using a service such as a transportation system: Mercedes coach, Alstom train or Airbus aircraft. Other examples can be found with health services equipment like a Siemens scanner.
- *Production Goods*: The people walking around can simply see them on a building site: Mack trucks or Fenwick forklift trucks. Another example are branded machine-tools seen during a factory visit.

Thus all types of industrial brands can be directly known by end users without any communication, only through observation of the goods as soon as they are visibly branded.

1.2   Industrial brands: reaching consumers through communication

The main way for industrial brands to reach end users is communication. Word-of-mouth is often the first type of communication allowing end users to learn about industrial brands. Not easy to control by companies, word of mouth can be diffused by employees, partners' employees, and by users who make comments on products to their professional or private contacts.

A lot of industrial companies still only communicate using their corporate brand, which is often the name of the company. In this case consumers can discover the brand cited in the press when new major contracts are obtained or when there are important events such as new product launchings or takeover bids.

Different messages to shareholders or employees use the same corporate brand and are known by end users without any advertising: corporate communication is quite effective in this case, thanks to the media (launching of new products, signing of contracts, announcement of hiring, company buyouts, etc.).

When an industrial brand begins advertising through a consumer media such as press or television, the number of consumers aware of its existence increases quickly. One of the best examples is provided by Intel, hardly known ten years ago. Today Intel's awareness rate is often higher than its customers – hardware integrators, like Compaq or Hewlett-Packard. Fiber suppliers like Lycra® or membrane makers like Gore-Tex® are better known than many of their clothing manufacturers. The best awareness rates can be obtained by industrial brands through using a combined strategy of communication actions and ensuring brand visibility on the finished products.

1.3 Industrial brands: reaching consumers through a change in strategy

Industrial product suppliers may decide to launch a product line for consumers. These products may or may not be the same as those used by their professional customers. Many examples of this can be found in do-it-yourself markets, such as ICI paintings, Hilti appliances, Red Devil hand-tools, Scotchgard® protector, Motorola or Nokia mobile phone systems. In this case the new consumer goods benefit from the technological prestige associated with the products' perceived higher performances in industrial fields.

The opposite process can be observed when a consumer brand tries to move into industrial markets. Detergents can be produced by a company such as Henkel for industrial users; mineral water suppliers like Evian can produce specialized packaging for restaurants. In these cases, high awareness rates are obtained among consumers who are sometimes unaware of the business strategies followed by these suppliers.

In the supply chain, the more a supplier brand is downstream, the easier its "purchaseability" is to final consumers (Figure 1). But the efficiency of industrial brands depends on their "purchaseability" and visibility strategies.

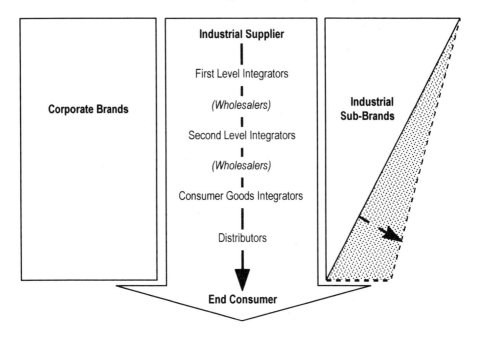

Figure 1. Reaching end consumers: the first role of corporate brands and development of industrial product sub-brands

2.   THE "PURCHASEABILITY" CONCEPT

For an industrial brand, "purchaseability" can be defined as the ability of end consumers to buy products or services separately from the final product purchase. The glass bottle, for instance, can only be obtained by end consumers when wine or orange juice is purchased. The same is true for an Airbag system, which cannot be bought separately from the car purchase. Given the diversity of industrial brands, there are different levels of "purchaseability".

2.1   The main levels of "purchaseability"

"Purchaseability" depends on internal factors linked to the company strategy and on external factors due to the complexity of the product category.

2.1.1 Product category

Depending on their technical complexity, industrial products can be divided into three categories: never, always and sometimes purchaseable (Figure 2).

• *Never purchaseable categories* include specialized machine-tools, electronic components, fibers, industrial packaging systems. The end consumer cannot obtain them under any circumstances.

• *Always purchaseable categories* include running car-parts or small appliances for do-it-yourself. Consumers can find these products through specialized distribution channels.

• *Sometimes purchaseable categories* include small industrial machines, office supplies, raw materials, processed materials (leather, wood, etc.). In this third category are to be found products of the same complexity level which can be purchaseable or not: this depends on an internal factor; the supplier brand strategy.

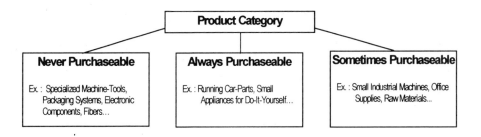

Figure 2. The different levels of product category "purchaseability"

2.1.2 The brand strategy

For the final consumer, an industrial brand can be purchased directly, through a professional middleman, or not at all.

• *Directly purchaseable goods* include relatively simple products like tires, windshield wipers for car equipment, electrical switches for housing, small office supplies. Consumers are free to buy them, need no special help, and can get the brand of their choice.

• *Purchaseable through a professional channel*: This includes housing equipment like Tapco shutters, Bessler stairways, etc. There are two situations:

-    The end consumer stipulates the brand of goods he wants.
-    The professional specificies the brand of goods to the end consumer.

In both cases, the end consumer needs the contractor (or other middleman) to procure the equipment.

• *Not purchaseable*: The end consumer cannot buy the industrial branded product directly. Entering goods are concerned because they are integrated by consumer goods producers. Consumers cannot buy empty food packaging, textile fibers or electronic microprocessors without buying the complete consumer product. Big equipment goods like trucks, trains, helicopters or aircraft are also not purchaseable by the end consumer. Another case concerns goods which could be purchaseable, but which are not, due to the supplier marketing strategy (Figure 3).

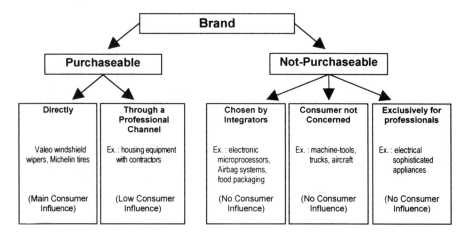

Figure 3. The criteria of "purchaseability" and "non-purchaseability" of industrial brands relative to final consumers

The two previous classifications of "purchaseability" levels can intersect. For instance, most of the "sometimes purchaseable goods" in the first classification can be found in different categories of the second grid. This depends on the marketing supplier strategy.

2.2   Factors explaining "purchaseability"

2.2.1   The product category's technical complexity

The implementation of the entering goods or the exploitation of equipment require, from a technical point of view, the use of:
- Sophisticated tools,
- Specific technical conditions such as constant hygrometry, temperature or ultra-clean air conditions,

- Specific technical skills (for assembling, integrating...),
- Respect of regulations, special safety conditions for workers and environmental norms for end users.

The different constraints require high investments. The more complex the product category, the less purchaseable it will be for end consumers.

2.2.2 The supplier marketing strategy

The second explanatory factor is due to the brand policy. The supplier may accept to sell directly to end consumers for one main reason: hope of larger sales owing to consumer channels such as do-it-yourself specialized stores. The size of the consumer market is an argument for a large diffusion from producers.

However, the supplier can refuse to give direct access for four reasons:
- Logistical constraints of delivering sophisticated goods and managing spare parts and after-sales activities for a diffused market,
- Concern about preserving a high level of quality. There is the risk that assembling norms and specifications may not be respected by end-users when doing it themselves. Safety conditions are too important to be left entirely to non-professionals,
- Contractual agreements with professional partners to guarantee them a regular income: they can get margins from spare-parts business, often necessary to keep them in business,
- Constraining regulations concerning safety, hygiene specifications, environmental protection, etc.

Thus the concept of "purchaseability" requires two explanatory variables: the technical complexity of the category and the brand's strategy of reaching the consumer, each with their respective components (Figure 4).

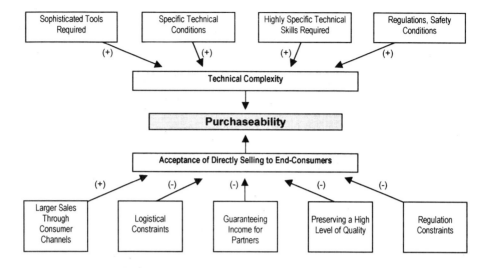

Figure 4. "Purchaseability" factors

3.   THE VISIBILITY CONCEPT

Industrial brands can be visible by end consumers thanks to communication actions and the visibility strategy on the product itself.

3.1   The different levels of "product-visibility"

The visibility of the brand on the product (called product visibility) can be considered from the perspective of the consumer or as a function of technical constraints.

3.1.1   For the end user

Entering and equipment goods brands can be analyzed in terms of the visibility moment, or when the consumer sees the brand. There are four possibilities:

• The end consumer can see the brand during purchasing but not when he is using the product. Good examples of this are lubricant for the car-industry and textile fibers for clothing: packaging or labels transmit the brand.

• The end consumer can see the brand during his purchase and throughout the product's lifetime. This is the case of consumer beverage packaging which often have their supplier brand name printed on them. This also applies to machine-tools or industrial vehicles, the brand of which lasts as long as the machine.

• The end user cannot see the brand, neither when purchasing nor when using the product. However the brand can be seen, for instance during repairs made by a professional. This is true for floor and wall coverings but also electronics and electromechanical parts in car engines.

• The end user cannot see the brand because it is not printed anywhere on the product. This is true of most raw materials but also the steel parts of a car body (Figure 5).

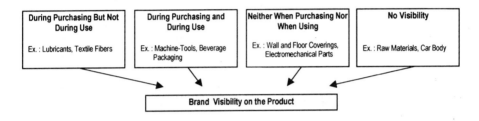

Figure 5. Presentation of the different visibility levels for end users

3.1.2   As a function of technical constraints

The visibility of industrial brands also depends on the technical possibilities of branding the product (which is linked to the physical characteristics) and on the visual accessibility of the brand for end-users.

There are four cases:

• The brand can be printed and "readable" thanks to ink or paint printing or engraving on glass, wood or metal, such as Michelin or Goodyear rubber tires, Saint-Gobain Sekurit glass panes, and Tetra Pak packaging.

• The brand can be transmitted by a separate support like a label or the packaging mentions. Lycra® textile fibers and Mobil Oil in cans are a case in point, so is cement stored in silos.

• The brand can be applied but cannot be seen as it is hidden by another technical part, for example, electrical mechanics in car engines, and cables in the housing industry.

• The brand could be printed from a technical point of view but is not for other reasons. This is true of plastic computer bodies, steel car bodies or car seats (Figure 6).

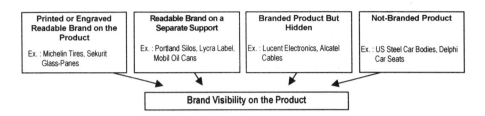

Figure 6. Presentation of the different visibility levels as a function of technical constraints

Thus there are four visibility levels which can be crossed between the two methods. For instance, "branded but hidden products" correspond in the first presentation to brands, which cannot be seen when purchased, and during use but are visible while being repaired by professionals. The two presentations are not redundant: the first one concerns the end user, the second concerns the producer.

3.2   Factors explaining brand visibility on products

The analysis of different visibility levels shows that brand visibility depends on whether the brand can be printed ("printability") or not. "Printability" can be defined as the ability for an individual to read the identity of the producer on the product when he purchases it or during the normal use of the product. The visibility depends on the choice of the supplier and of his client to let the supplier brand appear on the final goods or not.

3.2.1   Brand "printability"

Brand "printability" depends on four main factors which are the product's physical support, the identification longevity, the visual access to the product and product transformations after delivery.

• Branded products can be solid, liquid, gaseous or powdery. A solid product can be directly printed or engraved, when it is large enough. For instance, very small Motorola components cannot be branded. In the other cases – liquid, gas or powder – a separate support is needed such as labels, packaging bottles, bags or silos.

• Identification longevity depends on the support type. When the brand is printed on a label or an oil can, it is often thrown out after purchasing or first use: it lasts a very short time. On the other hand, the brand of machine-tools can be engraved and lasts as long as the machine.

• The visual access to the product depends on the consumer product design in which the industrial product is incorporated. For instance, in a building, electrical cables are less visible than a French window. Some engine components cannot be seen even though they are branded because other car parts hide their support. For legal reasons some parts are branded to allow tracking in case of accident. But they can be seen only while being repaired by professionals.

• Product transformations after delivery include semi-finished products such as metal bars or tannery leathers. The products delivered by producers are cut by the professional contractor or manufacturer. The industrial branded product cannot be readable after the next transformation step. Solutions to this problem are generally based on the use of labels, branded accessories like window handles, and integration of the supplier logo in the future consumer product design (Figure 7).

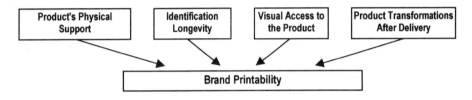

Figure 7. Main factors explaining the brand "printability"

Explaining industrial brand "printability" is necessary from a technical point of view. But to understand brand visibility, the marketing choices of suppliers and customers also need to be analyzed.

3.2.2 Supplier and customer marketing choices

Brand visibility involves high marketing stakes for both suppliers and industrial customers. Indeed, brand visibility depends on the marketing strategy of the supplier and on the commercial policy of the industrial customer whocan accept the presence of the supplier brand or not.

The supplier marketing policy

Why should a supplier wish to have its brand visible throughout the whole supply-chain? There are three main objectives:

• Transmitting information on the supplier's identity in order to increase awareness among professional customers and end users. For instance an equipment goods brand can be printed on machines to be seen by possible influencers. In this case the same Air Liquide brand will be printed on all types of supports, from trucks, production plants, and silos to commercial brochures, invoices and the workers' garments or employee uniforms. All branding rules are prescribed in the corporate identity code.

• Allowing the necessary tracking during and after use by authenticating the product. The company signature makes it possible to guarantee quality control from production to after-sales service.

• Preventing the risk of becoming commonplace versus competitors and unmarked products. Visibility is necessary to allow differentiation.

Customer commercial acceptance

Four main factors encourage the customer to accept or refuse the visibility of his supplier's brand. These are:

• Developing a long-term partnership with this supplier from quality control to after-sales service. This is possible when the identified supplier is perceived as continuing its activities in the long-term.

• Using the supplier's investments in terms of communication. The customer wishes to benefit from the credibility or prestige obtained by the supplier. This objective can lead to a co-branding strategy (supplier brand / customer brand). These two objectives incite customers to accept the visibility of their main suppliers' brands.

• Fear of dependence on this supplier. When the supplier brand becomes stronger, industrial customers have fewer opportunities to change their suppliers and to negotiate better purchasing prices.

• Fear its products look more and more like those of competitors. A strong supplier brand can be used by different industrial competitors, which reduces the perceived differences by end users.

The latter fears explain why so many customers do not accept the visibility of their suppliers' brands.

The "printability" of the product category on the one hand, and the supplier and customer marketing choices on the other, explain the brand visibility on the product. The following diagram represents the different factors of brand visibility (Figure 8).

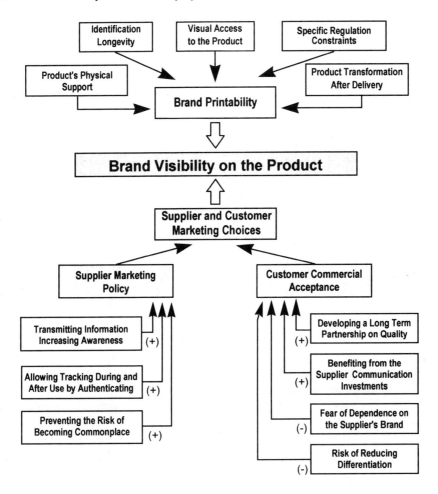

Figure 8. Factors explaining the brand visibility on the product

3.3 A communication strategy for greater brand visibility

Industrial brand visibility results, as was explained above, from the brand presence on the product itself and also from the communication strategy followed by the firm. Communication is necessary to transmit qualitative messages to professional customers and end users.

3.3.1 Non-organized communication

The company cannot control this type of communication, which does not use traditional media but contributes to the brand visibility. For instance, contractors and the other players within the supply chain make comments on the brand strengths and weaknesses. This word-of-mouth communication is completed by all the information transmitted by journalists after financial, technical or social events. Employees and partners' employees take part in this word of mouth communication when they give information to the people surrounding them. The content of this communication depends then on the in-house positive or negative environment as well as the company's in-house communication policy. This type of non-organized communication is linked with new information: the more events there are, the more brand visibility is developed.

3.3.2   Organized communication

This type of communication can use traditional media aimed at industrial customers and end users. But direct marketing and messages directly transmitted by the sales force remain the best ways to communicate in business to business. For instance, brochures, catalogues, and technical documents are diffused by marketing services, which can organize plant or site visits and other public relations events. Internet sites are used more and more to reach customers all over the world. Out of the different media vehicles, business publications and trade-shows represent the biggest advertising budget. Consumer media such as television, magazine press and billboards are used by a few brands such as Intel®, Lycra®, Gore-Tex®, Nutrasweet®, DHL, Monroe, and Boeing, among others. Their main objective is first to gain awareness among end users, and then to transmit information about their product advantages in terms of quality, design, technical characteristics, or user-friendliness. In this way, they are trying to develop consumer demand, which should in turn improve the battle of wills during business to business negotiations (Figure 9).

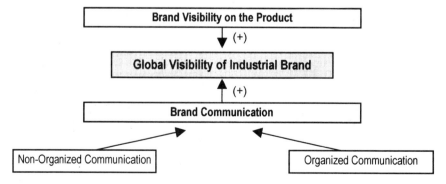

Figure 9. Factors explaining global brand visibility

3.3.3 The different types of industrial products or services advertised with customer media

There are three main product categories involving consumer communication. These are: combined consumer and professional products, entering goods for consumer products, and projects or products needing governmental decisions.

Combined consumer and professional goods

Both consumers and professional customers can buy these products and services.

• Small car parts are first and foremost produced as OEM goods. But some of them can also be bought by end users as repair parts: tires and windshield wipers for cars, small appliances for do-it yourself markets.

• Products which can be used by employees in companies but also at home by consumers: small office appliances, stapler, paper, fax, micro-computers, etc. 3M products are a good example in this category with Scotch brands: Scotch Magic®, Scotch Lite®, and Post-It® products now offered as small advertising gifts, branded with customer brands.

Even though there are no family consumers for these products, the number of potential professional users is very high. For this reason media like television correspond to this type of very large target: photocopier producers such as Xerox or Canon frequently use television and the consumer press.

Entering goods for consumer products

Entering goods are purchased by industrial customers who then integrate them into consumer products. Lycra®, a DuPont brand, has been one of the first industrial brands to develop a complete marketing strategy targeting multiple influencers within and outside of the customer organization:

• Production managers: to convince them Lycra® can improve yields and is usable with in-plant machinery.

• Technical departments such as quality control and maintenance to show them that their performances can still be improved with Lycra®.

• Marketing managers: to help them be more creative and benefit from upstream advertising investments by Lycra®.

• Sales force managers: to show them that new products will be easier to sell owing to Lycra® fibers demanded by final consumers. They are to become influencers on marketing departments.

• Research and development departments, to help them to better answer the needs of marketing departments which are in search of better solutions to consumer needs.

• Last but not least, purchasing departments: to convince them Lycra® is the best solution from an economic point of view in spite of higher purchasing prices versus competitors.

More recent examples are Tetra Pak packaging, which advertise directly to consumers in Europe, and Intel Corp., which does the same. Moreover, Intel will finance a part of its customers' advertising plans, when they explain the "Intel Inside®" concept and the presence of the recent Pentium III® or Celeron® microprocessors on TV ads.

Products or projects requiring governmental decisions

Obviously, citizens are end users. That's why they are concerned by energy issues like nuclear programs, or environmental protection plans. Similar situations can be found with aeronautics and space projects where citizens are concerned by noise pollution for instance. In these cases, main targets can be elected deciders such as members of Parliament and technical managers of Government departments, in charge of energy, space or environmental protection. Advertising to consumers allows companies to measure reactions and agreement rates of these consumer citizens. Institutional deciders will be more inclined to vote for a budget when they know their decision is backed up by their electors. These lobbying practices have been especially developed to modify technical norms (Figure 10).

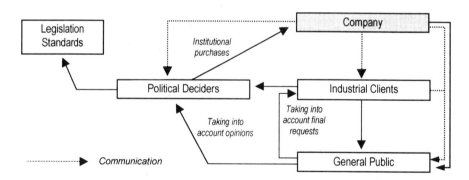

Figure 10. Influences and interactions to obtain new norms by governmental agencies

In these three cases ("Combined goods", "Entering goods", "Projects") and especially for entering goods, industrial branding uses three levels of influence within the supply chain. Brands try to increase end user demand, in order to better convince in-house and external influencers, who can at last influence the choices of purchasing departments (Figure 11).

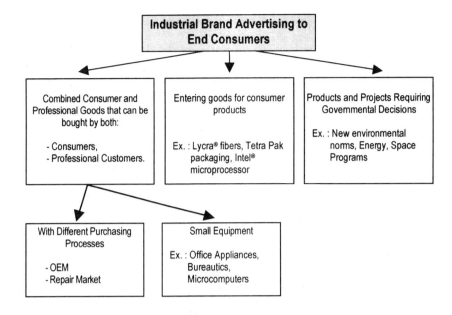

Figure 11. Three cases of industrial brand advertising with consumer media

As for the entering goods, the end consumer is revealed as an essential actor. Indeed, as the derived demand analysis shows, all upstream transactions (industrial purchases) depend on his final purchase. In this case, consumer communication can play a major role (Figure 12).

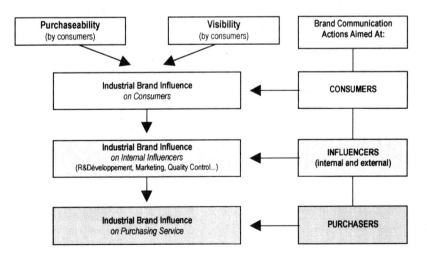

Figure 12. The different levels of industrial brand influence when advertising to end consumers

4.   HIGH VISIBILITY FOR SCOTCHGARD® BRAND (3M)[1]

4.1   A heavy-weight consumer advertising campaign across Europe

Representing an initial multi-million dollar investment over one year, a new heavy-weight consumer advertising campaign for Scotchgard® brand protector was launched in December in the UK and Germany. The press campaign will run into the spring; a second burst is set to break in the autumn, and will also run in France and Italy. Commenting on this new pan-European campaign, Scotchgard® protector European brand manager, Andy Lanes says: "This campaign is the start of a new era of sustained high visibility for the Scotchgard® brand. The new campaign is not a one-off; it is the latest evolution of a consistent consumer campaign that makes sure that Scotchgard® protector is the world's best-known brand for protection for floor-coverings, home furnishings, textiles, apparel and leather. The time is right to target consumers, to influence them to invest in home furnishings and fabrics, and to gain the added value of Scotchgard® protector when making a purchase; by doing this we are providing positive aid to our customers by maintaining the value of using Scotchgard® protector".

4.2   What kind of message?

A series of three innovative advertisements promotes the product performance benefits with a "Colors and Patterns" theme. The advertisements graphically display the benefits of carpets, upholstery, curtains, table-linen, garden furniture, awnings and leather goods treated with Scotchgard® protector to counter the everyday threats of stains and dirt. With this campaign, the company is not trying to impress the trade; it is Scotchgard® protector stepping out into the street to tell consumers what the product does, and to look for it at point of purchase. As a protection specialist, Scotchgard® is not advertising a carpet or a fiber with an addition. This campaign is a direct communication to consumers about the benefits of protection on all types of home furnishings, apparel and leather goods: Scotchgard® protector ensures furnishings look better for longer, and protects that investment. The development of the campaign resulted from extensive research across Europe with three major established factors: consumer demand for information on product performance and reputation; consumer recognition of Scotchgard® protector as the most widely recognized brand in fiber protection; the Scotchgard® brand as innovative, efficient, responsible and trustworthy. The "Colors and Patterns" concept reflects consumer purchasing decisions, which are based on choice of colors and patterns. The concept is accessible, easily understood, and identifies consumer concerns of accidental spilling and stains.

Further research has confirmed that the new advertisements communicate protection against stains and spills, and ease of fabric/carpet care as a result of using Scotchgard® protector. Consumers feel reassured, with greater awareness of the brand, which is perceived to be worth paying extra for the guarantee of quality. The full color page insertions appear in high readership home furnishing, home interest, women's interest, and lifestyle magazines. In Germany, these include: *Stern, Eltern, Brigitte, Freundin, Für Sie*, and *Meine Famille und Ich*. In the UK, the heavy-weight media schedule includes: *Good Housekeeping, She, Living, Woman & Home, Family Circle, Essentials, House Beautiful, Ideal Home, Homes & Gardens, Homes & Ideas, Prima, Bella, Sainsbury Magazine, Radio Times, Woman's Own, and Take A Break*. The advertising campaign will reach 75% of the target audience, a total of 55 million consumers across Europe with an OTS (opportunity to see) of 7/8 times throughout the double burst. In any area, the advertisement will be seen 5 times in each period.

4.3 Making the invisible, visible: communication program

A marketing communication program is now in place across Europe, making sure that the Scotchgard® brand maintains a high profile with the trade and consumers.

4.3.1 Point of Purchase

The same "Colors and Patterns" concept is the theme of new point of sale material, which is in thousands of retail outlets in carpet, textile and leather sectors across 15 EC countries, Switzerland and much of Eastern and Central Europe. It is available in 21 languages, including English, French, German, Italian, Spanish, Portuguese, Polish, Turkish, Russian, Hungarian, Czech, Slovak, Swedish, Danish, Finnish and Norwegian.

4.3.2 Trade Advertising Campaign

A pan-European trade advertising campaign has been visible across Europe and will continue through the whole year using the same heavy-weight media schedule. Promoting the message "Only Scotchgard® protector is recommended for them all", the campaign visibly communicates the product innovation and the versatility of Scotchgard® protector to treat more substrates than any other brand.

4.3.3   Promoting Innovation

A trade campaign for the high performance Scotchgard® leather protector makes a strong visual impact to promote 3M innovation and product development. The water-based leather protector is enjoying outstanding success because of its innovative properties: versatility of application, increased durability, and excellent compatibility with other chemicals used in the tanning process. Many leading tanneries across the world now use it to treat leathers for garments, upholstery, and shoes.

4.4   Fast track to success

Scotchgard® business growth is due to innovative product development, and high tech chemistry designed to respond to changing customer needs; in addition, pan-European sales and marketing activity has enhanced awareness of the Scotchgard® brand, product portfolio, and performance. With several hundred million meters of carpet and fabric treated with Scotchgard® protector throughout Europe, business growth is accelerating dramatically with important new areas of activity within high performance textiles, home furnishings, apparel, and leather. 3M has established a European-wide and global business management team responsible for the development of the Scotchgard® strategy; this central management is coupled with a strong subsidiary structure to provide local sales and technical support. With this finely-balanced combination, 3M is uniquely positioned to help its international customers who wish to sell across borders.

In this chapter, two concepts have been developed: "purchaseability" and visibility of industrial brands by end consumers. The main factors explaining "purchaseability" and industrial brand visibility have been presented ("printability", supplier and industrial customer choice, etc.). Global visibility can be obtained through the brand visibility on the product and through communication actions. The following chapter suggests a classification of industrial brands. Managerial involvement will be developed, taking into account the four main categories among industrial brands, i.e. brands of entering goods, intermediary equipment goods, equipment goods, and business to business services.

NOTES

1. Based on excerpts from *Scotchgard Protector Magazine*, European Edition n°3.

Chapter 7

Industrial Brand Classification

While much research has been done on the classification of consumer brands, the same cannot be said of industrial brands. The latter can be classified and characterized by applying traditional methods, analyzing the brand portfolio of major companies in the industrial sector, and finally, using the "purchaseability" and "visibility" concepts developed in Chapter 6.

1. CLASSIFICATION OF INDUSTRIAL BRANDS USING TRADITIONAL METHODS

1.1 Classification based on the main brand functions

The standard method of brand classification consists in distinguishing three brand categories according to their main functions: "functional brands", "symbolic brands", and "use-based brands". This method does not work for industrial brands, almost all of which belong to the functional category; in other words, they satisfy a need that is not linked to the personality, desires, or individual needs of the customer.

In fact, symbolic brands, which correspond to the customer's image needs, or that of the customer company in the business to business context, should be understood as a function of the brand's main global federating concept. This brand category is less applicable to industrial brands because professional buyers, when choosing suppliers, usually do not rely on intangible criteria such as the potential image projected by the supplier brand. A company might choose a computer equipment supplier like IBM because it projects an image of the company as serious, well-equipped, and able to afford the leading supplier on the market. However, while IBM brand may be good for the image of its customers, it cannot be classified as a symbolic brand insofar as it satisfies, above all, technical data management requirements. However, certain brands can be considered as having attained "reference brand status" thanks to the sheer size of their market share and to the power and reach of their communication strategy. This is the case of brands such as Tetra Pak, Intel, Michelin, Lycra® or Gore-Tex®. However, their status is still mainly based on technological know-how and expertise, which classifies them more in the functional brand category.

1.2   Classification according to the use of goods

Classification according to the use of goods distinguishes between those goods which are part of the composition of the final product ("entering goods"), those which directly enter into the production process ("production goods"), and those which contribute to it indirectly ("facilitating goods"). Classifying industrial brands in these terms gives the following table (Table 1).

Table 1. Classification of industrial brands according to the use of goods

Industrial brands by sector	Category of goods entering into the final product	Category of goods entering into the production process	Category of goods indirectly contributing to the production process
PACKING			
ELF ATOCHEM	X	X	
TETRA PAK	X	X	
SAINT-GOBAIN PACK.	X	X	
MOORE		X	X
GRACE CRYOVAC	X	X	
SIDEL		X	
SMURFIT			X
MEAD	X	X	
FOOD OR CONSUMER PRODUCTS			
NUTRASWEET	X	X	
SIAS FRUITS	X	X	
LYCRA	X	X	
GORE-TEX	X	X	
TEFLON	X	X	
SCOTCHGARD	X	X	
ELECTRONICS / COMMUNICATION			
INTEL		X	
XEROX			X
CANON	X		X
IBM		X	X
HEWLETT-PACKARD		X	X

From this table it can be seen that 15 out of the 19 industrial brands in the three different sectors fall into more than one category at the same time.

For example, Tetra Pak or Saint Gobain Packaging make up the container of the finished product (packaged fruit juice) but they also are part of the production process, as material suppliers. Similarly, Lycra® from Du Pont de Nemours is part of the final product and has also participated in the development and production phases of the finished product.

IBM and Hewlett-Packard are not part of the final product. However, the two computer equipment suppliers fall into the category of goods that are part of the production process (quality control of production lines), as well as the category of goods which indirectly contribute to the production process (computer/software for company management).

This method of classification, which works for industrial goods, does not apply to their brands. In fact, in business to business marketing, the brand represents as much the product or equipment as the service associated with it.

1.3 Classification of brands according to products or services

There are numerous ways of classifying products and services, taking into account their nature, complexity, and role in the industrial process (Wasson, 1976; Avlonitis, 1985; Dayan, 1985; Mahin, 1991).

However, consumer products that are sold to companies are usually not considered, such as a food product sold to company food services. Furthermore, for the producer goods category, it is difficult to distinguish between goods as different as machine tools and the construction of an airport or of a highway.

A more effective classification (Malaval, 1996) method divides industrial goods into nine categories: raw materials, transformed materials, consumables, entering goods and ingredients, detail parts, machine tool and office equipment, heavy equipment, services and consumer products for industry.

In the following table (Table 2), brands are classified according to their activity sector.

Out of the 34 examples chosen, most of the brands fall into only one category. At first, this classification would seem more to the point than the previous classification by goods.

Table 2. Classification of industrial brands according to products or services

Brands \ Categories	Raw Materials	Processed Materials	Supplies	Ingredients Entering goods	Parts	Office Supplies & Machine-tools	Heavy Equip-ment	Services	Consumer products for industry
Lafarge	X	X		X					
Bouygues	X	X					X		
Pechiney		X							
St-Gobain		X							
Air Liquide		X							
Aventis		X	X						
TotalFina			X						
EDF			X						
Motorola				X					
Lycra				X					
Gore-Tex				X					
Nutra-sweet				X					
Sias				X					
Kevlar				X					
Intel				X					
Valeo					X			X	
Monroe					X				
Somfy					X				
Fraikin					X				
Legrand					X				
Kärcher						X			
Mead						X			
Sidel						X		X	
Tetra Pak						X		X	
Mannes-mann						X		X	
Xerox						X		X	
Canon						X		X	
HP						X		X	
Schneider							X	X	
Sodexho								X	
Spot image								X	
Henkel									X
Evian									X
Yoplait									X

However, the analysis becomes more complex when you are dealing with the brands of major companies who haven't chosen to feature their corporate name. In fact, most of these companies have used vertical integration, which means that their brands/products fall into several different classes of industrial goods.

For example, Air Liquide, Bayer, Bouygues, Du Pont de Nemours, ICI and Aventis intervene with the same brand on extremely different markets such as raw materials, processed materials, heavy equipment goods, and services with industrial engineering. This is even more true for industrial brands of medium sized companies, which often use their corporate name whatever the service. For this reason, in business to business, the classification of industrial brands according to the type of products or services is not suitable.

2.   CLASSIFICATION OF INDUSTRIAL BRANDS ACCORDING TO BRAND PORTFOLIO MANAGEMENT

Certain companies choose to feature one brand, which is often the name of the company, while others invest in building up and maintaining a highly diversified brand portfolio. This means comparing brands in terms of investment and diffusion. For example, there would be no point in analyzing the Michelin brand and the Lexic brand, one of Legrand's product brands, in the same way, while comparing Michelin with Legrand could provide information on industrial brand management. Thus, it seems worthwhile to classify industrial brands as a function of their use.

2.1   Companies using mainly the corporate brand

In many industrial companies, the corporate name is also the brand. As such, the name projects the company image to all the market players: suppliers, bankers, financial markets, the job market (Malaval and Bénaroya, 1998). Corporate brands are much more frequent in industrial markets than in consumer markets, where branding has become more and more sophisticated (Cegarra, 1990). A sample of companies using their corporate name confirms this: Aerospatiale, Aga, Airbus Industrie, Air Liquide, Alcatel Space, Aventis, Boeing, Bosch, Eurocopter, IBM, Intel, Kimberly-Clark, Kompass, Lafarge, Legrand, Lexmark, Magneti-Marelli, Michelin, Motorola, Pechiney, Saint-Gobain, Schneider, Sidel, Siemens, Sodexho, Spot Image, Technal, Tetra Pak, Valeo, Xerox, etc.

Most of the brands in the preceding list are highly renowned; this is in part due to the frequent use of the corporate brand in industrial markets.

The use of corporate brands has certain major advantages and limitations. The main advantage of using a unique brand lies in the synergy possible between different marketing actions. A company can more easily exploit its name using traditional business to business communication media such as trade fairs, business publications, and direct, personalized measures targeting specific populations. Using the same logo for products and services backs up these actions. Furthermore, in-house communication is easier to manage, to the extent that personnel from different production and sales departments are grouped together under the same name.

The company saves money on creating the brand, advertising, and diffusion. The repeated use of the same brand reinforces awareness, making it more familiar to the different populations. Thus using the corporate brand would seem to bring savings in time and money and greater visibility and strength. The increased awareness for the company's new activities or products, resulting from using the corporate brand, can be compared to the advantages gained from brand extensions on consumer markets. However, the company cannot afford to risk any incoherence, whether in relation to external populations or in-house targets (Kapferer, 1995). In fact, a contradiction or weakness on a given new market could have negative spin-offs on other markets, which do not necessarily have anything to do with the counter-performance.

Furthermore, if the corporate brands which are used accompanied by product brands are removed from the above mentioned list, there are only a few companies that use almost exclusively their corporate name: Air Liquide, Kimberly-Clark, Saint-Gobain, Sidel, Siemens and Valeo. This would seem to suggest that the trend towards ever more sophisticated brand policies is equally true of industrial markets. Major companies, which have often used external growth to speed up their development, have chosen, for the most part, to feature their corporate brand even if it means modifying the name of other divisions. The name preceding the purchased companies thus becomes a complement to the main brand. Schneider is an example of this with today, Schneider Merlin Gerin, Schneider Telemecanique and Schneider Square-D. Pechiney, for its part, has unified its different subsidiaries such as Cebal, which today is Pechiney Cebal etc.

So as to unite the different companies purchased, another solution is to reuse the corporate identity code of the group logo, adapting it to the name of the integrated company. Bouygues, for example, has inserted the name of different companies such as GFC, Mistral, and Norpac, into the orange colored horizontal oval, the group's identifying symbol.

Quite often, in the industrial context, corporate brands are used alongside product references using only groups of letters and numbers (Table 3).

Table 3. Example of brands that associate a product reference with a corporate name

Brands	Reference Products
XEROX	Xerox 5815, Xerox 5043, Xerox 5088, Xerox 5310, Xerox 5365...; Xerox DocuPrint 180 NPS, XEROX DocuPrint NPS (4050, 4090, 4635, 4850, 4890), Xerox DocuPrint IPS (4090, 4250, 4635, 4850, 4890), Xerox DocuPrint (390-HC, 350-HC, et 390), Xerox DocuColor (40, 5750...), Xerox DocuPrint (N24, N32...)...
MICHELIN	Michelin XZA, XTA, XZE, XDE, XTE, XZT, Michelin Energy XZA, Michelin Energy XDA, Michelin Energy XTA, Michelin Pilote XZA1, Michelin Pilote XZY
SPIT	Spit Pulsa 1000, Spit P45, Spit P60, Spit P200, Spit P200 CI, Spit P250, Spit SB 72, Spit 315, Spit 327, Spit 215, Spit 322, Spit 355, Spit 490...
LEXMARK	Lexmark 3000, Lexmark 7000, Lexmark 2050 Photo Edition, Lexmark 2030, Lexmark 4227, Lexmark 4079 Plus, Lexmark 4079 Pro...

In general, the sets of letters and numbers correspond to technical specifications. For example, in the Xerox copier range, the last numbers correspond to the number of copies per minute (Xerox DocuPrint 4635 NPS: 135 pages/minute: Xerox DocuPrint 4890 NPS: 92 pages/minute; Xerox DocuPrint 4850 NPS: 50 pages/minute, etc.). These portfolios thus feature the corporate name while specifying the technical characteristics of the company's products. In this way, the corporate name acts as a brand-guarantee, while the reference serves as a product-brand.

Small and medium sized companies overwhelmingly use the corporate name alone. In their case, this often is the family name of the director or founder of the company: this process of brand creation is sometimes called "antonomasia" (Botton and Cegarra, 1990). Most of the time, these companies cannot afford to invest in different brands, both from a financial point of view, but also at the level of their organization. They stress the advantages of their size, close-by service and availability, in contrast to big companies. Big firms also use the name of a founder (whose personality is generally highlighted in the communication strategy). This is true of Procter & Gamble, Siemens, Dell, Boeing, John Deere, Gore, Michelin, Du Pont de Nemours, etc.

2.2 Companies with an extensive portfolio of industrial brands

Depending on the different brand objectives, such as differentiation from competitors, but also from other products and services proposed to customers, companies have started using different stages of brands. In fact, dual branding is more and more common in business to business. There is a big difference between companies managing a small number of specialized brands and multinationals that manage hundreds of brands worldwide, such as 3M. In all cases, the company backs up product brands by a more well known brand, whether it be corporate or not.

2.2.1 Brand portfolios based on the main brand

When a particular brand with its own communication strategy is added on to a main brand for a range of products or services, it is called an "affiliated brand". However, too many affiliated brands can weaken the main brand. Furthermore, owing to their sheer number, these new brands are not strong enough to really take hold. The brand policy must thus depend on the extent of the ranges and the size of the markets. It is often better to capitalize on the main brand than to create new brands for each new product. However when the products in question are highly specialized, it is worth developing affiliated brands so that they become a reference, thus facilitating memorization and recommendation. During a bid for example, the reference brand is indicated, potentially influencing which supplier is chosen.

Opting for an affiliated brand policy requires considerable promotion and a budget to back this up. Without this, there is no point: affiliated brands are unknown and thus will not be asked for. Yet, the promotion of such brands is often financed from the main brand's budget, which can weaken the latter. The launching of affiliated brands means that the company is faced with the problem of its competitors: individual cognitive capacity is limited and the challenge is to create a reference point for customers who already have numerous brands on their minds. If the brand succeeds in being retained, this might be to the disadvantage of the main brand, which has been weakened. This is one of the reasons why when a main brand launches affiliated brands, careful attention must be paid to their visual identity, watching out in particular for the coherence of the visual identity code with the main brand.

Brand portfolios that are based on the main brand are generally used by companies looking for a real synergy between their most known brand and the affiliated brands. There are brands which are based on the corporate brand (Table 4).

Table 4. Example of brand portfolios based on the corporate brand

Corporate Brands	Product Brands
SPOT IMAGE	Spotmap, Spotview, Spotview Basic, Spotview Plus, Geospot
GEMPLUS	Gemtel, Gemeasy, Gemxplore
GROHE	GroheTec, GroheArt, GroheDal, GroheAqua
RHÔNE-POULENC	Rhodopol, Rhoca Jet, Rhodocoat, Rhoditek, Rhodopas, Rhodigel
TETRA-LAVAL	Tetra Pak, Tetra Brik, Tetra Rex, Tetra Top, Tetra King, Tetra Classic, Tetra Prisma

Other companies rely on main brands which are not necessarily the corporate brand. This is true of 3M with the brand, Scotch, or Lafarge with the prefix, "Prégy" (Table 5).

Table 5. Example of brands derived from one of the main brands of the company

Main Brands	Product Brands
SCOTCH	Scotchban, Scotchbond, Scotch-Brite, Scotchcal, Scotchchrome, Scotch-Clad, Scotchcode, Scotch Color, Scotchdamp, Scotchflex, Mini-Scotchflex, Scotchgard, Scotchlite, Scotchlock, Scotchmark, Scotchply, Scotchprint, Scotch-Seal, Scotchtint
LAFARGE	Prégystyrène, Prégydéco, Prégyplac, Prégyflam, Prégydro, Prégyvapeur, Prégydur, Prégyroc, Prégycolle, Prégyréthane, Prégyroche, Prégymétal, Prégypan, Prégylis, Prégyfoam
HEWLETT-PACKARD	Desk Jet, Paint Jet, Think Jet, Laser Jet.... *(use of the "jet" suffix to signify printer with ink jet or laser jet technology)*

In this case, like in the preceding one, the brand logic is clear. The brand lines are sufficiently specified by the suffix which itself, often signifies the main function offered:

- For Scotch: Lite / light, Seal / sealing resin, Print / printing,
- For Prégy: Deco / interior decoration, etc.

The prefix serves as a guarantee by recalling the main, better known brand, and thus ensuring the federation of the different product concepts.

Adding suffixes or prefixes to the brand is generally motivated by the desire of the company to clarify its products and services. This involves adding to the company brand meaningful affiliated brands, capable of expressing the product function, its application, main characteristics, and the specific activity sector to which it is destined. While using brand equity covers all of the ranges offered, suffixes and prefixes make it easier to categorize, and segment the products and services. The names which designate the products are easier to memorize than a long series of alphanumeric references. The latter in general are " cold brands " which make it easier to see the ranges by an " objective " designation. Their name can be changed without affecting customer loyalty: it is an indication which is read and looked at without having to pay attention or make an effort to memorize.

Overall, affiliated brands are not necessarily meaningful brands, but rather brands that are qualified by their relationship to an identifying label. Unless it is a deliberate part of the company brand policy, the whole problem lies in not featuring these affiliated brands too much, for fear of erasing the main brand and confusing the customer.

Before making these changes, the company brand policy needs to be clearly established (later developments, management of future products, etc.) as well as the associated communication policy (budgets, targets, etc).

Certain companies use the renown of their corporate brand to develop the affiliated brands of their subsidiaries. This is true of Lafarge which includes Lafarge Ciments, Lafarge Plâtres (plaster), Lafarge Aluminates, Lafarge Produits Formulés, Lafarge Peintures, and Lafarge Bétons Granulats. This is also the case of the oil company Elf, whose subsidiaries include Elf Atochem, Elf Antar, Elf Antargaz, and Elf Lubrifiants, among others.

The decision to use affiliated brand names and industrial logos is a question of strategy: is it better to support subsidiaries by using the corporate name, or to leave them complete independence not appearing at all, or should the subsidiaries have limited independence by discretely featuring the corporate name right next to that of the subsidiary? Should the name of the subsidiary be changed? Should its visual identity be integrated into that of the group? The answer to these questions depends on the company's strategy, its culture, and markets. Using concrete examples, the different options can be illustrated.

2.2.2   Product brands portfolios which are not based on the main brand

These are product brands which do not recall the original brand (corporate brand). The original brand is then displayed on the company's technical documents, or on the products themselves using the logo of the main brand. Even highly renowned companies sometimes develop specific brands for new product launches.

Promoted and backed up by communication actions, these brands can become extremely well known without necessarily referring back to the parent brand. Brands such as Corian, Nakan, Pebax, Tactel and Tergal are well known but they are not immediately associated with ICI, Du Pont de Nemours, Elf Atochem or Rhone Poulenc (Aventis). In addition to the quality and performance of the products, these brands are so famous that the me-too products have an extremely hard time challenging their leadership.

The following table includes a list of companies using their corporate name as well as the main product-brands that they use for their commercial transactions (Table 6).

Table 6. Example of product brands not based on the corporate brand

Main Brand	Product Brands
LEGRAND	Diplomat, Diplomat Roc, Diplomat Light, Diplomat Skipper, Diplomat Couleur, Mosaic 45, Atlantic, Neptune, Armural, Martin Lunel Hypra, Starfix, Cab3, Duplix, Colring, Colson, Marina, Altis
DU PONT DE NEMOURS	Lycra, Kevlar, Teflon, Tyvek, Nomex, Zytel, Kapton, Corian, Tefzel, Hytrel, Mylar, Delrin, Suva, Centari, Minlon, Rynite, Spall Shield, Sentry Glass, Chromafusion, Butacite
RHÔNE-POULENC	Filifine, Miranol, Repel O Tex, Isceon, Oatrim, Neolor, Actalys, Microgard, Avgard, Oromoid, Technyl, Pontella, Comforto, Zéosil, Silcolease...
3M	Autohaler, Brittinox, Compublend, Conducer, Confirm, Controltac, Cubitron, Dual Lock, Duratrol, Dynatel, Ecart, Epx, Equisport, Excelerate, Express, Fibrlok, Filtrete, Finesse It, Firedam, Firestop, Floptical, Fluorad, Fluorel, Fluorinert, Flumequine, Flumiquil, Flumisol, Interam, Kennedy L.A.D., Light Water, Littmann, Magnus, Matchprint, Nextel, Nomad, Panaflex, Petrifilm, Photodyne, Post-It, Precise, Rainbow, Sarns, Scotch, Scotchban, Scotchbond, Scotch-Brite, Scotchcal, Scotchchrome, Scotch-Clad, Scotchcode, Scotch Color, Scotchdamp, Scotchflex, Mini-Scotchflex, Scotchgard, Scotchlite, Scotchlok, Scotchmark, Scotchply, Scotchprint, Scotch-Seal, Scotchtint, Stamark, Steri-Drape, Steri-Strip, Sulidene, Surface Saver, Tape Cure, Library Box, Tegaderm, Textool, Thinsulate, Tir'essuie, Trimatic, Trimax, Trinitrine, Vet Bond, Vetcast Plus, Vetrap, Vhb, Viking, Vitrotim
MOTOROLA	Bandit, Lifestyle Plus, Microtac, Mobius Mobile, Power Pc 603, Silverling, Ultralite
ELF ATOCHEM	Altuglas, Rilsan, Pebax, Norsorex, Orgater, Foraflon, Kynar, Voltalef, Sader, Topfix, Tps, Oniachlor, Surchlor, Prochinor, Clarcel, Acticarbone, Inipol, Gedeliant, Gedeflex, Penncab, Penncozeb, Thermoguard, Adine, Electrofine, Mixland, Orgalloy, Soarnol, Lotader, Aquakeep, Forane, Pyroforane, Foraperle, Forafac, Lucidol, Luperox, Norame, Liozan, Lacqtene, Evatane, Appryl, Gedex, Gedexcel, Lacqrene, Altene, Balmix, Baltane, Pertene, Wac, Jarylec, Ugilec, Lacovyl, Lucalor, Pressamine, Soluphene

2.2.3 Different affiliated brand policies

The wide range of types of brand portfolios is also reflected in the way that logos are managed. It is therefore interesting to note the main ways that brands are represented, from *uniform structures*, through *adapted structures* to *independent structures*.

• *Uniform structures* correspond to the identical and coherent use of the brand name and visual style of the company for all of its subsidiaries. Present in the names and logos of all the subsidiaries, the brand has a definite unifying role. This is particularly true of companies where internal growth has generated the creation of new activity sectors and where the external acquisition is then fully integrated into the company structure. The Lafarge group illustrates the coherence produced by this kind of brand policy. Serving the building industry, Lafarge is committed to producing materials that make life safer, more confortable, and more attractive. Thus Lafarge makes "materials for building the world". With a turnover of over 10 billion euros, the group is a world leader in numerous areas (number one in gravel, roofing, and aluminates and number two in cement, concrete, etc.).

The same Lafarge brand and logo are used for each of the main company activities: Lafarge Ciments, Lafarge Plâtres, Lafarge Aluminates, Lafarge Produits Formulés, Lafarge Peintures, and Lafarge Bétons Granulats. Lafarge's aim is to develop its position on different markets and its renown. Its brand policy is designed to increase exposure of the Lafarge brand.

• *Adapted structures*, which are similar to uniform ones, are when a company uses an identical visual style for all the brands (without necessarily having the brand appear). This is the case of Usinor, one of the biggest European steel companies, which uses the same image/logo and mentions its brand under that of its subsidiaries, e.g. Sollac or Ugine (Figure 7).

Figure 7. Some examples of Usinor brands: Sollac, Ugine, Ascometal, La Meusienne

This allows the company to endorse its brand with brands acquired through external growth, for example, by giving them a familiar visual identity. Without being directly mentioned, the parent brand is implicitly expressed by the visual. This is the case of Alcatel Alsthom[1], which used the same "visual language" for directly evocative brands such as Alcatel or Gec-Alsthom, as for brands such as Cegelec and Saft (Figure 8).

Figure 8. Alcatel Alsthom

• *Independent structures* are a characteristic of autonomous brand management policies. They can be the result of a deliberate discretion policy, or the choice not to capitalize on the group brand name. The decision to separate the different brands can come from the fact that they are highly renown, or that each has a highly specialized image. Independent structures can in fact be based on the desire to preserve the identity of the purchased companies. This is true of

Rexel, the world leader industrial distributor of electrical material, who maintains the identity of acquired brands (Electro-Midi, Facen, Omnitech-Sertronique, etc.). However, with its name, the brand can sometimes back up all or part of its activities and subsidiaries: a case in point is Bosch, whose name is under all the different brands of its subsidiaries each of which has a specific visual identity (Blaupunkt, Teldix, Bauer, Telenorma, etc.). Thus the fact of belonging to the Bosch group is indicated.

While there are many different policies for affiliated brand identities, there is even greater variety when it comes to the naming of brands. Policies used in other sectors can equally be found in industrial marketing[2].

2.3   Different policies for the creation of brand names

2.3.1   Brands whose names are explicit enough for the "customer-promise" to be directly understandable

- Armural from Legrand, for electrical tables which are both protective (armour) and decorative (mural art),
- Spallshield from Dupont for the composition of car windows with a safety system based on bullet-proof glass,
- Equisport from 3M, for a system of bandages which protect the ligaments and tendons of racehorses,
- Compublend from 3M, for an automated dosage system of abrasives,
- Firestop from 3M, for a process of treating apple and pear trees that prevents bacterial fire,
- Argelis from Gelis-GPS (a subsidiary of Imetal) for a brick made from clay (Argile in French) with a specific system that facilitates use (agile),
- Isover from Saint-Gobain for insulation based on fiber glass (verre = glass),
- Firedam from 3M for an endothermic material which stops the spreading of fire by the chemical transformation of heat,
- Sader and Topfix from Atochem for industrial glues (adhere/fix),
- Surchlor (literally over-chlorine) in the range for powerful water treatment in pools,
- Maniscopic from Manitou to designate a telescopic elevator,
- Aquakeep from Atochem for a very high capacity water retaining polymer.

Given the advantages of self-explanatory brand names particularly in terms of memorization and suggestion, some companies have replaced their product brands with more descriptive and meaningful brand names. The case of Elan Informatique illustrates the change from an evocative product brand name to a brand name with wider significance (see below).

Corporate names are also sometimes created so as to clearly describe the company activity: Respiron, Chronopost, Air Liquide, Microturbo, Turbomeca (mechanical), Carbone Industrie, Sextant Avionique (avionics), Aerospatiale, Airbus, Microsoft, Intel, Tetra Pak, Applied Materials, The Concrete Company, Micron Technology, Spot Image, Caryfast (road transport), Compaq (a merger between computer communication and pack, the letter q being easy to pronounce internationally). For these companies, diversifying activities can be more difficult under one name. Other companies have a name, which, while it may not describe their activity, is directly or indirectly meaningful (phonetically speaking). This is the case of corporate brands such as Valeo "I am well" in Latin. Velux, a company specialized in roof windows evokes its activity "V" for the slope of rooves and "lux" for the light given off by the windows. Finally, certain companies end up changing their corporate name by adopting the name of a leading product, system or activity. That was the case of CGE, which in 1990, took the name of its two well known brands, Alcatel-Alsthom and the case of Tokyo Tsuhin Kogyo, which became Sony in 1958. Other companies, in particular those whose name does not describe the activity or expertise (patronymic brands), specify their activity by adding descriptive suffixes such as Lafarge Plâtres (Plaster) or Lafarge Ciment (Cement), etc.

ELAN INFORMATIQUE "TEXT-TO-SPEECH"

Presentation of Elan Informatique

Created in 1979, Elan Informatique is a world leader in multi-lingual voice synthesis from text (Televox range, Proverbe range), as well as in sound digitalization and restitution (Echovox range). Specialized in the improvement of man/machine communication, Elan Informatique, working in cooperation with the French National Center for Research in Telecommunications, develops and commercializes software (Figure 9).

Figure 9. Elan logotype

This company runs on innovation. For example, in 1997, Elan Informatique obtained the European Prize for Information Technology, for the development of "Dial and Play E-Mail", the first reader of E-mail messages by telephone. The corporate brand name, Elan Informatique, expresses both this energy driving the company ("Elan" in French means viguour) and its sector of activity ("Informatique" means computers).

Elan Informatique has created computer assisted teaching programs, one of the many applications for voice technology, used by Airbus pilots. Aeronautics builders need flight simulators and training equipment. Elan Informatique's voice synthesis technology is also used in automotive navigators. The linguistic engineering technology of Elan can also be found in voice synthesis applications used by US Air Force pilots. Voice synthesis is used for applications in English or French but also in Spanish, German, Italian, or Portuguese. Thus Elan Informatique software are used to convert the yellow pages of the Argentinian phone book (in Spanish) or the telephone information from companies. Elan Informatique's innovative technology is of considerable interest to companies such as Aerospatiale-Matra, Alcatel, Bull, France Telecom, Suez-Lyonnaise des Eaux, Schlumberger, and Aventis, among others.

From suggestive to descriptive brands

For its range of products that generate high quality speech from all text, the company initially developed the ProVerbe brand. This name suggests the product function, to go "towards the verb", or in other words, to access speech. It also evokes professionalism with the prefix, "Pro". Furthermore, the first meaning of the word, "proverb", makes it easy to memorize. The complete product range offers voice synthesis from text with diverse applications such as:
- Messaging, sound commentaries, vocal word processing,
- Computer assisted teaching,
- Electronic data management,
- Games.

The "ProVerbe Speech" product brand has been used to name the entire product range. Meaningful words or prefixes are added to the brand name: the product brand thus is expressed in relation to the specific function of the applications.

With the growth of its international activity, Elan Informatique has become the world leader in voice synthesis technology used for converting text into speech. In light of its leadership position, the company decided to modify the range's brand name, as the message projected by the name, Proverbe, was not clear enough in different languages. Elan Informatique thus created a new brand to designate the Proverbe range: Text-to-Speech. Much more descriptive, this English sounding brand is easily understandable in an international context. It can be used in its complete form, "Text-to-Speech", or it can be abbreviated, "TTS" (Table 10).

Table 10. Evolution of Elan Informatique's brand portfolio

Former Names	Products	New Names
ProVerbe Speech Engine	Software motor	TTS Engine
ProVerbe Speech Platform	Electronic board for voice synthesis from text	TTS Platform
ProVerbe Speech Unit	Autonomous industrial unit for voice synthesis from text	TTS Unit
ProVerbe Dial & Play E-mail	Vocal provider for accessing E-mail	TTS Dial & Play E-mail

2.3.2 Brands formed from acronyms

These are the brands whose letters correspond, for example, to the initials of chemical formulas, that are easier to remember than the full names. This is the case of Pebax® Elf-Atochem, for "PolyEther Block Amides", a formula to which X was added to create the Atochem brand. This type of brand is often found in the medical sector. The acronym in its complete form indicates the product's specific characteristics, while its shortened form is easier to read and memorize. This is true of the computer system named "Socrate" used by the SNCF (the French National Train Company); Socrate, stands for the System Offering Customers Reservations for Business and Tourism (of course it also evokes the famous Greek philosopher).

2.3.3 Brands explained by the company history

Some examples are:
• Martin Lunel Hypra from Legrand, which allowed the new brand Hypra from Legrand to benefit from the excellent reputation of Martin Lunel, a company purchased by external growth,
• Oniachlor brand conserved by Atochem, but dating from the time when the manufacturing company was called "National Nitrogen Industries" (see Elf Atochem Case below).

2.3.4 Patronymic brands

These are brands that are named after the founder of the company (Malaval and Bénaroya, 1998). They are most common in small and medium sized companies but also in big multinationals. Some patronymic brands are: Andersen, Becton Dickinson, Boeing, Bosch, Bouygues, Dalsay Hillbloom Lynch (DHL), Coopers and Lybrand, Dassault, Dell, Du Pont de Nemours, Ford, Gore, Hertz, Hewlett Packard, Kimberly-Clark, Lafarge, Legrand, Magnetti-Marelli, Michelin, Monroe, Monsanto, Peter Kiewit, Renault, Schneider, Siemens, Smurfit, etc.

2.3.5 Brand names that are not in line with the product or service

There are industrial brands whose names have nothing to do with the product or services offered. The brand content is enriched by the originality of the name. At a time when most brands in the IT sector (which originally targeted professionals) were meaningful and descriptive, Steve Jobs and Steve Wozniak decided to call their company, Apple. The word "apple" has strong positive connotations (goodness, health, simplicity), thus expressing the simplicity and user-friendliness of the computers. The brand name was in contrast with the high technology of the product, which until then, had been the standard image projected by brand names in the IT sector.

2.3.6 Brands evoking high technology

These brands often finish in certain letter pairs, such as:
- ON: Mison (Aga), Teflon, Kapton, Minlon (DuPont), Cubitron (3M), Colson (Legrand),
- EL: Zytel, Tefzel, Hytrel, Tactel, Comforel (Du Pont de Nemours), Dynatel, Fluorel, Nextel (3M), Clarcel, Gedexcel (Atochem), Tencel (Courtaulds),
- EX: Nomex (DuPont), Panaflex, Scotchflex (3M), Gedex, Gedeflex (Atochem), Gore-Tex, Skyflex (Gore), Barex (BP), Sympatex (Akzo-Nobel), Kimtex (Kimberly-Clark), Bultex (Recticel), Cromadex (Courtaulds Coatings), Draincotex (Sommer), Gyprex (Placoplatre-BPB), Taraflex.,
- AX: Trimax (3M), Pebax (Atochem), Coolmax (Du Pont de Nemours),
- IX: Jetfix, Epomix (Spit),
- IUM and UM: Pentium (Intel), Truxium, Brakium, Plenium, Altimum, Traxium (Carbone Industry), Equium (Toshiba), Platinum (Packard-Bell), Magnum (truck cabs from Renault Industrial Vehicles), Maxium (Volvo trucks)...
- IS or XIS (to evoke the idea of Systems or Service Integration): Bloxys (Carbon Industry), Natexis (merger of Crédit *Nat*ional and the Banque Française du Commerce *Ext*érieur), Novartis (merger of Ciba and Sandoz), Numeris (France Telecom), Civis (Urban transport system from Matra Transport International and Renault), Citadis (tramway from Alstom),

Geodis (transport systems from Sceta: Calberson...), Agilis (Michelin tires for trucks).

One advantage of scientific sounding names is that they do not have any cultural connotations linked to a geographic region. As such, these brands seem better adapted to global strategies for the international market. The letter X expresses both that which is forbidden and mathematics. X suggests power, progress, efficiency, science, technology, a cutting-edge image, and an international vocation. "X" is often used in the names of medicines (Xanax, Microlax, Zovirax, Tranxene, Xatral, Maxillase, Clamoxyl, etc.) or in consumer products from detergents (Jex Four, Axion, Ajax, Spontex, etc) to cars (Lexus, Citroen Xantia, Xsara, AX, BX, CX, ZX, Renault Express, Peugeot Expert, Ford Galaxy, etc.) It can also be found in all financial sectors (Axa, Natexis, etc.) as well as services (Loxam, Sodexho, etc.), the chemical industry (brands from 3M, Du Pont, Atochem, BP), the office equipment and IT sector (Cyrix, Xerox, MMX Intel technology) and the building industry (Axter Akafix, Axter Paxalpha, Axter Stickflex).

2.3.7   Brands made up of initials

Some brand names, which are long and thus difficult to memorize or pronounce, are better broken down into their initials. Many companies prefer to highlight this type of brand name rather than the complete name. Some examples are: IBM (International Business Machines), EDS (Electronic Data System), ATR (Regional Transport Aircraft), Dalsay Hillbloom Lynch (DHL), EDF-GDF (Electricity of France – Gas of France), Sodexho Allliance (Société d'Exploitation Hôtelière), 3M (Minnesota Mining Manufacturing), CNRS (National Center for Scientific Research), CNES (National Center for Space Research), CFM (Compagnie Française de Motorisation), SFR (Société Française de Radiotéléphone), ABB (Asean Brown Bovery), PPG Industries, ATT, UPS, ICI, KPMG, NCR, SAP, etc.

BRANDING AT ELF ATOCHEM

A subsidiary of Elf Aquitaine created in 1983 from the merger of Ato Chimie, Chloé Chimie, and Produits Chimiques Ugine Kuhlmann (PCUK), Atochem took over the American company, Pennwalt in 1989, and the chemical activities of Charbonnages de France (Orkem, Norsolor), in 1990. In 1992, it became Elf Atochem. With over 33,000 employees and a turnover of 10 billion euros, Elf Atochem and its subsidiaries is one of the biggest chemical groups in the world. It is organized essentially around three main areas:

• Basic chemicals: petrochemicals and major plastics, chlorochemicals and vinyls (chlorine, sodium hydroxide, vinyl chloride, fluorine derivatives, solvents, vinyl polychloride, vinyl thermoplastics, PVC tubes and joints, sections), fertilizers and mineral chemicals (nitrogeneous fertilizers and complexes, carbonate of soda),

• Industrial chemicals: fluorine, sulphur, fine chemicals, resins, melanin, acrylics and derivatives, etc.,

• High performance polymers and chemical products: chemical products for galvanoplasty, adhesives, specialties, technical polymers, functional polymers, complex films for packaging.

Chemicals are used in numerous fields from packaging to the building industry, as well as sectors such as transport, agriculture, health, beauty, sports and entertainment, and water treatment. Thus Elf Atochem products are used in over 70 elements of a car, in the TGV high speed train, Airbus aircraft, or the Ariane V rocket. Yet end users are rarely aware of these numerous applications, as the products are incorporated into the final product or used during the manufacturing process. Chemical products can be raw or processed materials, minor additives, or major components of articles that are not perceived as chemical products by consumers; this is because the brand names of chemical products almost never appear on the final product. However, while brand visibility is not necessarily important for mass consumers, visible brand names are essential to make professional customers aware of the specific chemical products made by chemical companies (Table 11, Figure 12, Table 13, and Figure 14).

Table 11. Some examples of uses in consumer goods

Category of product containing the chemical component	Brands used by Elf Atochem and its subsidiaries
Roller blades	Orgalloy®
Toy figurines for children, CD boxes	Lacqrène®
Golf balls	Luperox®
Bicycle seats	Rilsan®
Athletic footwear	Pebax®

Figure 12. Master Mind® and Big Jim® helicopter: two examples of the use of Elf Atochem shock polystyrene Lacqrène®

Table 13. Some examples of the applications for semi-durable products

Category of product containing the chemical component	Brands used by Elf Atochem and its subsidiaries
Fuel lines, coating for aircraft engine blades	Rilsan®
Rail cushions	Evatane®
Interior trim for cars	Nakan®
Signalling icons, boat deck hatchways	Altuglas®
Fenders	Appryl®

Figure 14. Some examples of Elf Atochem brands used in cars: Rilsan®, Nakan®, Appryl®

Elf Atochem is developing a brand policy so as to send the right image to industrial firms, who are obviously looking at what is available on the market in terms of quality, properties and price; they will recall specific registered brand names easier than long (and not very distinctive) scientific or chemical ones. Elf Atochem's brand policy must take into consideration three types of constraints:

• *Legal constraints*: not all brands can be registered, particularly those which are too close to existing ones or those which are too descriptive, e.g. a super-absorbent material cannot be called "Superabsorb",

• *Market constraints*: the brand policy must be put into a "world" context. Brand names must take into account linguistic factors as well as the policies of international competitors,

• *Brand management constraints*: obviously the brand policy followed must have an internal logic and be externally coherent. Brands will then have the most impact because they are easy for customers to distinguish, recognize, and remember.

An analysis of brands registered by Elf Atochem reveals a certain diversity in the brand names, reflecting legal, market and management constraints as well as dates of creation (Table 15a&b). Elf Atochem has a well-stocked portfolio of brands whose varied origins can be largely explained by the company's history. In fact Elf Atochem has retained the brands of acquired companies so as to make the most out of their assets (capitalizing on the existing brands). Conversely, new products made by Elf Atochem call for the creation of new brand names.

Table 15.a Examples of names used by Elf Atochem

Combinations used to create the brands	Products	Names used
Code	• Polycondensing catalysers	• S21, S23, S24
Complete creation	• Vinyl compound • Vinylidene polyfluoride • Chlorinated PVC	• Nakan • Kynar • Lucalor
Chemical formula + Initials	• Styrene - maleic anhydride • Nitrogen + fertilizer	• SMA • AZF
Chemical formula + Initials + Translation	• Floculants (water treatment) Water + AluminiumChloride	• WAC (water cleaner)
Chemical formula + Syllable + Initials	• Polybutadiene	• Poly Bd
Chemical formula + Abbreviation + Function + Analogy	• Azocarbonamide(bubbling agent) • Fluorine + Alcane • Fluorine + Perle • Fluorine + Surfactant • Organic + EVA + compound	• Azobul • Forane • Foraperle • Forafac • Orevac
Chemical formula + Function	• Silicate/Porous • Porous/Silicate • Active carbon • Compressed wood/melamine • Phenol solution	• Siliporite • Porosil • Acticarbone • Pressamine • Soluphène

Table 15.b Examples of names used by Elf Atochem

Combinations used to create the brands	Products	Names used
Function	• Adhesive (for consumers also)/ "adheres" • "Double skinned" pipes PVC	• Sader • Bipeau (bi-skin)
Function + Translation	• Rust inhibitor • Insecticide • Weedkiller accelerator • Weedkiller	• Norust • Knox Out • Accelerate • Clairsol (~ground clear)
Function + Company + Abbreviation	• Fungicide/Refinery&Sulfur Reunited-RSR • Lubricants/cooling fluids for grinding	• Bordeaux mixture RSR • Atoguard
Function + Chemical formula + Company	• Stabilizer/vinyl/Norsolor	• Stavinor
Site	• Site Grande Paroisse (fertilizer) • Soferti	• GP • Soferti
Site + whole word + chemical formula + syllable	• Lacq (Elf Atochem Pyrénées Atlantiques site)/polystyrene • Polyethylene / Lacq • Vinyl polychloride /Lacq • Peroxide/Mont (Pyrénées Atlantiques site)	• Lacqrène • Lacqtène (" t" used to link) • Lacovyl • Peroximon
Site + Chemical formula + Abbreviation	• Balan (Elf Atochem Ain site) / Trichlorethane • Balan (Ain)/Trichlorethylene • Risle (name of river near production site) / Castor oil	• Baltane • Altène (no" B " to avoid confusion with Baltane) • Rilsan
Company + Abbreviation + Function + Whole word	• Alphacan / sheath • Alphacan /cable • Alphacan / telecom • Ceca / carbon	• Alphagaine • Alphacable • Alphatelec • Cecarbon
Company + Abbreviation + Chemical formula + Syllable	• Norsolor/acrylic • Onia/Chloride	• Norsocryl • Oniachlor
Company + Abbreviation + Translation	• Altulor (company)/Glas ("glass")	• Altuglas
Site + Analogy	• Lannemezan (Elf Atochem Pyrénées-Atlantiques site)	• Liozan
Site + Analogy + Domain + Syllable	• Jarrie (Elf Atochem Isère site /Electricity (chloride dielectric)	• Jarylec
Suggestion	• Swimming pool products	• Miami
Suggestion + Translation	• Material used for making sunglasses • Organic Alloy	• Sunprene • Orgalloy

Looking at the Elf Atochem portfolio overall shows the diversity of naming methods used to create brands.

• *Product origin*: several Elf Atochem brand names refer to the place where they were manufactured, including part of the company or subsidiary name (production site etc.). Examples are Lacqtène (the *Lacq* production site in the Pyrénées-Atlantiques + polye*thyl*e*ne*) or Jarylec (the *Jarrie* production site in the Isère + e*lec*tricity).

• *Product use*: the brand name of some products is based on their function. These names will differ according to whether there is a unique and narrow use or a very wide field of application. For the former, Jarylec denotes the electrical sector while for the latter, *Inipol* stresses the multifunction nature (*inhi*bits *po*llution) of a brand which absorbs and inhibits pollution in all domains (environment, paints, etc.).

• *Product complexity*: the use of a name which refers to the product's composition depends on its chemical complexity. For complex products such as alloys, the composition cannot be incorporated into the brand name. For example, an acrylic copolymer plastic additive was given the evocative name Durastrength rather than allude to its highly complex composition. Conversely, Evatane (copolymer *EVA*: *E*thylene + *V*inyl + *A*ce*t*ate + Alk*ane*), *Pertene* (*Per*chlorethyl*ene* + *t*) or *Pebax* (*P*oly*e*ther *B*lock *A*mides + *X*) take their names from their chemical formulae.

• *Product diffusion*: the necessity of creating, registering, and bringing to life a particular brand name depends on how much it will be diffused. For restricted diffusion there is no real need to differentiate it from other brands, whereas for products sold in large quantities, a specific brand needs to be created. To differentiate its pre-mixed "compounds", Elf Atochem chose the specific brand Nakan, to denote a multi-use material (interior trim for cars, leather look, electrical industry etc.).

• *Product target*: the brand name chosen must take into account the customer and his specific needs. The message carried by a particular brand name will change according to whether the customer is an industrial firm, a retailer or a consumer. These brand "limits" are an important constraint on the choice of brand name. In view of the diversity of product applications, to find an "individual" brand, covering only one product, is rare. A case in point is Appryl (*A* + *poly*propy*l*ene), a brand covering a family of different but chemically related products. Similarly Orgalloy, an organic alloy has various compositions according to its particular uses (automotive, electricity, packing, leisure). More often, the brand covers a range of products and so all those used together e.g. plastic + additives + adhesive for fixing the end product etc. are under the same brand name. This is true of the Miami range which in addition to swimming pool cleaning products includes brushes and nets under the same brand.

• *Product confidentiality*: a name may be chosen which has nothing to do with chemical composition, in the interests of confidentiality. This is the case for the molecular sieves, Cecagel or the highly technical Orgalloy alloys. In passing, it should be remembered that almost all chemical products are available in different concentrations, purities, and dilutions. The exact nature of a product is called the *grade* and is usually mentioned as a specific code after the brand name.

Thus there are many alternatives for creating a brand name (chemical formulae, function, company, production site or place, suggestions, codes, pure creations). Brand names can result from combinations of analogies, translation of words (English, Latin, Greek), fusion of whole words, abbreviations, syllables or initials. The diversity of examples bears witness to the richness of the brand portfolio and the variety of brand origins. The pragmatic approach is to favor the strongest brands. The prefixes Elf and Ato are not usually used because the policy is to separate company from product names. In particular, this allows a widening of the possibilities for creating and registering brands and eases the granting of licenses to companies not particularly enthusiastic about selling competitor brands. In addition, in the event of one-off problems with a product brand, only that particular image is concerned and not that of the company as a whole. Indeed, due to the increasing complexity of the search for brand names, Elf Atochem sometimes turns for help to specialized agencies (Nomen) e.g. for Nakan. The trend is to develop brand names which do not allude to a specific product function but rather leave the field open so that the brand can be extended to cover other applications even with variations of its name. As evocative brand names are often very similar it is better to go for completely invented brand names to distinguish between products. The development of Elf Atochem's compound activity, (addition of inhibitors, stabilizers, colorants etc.), reinforces the recent tendency to adopt creative brand names.

Having classified industrial brands using existing methods and as a function of the different portfolios, it is now possible to use the concept of purchaseability and visibility for a new classification.

3.   CLASSIFICATION ACCORDING TO BRAND VISIBILITY AND PURCHASEABILITY

As we have seen in the preceding chapter[3], "purchaseability" and "visibility" can be explained in terms of both brand policy and the product category.

• *Purchaseability* can be explained in terms of two main factors: the product's technical complexity and the sales strategy towards non-professionals (end consumers). Technical complexity depends largely on the nature of the product category, whether that be in terms of the level of equipment necessary, the conditions for setting up, the level of competence required to use the product or the specifications. Conversely, the sales policy towards non-professionals depends, above all, on the brand policy.

• The *visibility* of the brand on the product has two main components: "printability" and the drive of the people behind it. Printability depends on the product category characteristics, whether that be in terms of the actual physical nature of the product structure, the identification lifetime, the visual immediacy or the restrictions imposed by regulations. The drive of the people concerned depends on the sales strategy:

- of the supplier in terms of the awareness objective, the identification possibilities, and the differentiation objective,
- of the customer in terms of a long-term partnership, the synergy between sales and advertising, the dependence on the supplier, and the risk of making the final product commonplace.

Using the criteria for purchaseability and visibility, the following brands (Table 16) can be classified.

Table 16. Classification of some brands according to their purchaseability or visibility for a private customer

Brand	NOT PURCHASEABLE by the private customer	PURCHASEABLE by the private customer
VISIBLE by the private customer	Tetra Pak, Tetra Brik... Legrand, Diplomat, Altis... DuPont: Lycra, Tyvek, Dacron Scotchgard, Gore-Tex, Tactel, Tergal Grohe...	Xerox 5043, Canon, Toshiba, Olivetti Facom, Lexmark Michelin, Michelin Pilote Scotchmagic, Scotchvideo, Scotchbrite, Scotchlite, Scotchgard, Post-It Valeo Surchlor, Sader
NOT VISIBLE by the private customer	Gemplus, Gemxplore Xerox Docutech DuPont: Kevlar, Nomex, Hytrel, Teflon... Rilsan, Autohaler, Vitrotim Siemens Automotive, Motorola Automotive Elf Atochem, Sidel, Mead, PLM Bosch, Sollac Dorlastan, Isover, Lafarge Zurfluh-Feller	

This table separates the brands into three categories. There are no brands which are non-visible and purchaseable by the private customer. There are raw materials (e.g. sand, wood) and materials which have been transformed (e.g. wires, pipes) that can be supplied by small companies and by importers with unknown brand names. These products can be purchased in shops, and specialized supermarkets particularly DIY. There are products which are purchaseable and commercialized with a non-visible brand. In fact the latter are often sold inside new packing labelled with the distributor brand such as Point P for building materials, or Raja for packaging[4].

At the top right can be seen the purchaseable and visible brands. These are in the main "mixed products", that is those for professional as well as private customers. In these cases, companies can use traditional communication strategies relying on the main media: Michelin, Lexmark, etc.

At the top left are the brands which are visible to the private customer but not purchaseable, such as packaging brands, textile threads, electrical components. Although they are not directly purchaseable by consumers, many of these brands communicate through the general public media[5]: Tetra Pak, Gore-Tex, Legrand, etc. The strategy of these brands is to use the end customer as the driving force vis-à-vis the distributor with the object of getting the demand to travel right up to the finished product integrator.

At the bottom left are the brands which are neither visible nor purchaseable such as electrical and chemical components of car and building equipment. These brands generally communicate with their professional customers e.g. Kevlar, Sollac.

Nevertheless, this classification using visibility and purchaseability does not preclude the brand from being in several categories, because of the very different levels of complexity of the products:

• For Xerox, small photocopier parts can be bought by the private customer whereas the bigger material such as Docutech, essentially an integrated printing press costing more than a 150,000 €, cannot.

• For Valeo, window wipers are sold in car spare part centers aimed at private customers, whereas dashboards can only be bought by car manufacturers.

• For Dupont's Tyvek, non tearable envelopes are on sale to private customers, but the more technical products which make up the main part of sales are only sold to factories.

This way of classifying industrial brands can be combined with a classification based on the use of industrial goods.

4.   COMBINED APPROACH FOR CLASSIFYING INDUSTRIAL GOODS

Using the classifications explained earlier, it is possible to combine a purchaseability and visibility approach with a use-based approach. Thus industrial goods can be divided into those that are part of the end product, those that are directly involved in the manufacturing process, and those which contribute indirectly to the manufacturing process (Table 17).

Table 17. Cross-classification of several brands as a function of purchaseability, visibility and use of the industrial product

	NON PURCHASEABLE BRAND, VISIBLE by the private customer	NON PURCHASEABLE BRAND, NON VISIBLE by the private customer	PURCHASEABLE BRAND, VISIBLE by the private customer
Goods which are part of the end product	Tetra Pak Lycra Intel	Siemens Automotive Motorola Gemplus	Nutrasweet Villeroy & Boch
Goods which are part of the manufacturing process	Hilti Tetra Pak Case-Poclain	Sidel Mannesmann IBM	Facom Sader Scotchgard
Goods making an indirect contribution to the manufacturing process	Caterpillar John Deere	Xerox Big Systems IBM Kone	Xerox-Bureautics Canon Kärcher

Although the same brand can belong to two different categories depending on its application, this way of presenting the information highlights those industrial brands which could indirectly interest private customers. These are brands of goods which become part of the composition of the end product, regardless of their purchaseability or visibility vis-à-vis the private customer. In fact several of these brands have communication campaigns targeting the general public.

This classification is useful in that it presents a reasonably complete panorama of industrial brands as long as industrial services, also concerned by the analysis, are added. Indeed, in the non purchaseable and visible brands category, there are transport and logistics brands such as DHL and UPS (visibility on vehicles, delivery papers, invoices, work clothing, etc.), catering brands like Sodexho, Compass or cleaning ones like Industrial Cleaning Services International. In the non purchaseable, non visible brands category can be found the IT service brands such as EDS, Cap Gemini, money conveyers such as Brink's or consulting firms such as Andersen Consulting. In the third category, purchaseable and visible brands are those from the banking, leasing or insurance sector such as Citicorp, Chase Manhattan, Prudential Insurance, Metropolitan Life Insurance, etc.

These methods are a way of classifying industrial brands, taking into account their diversity and making them easier to understand. The classification method, based on the purchaseability and visibility of industrial brands by the general public can just as easily be applied to:

• Entering brands, i.e. brands which are found in the composition of the end product,

- Equipment brands, whether these make up part of the production process or whether they contribute to the functioning of the customer company,
- Professional services, whether they contribute to improving the functioning of the customer company, the in-house climate, or whether they play a role in improving the brand's image in the eyes of the customer.

The table below gives a classification of a certain number of brands from the different categories of products as a function of their purchaseability and visibility to the general public (Table 18).

Table 18. Cross-classification of several brands as a function of purchaseability, visibility and use of the industrial product

	Entering goods	Equipment goods	Services
Non purchaseable and visible	Saint-Gobain (Car glass) Air Liquide Lycra Gore-Tex Nutrasweet Intel Monroe Tetra Pak Villeroy & Boch Scotchgard Teflon (DuPont)	Sidel Hilti Case Poclain Caddie Fenwick Manitou Tetra Pak Airbus Industrie Alstom Fruehauf Otis	Fedex UPS Brink's DHL Chronopost Grosvenor Services Industrial Cleaning Services International Kimberly-Clark
Non purchaseable and non visible	Lafarge Cements Pechiney Saint-Gobain (Building) Aventis Motorola Kevlar Valeo Sommer-Allibert Delphi Mead Siemens Automotive Gemplus	Cogema Xerox Canon Hewlett-Packard IBM Bouygues Saint-Gobain Schneider Square D Kone Mead France Telecom Norton	Sodexho Spot Image Adecco Kompass Lloyd's Manpower VediorBis Andersen Coopers & Lybrand Servpro Rentokil Initial
Purchaseable and visible	TotalFinaElf Valeo Pass and Seymour Henkel Yoplait (Ingredients) Evian Post-It (3M)	Facom Kärcher Stanley Works	Wanadoo (France Telecom) New York Life Insurance Publications: *Advertising Age…*

5. AERONAUTICS SECTOR BRANDS

In addition to the methods described earlier, it is also possible to classify brands as a function of their main characteristics taken within a well-defined sector of activity. Without being exhaustive, it is thus possible to classify brands in the aeronautics sector as a function of their signification, evocative power and origin.

5.1 Family name corporate brands

The history of the brand often explains the present company name as well as certain of their models. Brand names and logos are thus the result of different strategies, of discoveries and technical advances, which have marked the history of the companies, some of which are named after their founders. Family name brands often go back a long way; they are created from the company founder's name and maintained over the years. On the other hand, the logos of many original, founding companies have changed over time, with technology and the creation of new sectors.

In civil aviation, Boeing McDonnell Douglas, which is the result of several mergers and buyouts, owes it name to three respective founders: William Boeing, James McDonnell and Donald Douglas. Dassault has also taken the name of its founder, Marcel Dassault. The planes have their own names: Falcon for the civil aircraft, Rafale, Mirage for the military aircraft. The name of the company has changed from Avions Marcel Dassault-Breguet Aviation, to Dassault Breguet Group and finally Dassault Aviation. Dassault aircraft adopted the four-leaf clover logo liked by the founder. In the same way, parts suppliers such as Latécoère or Rolls Royce have the name of their founders or co-founders, Pierre Georges Latécoère, Charles Rolls and Henry Royce.

While the founder's name can be used for the brand at the outset, it can also be used partially or totally to designate certain aircraft, even a whole range. This is the case of aircraft brands using their founders' names such as Andreï Tupolev, Ospiovitch Sukhoï, etc. The range uses certain parts of the name like, "LL", for Lirunov, "IL" for Ilyoushine, "YAK" for Yakovlev. This is the case for the "TU-144", Tupolev or the "AN-24", Antonov. McDonnell Douglas also use the name with DC for "Douglas and Co", while Lockheed use "L" and Vickers-Armstrong, "VC".

5.2 Evocative product brands

The old family name brands are usually immersed in the pioneer image surrounding the beginnings of aeronautics. With a long history, they are very well known and have developed a strong image over time. More recent brands such as Airbus, founded in 1967, owe their renown to the quality and success of their products.

The companies in this sector, quite apart from their corporate names, wanted to make their product names easy to remember. Their policy has been to derive their brand names from the corporate name or from something sounding highly technical. Some companies have pushed this reasoning even further and developed names which are easily recognizable not just by the aeronautics professionals concerned. In this way names have been thought up which are easily remembered by the media and the general public. Rather than a "dry" reference like XBF-885T, better to use something more meaningful.

In the military aeronautics sector, the names of predators have been used, like Aerospatiale Cougar (AS 532), Panther (AS 565 MB/SB) or Super Puma (AS 332 L1). The most recent helicopter is known as "Tiger". Aerospatiale then adds an abbreviation after the brand name to designate the type such as HAP for support/protection, UHU for multi-role, or HAC for anti-tank. The predator approach has also been used for the British Seacat, Tigercat, Python or Sidewinder (rattlesnake) missiles and in the Dassault Jaguar fighter aircraft. It should however be noted that predators and animal names are also used in civil aviation with Dassaults' Falcon or Rolls Royce's Viper 630 engine.

Warrior words are especially common names for missiles, witness the American Trident, Harpoon, Tomahawk, the French Arpon (harpoon), the Franco-British Scalp along with the European, Eurofighter. Brands are also taken from the weather and words for movement such as in the Franco-British Storm Shadow missiles (Matra BAe Dynamics), the British Skyflash and Thunderbird missiles, the American Tornado and the French Dassault, Mirage and Rafale fighter aircraft.

During the Gulf war, the media coverage given to the Boeing-developed American Patriot missiles was facilitated by the almost universal meaning in the name and the fact that it was easy to remember. Whether it be for civil or military brands, there is always the question of the language of the brand name. As a general rule, helped by the ubiquitousness of English, American aeronautic equipment keeps its name or sales name regardless of where it is sold; but this is equally the case for the French Aerospatiale helicopters with their Ecureuil (squirrel), Colibri (hummingbird), Dauphin (dolphin), Super Puma, Fennec (military version of the Ecureuil), Super Five, Panther and Cougar brands.

These strongly evocative brand names give the products an extra dimension, setting them apart and making them easy to remember. Indeed this branding policy is often accompanied in the military sector as much as the civil one, by a brand support and promotional communication policy. While engine and parts manufacturers deal essentially with professionals within the sector, plane builders also communicate with the general public. This can be directly through TV campaigns, PR, sponsorship or by the visibility of their brand on the aircraft, or indirectly through press relations or by customer companies citing their brand etc.

The following table is a classification of aeronautical brands as a function of the product category (planes, helicopters, missiles/rockets and equipment) and brand nature (family name brands, importance etc.) (Table 19 a&b).

Table 19a. A classification of some of the aeronautical brands

	Planes	Helicopters	Missiles / Rockets	Equipment
Family name brands	Breguet, Boeing, McDonnell, Douglas, Lockheed, Dassault, Tupolev, Antonov, Ilyoushine, Yakovlev, Mikoyan Gourevitch (*Mig*), de Havilland, Messerschmidt, Dornier, Fokker, Grumman	Bell, Sikorski, Grumman, McDonnell, Douglas,		Messier-Dowty, Messier-Bugatti, Latécoère, Pratt & Whitney, Rolls Royce, Lockheed-Martin, Renault-Morane
Meaningful brands	Airbus, Étendard, Caravelle, Concorde, Awacs (*Airborne Warning and Control System*), Aerospatiale	Eurocopter	Sidewinder, Iris-T (*Infrared Imagine Sidewinder Tailed Controled*), Slam, Pac-3 Patriot, Exocet, Matra BAe Dynamics (Matra: *mé*canique aviation traction)	Microturbo (Labinal), Turboméca (Labinal)
Brands which evoke natural phenomena	Mystère, Mirage, Tornado, Rafale	Typhoon, Thunderbold, Tempest, Hurricane	Meteor, Skyflash, Storm Shadow, Thunderbird, Aster, Hellfire	Airesearch (Garret)
Warrior brands	Eurofighter, Spitfire, Corsair, Crusader, Intruder, F5-Starfighter, Flying Fortress, Walkyrie	Apache, Commanche, Sea Knight, Kiowa Warrior	Trident, Arpoon, Harpon, Scalp, Tomahawk	

Table 19b. A classification of some of the aeronautical brands

	Planes	Helicopters	Missiles / Rockets	Equipment
Animal name brands	Jaguar, Faucon, Falcon, F22Raptor, F15Eagle, Vampire, F5-Tiger, F20-Tiger Shark, F18 Hornet, F14-Tomcat, Fockewolf	Ecureuil, Fennec, Tiger, Panther, Puma, Cougar, Cobra, Frelon (hornet), Gazelle, Lynx, SeaHawk, BlackHawk, SeaDragon, Alouette, Super Stallion, OceanHawk, RescueHawk, SkyHawk, Mosquito	Sidewinder (rattlesnake), Python, Seacat, Tigercat	Viper (Rolls Royce)
Divine or mythological brands	Mercure, Hercule		Ariane, Titan, Hermès, Apollo	

5.3   Product-brands with a " technical " dimension

Quite apart from brand names coming directly or indirectly from a founder's name, there are numerous aeronautical brand names with an important technical dimension. This often involves the use of letters and numbers and their various combinations. For Boeing and Douglas, the letter F added to the aircraft brand name means that it is a " freighter " or cargo plane, e.g. B747 F or DC7 F. The Boeing 747 SR (short range) is a model destined mainly for Japanese internal flights allowing a large load (500 passengers) to be carried over a distance of about 650 km (frequent medium range journeys). Conversely, the Boeing 747 SP (special performance) with a shorter body, can carry 331 passengers non-stop for distances of up to 9500 km. The American armed forces classify their aircraft using one or two-letter prefixes to denote the category to which it belongs, e.g. A for attack (A-10 tactical support aircraft), B for bomber (B-52), C for carrier (C-5 Galaxy transport aircraft), F for fighter (F15).

Letters and numbers are frequently used with aeronautical brands to show the chronological order of the generations of aircraft such as the McDonnell Douglas DC1, DC2, DC3, etc. or Dassault's Rafale A,B,C,D or the Ariane launcher models 1 to 5. For its missiles, Aerospatiale uses code letters to indicate the range and so there is Trigat MP (*Moyenne portée* = medium range; 2000m) or Trigat LP (*Longue portée* = long range; more than 7000m). Both Boeing and Airbus have a brand policy using a combination of the first letter of the company name with a number (to which other numbers are sometimes added to denote different variants) to designate their aircraft range.

Thus there are for example Airbus A300, A310, A318, A319, A320, A321, A330 and A340 or Boeing B707, B727, B737, B747, B757, B767, B777.

Brands can come from technical abbreviations such as in the case of the Patriot Advanced Capabilities missile or Pac-3 and the Sea Slam derived from Stand-off Land Attack Missile. The names of other American missiles use similar abbreviations: Slam Er (Stand-off land Attack Missile Expanded Response), GBU-15 (Guided Weapons System), Jassm (Joint Air-to-Surface Stand-off Missile), Jdam (Joint Direct Attack Munition) etc. In the same way Boeing's E-3A Awacs come from "Airborne Warning and Control Systems".

The technical sounds are sometimes very evocative as is the case with Snecma's commercial brands: Microturbo and Turbomeca, given to engines, turbines and turbojets for helicopters and planes. Microturbo, the manufacturer of aeronautical starters and propulsion systems sometimes uses abbreviated names as brands e.g. TGA15 (*turbo-générateur d'air*) for their air turbo generator. In a similar fashion Pratt & Whitney have developed evocative names like Turbojet or JT3D Turbofan, for engines fitted in particular to Boeing 707's.

Airbus[6] is doubtless one of the most well-known important brands, borne out of the political will of the British, French and German governments to create a 300 passenger European air "bus" to connect their different capitals, hence "European Airbus". The name A300 originally denoted the project for a 300 seat Airbus plane.

NOTES

1. Alcatel-Alsthom does not exist anymore. There are two separate and autonomous companies: Alcatel and Alstom.
2. See Chapter 8, Creating and Protecting Business to Business Brands.
3. See Chapter 6, Purchaseability and Visibility of Industrial Brands.
4. See Chapter 15, Industrial Distributor Brands.
5. See Chapter 3, The Characteristics of Business to Business Communication and Chapter 6, Purchaseability and Visibility of Industrial Brands.
6. See Chapter 13, Equipment Goods Brands, 8- The Airbus Case: Setting the Standards.

REFERENCES

Alba, J. W. and Chattopadhyay, A., (1986), Salience Effects in Brand Recall, *Journal of Marketing Research*, November.
Avlonitis, G.J., (1985), Revitalizing Weak Industrial Products, *Industrial Marketing Management*, n°14.
Botton, M. and Cegarra, J-J., (1990), *Le nom de marque*, Paris, McGraw-Hill.

Cegarra, J-J., (1990), L'identité nominale du produit, *Revue Française de Gestion*, n°84.

Dayan, A., (1985), *Marketing industriel*, Paris, Vuibert.

Kapferer, J-N., (1995), *La marque, capital de l'entreprise*, Paris, Éditions d'Organisation.

Mahin, P.W., (1991), *Business to Business Marketing*, Needham Heights, Allyn and Bacon.

Malaval, P and Bénaroya C., (1998), Radiographie des marques patronymiques, (Radiography of the Patronymic Brands), *La Revue des Marques,* n°24, October.

Malaval, P., (1996), *Marketing Business to Business*, Paris, Publi-Union.

Wasson, C.R., (1976), The Importance of the Product Life Cycle to Industrial Marketer, *Industrial Marketing Management*, n°5.

Chapter 8

Creating and Protecting Business to Business Brands

Brand classification, which was dealt with in Chapter 7, shows how diverse the origins of industrial brands are: company name brands, brands which have some sort of signification, and brands with a technological connotation, among others. As well as being the basic element of communication between the company and the customer and an indicator of the customer's loyalty and awareness, the brand is also the company's mouth piece conveying its values and promises. Considering what is at stake for industrial brands especially as regards the customer-supplier relationship, launching a new brand requires very serious preparation.

This preparation is of utmost importance at a strategic level to check the relevance of creating a new brand and its implications. Then once the decision to create a new brand has been made, preparation is necessary in order to draw up accurate specifications which are essential for the success of the creation. Finally, launching the new brand and applying it to different supports (visual, audio...) require a lot of work beforehand. This chapter deals with the brand creation process and with the principles of brand protection by looking at examples of successful industrial brands.

1.   CREATING BRANDS

The creation of a brand is a strategic decision, usually involving both top management and the heads of marketing. The brand creation process means drawing up specifications to outline the brand identity. It is important to specify the expected main characteristics of the future brand, as it requires a longer commitment from the company than do the other elements of the mix. It is precisely this brand durability which becomes capital.

Before continuing, one question should be asked: "who is (and who is not) this brand?" In fact, even before defining the intrinsic characteristics of the product, service, or company, it is important to know who is speaking, who is at the origin of the launch, who is signing it. Often the name of the company is retained. This is one of the strongest sources of brand identity, showing the company's commitment to the quality of services or goods which it guarantees. For cost purposes, brand-companies (i.e. using the corporate name) are frequently found in industry, especially in small and medium sized companies and industrial firms. However, they are also found among big international corporations such as Alcatel, Siemens, IBM, Novartis, Aventis, etc, which are both companies and brands. Brand identity and corporate identity are therefore closely linked.

When the brand represents the company this is called corporate branding, meaning that the brand conveys the company's merits, origin, image, strength, reputation and credibility. Yet there are other solutions to finding a name for the brand (names can be descriptive, meaningful, evocative, technical, strange...). When choosing a name certain criteria need to be respected:

• Impact: The function of a name is to make the company, product or service easier to remember. It is important to choose a name which has a strong impact: it should be easy to recognize, identify and remember. Cognitive response theories specify that brand memorization is stronger and more long-lasting when the public has to make a small effort to understand and remember it.

• Evocation: Although the name does not have to be necessarily descriptive, it should be evocative, suggesting a set of values directly or indirectly related to the company's products, services or general activity. A meaningful and descriptive name can turn out to be too restrictive by making future and possible brand extensions difficult. A feature, which is too linked to a name, can be a handicap. The total or partial use of its company name for its product brands makes it difficult for the company to transfer licenses. Should the activity concerned be sold to a competitor, the company could find itself competing with products bearing its own name. Moreover, if any problem (pollution, accident) occurs, not only is the product affected, the global image of the company is too. The brand should tend to suggest a meaning, a culture, a personality as well as the company's values.

• Differentiation: the vocation of a name is not to describe the product or service but to identify it while at the same time inciting a particular emotional response. The name fully contributes to differentiating the brand. Thus a brand which directly signifies a category of products cannot be used for it is very difficult to protect. Moreover, a product with a highly descriptive name limits the possibilities of extending the brand to other categories of goods, even to other international markets (problems of translation, of pronunciation, etc.).

• Flexibility: the fourth precaution to take when creating a name is to grant some freedom to the brand so as to make diversification easier. Future changes have to be taken into consideration (international, brand juxtaposition, possible uses, brand values, etc.).

These different preliminary precautions have to be taken into account in the brand creation process.

1.1   Creating and choosing a name

There are several ways to create a brand. The name can be created directly without any assistance or can be computer-aided. The latter method can reduce creation costs but sometimes leads to numerous in-house meetings or involves high legal expenses. Although the computer-aided creation process is often used, it is not always the easiest (need to check brand registration) nor the most efficient method (brand already patented, international transposition, etc.). Another solution consists in acquiring available registered brands.

Choosing a brand name has become a key decision. Because of the growing number of registered brands and the difficulty of finding brand names, the task of coming up with a brand name is increasingly being given to brand naming agencies. Taking into account the brand's legal complexity and the scope of brand registration (product categories and geographical territories concerned), companies prefer to use the services of an agency specialized in name creations. These specialists have developed a certain know-how using substantial data bases and proven procedures taking into account legal and language restrictions at an early stage of the creation process.

What about the brand names of brand creation agencies?

It is quite interesting to study the names of these agencies. For example, Hayden Group or Russell Mark Group opted for a company brand name (respectively Darrell Hayden and Susan Russell) whereas Hundred Monkeys, Comspring or StartStorm, MacroWorks, One Horse Rhino chose a more conceptual or imaginative name. Brand Institute, Namedesign (Bizword), Naming Company, Lexicon Branding, Namix, Catchword, Namestormers, are meaningful names which directly or indirectly suggest the notion of brand creation. The first four put forward aspects of new brand name search whereas the two others convey "agitated" creative phases, disorder leading to order. The logos used by these creation agencies also vary considerably from the simple typography of the brand name (Metaphor, Lexicon, Hayden Group, Master-McNeil, Hundred Monkeys, Catchword…) to the figurative representation: a magnifying glass for Startstorm, a black rhinoceros for One Horse Rhino, colored letters thrown in the air by the hands of a magician for Name-It, the company's name underlined by a "hand-made" red line for MacroWorks, a kind of circle for Ashton Adams, a circle with RM inside for Russell Mark, a global map for ABC Namebank, or the creative form using the capital N of "Nom" (name) for Nomen. This company chose the Latin word for "name" as its trade name. It also used the slogan "Nomen Omen" for a long time. This phrase by Cicero (the name is an omen) particularly suits brand name creation (Figure 1).

NOMEN

Figure 1. Nomen logo

Brand creation is a relatively long and meticulous process usually consisting of four main stages.

Stage 1: Definition of specifications

This stage consists in specifically defining the main characteristics of the future brand. This means establishing the conditions to be respected and defining the exact framework of the brand to be created so that it conforms both to objectives and to strategy. Several questions related to the brand are used to outline the approach. For example:

- What product will it be?
- What markets are targeted?
- What type of public (age, sex, level of income)?
- What distribution channel will be used?
- How much space will there be on the packaging product for the brand to be visible?
- In which language(s) should the brand be mainly used?

These questions make it easier to define the brand's content. This definition is based on using the tangible attributes of the products or services as well as the concepts conveyed by the brand such as service, warranty, price, technology, etc. Brand creations should thus take into account both the brand's tangible and intangible attributes.

An exhaustive list of the type of names suitable should be drawn up based on the characteristics of the future brand. At this level, any idea which could lead to the creation of a name is listed. This includes invented names, meaningless names, animals, celebrities, geographical locations, amusing jargon, etc. Although some of these names can be quite bizarre or illogical, they provide interesting creative themes as regards the name search.

Stage 2: Creation

Different methods are used for the brand name search such as brainstorming creativity sessions (Osborn method – Osborn, 1963 –, digital approach, arbitrary stimulus...) or semiological methods using computer programs and data bases (registered brands, potentially registered brands, lists of international words). The creation process requires pre-creation studies and post-creation tests.

Brainstorming consists in groups of five to ten people generating a maximum number of ideas. These groups include company employees, customers, and creation specialists. Computer programs can also contribute to the name creation process (combination of letters, groups of letters, phonetic filtration, similar words search). When using creation software, it is essential to choose the number of syllables, even the number of letters if possible and to specify the prefixes and suffixes to avoid because of negative evocations or an improper juxtaposition with the company's name. On request, they can produce names which evoke a language or a pre-defined culture: the software can then propose names of which the letters respect the possibility of occurrence in the chosen language.

Stage 3: Selection

This stage consists in narrowing down those names which come closest to the objectives and recommendations set out in the specifications (for instance the geographical area where the product or service is to be sold).

The name represents the symbolic materialization of the brand, it has to give a meaning to the product, service or company which it designates. A linguistic acceptability check is necessary at both a national and international level when the brands are intended for such usage. Market reactions to a new name of a product, service or company has to be checked. At an international level, evocation, memorization, euphonic and pronunciation tests are frequently used. These tests are qualitative (carried out one-to-one or in groups) and permit a sort of "mental map" of idea associations and links.

The selection process is often made among hundreds of names with preference being given to those which are suggestive, liable to be noticed, identified and easily memorized (impact value) as well as to those which are "flexible": names which offer future possibilities for extension, export or new names based on a part of the brand name (positive evocation, pronounceability, etc.). The selection phase should retain at least a dozen names in case some of them have already been registered. Above all, a "good" brand should be legally sound. That is why a legal check of the names available is essential.

Stage 4: Legal checks

First of all, it should be ascertained that there are no identical brands in the same sector. It is advisable to check the names available among national and international brands by using data bases such as Namewatcher or Lawmoney accessible on Internet. After this first check, a thorough search should be made at professional institutions and organizations. The US Patent and Trademark Office (USPTO) is the American organization in charge of receiving and centralizing registered brands.

1.2   Intel and its brands

1.2.1   Origin of the Intel brand

Intel, the current world leader in microprocessors, was initially and temporarily called "NM Electronics" for Noyce Moore, the two founders, (Gordon Moore and Bob Noyce – co-inventor of the integrated circuit). The other name envisaged, "More Noise", was not chosen because it sounded too pretentious. The definitive name INTegrated Electronics was chosen at the end of 1968 and rapidly became Intel, whose logo with the "e" lower than the other letters of the name indicates the meeting point of the two words (*inte*grated *el*ectronics) (Figure 2).

Figure 2. The Intel[R] logo

1.2.2   Origin of the Intel Pentium processor brand

In September 1986, Compaq introduced a new model called Deskpro 386, integrating Intel's 386 composed of 275000 transistors on a 1cm^2 chip, capable of handling 3 to 4 million instructions per second. By naming its product Deskpro 386, Compaq popularized Intel's 386 processor. It gave a sizeable reputation to one element. As American legislation does not allow brand names made up of numbers to be registered, within a few years the 386 processor had become a generic name to be freely used. In fact, as Intel patents were no longer protected, cloners launched into the CISC adventure by using Intel micro codes 386, 486, etc. At the beginning of the 1990s, the Intel name was not yet really known to the general public. To protect itself, Intel decided to communicate directly with the general public and launched its "Intel Inside" program so that consumers[1]:

- would understand the computer's added value, namely the microprocessor,
- would be able to tell the difference between an Intel 486 and a cloner 486.

Intel learned from its negative experience with the 386 processor, that is to say the numerous imitations of its products and the impossibility of protecting a brand name consisting of only numbers. So, in 1993, the company decided to create a specific name for its new processor, which was to follow the 486. The name of Intel's fifth microprocessor, "Pentium" was imagined by the Californian company Lexicon Branding, using both a Greek and Latin source "pente" meaning five in Greek (pentagon, pentathlon) to which the suffix "ium" was added to suggest the idea of strength and sophistication. The name Pentium is natural, international, neutral, and yet meaningful.

1.3 Search for precedence

Prior to registering the brand name, it is generally strongly recommended to carry out an availability search so as to make sure the registration will not undermine the rights of a third party and that the company will not lay itself open to future complaints or opposition. The search can obviously not be exhaustive. However, consulting data bases on registered brand names seriously reduces the risk of counterfeiting.

There are two types of precedence search:

• Identical: applied to the basic list, this initial search eliminates all unavailable names,

• Similarity: this requires a careful and legal interpretation as to the risks of similarity with the future brand name. Rules of comparison are in fact defined. This search is useful when the two brands compared designate identical or similar products. It also involves names, which are likely to be confused by a customer who does not necessarily have the two brands in front of him. There is a risk of confusion when:

- generally speaking, the phonetic and/or visual aspect is such that the buyer can be confused if he does not see both products at the same time,

- the newer brand name reproduces an existing brand name apart from one letter, sound or element that is added or removed. In this case, the public could think the products were from the same manufacturer (Table 3).

Table 3. The range of searches

Type of Search	Range
Searches for identical brands among those registered AND among company names, business names, acronyms and signs which are registered.	Shows up the existence of identical brand names already registered.
Searches for similarity among brand names already registered AND among company names, business names, acronyms and signs which are registered.	Shows up the existence of already registered brand names, which are visually and / or phonetically, and / or intellectually similar designating identical and / or similar products and / or services OR identical or complementary activities.

Whether searches for precedence are identical or similarity based, they are carried out on 5 categories of products and can be extended to the 42 categories defined in the Nice classification of February 1997.

They must be adapted to the needs of the company depending on its markets. The data banks suggested make it possible today to identify both national and international registered brands, but also the names of national or foreign companies, and Internet domain names. These can include national brands of a specific country and / or international brands (brands from one of the 43 countries which signed the Madrid Agreement or one of the 129 countries which signed the Paris Convention) and / or community brands (registered at the Harmonization Office of the Home Market at Alicante in Spain) and / or brands of member countries of the AOIP (African Organization of Intellectual Property). The research currently available does not allow brand-naming specialists to fully guarantee the availability of a brand name. However, if the recommendations are followed, there is little chance of a legal conflict. The name creation process is finished when all the searches have been carried out: this is followed by the brand protection phase.

1.4   The case of international brands

Choosing a name for an international brand is more difficult than for a national one in terms of pronunciation, evocation, and brand registration. For example, the Korean company Daewoo or the German company Hoechst carried out international communication campaigns to "teach" different target audiences how to pronounce their brand name ("Pronounce De-Ou" or "Just say Herkst"). If there is a lack of preparation and control when creating an international brand, the company image can be seriously affected. It is advisable to avoid names which can shock in a foreign language, be easily joked about (for instance: Chevrolet Nova meaning "No go" in Spanish) or sound too much like an already-existing brand name (especially if the name is already used for a product which is totally different and its reputation could be damaging). The word can also turn out to be impossible to pronounce in one or more languages.

Taking into account the variety of languages in which the new brand name has to be introduced if the product or service is exported, there is a big risk of unfortunate misunderstandings. For example, in 1985 (Hammel, 1997), when two American gas producers, Inter North of Omaha and Houston Natural Gas, merged, they chose the name Enteron to designate the new group. As the company had hoped, this name attracted a lot of attention but not for the right reasons: the Greek origin of the word "enteron" signifies the male anus. The company name was immediately changed to Enron.

The most frequently encountered problem cases are:
- slang or obscene meanings,
- names of political or religious movements,
- words which, although they have the same meaning in a foreign language, do not have the same connotations.

It is essential to consult local experts in order to avoid these pitfalls. In fact, using dictionaries or having knowledge of foreign languages is not enough to keep abreast of the rapid evolution of a language. It is also advisable to check the pronunciation of a word in every country concerned by using the international phonetic code.

These precautions were taken into account by the transport company Sceta (Calberson, France Express...) which, in 1996, used the brand name Geodis so as to enhance its concept "geodistribution of services integration". This new brand groups together all types of transport whether a small parcel or a container. The emblem, which existed before the name, represents the globe and human exchanges against a blue background, which is unusual in the transport sector. When Geodis chose to go international it was registered in a lot of countries. The search for precedence revealed that registering the brand was possible in the transport sector. The brand name is composed of "Odis" which evokes the Odyssey. "Dis" is a classical ending to express both distribution and distance (Figure 4).

Figure 4. The Geodis logo

2.   A NEW CORPORATE NAME FOR AN ESTABLISHED COMPANY: VIVENDI

2.1   Why a new name for the "Compagnie Générale des Eaux"?

The previous name Compagnie Générale des Eaux (General Water Company) no longer fit with the different activities of the group, from energy and water to Internet. The name could then not be flatly descriptive. The name looked for had to symbolize a major international group providing services in the environmental, communications, and construction fields and underline what unites those activities. It had to reflect the values shared by its business sectors and the 220,000 men and women who work for the group. The activities involved in everyday life, a vital, mobile Group.

• Services and accessibility: attentiveness, quality, and responsiveness in service to the customer,

• Improving the quality of daily life: all of the activities correspond to basic needs in the private and public sector in developed as well as in developing countries,

• Modernity and anticipation: one of the strong points of the group's culture has always been the ability to anticipate new needs and innovate (from water treatment to the Internet),

• International scope and strength without arrogance: present in 90 countries, the group always seeks to offer the solution best suited to local factors and the specific expectations of its customers.

2.2   Anatomy of the name

The brand name creation agency Nomen, which the company consulted came up with more than 5,500 names of which 400 were short-listed and

presented to the group (Coudray which evokes the hazel tree; E2C for Environment, Construction, Communication; Sequana which means the Paris river Seine in Latin; Ge which means the earth in Greek; Elegie; Egery; Eledia; Egedia; Primasty, etc.). A long linguistic and legal validation process followed this short-listing in order to check that the names could be pronounced in the 88 countries selected by La Générale des Eaux and that they could be easily applied to the fourteen product ranges retained. Vivendi was selected from a list of names tested in France, Germany, Italy, Spain, the U.K., the U.S., and China. These tests were conducted by Nomen Marketing among consumers (focus groups) and opinion leaders (qualitative interviews with economic leaders, local politicians, and financial analysts). Vivendi is derived from the Latin verb vivo / vivis / vivere / vixi / victum which means to live ("which has to be lived"). The Latin sentences "ars vivendi" and "modus vivendi" mean "quality of life" and "way of living, agreement to live together" (Figure 5). Vivendi was selected because:
- it evokes life...
- it evokes pure water, the source of life and the source of the group,
- it evokes movement, mobility...

Figure 5. The new name and new logo of the company: Vivendi

Among other names tested such as Anjou, Marly, Elegie, Egedia, Orya and Egery, Vivendi topped the list with strong approval rates:
• An international name that is easy to pronounce, that is pronounced the same throughout the world (Vee-Ven-Dee) and is rapidly recalled,
• Strong, practically identical connotations in all countries:
- the name evokes everything that contributes to and facilitates life, well-being, warmth, energy and nature,
- a rich, original personality, combining strength and vitality, competence and culture, openness and an enterprising spirit,
- a universe clearly oriented towards service, with both technological and cultural components,
- in China, there is a surprisingly close identification with the group's culture.

The Chinese ideograms (Wei Wan Di) representing the closest phonetic translation of Vivendi respectively denote:
- to join, to link,
- happiness,
- ten thousand, numerous,
- to advance, to progress.

All of these fit very well with the spirit and the vocation of Vivendi: "to advance together, progress in service to all, facilitate community life and create ties between people".

2.3   Steps in the name search

Finding a name that was:
- appealing and easy to pronounce in all languages,
- evocative of the group and its activities,
- legally available in France and abroad,
...was a long and complex undertaking.

• January 1997: preliminary studies consisting of two parts (a semiological analysis of the Générale des Eaux Group's communications and an analysis of existing studies).

• February 1997: launch of the name search using creative groups, documentary, computerized information and data bank research.

Simultaneously, the first legal searches were launched (initial filtering to exclude clearly unavailable names).

• At the end of April 1997, the first series of names was proposed. The total number of names (representing 4 successive searches from the end of April 1997 to the beginning of September 1997) amounted to 400.

• May to November 1997: intensified searches in France and abroad (including via the Internet) backed by linguistic controls in 57 countries covering 22 categories.

• September 1997 to February 1998: some twenty names were deposited for copyright in all appropriate categories (together with usage surveys and purchasing procedures).

• May 15, 1998: the name was submitted for approval at the general meeting of shareholders.

• 2000: evolution of the logo, simplification of the logo (birds disappear, stylizing the brand-name letters...) (Figure 6).

Figure 6. The evolution of the Vivendi logo

2.4   Summary of the market study per country (opinion leaders)

The following tables present the results of the study performed on opinion leaders in each of the targeted countries; they show the different associations linked to the Vivendi brand: evocations, image, personality (Tables 7a&b and 8a&b).

Table 7a. The market study per country

France	Italy	Spain	United Kingdom
- Musical, rhythmical - Lively, creative - Strong appeal +/++ - Good recall +/++	- Original - Contemporary - Strong appeal +/++ - Perfect recall ++	- "Arouses curiosity" - "Evokes happiness" - Good appeal + - Perfect recall ++	- Elegance, style, quality - A Latin ring - Strong appeal +/++ - Good recall +/++
Spontaneous associations	**Spontaneous associations**	**Spontaneous associations**	**Spontaneous associations**
Life, music, lightness, freshness, a way of life, art, conviviality, energy; subtlety, strength, refinement, Latin	Life, joy, a good lifestyle, harmony, elegance, "evviva" (hurrah!), viventi (lively), openness, sympathy, spontaneity, youth, everyday things	Life "vivencia", lifestyle, rhythm, vivacity "vivo, vivaz", vitality "vivador" and home "vivienda"	Music, joyousness, bright colors, brilliant ideas, beauty
Characteristics of the image	**Characteristics of the image**	**Characteristics of the image**	**Characteristics of the image**
Joyousness, openness, spontaneity, calmness, comprehension, communication	Status, strength, refinement, liveliness, lightness, sociability	Style, character, calmness, elegance, dynamism and comfort, well-being, quality and joyousness	Energy, feline, elegance, rapidity, dynamism
Personality	**Personality**	**Personality**	**Personality**
Accessible and aesthetic, dynamic, rational, spirited, character, ease, professionalism	Confident, concentrated, open and cultivated, presence, sense of autonomy	Connotes strong potential, culture, reliability, order, sociability	Creative, contemporary, open, dynamic, trendy, innovative and distinctive

Table 7b. The market study per country

France	Italy	Spain	United Kingdom
Characteristics of the group	**Characteristics of the group**	**Characteristics of the group**	**Characteristics of the group**
• Accessibility and strength • Services • Culture and technology • Very international • Traditional yet highly innovative Challenge spirit, quest for well-being and quality of life for people throughout the world	• Accessibility and strength • Industry and services • Cultural dimension • Relatively national • Very traditional yet innovative High quality, in pace with change, avant-garde	• Accessibility and strength • Services • Technology and culture • Relatively international • Very traditional but can be innovative Creative, proactive, lively, "major projects"	• Accessibility and strength • Industry and services • Technology and culture • Very international • Innovative with a traditional base Very creative, open, attentive to the customer
Overall appreciation	**Overall appreciation**	**Overall appreciation**	**Overall appreciation**
The most appropriate at D+8 (1st)	The most appropriate at D+8 (1st)	The most appropriate at D+8 (1st)	The most appropriate at D+8 (1st)

Table 8a. The market study per country

Germany	United States	China
- "Very musical" - Dynamic and positive - Strong appeal +/++ - Good recall +/++	- Simple, strong and different - "A lively ring" - Excellent appeal +++ - Perfect recall +++	- Western character - Dynamism thanks to "Vi" (as in "vi-tamin") - Good appeal + - Good recall +
Spontaneous associations	**Spontaneous associations**	**Spontaneous associations**
"Joie de vivre", life, energy, vivacity and dynamism (viva), culture, opera, quality of life	Music, femininity, life, freedom, elegance, sports, nature, health, vitality	Protection, vitality, size, wealth, health, elegance, strength, life, speed, generosity
Characteristics of the image	**Characteristics of the image**	**Characteristics of the image**
Altruism, sensitivity, attentiveness, joyousness, seriousness, well-being	Class, brilliant, energy, spirit, joyousness, vital force, Latin, youthfulness	Finesse, movement, gentleness, classicism, harmony, power, beauty
Personality	**Personality**	**Personality**
Positive, contemporary, youthful, in tune with the times, open to the future	Healthy, stable, harmonious, independent, appealing, enterprising, open, very contemporary, positive	Western, calm, contemporary, at home in the commercial and business worlds

Table 8b. The market study per country

Germany	United States	China
Characteristics of the group	**Characteristics of the group**	**Characteristics of the group**
• Accessibility above all • Services • Very cultured • Very international • Very innovative with a traditional base	• Exceptional accessibility and strength • Service vocation • Strong cultural dimension • Very international • Innovative above all	• Strength and accessibility • Relatively industrial • Cultural, technological • Very international • Traditional yet innovative
Up-to-date management, mutual respect, abreast of new trends	Really new, oriented towards well-being, very European	Very good management, industrial vocation
Overall appreciation	**Overall appreciation**	**Overall appreciation**
The most appropriate at D+8 (1st)	The most appropriate at D+8 (1st)	Very appropriate at D+8 (2nd)

2.5   Vivendi: "our 7 values"

Following the creation of the Vivendi brand, the group clearly defined 7 major corporate values (Source: vivendi.com).

Improving the quality of life

Throughout the world, our purpose is to provide services that help to improve the quality of everyday life. True to its traditions since 1853, Vivendi's vocation is to respond to the basic needs of the 21st century: the environment, communications and development, especially in urban areas.

Being close to our customers

Being attuned to and understanding our customers' needs, whether they are individuals, companies or communities; maintaining humility and ensuring availability while providing quality service at the best price and with a view to the long term. These are the engines that drive our daily activities. The confidence and loyalty of our customers are Vivendi's primary asset.

Creating and sharing value

Vivendi's goal is the creation of value in our sectors and through our growth, which is by nature international in scope. The primary beneficiaries are our shareholders, who provide the means to achieve this growth. But value created in the form of profits must also benefit our employees through profit-sharing and shareholding schemes, as well as funding our investments.

Developing a network of talents

The men and women who work for Vivendi are our greatest asset. Our enterprising spirit must be based on drive and the linking of skills. By decreasing emphasis on single individuals, separate disciplines and hierarchy, and within the context of a strategy defined by the group, Vivendi must encourage the emergence of new initiatives proposed by teams from different areas. This calls for the networking of talents.

Anticipating through innovation and imagination

Throughout the world, our customers' expectations are constantly changing. Anticipating needs, innovating, the creation and development of new products and services, all supported by expertise developed in our specific fields.

Affirming our ambition in social terms

Because all our activities correspond to basic needs, they have strong social utility which Vivendi demonstrates every day. At the same time, our service activities, above all, rely on the professionalism and motivation of the people that make up the group. Vivendi must also reflect this social utility within our companies: the drive for the most cost-effective performance must go hand in hand with social cohesion, raised to the level of a management priority.

Observing strict ethics

Improving the quality of everyday life requires an approach that demonstrates respect for mankind, which must correspond to a strict code of ethics. It must be observed in all our activities. Honesty, personal integrity, full compliance with local, national and international laws and anti-corruption regulations dictate our conduct. Honoring these ethics is a condition for being part of Vivendi.

2.6   Nomen: the creator of the name

Established in 1981, Nomen is the leading specialist in France for the creation of names and brand-names, and among the leaders worldwide (close to 200 creations per year). The Nomen group has created a lot of successful brands.

Among Nomen's recent creations:

- Arvie (flat spring water/Danone-Volvic),
- Goa (fruit juice/McCain),
- Grafic (hair styling products/Garnier),
- Chérie-FM (Radio FM/NRJ),
- Tribu (credit card for youth/Caisse d'Epargne),
- Wanadoo (Internet access/France Telecom),
- Episode (weekend packages/Accor Group),
- Natexis (merger of two banks/Crédit National-BFCE),
- Exor (company name),
- Artesis (company name/Paribas Belgium).

Marcel Botton, President of Nomen: "This name change was one of the most far-reaching projects of recent years when you consider the size of the Group, the extent of its activities and locations. Since it obviously required a worldwide perspective, we worked in close association with our 7 foreign subsidiaries and our correspondents in other countries. All precautions had to be taken to ensure that the name selected from the 5,500 considered were thoroughly checked in semantic, legal, and marketing terms. Clearly there was a risk of ending up with a compromise, a bland, mediocre name that wouldn't offend anyone, but that wouldn't excite anyone either. In the end, the exact opposite was achieved.

The chosen name is committed, expressive and conveys what seems to me to be the most timeless value of companies and individuals alike: life. Life, constant adaptation, evolution, change, mobility and the creative spirit. Nothing important happens without feeling. Consequently, the name had to vibrate, sing, seduce. In these terms, Vivendi is probably a turning point in the history of brand-names: after legions of family names, followed by arbitrary words, Vivendi opens the way to standard-bearing names."

3.   BRAND PROTECTION AND COUNTERFEITING

Legislation aimed at protecting product or service brand names has become increasingly necessary as abusive, illicit, and fraudulent uses of brands such as counterfeiting have become common practice.

Up until recently counterfeiting was most widespread in the luxury goods sector; however, today it is an ever greater problem in industry. Counterfeiting can be a genuine danger to both the end consumer (abuse of the product's quality and security) and to the company in terms of loss of customers. It is also dangerous for the State as its economy and revenue are affected and its laws ridiculed.

Counterfeiting is one of the most virulent types of unfair competition and is thus of great strategic importance.

Registering brands, patents, drawings and models with the US Patent and Trademark Office gives companies industrial property rights which allow them to take legal action, to have the counterfeited products seized, and to claim compensation.

3.1   Patenting

Patent registration is growing. In the United States, the US Patent and Trademark Office registered 200,000 new brands in 1996 compared to 125,000 in 1992.

Apart from the really famous brand names, patenting is the only formality which allows the company to be the exclusive owner of the brand. Patenting the brand name with a recognized organization such as the US Patent and Trademark Office is essential in that it asserts the rights of existence of the brand in favor of the company. It defines the duration of the brand rights and this almost indefinitely (a tax has to be paid every 10 years to renew these rights).

Patenting increases protection as the brand is protected for products and / or services designated in the registration and also for similar products and / or services. The patentee has the exclusive right which allows him to forbid any future use of the name without his permission in a field identical to the one which was initially protected or which is complementary. Finally, patenting makes it possible for the patentee to take action against counterfeiting.

In France, individuals, legal entities, associations and consortiums can patent brands with:

- the INPI (Institut National de la Propriété Industrielle, the French equivalent to the American USPTO),

- the Commercial Court registrar or the County Court, depending on where they are domiciled.

Brands can also be patented internationally with centralizing organizations (World Intellectual Property Organization, Paris Agreement, OHMI, OAPI) or in each of the targeted countries.

In all cases, national patents for the countries concerned are issued. International patent strategy depends on those countries in which the brand can be exploited immediately or in the near future (Table 9).

Table 9. Main Patent Offices in Europe

- Germany : the "Deutsches Patentantes" (Zweibrucken Strasse 12, 80297 Munchen), the "Branch Office Berlin" (Gitschiner Strasse 97 -103, 10958 Berlin) and the "Bundessortenamt" (Osterfelddamm 80, 30627 Hanover).

- Austria : the "Osterreichisches Patentamt" (Kohlmarkt 8-10, A-1010 Vienna).

- Benelux : the "Benelux Merkenbureau" (Bordewigklaan 15, 2591 XR DEN HAAG, The Netherlands), the "Ministère des affaires économiques, office de la propriété industrielle" (North Gate 111, Boulevard Emile Jacqmain 154, B-1210 Brussels, Belgium) and the "Service de la propriété industrielle" (12-2, Boulevard Royal, L-2910 Luxembourg-Grand Duchy).

- Spain : the "Officina Espanola de Patentes y Marcas" (Calle Panama n°1 Madrid, España).

- Italy : the "Ufficio Italiano Brevetti e Marchi, Ministero dell'Industria, del Commercio e dell'Artigianato" (19 Via Molise, Roma).

- Portugal : the "Instituto Nacional da Propriedad Industrial" (Campo das Cebolas, 1100 Lisbon).

- United Kingdom : "The Patent Office" (Cardiff Road, Newport - Gwent, United Kingdom, NPG 1RH).

3.2   Different patenting possibilities

Brand patenting covers the name under which products are circulated or services are sold as well as any other distinctive signs which accompany them: logo, packaging, label. It includes:
- Trademarks affixed to finished products or on intermediary goods, for example, Tactel or Teflon,
- Commercial brands affixed by the distributor on products he sells, for example, "Les Exclusifs by Point P"[2],
- Service brands which are used to designate services such as industrial equipment hire (United Rentals) or company catering (Sodexho Alliance...).
Articles L.711-2 and 711-3 of the Intellectual Property Code specify that the sign chosen as a brand has to be:
- Distinctive in relation to the designated products and / or services. The usual or generic names or signs are then devoid of any distinctive character. It is the same for signs or names which notably characterize the type, quality,

destination, value, geographical origin, the year the good was produced or the service provided or any other characteristic of the product or service.

• Authorized or not specifically forbidden, or morally offensive. It should also not be deceptive so as not to mislead the public (especially as regards the nature, quality or geographical origin of the product or service). Other exclusions include any appropriation of coats of arms, flags, state or international organization emblems, official signs and stamps of inspection and guarantee, international organization names or acronyms.

• Available: the chosen brand should not infringe previously acquired rights.

These can consist of:
- a patented brand or one which is extremely well-known,
-   a name or trade name which could lead to confusion in the public's mind,
- a protected trade name,
- a copyright,
- a drawing or model,
- third party personality rights (own name, pseudonym, image),
- the name, image or reputation of a territorial administration.

There are three main categories of signs which can be protected as a brand:
• Names,
• Representational signs,
• Sound - based signs.

3.2.1   Names or verbal signs

Names include:
• Simple or compound words found in everyday language: Air Liquide (gas),
• Neologisms: Tetra Pak (packaging),
• Combined words (MicronTechnology, Uniroyal), random or fantasy names such as pseudonyms or words diverted from their meaning,
• Slogans or mottos: "Hi-speed Company" (Alcatel's tag-line),
• Foreign words: Jumper (Citroen),
• Surnames: Boeing,
• First names: Mercedes,
• Geographical names (provided there is no confusion with origin): British Airways, Texas Instrument,
• Letters, numbers, acronyms: 3M, UPS.

3.2.2   Representational signs

These include:
• Two or three-dimensional signs such as drawings, labels, stamps, stickers, holograms, logos or computer-aided drawings,
• Shapes such as those of the product or of its packaging,
• Combinations, or shades of colors.
Most brands associate several verbal and representational elements so as to create complex brands. In general, a company uses several distinctive signs such as its name, its logo, and its brands.

3.2.3   Sound - based signs

These include simple sounds, musical phrases, rhythmic sequences, jingles, radio or television spots.

3.3   Brand protection methods

Brand patenting is the first legal element used to protect the brand. In order for this to be possible, the essential condition is to use the brand or sign in question so that it is:
- able to use the acquired rights for defense purposes,
- protected from any loss of rights.

3.3.1   Patent watch and brand use verification

This "passive" form of protection has to be completed by an active approach. So as to protect the brand, it is necessary to keep track of the registration of similar or parasite products as well as opportunities and threats due to sector changes. Occasional or permanent watch operations make it possible to:
• Detect any subsequent brand registration which could be harmful and if this is the case, to envisage a quick reaction so as to stop the conflicting situation appropriately and in due time,
• Know the existence of brands registered by a competitor and / or in the name of a specific individual or legal entity.
Although this watch is essential from a legal point of view, it is also part of brand image control. Rigorous brand management means specifically defining and carefully supervising the conditions of the brand's use. So as to prevent the brand from becoming too commonplace like the "branduits" (branded-product[3]) (such as Scotch, Pantone, Neiman, Cromalin...) a solid framework for use has to be established. Once a brand becomes part of

everyday language, this leads to a loss of sovereignty or even to a loss of rights from a legal point of view. Moreover, the brand is then used to designate rival products who take advantage of the advertising, reputation, and image of the brand. This can seriously affect the brand's credibility by tapping its territory and reducing the chances of imposing the brand on foreign products. That is why industrial companies, especially those which devote substantial budgets to backing their brands are very vigilant concerning the use of their brands[4]. Apart from the use of visual identity codes (developed further on in Chapter 9), companies check that their brands:

• Are accompanied by the generic designation of the product (for example to say and write "Scotch adhesive" roll and not "Scotch" as it is called in French),

• Are distinguished from the surrounding text on all documents (for example by putting the brand name in capital letters or italics),

• Do not become a verb (as with Xerox in the United States where to Xerox means to photocopy "If you want to xerox a document, choose a Xerox"),

• Are not used in the plural form (not to write Toshibas but Toshiba laptop computers) nor be deformed (to write Wanadoo and not Wannadu for example),

• Always use the same graphic style, logotype, and emblem on all documents where it is found (see *visual identity code*),

• Are accompanied by the owner's name which is legible (Post-It® is a 3M patent) or specifying that their name is registered and protected (international symbol: ®).

3.3.2   Brand protection: the Intel case

The use of the different Intel brands depends on the charter drawn up by the company in order to avoid their trivialization or devalorization. The brands should not be shortened or used with a hyphen. The Pentium, Pentium Pro, Pentium II and MMX brands should be used as adjectives and followed by an appropriate designation, for example "system equipped with a Pentium II processor, Pentium processor with MMX technology, Pentium 166 MHz microchip...». The appropriate words associated with Pentium and Pentium Pro are: microchip, processor, microprocessor, brand, name and logo. Concerning the Pentium II brand, the same words can be used except for "microchip". The MMX designates Intel as being at the origin of the technology which improves sound and image and which especially accelerates multimedia and communication software. Concerning MMX the appropriate words are: technology, instructions, brand, name, and logo.

The recommendations are specific. For example, for all the Pentium, Pentium Pro, Pentium II and MMX brands, the following words cannot be used: motherboard, power, system, computer, PC, class, notebook or laptop. Among other conditions of use is that the word which follows the brand should be in small letters (except if it is a title). Moreover the plural of Pentium is Pentium and not Pentiums (this is true for all the brands). Intel brands cannot be incorporated into the trade name, product name or the reference of another company's model. Finally, the use of Intel logos is reserved to those companies which have signed a licensing agreement with Intel.

3.3.3   The necessary fight against counterfeiting

Although brand registration and patenting are the first protection, more than 50% of industrial companies do not use any protection. Patenting is not just a defensive and dissuasive weapon, it is also strategic and offensive. Numerous companies have at their origin a patent registration such as Air Liquide with its Claude patents on gas liquefaction techniques or Innovatron with its invention of the smart card. As with patents which give an image of technical skill and know-how, brands reassure customers and partners. However, registering a brand with the US Patent and Trademark Office does not stop counterfeiting.

Automakers such as Volkswagen, General Motors, PSA-Peugeot-Citroen or Renault and also autoparts manufacturers such as Valeo or Delphi are subject to a specific type of counterfeiting which affects spare parts. This damage runs up to several hundred millions of euros. Counterfeiters, based in Taiwan, Turkey, ex-Yugoslavia, Spain and Italy copy those parts which are most often replaced.

However, the safety of these parts is often deplorable: for example, counterfeited hoods are not solid at the hinges and the bad quality of their inside flanges stops them from bending in the event of a collision. In fact, they can breakthrough the wind screen and end up inside the automobile. Similarly, counterfeited brake pads increase braking distances by 30 meters at 90 km / hr. and by 60 meters at 130 km / hr. Auto users attribute these defects to the Automakers and thus undermine their image. Regulations adopted by the European Commission in June 1995, allowing autoparts makers to affix their brands to products have contributed not only to restoring the balance between customers and suppliers in the automotive industry but also to slowing down the development of counterfeiting. The fight led by autoparts makers consists in informing their customers of the distinctive signs of their brand by means of information booklets and information seminars (this information is on the products; packaging authenticity; related documents; the name, address and type of supplier, etc.). Distributors are thus able to detect counterfeited parts and so alert the autoparts makers as to the prejudice suffered (price, terms of sales, sales volume, documents, publicity supports giving rise to confusion, etc.).

3.3.4   Action against counterfeiting

• The owner of a brand or exclusive rights can take legal action against counterfeiting to obtain compensation for any damages suffered. This action is often accompanied by impoundment of the goods.

• The action is brought before the Criminal Court or County Court if the prejudice to the brand is a penal offense. Penal sanctions concerning counterfeiting are a two-year prison sentence and a fine of a half million euros.

Additional sanctions can be applied, including the publication of the judgement in the newspapers, confiscation of products and materials, or their destruction. The law of February 5, 1994, extended legal responsibility to individuals, including companies, and made easier their application as well reinforcing sanctions.

• Civil action against counterfeiting depends exclusively on the County Court. The civil sanctions for counterfeiting are the payment of compensation and interest to the victim, discontinuance of exploiting the disputable brand and the confiscation of the counterfeited products.

Nearly 200,000 seizures were carried out in 1994, 300,000 in 1995, and more than 600,000 in 1996. Legal action has increased and companies which have lodged a complaint win in 86% of the cases, however the procedures are so long, complex, and heavy that more than a quarter of the companies victim of counterfeiting renounce legal action.

The other possible solution for companies is to negotiate with the counterfeiters. Indeed, nearly one third of them opt for this solution. This means of fighting against counterfeiting is quicker and less onerous than legal action. It is also useful if the counterfeiter is in good faith and offers to withdraw the product in question. All these actions allow companies to fight more efficiently against counterfeiters within the European Union and the United States. Outside these regions, the fight is a lot more difficult as not all countries have repressive regulations.

3.3.5   Action against unfair competition

This is based on punishable civil responsibility meaning that the party at fault has to have committed a fault and that the victim has had to suffer a prejudice. There has to be a link of causality between the fault and the prejudice. The author and the victim must be in direct competition.

Unfair competition covers diverse situations such as denigrating a competitor, disorganizing a competing company, or deliberately creating confusion by using unprotected distinctive signs: a servile or quasi-servile copy of the labels or packaging of a competitor's product.

Taking action against unfair competition can be carried out alone (in the case of abusive copying of a "usual brand" which is not registered) or jointly with an action against counterfeiting when the unfair competition act is distinct from the counterfeiting.

3.3.6   Action against parasite manoeuvres

Most often, in the absence of direct competition, this means taking action against the dealings of a company which damage the activities of another company and notably its brand image. There is damage done to the brand when the protected sign is reproduced or imitated to designate products and / or services which are identical or similar to those for which the brand is protected or complementary to them. Any attack on the brand holder's rights constitutes a counterfeit act.

Article L713-5 of the Intellectual Property Code states that the use of a recognized brand for products or services other than those designated in the registration, is the civil responsibility of the author, if this action is damaging to the owner of the brand, or if the use of the brand is deemed unjustifiable.

Article L.713-2 of the Intellectual Property Code concerning the identity of products and services specifies that "the reproduction, use or affixation of a brand, even with adding words such as "formula, way, system, imitation, type, method"; use of a reproduced brand for products or services identical to those designated in the registration as well as the suppression or modification of a regularly affixed brand are forbidden unless the brand holder expressly authorizes so". The law distinguishes several cases ranging from partial, almost servile or servile reproductions, representations with an addition, the abusive public or business use of another brand (in its advertising, its trade name, its sign) to the offense of commercializing a product under a false name on the container.

Moreover, article L.713-3 of the Intellectual Property Code concerning the similarity of products and services states that "the reproduction, use or affixation of a brand as well as the use of a reproduced brand for products or services similar to those designated in the registration, the imitation of a brand and the use of an imitated brand for products or services identical or similar to those designated in the registration are forbidden if they lead to confusion in the public's mind unless the brand holder expressly authorizes so".

3.4   **Brands and the Internet**

In Europe, the media-coverage of the Internet development for the general public has almost hidden its explosion in industry. The business to business sector is more directly involved by these developments than the general public, with numerous sites everyday appearing.

Although initially designed to project the company image and provide information on the company's activity, history, and products and services, company Web pages have since widened their fields of action. The Web is used to give prices, product availability, information for financial markets, sales of goods, on-line service. For industrial companies, the interest of the Internet lies in the growing overlapping of customers and suppliers: being able to visualize his customer's level of stock allows the supplier to better anticipate renewals. Other advantages include E-mailing, price proposals, bids, and new product development.

The growth of Internet development at a professional level has encouraged numerous companies to open sites (identified by a domain name) for promoting their brands. However, the rules for the attribution of a domain name are very different to those classically characterizing brand rights. For example, names are registered with a national centralizing organization on a "first come, first served" basis. These rules do not follow usual brand regulations.

In essence, the Internet aims at abolishing all frontiers and so questions the old principle of brand territoriality, which asserts the rights of the brand only in those countries where they are claimed. The domain name envisaged by a company is no more limited to a geographical zone than it is in its field of application. In fact, the principle of brand specificity is also questioned. Contrary to the brand, the rights of the domain name are valid not just for specifically designated products and services provided by the company but also for all the products and services.

Taking account of these fundamental differences between the rigor of brand rights and the ease with which domain names are attributed, numerous conflicts have appeared which will probably lead to the creation of an international commission for attribution check and control. For the moment, certain fraudulent appropriations of brands and trade names as domain names have been observed, motivated by the obvious intention to cash in on them. Apart from these situations, it often happens that the domain name, which a company would like to have, is already being used by a company with an identical brand or by an entity with the same trade name. For example, this is the case for the aluminium frame company Technal whose address is "http://www.technal.fr which exists alongside another web site used by an R & D company specialized in management software

(http://www.technal.com). As with the classical registration and defense of a brand, in order to register its domain name, a company has to:
- Search for the availability of the name on Internet,
- Watch those domain names which could be harmful for it.

While in the United States no documents have to be supplied for field registration, in France, a name ownership certificate has to be presented ("kbis", business registration number, INPI registration certificate) confirming the usefulness of brand registration.

Effective brand registration on the Internet depends on the level of vigilance which companies have concerning their brands: active surveillance, utilization guides, and authorization for use grids. Some companies such as Microsoft® have already drawn up graphic, visual, and legal charters for use of their brands on Internet.

3.4.1 Logotype utilization on the Internet: the Microsoft® example

With the development of the Internet and with easy access to information for all users, companies have had to start thinking about new ways of protecting their brands. Companies in the computer sector have been among the first concerned. Microsoft® thus drew up a Microsoft® logo utilization charter for non-Microsoft® web sites. These non-official sites, meaning that they are not affiliated to Microsoft®, can in fact use the Microsoft® logo simply by downloading it off "Logo-gif". This downloading is possible if the logo's utilization is limited to the site which requested it and if it includes a link to Microsoft®'s visitor page. The supplied logo mentions this link. The logo can only be used if the site specifically refers to Microsoft® or to its services and products. However, it is not a licensing agreement for the company's different brands and logos: it is not a guarantee, a sponsor, or a certificate of approval. The logo cannot be used on a site which denigrates the company, its products or services (counterfeiting, patent infringement), nor can it bring prejudice to a country (national, international laws, etc.). Should this happen, legal action would be taken as for any fraudulent and illegal use of the Logo. More formally, Microsoft® asks the site which downloads the Microsoft® Logo to have its own identity (name, logo) at least the same size as the Microsoft® Logo. Moreover, the Microsoft® Logo has to appear on its own with a space of 30 pixels around each side. It cannot be directly modified in size, proportions, colors or movement nor indirectly on its elements and attributes.

Having discussed the different stages of brand creation, registration and protection, it is interesting to look more closely at those elements which often incarnate and even sum up the brand: the logotype, slogan, and jingle.

NOTES

1. See Chapter 3, The Characteristics of Business to Business Communication.
2. See Chapter 15, Industrial Distributor Brands.
3. See Chapter 1, Development of the Concept of Brands.
4. See Chapter 11, "Entering Goods" Brands: The Development of Co-Branding, 5-Lycra® Only By DuPont: A Commercial and Technical Partnership.

REFERENCES

Hammel, S., (1997), *US News & World Report*, Washington, quoted in *Courrier International* n°368, Brands: what a bummer finding a name, 20-26 November.
Osborn, A.F., (1963), *Applied Imagination*, 3rd ed, New York: Charles Scribner's Sons.

Chapter 9

The Logotype and The Visual Identity Code

A brand can only rarely be summed up by its name: various different elements contribute to its identity, which progressively develops throughout its life. Brand identity is multidimensional. In addition to the numerous evocations and associations, and tangible product or service attributes brought to mind by the brand, identity is also built on distinctive elements such as the logo, slogan or jingle. Representing the brand and communicating its basic values, these elements must be carefully managed starting with establishing an effective visual identity code.

1. THE ESSENTIAL ROLE OF THE LOGOTYPE

The brand and the different elements displayed with it become so inextricably associated that the brand might be unidentifiable without them. The graphic unity of these different components form the brand's *visual identity*. The latter is strictly defined in order to preserve coherency whatever the support used (poster, brochure, Internet site, company car, work-clothes, TV ad, etc.). A company's visual identity should reflect its values – in other words, its culture, personality, vocation and projects for the future – in a recognizable tone and style. The defined visual identity may contain up to four elements: a typographic transcription of the brand (name, slogan), a visual symbol (logo), a color or aural code (jingle or associated musical theme). Visual identity should be long term to have a significant effect on company awareness and strength. Evolving with time, it should follow the different phases of company development, reflecting any changes in company image (Brun and Rasquinet, 1996; Behaeghel, 1990).

Thirty years after its creation, the Accor group is now in four complementary sectors of activity: the hotel trade, travel agencies, car rental, and service vouchers. In 1997, it entered a new development phase and adopted a new visual identity, which expressed both the strength of its network and the coherence of the group. Accor's new modernized logotype was clear and forceful. More graceful, compact and easier to read, it recomposed the graphic heritage of the group while capitalizing on its strengths and acquisitions (Figure 1).

Figure 1. Accor logotype

Visually, the design forms a triangle; its left side is a prolongation of the A of Accord. The group's brand strategy is clearly visible through this design, which projects a reassuring image. There are fewer birds (three instead of the original five) and they are more precisely drawn; they portray the idea of travelling and movement. This single, emblematic sign – the new logo – is not a rupture with the past, rather it is a progression, opening the way to an even simpler design for the future (a single bird perhaps). It visibly communicates both change and the group's continuity of values and traditions. All the different subsidiaries (Novotel, Ticket-Restaurant, Formule 1, Ibis...) are thus grouped under one banner, using the logo alongside the individual hotel and service brand names. In line with the group's strategy, the logo has become a sign of excellence and cooperation between clients, partners, and in-house teams.

The logo constitutes the main element in brand identity. In the past, military colors showed who was friend or foe; heraldic arms communicated the identity of the family or country. Today, the logo has the same role, both in-house and in "commercial and marketing battles", each company adopts its own "crest" with color code, type face, motto, and slogan.

The logotype or symbol represents a complementary – often indispensable – element for building brand awareness and consolidating associations. The logotype makes the brand easier to recognize and quicker to identify; image processing rather than word processing is in fact easier for the brain.

Thus the logo should:

• Translate, over the long term, the image of the company (and its possible evolution),

• Be easy to spot,

• Be easy to read and to memorize, whatever the media support,

• Be accepted from the outset by the different populations connected with its use (federating role of the brand).

Certain logos also communicate the brand's activity: the Legrand logotype symbolizes an electric circuit, thus evoking the company's position in the electrical sector. Other logotypes are not as referential, but nevertheless clearly identify the company. Used alone, they identify the company on packaging, vehicles or work clothes.

To build a solid image, the logotype should be the graphic transcription of the company, coherently combining the brand, type face and graphics chosen. Different impressions will be created by juggling with the complexity, colors, modernism or classicism of the type face. Narrow or italic letters give a dynamic feeling; *Helvetica*, *Arial* or *Universe* type convey brand force and aggressivity; *Times* suggests balance, elegance and classicism. In the same way, different colors evoke different sectors of activity, concepts, and references depending on the culture. Colors may even have opposing associations: warm colors may evoke a friendly atmosphere – or danger.

Because of the relatively low cost of creating a logotype and its efficacy in terms of memorization, many industrial firms, even small ones, have developed strong visual identities. In fact, the logo is one of the first items of information communicated by the company to its clients or suppliers. A well-designed logo can strengthen a company's position, increase awareness and memorization of the company name, even reinforce its meaning and consolidate brand positioning.

Although it would seem relatively easy to create a logo, it does in fact require serious thought and often creates problems. When creating a logo one must take into consideration the fundamental values of the company, its competence and know-how, markets, partners, etc. The logo should not detract from the existing image of the company but rather reinforce it. When it is necessary to change symbols, there is not only the difficulty of harmonizing the new with the old, but also the problem of re-educating the various target populations (beginning with in-house). However, such changes can inspire new energy, communicating a new company dynamic; the brand identity should progress while preserving the heritage of the former symbol (Aaker, 1991). Often a transitional period is necessary: this is the case of Usinor, number two internationally in steel, which progressively harmonized the visual identity of its subsidiaries (Ascométal, Ugine, Sollac, CLI...) while keeping their name. In 1997, the Usinor Group was thus able to rely upon a solid unified image to reinforce its visibility, particularly on an international level.

Changes in brand or logotype identity often correspond to a change in strategy (new markets, new leadership position, change in sector, etc.) or to major events in the management of the company (take-over, merger, new products, etc.). Michelin is a case in point: the world leader in tires changed logos for its centenary in 1998.

A new logo for Michelin's Centenary Anniversary

The famous Bibendum first appeared in 1898. Drawn by the artist O'Galop – alias Marius Rossillon – it was originally used quite by chance[1]. The character Bibendum has been ranked among the ten most well-known symbols in the world today (Figure 2); However, for Michelin's anniversary, it was modified. With the approach of the year 2000, the decision was made to update the traditional design, which had epitomized the company for almost a century. The difficulty was to modify without spoiling or diluting the image acquired by the brand in more than 170 countries. To do this, all the brand supports and associated items (products, advertising, media, signs, etc.) were collected in each country. In addition, a client and in-house management study was conducted in each geographical zone.

Figure 2. Michelin's former logo: Before the facelift Bibendum is 99 years old

As the personification and embodiment of the Michelin brand, Bibendum carried a promise: to be close to the client, reassuring, available, and service-orientated. Bibendum expressed brand values of confidence and quality. It was important that any change should not break with this continuity, while "rejuvening" Bibendum. The jovial corporate Bibendum had sometimes been perceived as obese. Over the years, he had adopted a variety of postures, giving varying messages, sometimes pushing a tire, waving or running, etc. Because of this, in certain countries, Bibendum was more well-known than the brand Michelin and not necessarily associated with the sector concerned.

The company's new identity created by the Carré Noir agency gave it more weight and assured better coherence and visibility of the brand and logo together. The Michelin name and its sector of activity were reaffirmed next to a more youthful Bibendum. Taller and slimmer, the character became stronger and more dynamic (Figure 3).

Figure 3. The new logo: Bibendum is 100 years old and weighs 100 kilos less

The facelift worked on three areas:
- The color code: the first element of visual recognition. It is recognizable even before shape and the reading of the name. The new design uses the original four colors (blue, white, black, and yellow), but the new identity is more "technological" and brings out the maturity of the company with the color blue. Its universal character communicates its values and the international dimension of the brand. The use of white gives the brand elegance and modernity, in coherence with Bibendum and the brand name. There is visual synergy in the "brand + logo" unit. The color yellow underlines the logo and brings a touch of warmth and sensitivity.
- The Michelin brand: the previous typeface used large capitals to emphasize the solidity of the brand. The capitals were kept, but reworked to give them flow and elegance. The new logo is in italics to convey a sense of movement and innovation.
- Bibendum's new look: the character stands squarely on its two feet, embodying the brand's leadership. He opens his arms in a friendly and human way, welcoming us. It is frank and direct. The visual message thus expresses the image's new dynamism and Michelin's commitment to customer service.

In 1998, the new identity was progressively used on all supports throughout the world. Because of the diversity of applications and the variety of products involved (50,000 items), Michelin used on-line consultation between its design agency and the different management levels concerned to normalize the new brand graphics.

2.   CLASSIFICATION OF DIFFERENT LOGOTYPES

After careful observation of the huge variety of different logotypes, it is clear that a unique definition is hardly possible. Several suggestions, however, can be made. The logotype is:

- a synonym of the brand,
- a summary of the brand,
- a brand attribute (indispensable, useless...),
- a sign (complex, simple...),
- a graphic symbol (incomprehensible, descriptive...),
- a simple shape using stylized writing,
- a mark, pictogram, emblem, initials.

None of these suggestions is satisfactory alone, the definition of a logotype is rather a combination of several ideas. Thus, we can define a logotype as an association of graphic and visual elements which durably and specifically symbolize the brand, the name, and the company (or organization).

The great diversity in the consumer and business-to-business sectors makes categorization difficult. The development of industrial brands has been accompanied by more creative, efficient and coherent logos, and it is interesting to study both their styles and visual identities. Two main groups can be distinguished: logos 'to read' and logos 'to see' (sometimes called 'icotypes') (Veys, 1991).

2.1   "Logos to read" or explicit logos

These include brands which simply transcribe their name as a logo using a particular type face, size or style of lettering. The transcription of the brand name varies greatly in its complexity within this category; it ranges from the simple association of brand name and a unique color (such as the Toshiba brand name written in red) to a stylized rendering in specific colors (Digital) or special graphic design.

Logos which use simple lettering are more versatile and adapt to many different media and a variety of forms: from monochrome posters to a roof sign or a press advertisement (color or black and white). Brands written in capitals or in large characters suggest solidity and strength – those in small letters tend to evoke a notion of service.

Some logos are also recognizable by a particular slanting of the letters (the O in Canon, the E in Intel or in Dell), or even by a particular anomaly in the letters, etc.

In the same category of "logos to read", a sub-group can be created. This includes logos which are easy to read and to which a line or other external element has been added to the name. The logo thus endowed with another dimension, the image enhances the word (Figure 4).

Figure 4. Some examples of explicit logos using simple typography

The Valeo Logo

Founded in 1923, the French company Ferodo originally produced car friction fittings. In 1980, because of the group's diversification into other activities, a new name was adopted with the aim of federating the market offer: Valeo (Figure 5).

Figure 5. Valeo logo

Since then, the group has developed into gearboxes, heating and air-conditioning units, lighting and electrical systems. The different brands of the group – Ferodo, Sofica, SEV Marchal, Cibié, Paris-Rhône, Ducellier – and the various product lines have been organized by branch of activity.

But it was only in 1987 that Valeo decided to specialize in automotive components, developing its expertise in electronics and systems. The international expansion of Valeo had begun, making the company a leader in the world automotive and heavy goods vehicle component supply market. This development has been reinforced by:

• Associations (with Osram Sylvania for example which produce automobile lights),

• Internal growth (Neiman for passenger space, Delanair for temperature control, Blackstone for the engine, Thermal for thermic regulation and air-conditioning systems for heavy goods vehicles and coaches, Univel for passenger safety, Sagar Richards for gearbox synchronizers, etc.),

• Creation of joint ventures (for example, with Siemens Automotive for heating and air-conditioning systems in 1995).

Today, the group specializes in the design, production, and commercialization of automotive and heavy goods vehicle equipment. It has 104 factories and 21 research centers in over twenty countries. Its ten different industrial branches are federated under the corporate name Valeo. Each specialized industrial branch also has a separate sub-brand, examples of this are Valeo Climate Control or Valeo Electronics. This branding policy will allow the company to develop and incorporate other activities in the future, without compromising the advantages gained by the Valeo brand name and the recognized quality image of products in the other branches.

Figure 6. Valeo's different branches of activity: an umbrella logotype couples with a branch of activity

The Valeo logo is a variant of the explicit logo with elements added. It also uses the idea of framing, which isolates and emphasizes the brand. This technique is particularly interesting because the logo can be used on a variety of supports without worrying about the surrounding background colors. A logo with no border must necessarily take into consideration the color of its support: if the background color is black for example, a brand usually printed in black may have to be changed to white. In this way, the border of the framed logo assures its unchanging representation.

We can also add to this category those logos which are in fact the initials of the company or institution they visually represent (IBM, DHL). These 'logos to read' are very similar to the general definition that most lay people would give of a logo: a symbol associated with a brand name (Figure 7).

Figure 7. Some examples of more complex explicit logos

2.2   "Logos to see" or "icotypes"

The symbols often associated with a brand name enable it to be more easily recognized. In the same way, it is easier for the brain to take in a symbol than to read a brand name, it is easier to memorize images than words. The very fact that a symbol can conjure up a wealth of images and emotions makes it a valuable asset for the company. Logos to see, also called 'icotypes', include those which use visual signs to represent the identity of the company (ranging from characters, vegetables, animals, to geometrical shapes, even imaginary figures).

Depending on their nature, such logos facilitate the creation of emotional ties, or help to position the brand, reinforcing and even creating product attributes. Thus, thanks to the presence of a particularly meaningful symbol, the activity of a company may be recognized at a glance. Examples of this are the steel sheeting for the Usinor logo, electricity for Legrand and satellite imagery for the Spot Image logo (Figure 8). It must be said, however, that such logos may be limiting in that they correspond to a specific company activity and thus may have to be changed later if diversification takes place.

Figure 8. Some examples of "logos to see": representative symbols or symbols evoking a particular sector of activity

One of the ways in which symbols can create emotional ties is, as already mentioned, to use characters or real or imaginary animals (Figure 9). This renders the brand more familiar, friendly, less distant; Michelin's Bibendum is a good example of this – in addition to the fact that the tires used to create the figure reinforce the product attributes of the brand. Dulux Valentine's panther is greatly loved by the public, the animal evokes sleek beauty and strength – ideal to describe paint.

Figure 9. Some examples of 'logos to see' with emotion-inducing symbols

Among other logos using symbols, it is interesting to note that some stylize the initials of the brand name. This is the case of the M in Motorola, the AL in Air Liquide or the DE in Dassault Electronique. These "synthesizing" logos "summarize" the brand, giving it an independent existence. This is particularly important for industrial brand visibility policy concerning semi-finished products. Despite its small size, the "shortened" brand is seen on certain components – the M in Motorola can easily be put on a microprocessor for example (Figure 10).

Figure 10. Some examples of summarized "logos to see"

Some logos also use underlining and framing as mentioned above. Geometrical shapes such as squares, rectangles, triangles or circles in a 2D representation (cubes, spheres, pyramids in 3D) are often used in "logos to see" and their association with the many and varied other symbols can inspire confidence, suggest technical performance (square), importance and progress (triangle), quality (circle), reliability and speed, etc. (Figure 11).

Figure 11. Some examples of "logos to see" incorporating various geometrical designs

Besides these traditional shapes, there are numerous other symbols for expressing the company image, such as arrows (which can signify dynamism, opening, expansion, and action). Other types of logos can be grouped according to their structure. In general, they are composed of imaginative forms (often with no particular meaning) or general elements (with no specific link to company activity). These forms are often highly simplified representations, with different colors and suggestive shapes (Figure 12).

By choosing this type of logo, the company is entirely free to decide that a particular color designates an activity, a particular shape suggests a specific product or an element symbolizes a specific company value, etc. The use of a human silhouette is quite common in the chemical industry or life sciences – and also in the service sector.

Figure 12. Some examples of creative "logos to see"

3. SLOGANS AND BRAND SIGNATURES

3.1 Slogans

Slogans are generally very concisely formulated in order to make memorization easier and facilitate automatic association with a product or service, the company and/or the brand advertised. When associated with a logo, a brand, or a company name, the slogan is the translation of the company's key message, its signature and even its philosophy. Just as there is a variety of logos, there are many different types of slogans: from highly descriptive ones to the more general, from those that are almost aphorisms, to those that are quasi esoteric. Slogans are often registered in the same way as the brands themselves.

When a brand name does not adequately describe the activity, it is sometimes necessary to add an "explanatory" slogan as a signature. For example, Alcatel signed with "The Hi-Speed Company", referring to the high speed train and information technology.

Microsoft France has had four different brand signatures (tag lines) in 15 years. The first, chronologically, for the French market emphasized the product: Microsoft products were the first to be so user-friendly. The following signature underlined the importance of the software as a factor of progress – this particular tag line was not welcomed unanimously by constructors and users who considered it as somewhat arrogant. The next signature privileged user benefits. Since 1994 Microsoft Corporation has imposed the tag line: "Where do you want to go today?®" as part of its global management policy. This has been translated or adapted in each country. The French version is the one with the highest unprompted recall:

- 1984-1988   "Software for an easy life"
- 1988-1991   "We civilize computers"
- 1991-1994   "Software to fly"
- Since 1994   "Where do you want to go today?"

Slogans enrich emotions and associations induced by the brand name, facilitating memorization of information concerning activity and values. The slogan is also a complementary support capable of rectifying the image of a brand. Compared to the brand name, which is a real summary of information, the slogan is generally placed in a discreet position – in support – to recall the essential message. Its life is usually shorter than that of the brand name. Because of its discreet role, the slogan can communicate new messages for the brand (new activities, mergers, and new strategies). To avoid changing slogans too often, a general signature is mainly used in order to translate the basic spirit of the company (Table 13a &b).

Table 13a. Some examples of slogans

Company	Activities	Slogans
Air Liquide	Gas	Imagine just what your performance could be
Alcatel	Telecom, energy, transport	The Hi-Speed Company
Chronopost	Express	The masters of time
Elf Atochem	Chemicals	The chemistry of challenges
Compass-Eurest	Catering	Our difference, it's to integrate yours
Hoechst	Chemicals	Finding new ways

Table 13b. Some examples of slogans

Company	Activities	Slogans
IBM	Computers	Solutions for a small planet
Lafarge	Construction	Material to build the world
Lexmark	Computers	To go further in the art of printing
Manpower	Temporary work	The skills network
Microsoft	Software	Where do you want to go today?
Motorola	Semiconductors, telecom	What you never thought possible
Novartis	Health, agriculture, nutrition	New strengths for the science of life
Sodexho	Catering and services	Satisfy a world of differences
Sun Microsystems	Computers	The Network is The Computer
Tetra Pak	Packaging	More than the package
Vivendi	Water, building and Public Works, services, communication	Create what changes your life

Slogans are usually placed under the brand name or to the side. Certain are deliberately placed at a slight distance to give the effect of a brand echo. When logos are communicated in an audiovisual form rather than a written one, the slogans reappear on the screen or on voice-off to reinforce the contents of the brand and its message. Some industrial brands also use jingles or music as a signature.

3.2   Jingles

Jingles are a musical or audible signature added to the brand, logo or slogan. The aim is to facilitate memorization of the brand, its logo, slogan, and message by the memorization of the musical accompaniment.

Although this technique is used less in the industrial sector, it has become quite popular in business to business with the development of industrial brand mass communication to the general public (via television, radio, etc.). It is mainly used, however, by those companies with a mixed clientele (general public/professionals). Service companies such as temporary work agencies, banks and insurance companies also use jingles. Such is the case for France Telecom whose eight characteristic notes are to be found in its television commercials but also radio advertisements targeted towards the professional client. For its audiovisual campaign, IBM has used the same music for the last few years.

The classic example is Intel whose five notes are systematically played in each advertisement every time the brand is mentioned – that means not only when it is an Intel campaign but also those of its clients like Compaq, Hewlett-Packard, Siemens, etc. As the memorization rate of a jingle is high, Intel's reputation and brand awareness grows accordingly. The use of the Intel jingle results from an agreement between the company and its clients to mention the presence of Intel components in their products [2].

4.   THE VISUAL IDENTITY CODE

Because of the diversity of elements which could be associated with a brand and its evolution (changes, abandon, new creations, etc.) it is vital to have a general guidelines containing details of just how the various entities linked to the brand should be used. These guidelines, which are a sort of internal reference document, help the company to coordinate the elements contributing to brand image. They define in a concrete manner how the brand should be written, the reproduction of the logo, any size and placement constraints regarding the logo, slogan, brand-name, and the jingle. In general, these guidelines serve as a visual identity code (even though they may include reference to a jingle). It is of particular importance when companies are set up around the world [3].

Visual identity codes or normalization guidelines define a standard usage and application of the logo, be it on the product, packaging, letter-heading, vehicles or any other visual support used by the company. By respecting the established code – whatever the means of communication – a greater global brand coherence is perceived by the different target populations. The visual code specifically covers:

- the make-up of the logo and the different elements it contains,
- the position of these elements, their size and relative proportions,
- the overall size of the logo and the smallest permissible size when printed,
- the black and white version specifying the nuances of black,
- the exact composition of the colors used (single or four-color),
- the possible different backgrounds on which the logo can be used, and how it should be adapted (colored background, four-color, very dark background, etc.),
- the exact position of the logo on headed paper. The type face and any modifications which may be necessary (spacing, style), size, line spacing, incorporation of the company address and corporate name,
- the exact position of the logo and the details to appear on business cards; the typography and use of color for envelopes, letter paper and bills are also defined,
- the characteristics of the logotype (position, color, typography, size..) defined for all possible applications: on vehicles (stickers...), press ads, television commercials, signs, banners, flags, neon signs, street signs, totems, exhibition hall and stand decor, etc.

The visual identity code enables a company to reinforce its visual identity, making its communication policy more effective. There is greater consistency between brands, as well as a rallying of the company's different activities. Internationalization is facilitated by the adoption of a universal "language" and by the consolidation of a sense of belonging within the company. By controlling the image more closely, the company is better recognized by the market and improves its reputation.

NOTES

1. The origin of the character can be traced back to a combination of heterogeneous events and circumstances:
   - A famous sentence: the slogan launched in 1892 by André Michelin, "*le pneu boit les obstacles*" (meaning approximately the tire can eat up the miles on any road),
   - A pile of tires resembling a human figure, seen by André and Édouard Michelin at the Universal Exposition in Lyon in 1894,
   - A poster artist, Marius Rossillon, who in 1898 suggested a poster in which a heavy character made up of tires raises his glass at a dinner declaring, "Nunc est Bibendum". This is an extract from a text by Horace: *Nunc est Bibendum, nunc pede libero pulsanda tellus, nunc Saliaribus ornare puluinar deorum tempus erat dapibus, sodales* which, by association, evolved into the slogan launched by André Michelin,
   - A race car driver, Théry, who on meeting André Michelin at the end of the Paris-Amsterdam-Paris race declared: "Voilà Bibendum!"
2. See Chapter 3, The Characteristics of Business to Business Communication, 5- The Intel Communication Strategy.
3. See Chapter 10, Managing the International Brand, Air Liquide: the Global Strategy for a World Leader.

REFERENCES

Aaker D. A., (1991), *Managing Brand Equity: Capitalizing on the Value of a Brand Name*, New York, Free Press.

Behaeghel, J., (1990), A Corporate Identity… to be Identified, *Gestion 2000*, p 91-106.

Brun, M. and Rasquinet, Ph., (1996), *L'identité visuelle de l'entreprise au-delà du logo*, Paris, Éditions d'Organisation.

Veys, P., (1991), *Le secteur tertiaire*, Paris, Vuibert.

Chapter 10

Managing the International Brand

Over the last few years several factors have contributed to reducing trade restrictions such as:

- International agreements (Gatt, lower customs duties...),
- Improvements in the means of transport and logistics,
- Rapidity and availability of information,
- Global media coverage,
- Growth of industry worldwide,
- Changes in financial context.

These changes have generated a multitude of business opportunities and international transactions and, at the same time, have greatly increased international competition.

Until recently, industrial sectors tended to evolve within mainly local contexts. But with markets going global at full speed, companies have had to rethink their strategy and include industry in an international environment. This is especially the case in business to business. In this sector, socio-cultural differences are less important than in the consumer sector and it is also where more and more contracts are being signed at a world level. The strategic positions of companies are increasingly defined according to what is at stake worldwide. Often companies can no longer limit themselves to the home market only. They have to operate at a world level and are thus inclined to search for the critical size in their activity.

This has created the need to find new markets for brands. This geographic extension has many reasons such as production over-capacity, opportunities abroad, the ability to better resist to the arrival of global brands on their usual markets or quite simply for reasons of survival. By their very functioning, brands have to be open and to adopt an internationalization policy if they are to be able to evolve, develop and keep their competitive advantage. This policy of going global has already been the subject of marketing and strategy research for several decades and has given rise to new disciplines such as international marketing and strategy. Because of the risks involved (countries which are politically or economically unstable, regulations, technological leaks, etc.), globalization imposes the need for the company to adopt a rigorous approach and to develop a marketing strategy suitable for zones made up of several countries. International marketing strategy and the very principle of internationalization have become essential because firms have to face the growth and size of international trade and also companies converging and overlapping within the "global village". However, the way to implement an internationalization policy has been much debated. On the one hand, there are those who favor a uniform (global) strategy, whereas others argue for adapting strategy, or in other words, customized (localized) marketing.

Driven by the will to reach economies of scale and by the certainty that needs are homogenous, a uniform strategy advocates standardization of the same mix in all countries. On the contrary, a customized strategy favors the systematic adaptation of supply so as to stick as closely as possible to the specifics of the different markets. This almost ideological confrontation has, over time, shown its limits. In fact, companies have very pragmatically opted for strategies which oscillate between these two conceptions of international marketing. Globalization does not necessarily focus on all the elements of the mix (price, position, brand, etc.). The same is true of localized strategy which is only applied to certain elements, for example, product distribution or communication policy. In practice, companies opt for a "*glocal*" strategy rather than choosing either a global or a local strategy. The difficulty for company managers is to determine on what level their marketing strategy and offer need to be adapted.

This difficulty rebounds on brand management internationally. In fact the brand plays a determining role in the international strategy of industrial companies. Brands symbolize the company, its products and/or services and contribute to the added value of the offer. They also provide information and indicate quality by conveying a certain number of values. The brand often represents the first vector of the company and the first perceived element on much sought after new markets. By reflecting very different levels of abstraction, it corresponds to all the images connected with the company, its products and services. The brand also exerts an influence on the way customers perceive the company which it represents. Thus, international buyers use the reputation of industrial brands as one of the criteria when short listing suppliers.

The stakes connected to local or global brand management have to be taken into account when industrial companies plan their international strategy. Both multinational corporations and local companies are concerned by international brand management, the former in order to harmonize their brand management strategies, the latter so as to define their export policy. Therefore it is important to look at different possible brand strategies and to underline their advantages and limitations. The Legrand case shows a successful implementation of a global product-brand strategy. The Air Liquide case notably illustrates the move from local brand strategy to a global brand strategy. The Sodexho-Marriott case shows a mainly global brand strategy whereas the Saint-Gobain Containers case illustrates a dual brand strategy – global or local – depending on the markets targeted.

1. GLOBAL BRAND STRATEGY

1.1 The trend towards the internationalization of industrial brands

Compared to companies which sell to the general public, industrial companies, by their very nature, tend to be more international or even global. In fact, because of the limited number of prospective customers, these companies, be they large or small, often have to look towards international markets very early on. The adoption of international technical norms reinforces this trend to internationalize industrial brands. Thus, industrial goods which are characterized by their technological rather than cultural nature (and so less restricted) can satisfy technically complex, specific, and homogenous needs without requiring too many modifications. The same brand is then likely to have customers situated in several different countries. Moreover, industrial brands increase their presence internationally in diverse ways such as:
- Direct exporting by the export service or by an international sales team,
- Indirect exporting by means of import-export companies, co-operatives, buying groups, distributors and local agents or by a *piggyback* process,
- Transfer of licenses to use production procedures, patents or brands,
- Partnerships such as joint ventures,
- Compensation agreements such as reciprocal buying,
- Direct investment in the different countries in terms of production units, sales offices, etc.

The international dimension makes brand management more complex. In fact, it is a question of taking into account a greater number of parameters: changes which are less predictable and less explicable, a multiplicity of interactions between the company and its environment, increased media coverage, etc. The international presence of the brand is necessarily accompanied by the decision of whether or not to adapt the organization and marketing mix. It is especially a question of determining if the company should maintain the same offer under the same brand. Taking into account the diversity of the possible situations in terms of international presence, of the type of offer and brands concerned (corporate, products, patronymic, evocative, etc.) and the geographical zones targeted, there is no one best brand strategy. It is a question of companies measuring the interests and drawbacks linked to their choice of a global brand strategy for their products or for their own company corporate name.

LEXIC BY LEGRAND: A FEDERATING PRODUCT-BRAND

Created in 1896 in Limoges, France, the Legrand company today is a leader in low voltage fittings and accessories for industrial, service, and home usage. With a 2.3 billion euro turnover and a workforce of about 25,000 people in the world, Legrand has become a multinational in 56 countries while preserving its regional roots; it is present under the corporate brand as well as those of its subsidiaries (Bticino in Italy, Pass & Seymour, Ortronics, the Watt Stopper in the US, etc.).

Legrand designs, manufactures, and commercializes a very wide range of products including all of the functions and cabinets required for complete electrical installations (Figure 1).

Figure 1. Legrand logotype

Each electrical installation must be controlled by one or more distribution boards providing the protection of circuits, people, and additional control, programming, and signalling functions, among others. The boards are made from different sized cabinets depending on the installation and the quantity of units used (disjunctors, differentials, circuit breakers, clocks, operating boxes, etc.). The Legrand range includes all of the above elements and by the 1990's had become relatively heterogenous.

Defining a new "distribution-protection" range

Legrand decided to replace the former range by an entirely new series, completely redesigned to be perfectly homogenous and to better meet the requirements of distributors, electricians, and users. The range offers numerous plus-products such as:

- Easy setting up: a crimping tool for even safer connections, a mixed print screw head compatible with flat or Philips screwdrivers allowing manual or automatic screwing, easy association of differential blocks and control aids, etc.
- Higher performance: performance and safety up to 1600 A, reduction of the space required for cabling, etc.
- Easy locating of circuits on the front side of the unit.

In defining the new product offer, it was important to respect the needs of professionals by offering complete, more homogenous, and more efficient "distribution-protection" systems. The new range was developed with the following objectives in mind:

- Simple, easy to understand, and rapid installation,
- Safety of personnel and equipment: both for professionals and home users,
- Freedom: user-friendly and comfortable installation, respect for working methods.

The new range was commercialized in different phases. Products were first launched in the service sector, then in industry, and finally in the household market. Every year, new additions are added to the range to adapt to the specific norms and customs of different countries around the world.

Creating Lexic, an international product-brand

To establish the new range, Legrand sought to develop a product-brand that would give it a strong and coherent identity. In addition to being a guarantee, the product brand had to make it easier for professionals to recognize and memorize the new range, ensuring its inclusion in specifications.

The new name and identity had to meet several requirements. First, the product brand had to be truly international with a name that could be easily pronounced in over 20 countries without any negative connotations in the different languages involved. Furthermore, the brand had to reflect the full extent of the range and product advantages. Another consideration was that certain product names (in particular with the reference "X" such as DX, DNX, or DPX disjunctors) were maintained in the range and had to be reflected in the new name.

The name "Lexic" was finally chosen for the new coherent range including all of the distribution-production components and equipment. Thanks to its phonetic and semantic similarity with the word "lexical", this name suggests a more complete range and includes an "X", which is also evocative and easy to pronounce in most European and American languages.

Brand identity: the importance of symbol

The identity of the product brand begins with its graphic design and in particular the branding on the front side. In a very limited area, the branding includes technical characteristics (references, performance) and identifying elements. The Legrand brand is black between two red lines. The reference is included in a red rectangle. For greater brand visibility, Lexic is associated with a symbol which comes directly from the product branding. This symbol is a red rectangle with a white dot, identical to the rectangle including the reference on the front of the units.

An international visual identity code was established for Lexic to ensure the stylistic unity of communication on this range in all the countries where it is sold (Figure 2).

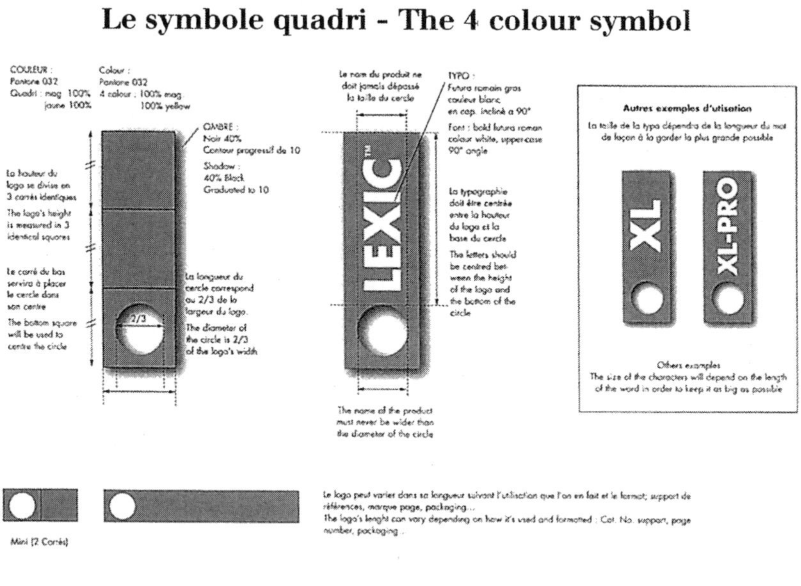

Le symbole quadri - The 4 colour symbol

Figure 2. The choice of the logo: a red rectangle with a white point

All of the products in the range now use the red rectangle with a white dot. The Lexic brand can also be printed repeatedly on point of sales advertising for greater visibility. Assembly instructions and any indications on packaging were also standardized as these products are manufactured in different factories in France and Europe.

The Lexic visual identity code includes:

• Specific rules defining the use of the name and the symbol: typography, color, position, etc.,

• Examples of usage on different communication media: documents, point of sale, displays, catalogs, promotions, gadgets...,

• A visual type for coverings, which can be used depending on the technical specifications of different countries,

• Free photographs of worksites.

All these visuals are subjected to the overall Legrand visual identity code before finalization.

Launching the Lexic brand

Considering the strategy of progressively launching the new product range, Legrand could not immediately reveal the new name. At first Legrand used the Lexic symbol without mentioning the name to launch the new XL cabinets. The XL name was integrated into the rectangle.

A "teasing" strategy was used to announce the launching of the Lexic range: a question mark whose dot was formed from the Lexic symbol. Later, the Lexic brand was finally revealed.

With later launchings, a visual family developed around the federating symbol and the Lexic brand. The symbol used first in France for the launching of the XL distribution cabinets and enclosures, today internationally federates the entire "distribution-protection" range (Figure 3).

Figure 3. Examples of Lexic documents from different countries

For the launching of Lexic, commercial and technical aids in line with the visual identity code were provided for the Legrand sales force and professionals. These included technical demonstration kits and samples, point of sale displays, brochures and catalogs, SL-Pro software (assembly assistance, etc).

Furthermore, to backup sales, gain new customers and increase loyalty, promotional operations were launched (Figure 4). Professional customers were given samples, catalogs, and other gifts such as folders or notepads to incite them to try the Lexic range.

 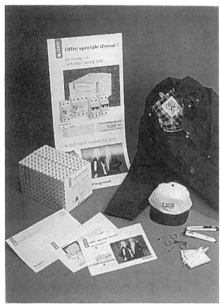

Figure 4. Some examples of Lexic advertising and promotional aids

The Legrand case illustrates a company whose international strategy is based on a product brand. Thus before looking at the Air Liquide case, it is useful to present the objectives of a global brand strategy.

1.2   Factors favoring the adoption of a global strategy

Global brand strategy refers to the use of a common name, symbol, image, signature, and slogan for all markets. A global brand therefore supposes that all international markets can be approached in the same way given that they all have the same expectations and perceptions. It also supposes that brands function in the same way and play the same roles whatever the country considered. This includes offering the same operational benefits of security and guarantee, identification and indication. Global brands offer advantages such as saving time and effort and facilitating performance. In the industrial context, these suppositions are often confirmed and so make the use of a global brand particularly relevant. This is why Tetra Pak is a global corporate brand which also offers a portfolio of global brand products such as Tetra Prisma, Tetra Brik, Tetra Rex, Tetra Top, etc. In the same way, Intel is a global brand with the same identity in all the countries where it is present.

Several factors argue in favor of adopting a single global brand. On top of the technical and technological considerations already mentioned, transnational media and the Internet also offer a homogenizing character favoring the development of global brands. The visibility of the brand can in fact be considerably increased by international presence and exposure. The manager who is doing business abroad is therefore satisfied to note the presence of brands which exist in his own country. In general, several combined factors lead to choosing a global brand strategy. It is especially a question of marketing, commercial, financial and organizational motives:

- Making savings by minimizing costs in terms of brand supports, advertising, general working and structure thanks to "standardization" or harmonization of the brand (development costs spread out over a market, better distribution of resources and investments),
- Enhancing the company and the investments which have been successively devoted to the brand,
- Reducing market fluctuation and diluting industrial and business risks,
- Increasing the reputation of the brand and improving its image,
- Improving the perceived quality of the brands whose international presence is a sign of expertise, specific quality, sturdiness and guarantee,
- Increasing the brand's visibility by making its presence more frequent,
- Increasing the brand's power and strength notably in terms of credibility and legitimacy by an international extension,
- Contributing to increasing international buyers' trust in the brand: the stability of the brand internationally is considered as proof of superior performance and efficiency,
- Making it easier for the brands to be short-listed by international buyers,
- Benefiting from a good image and reputation which have already been acquired in a geographical zone in order to guarantee its offer in another larger region,
- Making it easier to transfer acquired experience and better solutions tested by the brand from one market to another,
- Increasing the brand's persuasion power and so making it easier to extend the brand to other categories of goods,

- Consolidating the company's "cultural leadership" and developing the brand's autonomy,
- Allowing the company to quickly and solidly construct a new global identity for itself, made necessary following takeovers or mergers for example,
- Allowing worldwide advertising campaigns to be launched by relying on the development of a multinational media audience.

Global brand strategy is therefore essentially pursued in order to rationalize management (economic, enhancement), to improve the brand's reputation and image and make brand development easier (extensions, launches, etc.). Possessing a single international brand corresponds to a brand extension strategy, thereby allowing the company to capitalize on and extend its brand to other products.

It also fits into the framework of a global strategy: the competitive position of the brand in one country can be influenced by its position in another and more largely by the international stakes involved. The use of a global brand is particularly efficient when it is present in zones where there is no reference and where local competition is relatively weak. A global brand strategy can also be applied to new activities as there are no past values and references. This is the case in high tech sectors such as computers, electronics, or telecommunications. In this type of sector, the brand depends on strong innovation and so tends to be imposed everywhere without any modifications.

Likewise, a single global brand strategy is particularly relevant to markets where the purchases are negotiated and made at a world level. This is notably the case for capital goods brands or entering goods brands: once the goods have been bought, the same brand can then be found in the customer's operations. Finally, like designer labels in the clothing trade, it is possible to opt for a global brand when it represents a designer's label or signature. In industrial design, the names of people like Philippe Starck or Norman Foster have become genuine international brands.

AIR LIQUIDE: THE GLOBAL STRATEGY OF A WORLD LEADER

Founded in 1902, Air Liquide is an international group specializing in industrial and medical gases and adapted services. Within the first ten years of existence, the group set up in Canada, Greece, Japan and Sweden in order to produce industrial gases there where the customers use them. Air Liquide rapidly gained a foothold on the world market (Figure 5).

Figure 5. Air Liquide Logotype

Today Air Liquide has 125 subsidiaries in more than 60 countries, has nearly 29,000 employees and over one million customers all over the world. Its annual turnover is more than 6.5 billion euros.

Customer convenience and performance improvement policy

Along with engineering, industrial gases make up 70% of the group's activities. Regarding gases, Air Liquide aims to cater to both individual entrepreneurs as well as huge industrial companies. Over the last few years, Air Liquide has set up Regional Service Centers in each country so as to offer better service to its regional and local customers. This decentralized structure allows the numerous regional teams to have greater customer awareness and to bring them a tangible added value: customer gains in terms of easier management, better productivity, reduced costs, respect of the environment. In the same way, Air Liquide caters to customers belonging to world industrial sectors such as iron and steel, chemicals, refining, glass, energy, electronics, metallurgy, foodstuffs, health, space and paper pulp, etc. In order to better meet the requirements of such sectors, Air Liquide has specific teams in charge of those markets at a world level.

The permanent sharing of market and new technology experiences enables the company to make offers which are continually better adapted to customers' needs.

These teams put the group's technological developments at customers' disposal and offers them the same high level of service everywhere in the world. Apart from gases and usual services such as piped oxygen and nitrogen, Air Liquide also offers its big industrial customers innovating solutions and extends its offers to include other products such as hydrogen, steam, or energy. The combined production of the last two, while respecting the environment, is also a cost-saving factor which in turn contributes to improving performance.

This strategy of being near the customers (intimacy) has resulted in the setting up of small, autonomous units all over the world which satisfy industrial demand and fully take the customer relationship into account. However, for historical reasons, this worldwide expansion has not been accompanied by a genuine international brand image. The gas subsidiaries in particular, have had diverse and varied names: SIO in Italy, La Oxigena in Argentine, Oxigeno do Brasil in Brasil, Liquid Air in the USA, SEO in Spain, Canadian Liquid Air in Canada, Teisan in Japan, etc. Furthermore, the visual identities of its subsidiaries were well established by means of a long term local brand strategy. This led to Air Liquide having a globally confused and dispersed image which prevented the group from taking full advantage of a coherent image. It also prevented them from internationalizing its research, marketing, finance and recruitment. During business negotiations with international groups, the sales teams often had to remind the latter that they were in fact a world leader in industrial and medical gases.

In 1987, Air Liquide decided to move towards a global brand strategy so as to extend the international influence of its brand and to accompany the development of its international activities.

Corporate identity harmonization

The implementation of a global strategy for the Air Liquide brand was decided in order to:
 • Bring the company closer to its customers,
 • Illustrate its global size,
 • Show its ability to make homogenous offers to its customers all over the world.

So as to increase its brand impact, Air Liquide standardized its graphic image in 1987. A visual identity code was drawn up so as to, first of all, normalize the way in which the gas subsidiaries' names were written by means of a common logo. The advantages of having just one logo were that the group's identity was personalized and symbolized, and also the company's values were better reflected. Moreover it allowed the company to organize its approach in a more coherent way. The generalization of the visual identity code and color system was the first step towards bringing the subsidiaries together. A normalization procedure was carried out to harmonize the variations so as to obtain a more homogenous visual unity. The visual identity had to be respected if the company's image and reputation were to be improved (Figure 6).

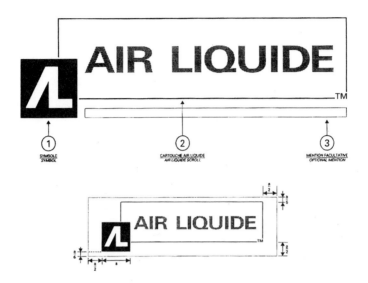

Figure 6. The logo: general principles relating to the logo's components and zones

However, the extremely varied names of the some 120 subsidiaries prevented the group from taking advantage of a coherent global image (Figure 7).

The title phrase "an Air Liquide Group company" was far too discreet. The visibility ratio of the Air Liquide brand to that of the local subsidiary was only 18%: only the subsidiary's brand was being remembered.

Everybody, whether they were customers, students, financial experts or public authority representatives were more inclined to know Teisan, SIO or Oxigeno do Brasil.

Figure 7. Example of a reference to the former Japanese brand name Teisan alongside the
Air Liquide logo for reasons of corporate image

In 1993, following both internal (subsidiaries) and external studies on its image policy, Air Liquide decided to develop its global brand strategy. The group entered another stage of its globalization process by deciding to adopt the brand name "Air Liquide" on the five continents in the short run. On markets which were starting to become more and more international, Air Liquide thus applied a global brand strategy in all of its industrial gas subsidiaries. For international customers, this step was a sign of Air Liquide's ability to provide them with homogenous products all over the world, in accordance with their requirements. Moreover, the standardized brand image "Air Liquide" highlighted the fact that the strong local presence of Air Liquide was based on the resources and competence of a world leader.

One of the strategic priorities consisted in asserting the international status of the group. It was a question of establishing a strong international identity in the eyes of its customers, many of which were operating worldwide. The mere name Air Liquide clearly identified the technological, marketing and financial know-how of the group everywhere in the world. Moreover, this unified image aimed at making its staff feel they belonged to the same group.

A new visual identity code was then developed specifically defining the usage of the new united brand image of Air Liquide for all the usual vectors (buildings, factories, storage, vehicles, writing paper, envelopes, etc). The "L" (as in L'air liquide) was suppressed as it was considered to be too French. The charter went as far as specifying the amount of exterior lighting required on company sites in order to optimize the legibility of Air Liquide's identity around the clock. From then on, the brand was presented on the gas market and had to put forward a strong and homogenous image enhancing the company's dealings throughout the world despite competition and enabling customers to clearly recognize the group's identity. In more than 500 company sites the buildings, storage, vehicles, employee uniforms, and communication aids were modified to introduce unity, standardization, and perceived quality harmonization. The Air Liquide brand increased its visibility by having a greater presence on its markets.

On national markets, regionalism and a single image complement each other: the Air Liquide brand expresses the competence and experience of an international group catering to local and reactive structures. It reinforces the autonomous units situated all over the world and backs the development of activities which bring the company closer to the customer such as maintenance or equipment installation. The visual identity code specifically defined the new standard logo (showing the brand and its graphic structure) as well as instructions on using complementary optional references allowing the subsidiaries to assert their local image if necessary. References such as the activity, specialization, geographical source even the former brand name could be added to the logo when they represented a genuine business asset. Moreover, it was a sign of cultural respect for the regions in which Air Liquide was present.

Although the subsidiaries' brand names were changed, their corporate names for example: Three Incorporated or La Oxygena SAIC, remained the same: these latter were still put on invoices and paychecks along with the Air Liquide brand name (Table 8).

Table 8. Global brand strategy: Air Liquide brand adopted by its subsidiaries

Corporate name	Brand	Product or range name
SIO	Air Liquide	Aligal, Atal, Arcal...
Canadian Liquid Air	Air Liquide	Floxal...

In 1995, a significant effort was made to establish the Air Liquide brand in the field. The new image was applied to thousands of vehicles, stock and regional service centers. The principle of a single brand was next extended to the group's health activities under the brand "Air Liquide Santé". In 1996, its welding activities followed suit ("Air Liquide Welding").

All these actions reinforced the global image of Air Liquide. At the same time, they relied on:

• A new architectural policy for the Group's establishments so as to give an image of quality,

• A harmonization of marketing literature,

• A new visual identity for the group's products and equipment.

In fact, a brand's internationalization has to be accompanied by actions carried out at a world level. The Air Liquide Group wanted to harmonize the identity of its products and its branded products. Taking into account the diversity and wealth of its portfolios, the rationalization used had to be quick and easy to implement. That is why the solution applied to product recognition principally concerned the color. The Air Liquide's logo colors – white, blue and red – were chosen depending on the markets. For example, white was the main color chosen for its medical activities whereas to project its image of high technology services, three quarters white and a quarter blue were chosen. To project strength and soundness, blue became the principal color for its welding equipment (Table 9).

Table 9. Colors chosen to represent the different sectors

Equipment	Colors allocated
Gas	75% white, 25% blue and a red spot
Medical	90% white, 10% blue
Welding	80% blue, 20% white

This product design harmonization strengthened the coherence of the products and services offered. Product brands also underwent the same changes. Numerous international parties were associated with carrying out these modifications. The variety and fantasy of the symbols which had existed up to then can be illustrated by merely juxtaposing the former logos of Alnat, Floxal, Blue Shield, Arial and Alix (Figure 10).

Figure 10. Some examples of product brands before the identity harmonization process

To homogenize product brands, it was necessary to introduce specific rules regarding the creation and use of logos which enabled product brands to have both their own personality as well as common features (Figure 11). Specific logos were developed for certain product brands and the same typography was used for all the products (Antique North Olive Italic in capital letters).

ALARC · ALECT · ALCASTING · AIROXAL · ALIGAL
MAGNUM · ASPAL · ALNAT · ALPHAGAZ · ATAL · ALIX
ALIGAL · ALIX R · ARCAL · ALGLASS · ALBLACK · ALIX W
ALARC AS · ALIX LT · ALIGAL FLO · ALARC PC
BICONE · BARAL · BLUESHIELD · CARBOMAT
CLAUSPLUS · COSOLV · CLEANBLAST · CONSPAL CLAL
CLIP-ON · CRYOSAUCE · CRYLENE · CARGAL · COMPACT
VSA · CRUSTFLOW · CRYODROP · CRYOSAS
CARBOSUB · CARBOSTAT · CRISTAL · CUTAX
CARBOVAL · DINEXTRAL · DROPPEL · DATAL
EXELLENE · EMIXAL · ELOXAL · ECOGAL · FLAMOXAL
FLAMAL · FLAMATIC · FLOXAL · FERENE
FLUXOMATIC · GRAVITAL · GAZAL · HEMIXAM · ISOXAL
INARC · KIT CRYO-B · KYRENE · KRYTENE · LASAL
LUCIFER · LUCIFLAM · LUCIPACK · LOGATOME · MAPP
MIXAL · MINICOOL MXI · MEDAL · NERTAL · NOXALIC
NOXAL · NATAL · NOVITOME · NICOOL · OXYFLAM
OXAL · OXYMECC · PRACTICGAZ · PROTOXAL
ROLLERFLAM · ROCJET · RANGER REMBO · SOLVAL
SCAL · STABIGAZ · SILVERLINE SAROX · SPRAL
SILVERSAS · SPAL SAF · SPIROTECHNIQUE · STEROXAL
SULFIMETRAL SPI · SAFMATIC · TURBOXAL · TERAL
TETRENE · TOM POUSSE · TOM JAUNE · TELEFLO
ULTRAFREEZE · VENTOXAL · VIDOXAL · VINIKIT
ZIPSAUCE · ZIPFREEZE · ZIPROLL · ZIPFLOW · ZIPSAS

Figure 11. Typography used for Air Liquide's product names

Product brand logos were attributed according to specifically defined graphic principles (Figure 12):

• Presence of a blue square, symbol of Air Liquide's identity since 1960 (1),

• Use of typography: blue outside the square, white inside the square (2),

• Creation of a symbol representing the product or service so as to express its personality (3). For example, a flame representing its welding activity.

Figure 12. Blue square (1) + typography (2) + symbol (3) = logo

Progressively, Air Liquide product brands such as Arcal, Lasal, Spran, Aligal, Alix, or Alphagaz adopted the defined identity. Characterized by high visibility and a strong personality, they could now take better advantage of advertising (Table 13).

Table 13. Examples of Air Liquide brands

Brands	Products or Services
Floxal	Nitrogen production service on customer's site
Datal	Video surveillance + management service
Arcal	Ranges of argon based welding gas mixture
Aligal	Range of gases used in foodstuff preservation
Aljet	Oxygen combustion system for rotary iron melting ovens

The harmonization of product and corporate identity gave the Air Liquide group a global homogenous image, facilitating advertising and the projection of the brand's values at a world level (Figure 14). In 1996, Air Liquide launched a worldwide advertising campaign to prove that its global brand strategy represented a genuine asset for growth. It was a question of strengthening its image and developing its international reputation.

EXEMPLES   **EXAMPLE**

Figure 14. Examples of product brand logos

International brand management: the international image identity guide

Air Liquide drew up an international communication and marketing visual identity code so as to coherently manage the brand especially regarding advertising. This charter specified the framework of the advertising policy decided upon. It was a question of reflecting the group's personality: total availability and active listening to customers. The group's identity is built on "bringing added-value to customers". Externally, this identity is expressed by the characteristic Air Liquide slogan "Imagine what your performance could be". So as to assert the spirit of the global strategy, it was essential to respect the editorial and visual codes defined. The Air Liquide image was highly regarded by its partners and clients.

The international image identity guide defined the company's values and the specific global language of the brand. The guide specified:

• The editorial charter: hierarchy of texts, style of writing, number of words per paragraph, those expressions to favor, those to avoid, the tone to use ("you" for the customer and "we" for Air Liquide),

• Style of layout: visual balance, typography,

• Style of visual: the sky as the visual generic representing "Air of Life" (Air de la Vie), centering of the company's blue and white colors,

• Style of brochures: sizes, space reserved for visuals, colors, typography,

Applied coherently to the whole group, this style has given new life to the Air Liquide corporate brand.

World advertising campaign

Thanks to the brand strategy adopted, the Air Liquide brand successfully went global and increased its visibility. The next step consisted in developing the reputation of the Air Liquide name, especially regarding customers and the group's prospects. Air Liquide had a long tradition of discretion in terms of company advertising. In fact, Air Liquide only advertised occasionally, depending on local needs and using the names of its local subsidiaries. The discreet reminder "an Air Liquide Company" showing that a subsidiary belonged to the group did not allow the Air Liquide brand to have a significant impact on customers. Moreover, the image put forward by the Air Liquide brand was often very different from one subsidiary to another in the world. The company did not have just one image, but several and none of them were well defined. In these conditions, it was difficult to elaborate an international campaign.

At the end of 1995, Air Liquide prepared a world international campaign with the help of DDB & Co., an advertising agency chosen for its international experience. An international work team carefully thought about what best characterized the group so as to single out a common position for the Air Liquide brand: industrial gas specialist supplying added value to its customers.

In June 1996, the communication managers of the seven main countries where Air Liquide was located (France, Germany, Italy, Spain, the United States, Canada and Japan which together represent nearly 70% of the group's turnover) defined the positioning and the strong message of this campaign. They decided on the following positioning: "Air Liquide, industrial performance inventor". This fulfilled the group's objective of highlighting the common characteristic of its activity worldwide. So as to ensure optimal adaptation of the campaign in different countries, several messages were elaborated taking into account local realities and the different types of clientele. Each subsidiary was then able to adapt the campaign to its own national context by insisting more or less on one message or another. Once the global concept was defined, the slogan, lead-ins, and visuals had to be found. The campaign slogan "Imagine what your performance could be" and the lead-ins were overall the same for the seven countries. Sometimes they just had to be adapted for language or cultural reasons. The messages were built on customer expectations. The five advertisements produced (single or spread) were pre-tested. They were designed around a sort of dialogue in which Air Liquide answered customer questions. For example, in one advertisement it was asked: "You want every type of industrial gas, applications and related service, anywhere in the world? Let's talk". The texts were set off by visuals chosen deliberately for their universal character in order to illustrate and convey the scope of their business (Figure 15).

Figure 15. Air Liquide's worldwide press campaign

Apart from the generic message of the group's activity suitable for all countries, the advertisements had specific themes focusing on very big international customers, big national customers, small customers, commitment to service, and new applications. Thus the campaign reflected the nature and strength of Air Liquide's offer: the ability to bring added value to its customers through its adapted products and services, the resources and expertise of an international group accessible through a flexible and reactive proximity structure, and in-depth knowledge of its customers' activities.

The media plan included a three-phrase launch over fifteen months. The campaign started first in America in October 1996, then in Europe and Japan in February 1997, and finally in 1998, in the international trade press such as *Chemical Week*, *Semiconductor Electronics*, *Hydrocarbon Processing*, *Pulp and Paper International*, and *Glass Digest*, among others. Taking account the target, the trade press was favored over economic reviews. Each country adapted its media plan and bought its space depending on the structure of its clientele and the local trade press. Finally, the campaign launch was accompanied by an internal communication operation (special issue of the internal journal Alizé, advertisements, etc.) which allowed the staff to be informed in advance of the objectives of the world campaign.

Using essentially the trade press, the campaign confirmed that the Air Liquide group was physically near its customers and integrated in the local industrial fabric. Its objective was to satisfy customer needs and concerns about performance improvement by putting the group's internationally acquired expertise at their customers' disposal. The 1998 campaign enabled the Air Liquide brand to strengthen its reputation and to better its image with concepts such as proximity, services, and innovation, while at the same time differentiating the group from its competitors. Overall, the global brand strategy pursued by Air Liquide enabled it to associate the resources and know-how of a group with a global image to that of strong local proximity with autonomous teams at the customers' service.

1.3   Precautions and limits of a global strategy

Global brand strategy is more often adopted for the corporate brand which generally functions as a global guarantee on the offer than for product brands which often have to adapt to the countries targeted. In fact, a global product does not necessarily mean a global brand: sometimes it is preferable to modify the product brand name or to create a specific one for certain markets targeted. For example, this is why Ricoh photocopiers are sold under the name Savin in the United States and under Nashua in France. The company can decide to adapt its global brand policy, for example by translating it into Cyrillic writing for Russia or Katakana writing for Japan. If the company wants to optimize its choice, it must favor a global brand which corresponds to a universal concept or which is linked to a characteristic of the product or service it sells.

This is perfectly illustrated by the group La Générale des Eaux's name change in 1998 (see Chapter 8 for further information on this case of name creation: pp 188-195). The group's top management decided to look for a new name so as to develop its international reputation and an image better suited to its activities.

Tests carried out in France, Italy, Spain, United Kingdom, Germany and the United States led the group to opt for the name Vivendi. This joyful name conveys global notions of life and movement which correspond to the group's values and its vocation to supply "professional proximity services which improve daily life". The name Vivendi, pronounced the same way in every language, has enabled the construction of a strong international reputation around this global corporate brand.

If a company wants to develop a global product brand name – it is better to choose an international name which can be easily exported to other countries or else to invent a name. On the other hand, brand names which are too descriptive in one language are often very hard to internationalize. Once they are exported, they lose their meaning and their substance. That is why "neutral" brand names are becoming more and more frequent as they have no meaning. It is then a question of elaborating the contents.

Global brand strategy is not always applied to corporate brands. Because of their internationalization, companies sometimes have to modify or even change their name so as not to be offensive in other countries or quite simply to have a name which can be pronounced. They can also be forced to do so because of the presence of a similar or identical brand on a target market or one which has already been patented by another company. For companies to sell their goods under the one brand, they have to redefine or readjust their brands while at the same time making sure that the new name does not dilute the established identity. This is the case of new global brands which have been created following takeovers and mergers. Their role is to be an umbrella brand and include in the one entity, all of a group's activities. For example, Novartis was created after the Sandoz-Ciba Ceigy merger or Aventis (merger of Hoechst and Rhône-Poulenc).

Generally, as the immaterial, affective, psychological and socio-cultural values of a brand can differ depending on the country concerned, the global brand strategy needs to be adapted and managed so as to suit local requirements. For example, the cultural values related to a brand are very hard to transfer from one country to another. The same idea can have different meanings depending on the country. Using the same brand name in every country does not necessarily mean that the brand stays closest to its key concept. Therefore, global brand strategy cannot always be systematically and unilaterally applied.

When deciding to globalize their brands, companies have to take into account the international potential of every name in their brand portfolio and the number and type of countries concerned (to include geographical, demographic, economic, political, cultural and linguistic factors). They also have to evaluate the risks involved should they drop a specific name in favor of a brand name which would be unknown on markets. It is therefore necessary to carefully study the brand's different attributes in order to evaluate the relevance of a brand globalization. This can define the homogenous "prisms" of a brand's identity, i.e. the main elements which make up the brand or in other words the heart of the brand. The brand's internationalization often reveals its strong and weak points. Apart from this fundamental basis of a brand, it is a question of meticulously defining the global visual identity code to adopt and also the possibilities of common advertising creations (key words, slogans, style, typography, what should be avoided and the major outlines of the approach to take, etc.). Every brand of the 3M group is global by vocation. Therefore an internal document "Brand Asset Management" was drawn up providing the brand management framework. This document, for example, prohibits the creation of any form of local brand and also lays out the conditions for creating new global brands or names or brand nicknames (first names). This brand portfolio management enables newly created brand names to live, to be valued and to increase their power.

Finally, another limitation to using a global corporate brand name has to be mentioned. This limitation concerns the risks of using a single brand name. Information published about the company such as accidents, social or legal problems can have serious consequences on the brand image or even a negative impact on sales and on the group's financial health.

1.4   Brand globalization levels

The level of brand globalization varies depending on its components. One of the main elements of the image, i.e. the brand name, is generally standardized. When using a global brand, it is necessary to be careful that there are no negative connotations and that the name can be pronounced and registered in all the countries targeted. Although most firms do not want to modify their strong global identity acquired on a lot of foreign markets, for legal, regulatory or semiological reasons, some companies are forced to develop a specific brand name for certain countries while at the same time trying to follow the group's global visual identity code.

The graphic identity and logo are also very often global: they represent an essential anchor for the brand. For the brand's unity and cohesion it is important that the brand have the same code in all countries, even if its name is different. In fact, customers have to be able to recognize and find the brand all over the world: it has to project the same concept everywhere. The visual identity code includes all the requirements linked to the brand's identity and to its good use. It is necessary to validate the emblems, symbols or images related to the brand as their meanings can considerably differ depending on the country. Any symbolic representation which can be damaging anywhere, even at a local level, should be avoided. The ideal situation would be that companies, when starting a business, foresee the future possibility of going international and take this factor into account when deciding on its name, registering their brand name and creating their visual identity. On top of audio or visual brand signatures, a lot of companies such as Alcatel use the same global slogan "The Hi-Speed Company". This can sometimes be translated into other languages like Microsoft's "Where do you want to go today" which in France, has become "Jusqu'où irez-vous?"

In 1998, 3M decided to launch a new logo for its Scotchgard brand in order to be better identified throughout the world. Uniformity is indeed essential for brand capitalization and to enhance a competitive advantage. Including a written description of the product and of its application fields, the Scotchgard logo was designed to facilitate the translation-adaptation of these mentions in other languages.

Rather than globalize their logo, some companies prefer to take advantage of their subsidiaries' logos so as not to undermine their acquired image nor their local brand's own identity. It can also keep these logos to avoid any negative reaction due to a brutal visual change or the arrival of a foreign brand. In fact, although a global brand has a worldwide vocation, it also has cultural connotations as well as national roots to which its image is often strongly associated. Renaming a local brand with a strong identity undermines its integrity. It is very risky to replace it by a lesser known global brand. Rather, single brand strategy consists more in pursuing a global dynamic while maintaining a strong presence at a local level.

SODEXHO-MARRIOTT: ADOPTING A WORLDWIDE IDENTITY

Sodexho (Société d'Exploitation Hôteliere) was created and presided since then by Pierre Bellon in 1966. In 1995, it formed an alliance with the British company Gardner Merchant and the Swedish company Partena to become the first group in the industrial catering business worldwide. Now, nearly 150,000 people of 70 different nationalities were employees of the group and nearly 80% of its turnover (9,2 billion euros) was made abroad thanks to its 13,500 sites in 62 countries.

Sodexho is the leader in several fields of service activities:

• N°1 in the catering business worldwide (companies, public administrations, schools, universities, hospitals, establishments for the elderly, etc.),

• N°1 in essential services to industry worldwide (oil rigs, mines, industrial building sites),

• N°2 in service vouchers worldwide (restaurant vouchers, gift vouchers, gas vouchers, job vouchers, medical vouchers, etc.),

• N°1 in port and river tourism.

This strong international dimension was an essential characteristic of the group and it was further strengthened by its alliances with Gardner Merchant and Partena. So as to symbolize its successful alliances and its new situation, the group decided to look for a new visual identity. This identity was the first step of the global brand policy decided by the group (Figure 16).

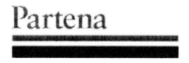

Figure 16. Visual identities of Sodexho, Gardner Merchant and Partena before their alliance

First step: creating a new visual identity

An international task force was formed in order to think about how to change the logo. The initial idea of creating a totally new logo was dismissed. Their second idea of creating a new logo using the existing logos of Sodexho, Gardner Merchant and Partena was preferred. In addition to the three logos, the creation also had to take into consideration the defined specifications and the criteria which the new logo had to fulfill:

• A harmonious combination,

• The human dimension,

- An international scale,
- Reliability,
- Flexibility.

This last aspect was especially important for Sodexho's international strategy: in fact the emblem had to be usable by all of the group's companies. These conditions led the task force to look for:

- A more human style of writing so as to minimize the industrial aspect of "Sodexho",
- A friendlier logo so as to better put forward one of the vital characteristics of its activity.

The brand name Sodexho Alliance was retained so as to specifically reflect the group's philosophy founded on the will to respect the history, culture and personality of the women and men in the group. The word Alliance was strictly associated with the name of the holding which brings together the human energies of the different subsidiaries. The chosen name offered the possibility to include other companies in the future. The company's new logo was also created so as to be able to accompany its international development (Figure 17).

Figure 17. Sodexho Alliance's new identity

The star was the essential emblem of the logo as it symbolized the unity of all the group's companies in the world. In fact, the logo had 5 blue stars in a semi-circle, to represent the five continents. Already present in the Gardner Merchant logo, the star was seen as the most vivid symbol to emphasize dimension. Easy to remember, the star allowed the new visual identity to be instantly recognized. Its visual impact fulfilled the need for an aatractive and pleasant looking logo. The star is an immediately recognizable symbol. As it is shiny and bright, it gives rise to positive feelings. For thousands of years the star has played a role in legends, tales and mythology throughout the five continents. It also figures on more than one third of all the national flags. Moreover, the star is also a reminder of the notion "five star quality", a point of particular relevance given the group's activity. The "starry" logo of the Sodexho group is simple, recognizable and highly meaning in any language.

This logo is graphically animated by a circular movement which symbolizes the notions of openess and friendliness. A "graphic mistake" was made with the "e" and "x" and this tends to reinforce the elegance and

warmth of the Sodexho brand. It was also decided to write Gardner
Merchant on two separate lines so as to avoid any problems linked to the
length of the name. The task force opted for a two-colored logo so as to
simplify use, maintain the same impression of quality and minimize
production costs. The colors chosen were:

• Blue which is a dominant color and was already in the Sodexho and
Gardner Merchant logos,

• Red which is a warm color and draws a link with Partena. It also
makes the logo more dynamic.

The new logo with its blue, red and white color scheme also refers to the
colors of the flags of the principal countries where Sodexho Alliance is
present: France, Great Britain, United States, Holland, South Africa,
Australia, and Chile...

A code was drawn up to ensure that the new visual identity would be
respected and coherently implemented. Presented in October 1996, the new
visual identity was officially launched in February 1997. Since then it has
been progressively applied to stock renewal and so has generated no extra
cost.

Sodexho's new visual identity has allowed it to establish its international
brand strategy by grouping its different brands under the brand name
Sodexho Alliance while at the same time respecting the identity of each of
them. Taking into account Sodexho's corporate culture and the importance
of the human aspect of its activity, there is a definite respect of the history,
culture and personality of its personnel and the subsidiaries in which they
work. The company applied its international visual identity to the brands of
its different subsidiaries which were thereby preserved.

Second step: shifting to a new unique global brand

The setting up of a new visual identity code allowed the company to
move on to the next phase of its brand policy: firmly establishing Sodexho in
the ranks of the major world brand leaders. The aim was to capitalize on the
unique global Sodexho brand by progressively applying it to different
sectors and market segments, thus clarifying the group's identity, facilitating
the immediate comprehension of its activities, and improving the visibility of
brands. In this way Sodexho also sought to more clearly affirm the expertise
and know-how of its leading sectors.

This brand policy was solidly reflected in a specific visual identity code
establishing the major guidelines for use of the brand. For example, while
the commercial brand of the group is Sodexho, the name Sodexho Alliance
is reserved for the company as it is listed on the Stock Exchange. In the same
way, all companies in the group must include the words, "Member of

Sodexho Alliance" (in the local language) on all their documents, bills, brochures etc.

The decision to transform Sodexho into a unique global brand was determined in particular by the increasing importance of brands in the service sector as a factor in differentiation, loyalty building, and mobilization. Moreover, in the major international markets worldwide brands predominate. Thus a global brand is a real asset for international competition as well as for building future alliances or acquisitions.

This policy has also reinforced Sodexho's role as a channel for the company values and image. The brand can now bring together consumers, customers, partners, and shareholders, thus improving the efficiency of communication investments (both in-house and external). The brand can now benefit from all the media events, press relations, and public relations launched by Sodexho all over the world (sponsoring, corporate communication, financial communication, etc.). In terms of awareness and image, it can take advantage of the positive spinoffs of these measures in the international media. In the eyes of customers and prospective customers, the media, opinion leaders, and influencers from the financial community, Sodexho's shift to a unique global brand is just one more proof of the group's professionalism, expertise, and international experience.

Overall, this unique global brand policy went hand in hand with the development of the group and significantly strengthened its leadership position.

Internal branding

In addition to this international strategy, Sodexho has developed an original brand policy. Its subsidiaries have entirely designed and developed brands which enable them to differentiate their offers. Called "internal branding", this approach satisfies a growing demand for business catering to offer menus comparable to those found in normal restaurants. Sodexho does not just want to supply a meal to its customers' personnel, it also offers them the possibility of choosing their menu for example "Tasty Lite Cuisine", "Spitfires". Indeed, thanks to the diversity of the menus offered and the fact that they are easy to recognize, a company's canteen facilities can become more and more like a genuine restaurant. Specific brands for each type of menu enable the services offered to be very varied ranging from Italian-style cooking to light cuisine, including exotic food, hamburgers, sandwiches, and traditional dishes.

For example, Italian-style meal brands are easy to recognize, in the United States they are called "Pastabilities", in France "La Pasta", in Great Britain "Pizza Gusta". Internal branding makes the choices more visible, attractive and also makes companies' canteen facilities more like those found in normal restaurants and less like impersonal, bland canteens.

The following sample of brands gives a general idea of the menus elaborated by Sodexho's subsidiaries (Figure 18).

Figure 18. Examples of internal brands created by Sodexho Alliance's subsidiaries

2. LOCAL BRAND STRATEGY

2.1 Factors favoring a local brand strategy

Global brand strategy is a voluntary approach to rationalize management generally with the aim of taking advantage of opportunities in marketing, research, production, logistics and sales due to similarities and convergence between countries.

However, it is not always applicable because it can encounter problems linked to:

- Restricted possibilities concerning brand patenting and legal protection,
- Cultural and perception differences,
- Heterogeneous markets (life cycle...),
- Change of name and brand dilution,
- Decentralized structure and internal brakes on global brand management.

Instead of adopting a global brand approach, some multinationals prefer to opt for a "multi-local approach" so as to take advantage of the specific image linked to the local character of different national brands. Local brand strategy expresses the will to adopt differentiated marketing in order to exploit the slightest differences between markets. This consists mainly in adapting to local specificities. With this in mind, certain international corporations opt for a decentralized organization. Subsidiaries can then develop competence which can be adapted to a specific market or territory.

Thanks to a better knowledge of the market, of competitors, of middlemen, the physical or psychological characteristics of the offer can be modified and adapted to each market targeted (norms, distribution and transport regulations and restrictions). When selling under a local brand name, it is possible to adopt a specific positioning of worldwide products, for example, in terms of price or advertising. Global brand strategy ensures the coherence of positioning, the brand and the level of price, resulting in a certain level of perceived quality and performance. However, this type of strategy cannot easily justify big differences in price for the same product and brand on two different markets. On the other hand, a local brand strategy makes it easier to have different pricing policies in different countries. National markets are not always at the same stage of development: technology and product life cycles are not always at the same stage everywhere. Local brand strategy enables an international corporation to make an offer on a market which is adapted to its context and so cannot really be compared to other offers made to other markets under a different brand name.

Moreover, it is often difficult to use the same name, the same symbol or image everywhere. Using the same name does not always mean that the brand stays closest to its fundamental values. Choosing a local brand allows for more creativity especially as regards names suitable for local markets (meaningful or evocative brands). The subsidiaries have a local identity which may be better perceived by their markets. This is why an international brand sometimes has to be represented by a local brand. International corporations often acquire local companies so as to take advantage of their solid implantation and their good brand image. A local brand makes it easier for them to enter a new market. The notion behind a local brand strategy is to stick to the market so as to enable the company's offer to better meet local demand. Its objective is to maximize the brand's perceived values and so strengthen its impact.

SAINT-GOBAIN CONTAINERS: A LOCAL BRAND STRATEGY

Introducing the Saint-Gobain group

Founded in 1665, Saint-Gobain has a special place in French industrial history. It started internationalizing its activities more than a hundred years ago and today it has more than 350 companies, in over 40 countries, employs 110,000 people and had a turnover of more than 15,5 billion euros. The group is decentralized and its parent company "La Compagnie de Saint-Gobain" co-ordinates everything. The group is built on a European basis and on a worldwide presence and in each of its main activities, it is an international leader (Figure 19). For example:

• N°1 worldwide for industrial ceramic applications (melted quartz used in the space industry, ceramic balls used to treat metal surfaces, crystals for transmission optics, ceramic fibers ...),
• N°3 worldwide in the windows business (automobiles and building),
• N°1 worldwide for cast-iron duct piping,
• N°1 worldwide for insulation (rockwool, glasswool),
• N°1 worldwide for abrasives,
• N°1 in Europe and n°2 worldwide for reinforced fibers (glass fibers used to strengthen heterogeneous materials used in automobiles, aeronautics, industrial and agriculture equipment, building, electronics and sports and leisure equipment),
• N°2 worldwide for products used in coating the exterior of buildings (building materials).

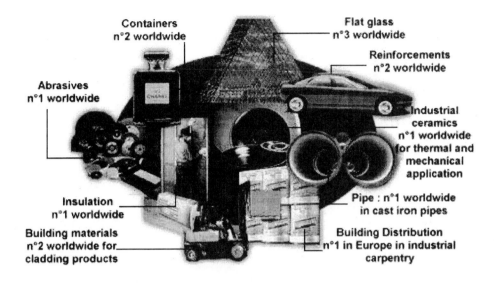

Figure 19. Saint-Gobain's different fields of competence and its worldwide leadership

Saint-Gobain's international brand strategy differs depending on the sector considered. For its glass activity it pursues a global strategy with the brand Sekurit for automobile windows. Figuring among the worldwide leaders of packaging, Saint-Gobain has however adopted a local brand strategy.

Saint-Gobain Containers: a local brand strategy so as to be near customers

Saint-Gobain Containers has progressively developed its three activities: bottles and jars (Figure 20), perfume and medicine bottles and other glass containers, by relying on its fundamental values: careful workmanship, multiple know-how and technology to be used to better serve customers. Its packaging activity is determined as a group of companies having the same values and adhering to the same philosophy. These companies are actively present in numerous countries.

Figure 20. The packaging sector: committed to total clarity and modernity for each market

Organization is decentralized for better proximity to customers. Each company maintains its name, personality, independence, and own customer culture. Thus the bottles are commercialized in the main countries with different brands (Table 21).

Table 21. Packaging activity's local brand strategy and the window activity's global brand use

Country	Brands of Bottles	Automobile glass brand
France	Saint-Gobain Emballage	
Portugal	Vidreira do Mondego	
United States	Ball-Foster Glass Containers (Ball Glass & Foster Forbes merger)	
Spain	Vicasa	Sekurit
Brazil	Santa Marina	
Italy	Vetri	
Germany	Oberland	

Saint-Gobain's local brand strategy expresses the group's total customer commitment. Although its different companies are autonomous, they are not decompartmentalized. They are constantly developing their synergies and go as far as regularly setting up "ad hoc" organizations to carry out their specific projects. This allows for mutual enrichment and a higher level of reactivity.

By means of top level design and production as well as a flexible and reactive customer-oriented organization, Saint-Gobain Containers branch has become the world leader in glass. With 26 industrial sites and 63 ovens in Europe, Saint-Gobain Containers employs 10,000 people, has a turnover of 1.6 billion euros and produces over 4 million tons (15.8 billions pieces) which is more than on quarter of the total European production.

Saint-Gobain's success depends on the will to contribute to its customers' performance. In the same way, its packaging branch tries to satisfy customer demand by creating that difference liable to help the customer gain market share. Thanks to its thermal, technical and mechanical skills, it develops glass which, apart from its functional aspect, aims to seduce and reassure. Its expertise in glass takes into account technological realities which differ depending on the needs. It has to adapt to specific demands: light glass for bottles and jars, sturdy or attractive glass for perfume and other bottles, harmonious glass for drinking glasses.

It is a question of reducing the weight of bottles and jars without removing any of their qualities. It is also about designing new shapes, sizes, stoppers and colors which are always more varied and creative. That is why bottles can be engraved, such as Châteauneuf-du-Pape wine bottles. They can also be used in serigraphy with a permanent and anti-abrasive enamel decoration, for example, the Provence line of aperitif drink Ricard bottles. Always with the same concern for its customers' sales performance, it uses several types of printing such as quadrichrome, and printing on a flat or three-dimensional surface. The glass itself can be colored in different ways (satin effect, sleeve). So as to increase both its own performance and that of its customers, Saint-Gobain seeks productivity gains on glass material while respecting the environment.

2.2 The different levels of local brand strategy

Local brand strategy is based on a certain autonomy and a decentralized organization. However, it is part of a global framework with an overall coherent strategy. The local brand generally satisfies global objectives by means of local plans of action and measures. For example, local brand strategy makes it possible to locally sign a product which has been globally designed. It intervenes in product harmonization (performance, packaging, format, etc.) and backs up a differentiation policy (promotion, brand image, positioning, etc.). The adoption of a local brand strategy requires a perfect general organizational management, in particular defining the exact level of local brand autonomy and the extent of positioning homogeneity.

The company has several possibilities depending on whether it wants to remind its customers of its subsidiaries or not (Table 22). The subsidiaries can have total autonomy as regards their name, logo, identity and their general brand management. They define their own visual identity code independent of the group to which they belong. This is the case for Legrand's local brands such as Pass and Seymour in the United States or Bticino in Italy.

Table 22. Different strategies possible for the company brand internationally

	"Identical"	"Adapted"	"Suggested"	"Indicated"	"Not Used"
Use of corporate brand name	Same in every country	Translated and written in different languages	Local subsidiary brand names are kept but the graphic style of the parent company is used	Local brand names are kept. The belonging to the global brand is indicated	Total local brand
Type of brand strategy used	Global brand strategy	Adapted global brand strategy	A combined global identity and local brand strategy	Local brand strategy	Local brand strategy

It can also be a question of maintaining local brands and their identity while at the same time, being more or less discreet about their belonging to an international group, for example by mentioning the group's name and logo. In this case, the group defines a very general brand management framework (use of corporate name, local brand creation). Another possibility consists in keeping local names by "blending" them into the group's visual identity code. Although this is a form of local brand strategy, it is more controlled by the group: local customers perceive both the local nature of the subsidiaries' names and the fact that they are part of an international group.

Local brand strategy should not necessarily be applied systematically and uniformly: indeed, different variants of such a strategy can coexist. For example, there can be opportunities to extend the local brand range to certain homogeneous markets. Depending on the position of the brand in different local markets, the company could leave brand management autonomous in one zone or, on the contrary, harmonize it in another one. The company might also mention the group's global dimension in every market where its brands are present: the parent company's brand is represented in different markets to varied degrees, depending on its life cycle.

2.3   Local brand strategy limitations

Local brand strategy is generally criticized for the cost it entails. It requires the presence of a local marketing structure and the launching of specific action plans, and adapted products, among other things. On top of these increased marketing costs can be added higher storage costs and a loss of economies of scale because of a lack of product standardization. In fact, excessive adaptation can lead to very heavy brand management costs. Moreover, local brand strategy makes it extremely difficult for companies to capitalize on their global brands in terms of image and reputation. Local brand positions are not the same on different markets: the company's global image is diffuse. For this reason, some companies try hard to reduce their brands, and optimizing on those retained for a maximum turnover: they can then take advantage of brand leverage.

In general, it is clear that companies are led to planning and adapting a pragmatic strategy. They take into account particulars as much as possible for example by developing a brand in a local niche while at the same time trying to globally homogenize the heart of the brand, their positioning. Today this trend is developing with the construction of strong global parent company brands which guarantee local brands and federate the image of groups.

This pragmatic international brand management can consist in adopting both a market-leader strategy in its home market and a market-challenger policy in a new market for the same product. Companies favor a flexible global market strategy over having a brand which is too mono-national, as this could seriously suffer in a global context. This is in line with the expression "Think global. Act local". In fact, globalization does not have to involve all the elements of the brand and marketing plan, but can selectively apply to the name, symbol, slogan or certain characteristics of brand image.

Chapter 11

"Entering Goods" Brands: The Development of Co-Branding

1. "PURCHASEABILITY" AND VISIBILITY OF "ENTERING GOODS"

"Entering goods" have three main characteristics. They are generally not purchaseable by end consumers. They are selected by industrial customers and then integrated into the production process. Physically they are delivered in a way which does not allow end users to use them. For instance, Lycra® fibers such as Tetra Pak packaging are delivered in reels which require industrial equipment to be transformed into underwear, clothing and pre-finished packaging.

Secondly, in general, entering goods cannot be identified after transformation and integration in a consumer product. This is the case for food ingredients, textile fibers, or chemical compounds, which can be found in sports shoes or other equipment, from snowboards to tennis rackets. The brand visibility of entering goods is quite difficult to establish on the products of industrial customers (Malaval, 1998). For this reason, information labels are used to identify the supplier brand. When the supplier delivers already assembled goods, such as microprocessors, they can be considered as "intermediary equipment goods" described in Chapter 12.

"Entering goods" essentially concern consumer products, which explains why suppliers are interested in advertising directly to final consumers.

2.   TECHNICAL PARTNERSHIP FIRST

In keeping with the surveys described in previous chapters, the product advantages demanded by industrial customers are first and foremost technical[1]. For this reason, the credibility of "entering goods" brands is based on improving technical performance. A technical partnership means:
- Added-value for the end consumer,
- And/or added-value for industrial customers.

Added value for end consumers is essentially about the new product advantages obtained thanks to the integration of the entering goods. For instance, clothes made with Gore-Tex® membranes are appreciated by the end consumer because they are supposed to be durably waterproof and breathable. Thus, these membranes improve the efficiency of outerwear and shoes used essentially for winter sports.

Added value for industrial customers means:
- Innovation and help developing new products,
- Production management and controlling costs,
- Quality control during the production process,
- Product support and help maintaining machinery,
- After-sales service and tracking ("traceability").

For the brand, establishing a technical partnership is the prerequisite to developing a potential commercial partnership. Depending on the company's technical expertise and its desire to seduce end users, a commercial partnership can be developed with industrial customers to make the marketing of their consumer product easier. This partnership requires a visibility strategy.

3.   CO-BRANDING DEVELOPMENT: A VISIBILITY-BASED STRATEGY

To be part of the attractiveness of the consumer product, the brand must become visible to the end user. This strategy must be backed up by advertising. With this decision, a commercial partnership becomes the visible side of the relationship between a supplier and an industrial customer. "*Industrial brand & consumer brand*" co-branding can be developed to make marketing of the consumer product more effective.

But a long term co-branding strategy must be based on a double partnership, both technical and commercial. It must allow the following deal: better product advantages for consumers in exchange for clear industrial brand visibility. Visibility strategy is linked to product category "printability"[2], which depends on the physical product support, visual access to the product, and identification longevity. But it is also linked to after-delivery product transformations (Figure 1).

Leather production illustrates "printability" constraints for "entering goods". Soft lambskin is delivered by raw-leather producers to manufacturers. For example, the latter must cut the skin to assemble trouser parts. For upstream brands, the "printability" possibilities are then reduced:

- if a logo is engraved on the skin, its future visibility cannot be guaranteed after parts assembling,
- if it is engraved repeatedly on the back side, it will be hidden from the end consumer after assembling,
- if it is engraved repeatedly on the flower side (external), it modifies the visual look altering the natural appearance of the skin,
- the logo can be printed on a separate label, but in this case the risk of imitation is very high, especially by developing country companies.

Figure 1. Difficult printability for the leather industry

For the food industry, however, brand visibility is being developed with industrial brand strategies. The Monsanto group, for instance, has launched the Nutrasweet brand with its spiral logo. This logo can be seen on consumer products such as Nestlé or Orangina. For paper products such as stickers or writing paper, industrial brand visibility often consists in printing the name on the back or watermarking it.

Another example can be found in computer supplies with Verbatim diskettes co-branded with the Teflon process by DuPont. Co-branding-based partnerships are frequently used in the shoes and clothing industry. For instance, Ingemar or Car Polol outerwear for snowboarding integrates the Pontella brand (Rhône-Poulenc polyester), the Scotchgard brand for its anti-stain process (3M), or the Gore-Tex® brand for its breathable membrane (Gore). The following table shows several co-branding examples taken from three "entering goods" categories: fibers, membranes, and fabrics (Table 2).

Table 2. Some examples of textile co-branding (industrial / consumer brands)

Entering Goods	Brands	Companies	Examples
FIBERS	Enka Sun	Akzo Nobel	—
	Dorlastan	Bayer	—
	Dynactyl	Damart	—
	Kevlar	Du Pont de Nemours	Garmont (shoes)
	Cordura	Du Pont de Nemours	Bestaro (shoes), Fusalp, Cimalp (outerwear)
	Lycra	Du Pont de Nemours	Dim (stockings)
	Tactel	Du Pont de Nemours	Moncler (jackets)
	Thermolite Extreme	Du Pont de Nemours	—
	Thermastat	Du Pont de Nemours	Decathlon, Bridgedale (socks)
	Meryl Micro	Nylstar (Rhône-Poulenc/Snia Fibre)	Eider (jackets)
	Filifine Tergal	Rhône-Poulenc	(suits)
	Setila Micro	Rhône-Poulenc	Adidas Climateam (outerwear)
	Rhovyl'Eco	Rhovyl	—
	Rhovyl'On	Rhovyl	—
	Rhovyl'Up	Rhovyl	Himal Sport (T-shirts)
	Rhovyl'Fr	Rhovyl	—
	Rhovyl'As	Rhovyl	Rywan (socks)
	Etaproof	Stotz and Co	—
	Breathe	UCB	Wilsa-Sport (outerwear)
MEMBRANES	Comfortex		—
	Sympatex	Akzo Nobel	Vaude (jackets)
	Skinflex	Calamai Company	—
	Alpex	Dickson PTL	Technica (shoes)
	Coolmax	Du Pont de Nemours	Decathlon (Tracksuit jogging), Duofold (underwear), Bridgedale (socks)
	Gore-Tex	W.L. Gore et Associés	Salomon, Nordica (gloves), Dolomite, Bestera, Meindl, Salomon Technica (shoes)
FABRICS	Duratex		Reusch (ski gloves)
	Taslan		Decathlon (outerwear)
	Micro-loft	Du Pont de Nemours	Padding for Aigle parkas
	Triple Point Ceramic	Lowe Alpine	Lowe Alpine (outerwear)
	Polartec	Malden Mills	Aigle (parka), Karrimor, Trespass, Eider (outerwear)

4. GORE-TEX®: A PARTNER BRAND, FROM INNOVATION TO QUALITY CONTROL OF THE CUSTOMER PRODUCT *

The company was founded in 1958 by Wilbert L. Gore and today is managed by his son Bob, a chemical engineer. Gore company initially produced insulation products out of PTFE (polytetrafluoroethylen) for the electronics market (cable insulation). In 1969, Bob Gore discovered and

* *Reproduced with the permission of W.L. Gore*

patented a new combination of PTFE characterized by waterproofness and breathability. This innovation started the company in the textile industry. Thanks to this microporous membrane, Gore today employs about 8,000 people and makes a large part of its 1 billion dollar turnover in the textiles sector (Figure 3).

Figure 3. W.L. Gore corporate logo

Today Gore-Tex® is a must for hiking equipment, but it is also essential for astronaut clothing and is used for many applications in the medical and electronics fields. Gore-Tex® outerwear is designed to be waterproof and "guaranteed to keep you dry". As a matter of fact, Gore-Tex® fabric is the world's first and still the most durably waterproof, breathable and windproof fabric available. It is made of two different substances. The first one contains 9 billion pores per square inch, which makes it hydrophobic or "water hating". The second one is an oleophobic or "oil-hating" substance, which prevents penetration of contaminants that might effect its waterproof or breathability qualities.

Besides the textiles sector, Gore-Tex® membranes are used in environmental protection from the chemical to the automotive industry. All these applications have been made possible thanks to technical and commercial partnerships with business customers and the company commitment to end users.

4.1   Facilitating technical performance

The Gore brand tag-line "Creative Technologies Worldwide" shows the importance of innovation in the corporate culture. Mastering polymer transformation allowed Gore to develop new processes and solutions for different markets such as:

- Dryloft® for down protection, keeping insulation dry from the inside to stay warm,
- Activent®, an extremely breathable, water resistant and windproof garment, developed for outdoor activities from warm-up to cool-down,
- Windstopper® to protect durably against winds. Very breathable, it assures warmth with less bulk (Figure 4),
- Skyflex® for waterproof seals in aeronautics,

- Gore Immersion® to protect products in deep water,
- Gore Ocean® waterproof products for offshore and coastal sailing.

Figure 4. Windstopper® logo

The fabric line integrating Gore-Tex® microporous membranes is called Gore Windstopper. It provides windproof liners for sweaters, pants and casual wear which eliminate the need for a jacket in cooler weather, giving athletes less bulk and greater freedom of movement and versatility indoors and out. To enlarge its application possibilities, Gore has developed a strategy based on specialized equipment for the army, the police, and firemen. Most innovations have resulted from partnerships with industrial customers in terms of research and development and technical know-how. Gore does not only deliver fabrics to its industrial customers. It helps them in finding new applications and the best material combinations.

Working with customers does not end when the new product is launched: the partnership continues throughout the production phase, for instance, for new adhesive processes, or sealed seams. Waterproof outerwear means that liquid from the outside won't get inside. That's why Gore-Tex® outerwear is truly waterproof, an absolutely impermeable barrier against rain and snow. Every detail of the design and construction is considered to ensure this. Every design is tested in rain simulation to ensure that it meets Gore-Tex® waterproof standards. Thus quality manufacturers (industrial customers) must be members of the Gore-Tex® "Partners in Performance TM" program, especially for waterproof design and seam-sealing technology. This technical partnership is necessary to warrant the Gore-Tex® promise "guaranteed to keep you dry®".

All these partnerships allow:
- Gore-Tex® to control the true and perceived brand quality by end users,
- Industrial customers to best benefit from the membrane properties and to be helped from a technical point of view,
- The end user to benefit from true waterproof quality with his consumer purchase.

Thus Gore-Tex® guarantees the performance of its own supplies and its customer products in:

- *Waterproofness*: droplets of water are 20,000 times bigger than Gore-Tex® membrane pores(0.2 micron). They cannot penetrate these pores with humanly bearable pressure conditions,
- *Breathability* or perspiration escape: molecules of water vapor are 700 times smaller than Gore-Tex® membrane pores: moisture from perspiration can easily escape,
- *Windproofness*: determined by measuring air permeability, it allows a fabric to prevent wind penetration and resist heat loss.

This commitment is written on the Gore-Tex® label which can be seen by consumers: technical know-how is essential but it must be visible to consumers too.

4.2   Facilitating commercial performance

Gore-Tex® invests in improving its customers' commercial performance. For this reason advertising has been developed to increase brand awareness. The aim of this pull strategy is to help better develop sales of manufacturers integrating Gore-Tex® membranes. This support is provided to industrial customers before, during and after sales. It is based on three main points:
- Communication actions,
- A brand visibility strategy,
- A warranty strategy.

4.2.1   Communication actions

Gore-Tex® is the membrane brand which has the best top of mind awareness results in Europe. Gore-Tex® brand awareness is the fruit of a long-term communication strategy. At the beginning, in 1980, Gore-Tex® advertised essentially towards industrial customers through trade-shows, business publications and documentation. Since 1983, the consumer public has also been targeted with specialized magazines on hiking, mountain climbing, and hunting: adverts explain Gore-Tex® is selling a concept (waterproof, windproof...) not a raw material. Since 1994, mass media such as television have been used to increase brand awareness and to improve brand image. For example, in 1997, most European top TV programs were chosen to diffuse a new ad: after walking through a carwash machine, a man pulls a chick out of his trench-coat: protected by the Gore-Tex® processed outerwear, the chick is dry. In the US, three different TV-ads show the reliability of the Gore-Tex® membrane (waterproof, windproof...). The press ads conclude with this tag-line "it's what's on the inside that really counts" (Figure 5).

Figure 5. Recent Gore-Tex® press ad "it's what's on the inside that really counts"

4.2.2   A brand visibility strategy

This visibility strategy is based on the choice of a specific visual label, which allows final consumers to identify the Gore-Tex® entering good. Each item of clothing or pair of shoes manufactured with a Gore-Tex® membrane has a separate label with brand logo, explaining the type of fabric, its characteristics and advantages. This visual aid contributes to building technical legitimacy. End users are careful when choosing the consumer brand to check for the presence of Gore-Tex® in its composition. Thus the "upstream" brand provides added-value to the consumer product.

Gore-Tex® brand uses a black 45° sloping square written in golden letters. On the bottom is the corporate Gore logo in white and red colors. Today, the Gore-Tex® logo has become a symbol for microporous membrane. While "Gore" is the name of the founder of the company, the "Tex" suffix phonetically evokes "tech", the abbreviated form of technology. This allows Gore-Tex® to guarantee other products than the original textile category (Figure 6).

Figure 6. Gore-Tex[®] logo

4.2.3   A warranty strategy

The Gore-Tex[®] label is featured next to the manufacturer's label on the product. It is a guarantee for consumers: even in the case of an unsatisfactory product, they know not only the manufacturer's identity but also the membrane supplier. The Gore-Tex[®] "signature" is a double guarantee for both industrial and end customers. Gore-Tex[®] has developed the warranty function of its brand by providing a consumer toll-free number. Six days a week, from 9 to 7 o'clock consumers can get any information they wish: shops with available products, washing advice, or they can make a complaint. At the same time, information collected from consumers can be a useful source for new product development.

This service reassures end users and provides visible support to industrial customers in their sales approach. Perceived as a warranty label by consumers, Gore-Tex[®] improves the sales performance of its industrial customers.

With the same aim of increasing efficiency, Gore helps distributors to train their salespeople. The latter can improve their sales arguments when they know the fabrics as well as the final products. For the training program, a Gore visiting team gives technical and merchandising advice to the distributor's sales staff. This improves the efficiency of distributors and the quality of the information given to final consumers. With actions aimed at industrial customers, distributors, and end users, Gore-Tex[®] has chosen a new position: a partnership for better business efficiency.

5.   LYCRA® ONLY BY DUPONT: A COMMERCIAL AND TECHNICAL PARTNERSHIP *

5.1   Du Pont de Nemours Company and its Lycra® brand

Figure 7. Du Pont de Nemours corporate logo

In 1802, Eleuthère Irénée Du Pont de Nemours was a scientist and a student of Lavoisier. Fleeing the French revolution, he founded a black-powder mill in the American State of Delaware. Two centuries later, Du Pont de Nemours has become a diversified petrochemical group employing 98,000 people all over the world with a 45 billion dollar turnover in 1997.

The company has developed activities in chemicals, energy and life sciences, as well as speciality products, but it is better known for its innovations such as the discovery of nylon and different brands like Dacron® polyester, Tactel® polyamid, Orlon® acrylic, Nomex® meta-aramid, Kevlar® para-amid and Lycra® elastane. This man-made polyurethane type fiber is elastic and was invented in 1959. Today it is produced in 9 different sites employing a total of 3,500 people.

Lycra® fiber is used in a lot of textile combinations: its remarkable properties of stretch and recovery enhance fabrics adding new dimensions of fit, comfort and drape to clothing. Swimsuits and lingerie owe their gentle, figure-flattering fit to Lycra®. Quality hosiery is smoother, softer and wrinkle-free thanks to a little Lycra® in the leg. The elasticity Lycra® imparts allows active sportswear to be cut aerodynamically close to the body without impairing movement. Lycra® in weaving and knits for leisure and fashion wear improves their drape and shape retention and eliminates wrinkles quickly. Even loose-fitting clothes feel better when made of fabrics containing Lycra®. Stronger and more durable than rubber, Lycra® adds a special liveliness to fabrics of all kinds.

5.2   Lycra® only by DuPont: a reference brand for the supply chain

Since 1980, Du Pont de Nemours has developed a pull strategy for its Lycra® brand. This has been possible thanks to the technical added value

* Reproduced with the permission of Du Pont de Nemours.

given by this fiber to consumer products. To this end, DuPont has decided to take steps, for each level of the supply chain, to control the appropriate use of its product (Malaval, 1996). Marketing tools have been developed to increase the Lycra® brand awareness. Beyond Lycra®'s own technical excellence, a highly effective marketing strategy has helped to create the best conditions for greater distribution. A strong brand policy has been implemented to indicate the presence of Lycra® on consumer products. This signature has become a guarantee of high level quality.

This brand visibility strategy provides a technical and commercial guarantee to consumer products. Initiated in 1960, this strategy involves four steps.

5.2.1   Step one

The objective is to be known by end consumers. The Lycra® brand must be associated with elastane fiber. And it must be perceived as more innovative than competing fibers. Its stretch and recovery properties must be seen by end consumers as product advantages in terms of smoothness, softness and wrinkle-free quality. This is an objective to be achieved by the sales force who are supported by technical departments. This sales force is to meet industrial customers in order to convince the different members of the buying center: production managers, research and development, marketing and sales managers, quality control and purchasing department managers. The enhanced arguments depend on each function and each level of influence.

5.2.2   Step two

The Lycra® brand's main objective is to be recommended. This brand must be perceived as the best choice by industrial customers, providing product advantages in terms of differentiation and better positioning. For this purpose, Lycra® brand must be requested by downstream actors: all along the line, from distributors and manufacturers, to weavers or knitters, depending on the product type. This derived demand strategy consists in influencing the most downstream actors: consumers. That is why the Lycra® brand must be visible on consumer products using separate labels or adhesive on packaging. The Lycra® label, or printed logo on the consumer packaging is proof of the supplier's commitment to quality. It reassures consumers, giving them information about the supplier, the product's technical performance, the use and washing instructions. The Lycra® brand and its logo are visible on the consumer product, beside the consumer brand which can be a manufacturer like Dim or Chesterfield for stockings, or a private label like St-Michael (Marks and Spencer) and also for ready-to-wear clothes brands such as Hugo Boss, Max Mara or Hechter (Figure 8).

Figure 8. Lycra® logo

For the visibility strategy to work, a specific corporate identity code must be respected, with given constraints for different brochures, sales documents and catalogs, as well as for advertising messages. Whatever the support, it bears the Lycra® logo and the main promise "Freedom of movement". The new Lycra® logo evokes this idea of movement, thanks to its wave-shape. It is called the swing ticket (Figure 9).

Figure 9. Swing ticket Lycra®

5.2.3 Step three

This third step consists in being requested by consumers in order to obtain partnerships with industrial customers. The product strategy is backed up by a communication plan targeting distributors and consumers. Distributors receive documented files with consumer surveys describing new behavioral trends. They also receive communication plans aimed at end consumers with advertising and promotion actions. These distributors will be more inclined to accept new products – composed of Lycra® fibers – in their shelf spaces. They are also influenced in the definition of their own label product-brands including Lycra® fibers.

Because DuPont places such a high premium on quality throughout the complete manufacturing/distribution chain, it has established a licensing program for woven fabrics containing Lycra®. This program works to the advantage of both apparel manufacturers and retailers. The garment manufacturer knows that approved fabrics satisfy criteria established by DuPont. Retailers know that garments displaying the Lycra® swing ticket are made with properly constructed fabrics that fully meet consumer expectations.

Another objective in this step is to make sure that Lycra does not become something trivial. In the beginning, Lycra® was synonymous with "stretch". This handy catchword became a simple marketing tool that attracted some opportunistic fabric and garment producers whose products might stretch, but don't contain Lycra®. And they don't perform up to Lycra® standards. No one "owns" stretch. It is merely a look, an ephemeral fashion, and a marketing gimmick. Lycra®, on the other hand, carries the weight of DuPont's continuing research and development and its unfailing commitment to quality and performance. There's a big difference between Lycra® and "stretch", a difference every responsible garment manufacturer and retailer should be aware of.

The communication plan has been developed with a simple and direct message "Feel the freedom a little Lycra® brings". Ads for women's wear with Lycra® appeared in 1998 in leading fashion magazines in France, Germany, Spain, Italy and the UK, including *Marie-Claire*, *Elle*, *Cosmopolitan*, *Vogue*, *Freundin* and *Donna Moderna*. Men's wear with Lycra® will be featured in *GQ*, *Der Spiegel*, *L'Équipe*, *Il Mondo*, *L'Espresso*, *Financial Times* and *The Economist*, mostly in cooperation with high image brands. The Lycra® brand enjoys an extremely high level of recognition worldwide, which has been rising steadily to **88** percent of female consumers and **50** percent of male consumers, according to a 1997 study conducted in major European countries by the Research Bureau

International. The Lycra® swing ticket has become a universal sign of quality (Figure 10).

Shape up your sweaters and knits?
Happy to help.

Freedom of movement for your suits and skirts?
Go right ahead.

Breathe more life into your sportswear?
Delighted if you do.

Put more comfort in your underwear line?
Fine with us.

Looking for hosiery that feels and fits better?
Be our guest.

Want your swimwear to stay smarter longer?
No problem.

Abuse our trademark?
See you in court.

If you are using LYCRA® in your products and you're not sure how to advertise the fact, call us.

And if you're using another elastane and *calling* it "Lycra" you'd better also call your lawyer.

Because the next time you see us it'll be in court.

When you use LYCRA®, it really pays to tell your customers about it. By adding our hang-tag or label to your garments, or our logo to your packaging or advertising, you are also adding

the quality and performance reassurance of one of the world's best-known, most-valued brand names – a name that DuPont has actively and successfully promoted for more than two decades.

You already know the comfort, fit and freedom of movement that LYCRA® can bring. So if you're using it, it makes good marketing sense to use our trademark too. But if you're not, don't even think about it.

Figure 10. The controlled use of Lycra® brand: ad for business publications

5.2.4   Fourth step

This step consists essentially in gaining customer loyalty. This means making sure that the Lycra® brand is an essential key to success, one that industrial customers cannot avoid if they want to succeed in launching new products.

In order to respect customer independence within the supply chain, Lycra® develops tailor-made marketing plans. Each customer understands the advantages of working with Lycra®. Moreover, industrial customers can elaborate their media planning in combination with Lycra®. They can use the same arguments as those chosen by Lycra® (recovery, wrinkle-free...). Depending on their esthetic or innovative properties, some products of industrial customers can be selected to illustrate a Lycra® campaign. In this case, the customers can benefit from very favorable cooperation from Lycra®, which can help them in elaborating their own promotion campaign.

By helping industrial customers during the launching of new products, Lycra® is facilitating the product's success on the market (Figure 11).

Figure 11. Example of partnership and innovation: "Wool plus Lycra®" with Chargeurs Company

This is the case of Lycra®'s partnership with IWS (International Wool Organization) combining Woolblendmark wool with Lycra® fibers. Thus, new aspects and surface effects have been obtained from this cooperation "Wool plus Lycra®". This type of partnership has been developed with many actors within the supply chain.

Du Pont de Nemours also supports thread producers by:
- Helping them to develop new threads,
- Providing technical support for launching new products,
- Giving them coverage with marketing surveys, trends, and data bases.

Help is also provided to the customer's customers, the weavers, in terms of:

- Technical support for woven goods (providing a test laboratory for new fabrics, technical brochures and advice...),

- Marketing support with forecasts on new trends, fashions, color-lines, videos...

- Exclusive development of fabrics inciting higher innovation (use of new threads, creative samples, etc.).

Du Pont de Nemours also facilitates the performance of the next customer in the chain: manufacturers. The objective is to promote new fabrics including Lycra® for female and male consumers. That is why a specialized "fabrics-library" for the American, European, and Asian markets are presented to manufacturers during textile tradeshows such as Première Vision in Paris, Modamilano in Milan, Modtissimo in Portugal or at the Semana de la Moda in Barcelona. During these events, Lycra® provides brochures with information about trends, creative styling with their technical characteristics and the names of the fashion-show suppliers. Thus, manufacturers can draw on creative ideas integrating Lycra®.

With fashion shows, Lycra® influences the most upstream actors. At the same time, Lycra® tries to influence the most downstream actor, the customer. Backing up the "feel of freedom" advertising campaign will be valuable point-of-sale merchandising material including posters, cardboard display units and door-and-window stickers. This will increase visibility, reinforce the advertising message and serve as a reminder of the value-added benefits of Lycra® at the critical point of purchase.

These technical and commercial partnerships have been developed on different supply chain levels. This strategy enables the Lycra® brand to catch and keep more and more loyal customers.

NOTES

1. See Chapter 5, Brand Functions.
2. See Chapter 6, Purchaseability and Visibility of the Industrial Brands.
3. See Chapter 7, Industrial Brand Classification, 2-3-6 Brands Evoking High Technologies.

REFERENCES

Malaval, Ph., (1996), *Marketing Business to Business*, Paris, Publi-Union.
Malaval, Ph., (1998), The New Visibility of the Industrial Products, *Figaro,* 18th September.

Chapter 12

Brands of Intermediary Equipment Goods

1. BRANDS OF INTERMEDIARY EQUIPMENT GOODS

Intermediary equipment goods are similar to entering goods in that they are often found as an integrated part in an assembled product such as a house or car sold by an industrial client. The purchaseability of such products by the consumer is higher than for entering goods and is dependent on the supplier brand strategy and on the technical complexity of the product category. Purchaseability in fact applies to independent units, easily used by the final consumer. Such renewable parts include windscreen wipers for cars, tools, radiators, carpets or electrical appliances for the home. More complex sub-assemblies such as microprocessors or alternators are generally not available for purchase by the final consumer.

As with the entering goods, brand visibility varies with the type of product. In the case of room partitions, plaster and cement brands such as Lafarge or Placoplatre will not appear, as they are ultimately hidden by the paint or wall covering. Visibility is directly linked with the difficulty encountered in terms of "printability". For example, aluminium profiling is not produced as individual units – this makes branding during manufacture impossible. However, three other solutions are possible:

- Ex-works branding for "mounted" assemblies i.e. those sold to artisans,
- Post-branding for products mounted later by an artisan (windows, verandas),
- Logo branding on the accessory (window handle).

Visibility also depends on the willingness to cooperate of all those concerned in the purchase process: from supplier to the acceptance or refusal of clients.

Intermediary equipment goods brands may be perceived as facilitators from both a technical and commercial viewpoint. The concept of brand as commercial facilitator only applies where a technical partnership is already established. It is interesting to study brands recognized as performance facilitators in their sectors of activity. In the automobile sector, the Valeo study illustrates the role of performance facilitator on a technical level. The Zodiac case illustrates technical facilitation extending over to influence commercial performance. In the domain of microprocessors, Intel is an example of how a partnership can be developed on both a technical and commercial basis.

2.   VALEO: CUSTOM-MADE SPARE PARTS, FROM THE DRAWING BOARD TO FINAL PACKAGING

2.1   Presentation of Valeo and its different activities

Valeo is an independent industrial group whose entire business activity is focused on the automotive industry. Valeo designs, manufactures and sells components, integrated systems, and modules for cars and trucks, both in original equipment and aftermarket segments. The Valeo group is among the top six automotive suppliers in the world; it has over 50,000 personnel in 20 countries and a turnover of 8.3 billion euros.

Valeo is the world leader in engine cooling, lighting systems, wiper systems, electric motors, switches, clutches, manual transmissions and friction materials; it is the European leader for climate control systems and access and security systems. Valeo's starters and alternators business ranks among the top 3 in its sector worldwide. Valeo is present in all the essential functions associated with vehicles: engine, chassis, transmission, style, bodywork, access and security, as well as electronics and electric motors. The activities of the group are divided up into ten industrial branches (Figure 1), one for each product line and system, and one dedicated to aftermarket distribution (replacement parts) – which includes a wide range of Valeo products and also those of other brands in the group (Cibié, Marchal, Paul Journée).

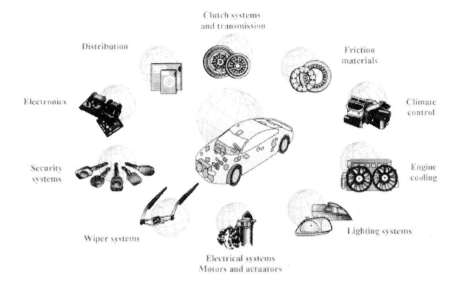

Figure 1. Valeo's different industrial branches

The industrial branches are:

• *Clutch systems and transmission* for automobile and industrial vehicles: complete clutch systems (from pedal to crankshaft), clutch cover assemblies, discs, release bearings, hydraulic clutch actuators, electronic clutches, torque converters absorbers (double flywheel radial absorbers), lock-ups (double-sided lockups for automatic gear boxes),

• *Friction materials*: dry clutch facings, friction materials for automatic transmissions, synchronizer rings, cabin air filters,

• *Climate control* (cockpit): heating and air-conditioning systems, heater cores, evaporators, condensers, ventilators, A/C control panels (automobiles, heavy goods vehicles, coaches),

• *Engine cooling*: powertrain cooling systems, radiators, condensers, charge air coolers, oil coolers and exhaust gas recirculation coolers, fan/motor systems, cooling modules, front end modules,

• *Lighting systems*: main and auxiliary headlamps (halogen and HID), headlamp leveling actuators and headlamp washers, fog lamps, signal lighting, cigar lighters and multifunction connectors,

• *Electrical systems*: alternators and starters for passenger cars, utility vehicles and trucks, remanufacturing of alternators and starters,

• *Wiper systems*: complete wiper systems (arms, blades, linkages, motors), rain sensors, wash systems, modules,

• *Motors and actuators*: climate control motors, engine cooling motors, seat adjustment and head rest motors, steering column adjustment motors,

ABS motors, window lift motors, sun roof motors, seat belt adjustment motors, door latch actuators, air compressors for adjustable suspensions,

• *Security systems*: steering column locks, ignition switches, locks and handles, (door and trunk), latches (door, trunk, tailgate, hood, seatback), RF remote controllers and receivers, transponder-based immobilizer systems, electronic central door locking modules, hands-free keyless entry and ignition systems, door modules,

• *Electronics*: body controllers, control panels, electronic modules, park assist systems, switches, sensors.

2.2   The Valeo brand: technical facilitator in design, innovation and production

Partner to automobile and industrial vehicle manufacturers, Valeo devotes between 12 and 15% of its annual turnover to research and development and the improvement of quality and productivity (increased capacity, total quality...). It has 21 research centers and technical bases (design offices and test laboratories), 2,500 highly skilled engineers and technicians; it registers over 500 patents worldwide every year.

Its innovation strategy has meant that the company is acknowledged as "design partner" by the majority of car and truck manufacturers in the world. This strategy has been developed along four lines:

• A worldwide presence (to ensure the closest possible proximity to the client),
• Advanced technology,
• The search for competitive costs,
• The search for total quality.

The role of equipment manufacturer has effectively evolved. More than simply supplying vehicle parts, it means accompanying, even anticipating, the needs of the automotive market – that is to say, both those of the manufacturer and the final user.

2.3   Taking into account the needs of the manufacturer customer and the final consumer

In the case of manufacturers, this would mean having for example a development organization in phase with the platforms used by the large production plants. In addition to such organizational demands, competitive costs and total quality, there must also be consideration for reliability in line with longer vehicle warranty period and less frequent maintenance.

Furthermore, product and system recyclability must be taken into account from the design stage, and throughout the production process. It is undoubtedly a major concern for automobile manufacturers – for reasons including respect for the environment, as well as a desire to make better use of energy resources and raw materials. In close partnership with manufacturers, Valeo is actively preparing new developments such as the possibility of recycling 90% of vehicle components. Along the same lines, the company is also developing its renovation activity aimed at partially reusing products which have come to the end of their normal life. To do this, Valeo Electrical Systems has sites devoted specifically to renovating alternators and starters: they are situated in Angers in France, and Lincoln in Great Britain.

In order to meet the demands of car buyers, manufacturers bring out new models more often, and offer a wider range of vehicles: monospaces, estate cars, coupés, convertibles, roadsters, leisure vehicles and commercial vehicles complete the range of the traditional car. With development times becoming shorter, Valeo must now anticipate needs: a project which once took five years from the first drawing to mass production, now takes three years, and soon will take only two. These new constraints are added to those of quality reliability and cost cutting – not forgetting the problems due to the application of stricter legislation concerning safety, exhaust emissions and more generally, respect for the environment.

The safety and comfort of car users and their passengers are a constant preoccupation for both manufacturers and equipment suppliers: temperature control, acoustics, visual comfort, easy handling – all of which, allow the driver time to concentrate exclusively on driving.

For these reasons, equipment suppliers need to have more and more specific know-how, as well expertise in the main functions of the automobile. In this way, they become real partners with the manufacturers, involved earlier and earlier on in vehicle development, generating major technological innovations.

2.4   Innovation

For Valeo, innovation has taken off in many directions: compactness, weight reduction, noise and vibration elimination, reliability, respect for the environment by giving priority to all applications contributing to safety and comfort. This means that Valeo carefully studies the needs of the market and analyzes its own potential in order to be in a position to offer attractive ideas to automobile and industrial vehicle manufacturers (their direct customers). Such offers include innovative products and systems, ready-to-mount, compatible with the standardization of components, the simplification and ease of recycling processes.

Although the systems integrated into vehicles are becoming more and more complex from a technical point of view, Valeo is turning its efforts towards simplicity and ergonomy both in their use and assembly – for the reasons given above. It is also necessary to anticipate the vehicles of tomorrow which will be non-polluting, comfortable, safe, but which will still have real identities, differentiated by their style and performance (Figure 2).

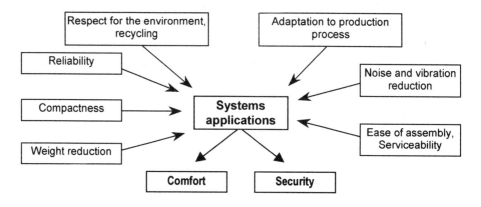

Figure 2. Valeo: for the manufacturer, a partner in innovation

Through its innovations, Valeo hopes to improve the technical performance of its customers in terms of design and production processes: ease of assembly, modularity of technical solutions, flexibility and freedom of design, etc. It also hopes to contribute to their commercial success by providing technological innovations aimed at increasing the comfort and safety of car owners.

2.5   Examples of Valeo's technical contribution and innovations

2.5.1   Increased safety with optimum lighting

With the idea of increased safety on the road, the Valeo Lighting Systems Branch works on new lighting sources (LED, discharge lights, neons) and also the optimization of reflectors (complex surfaces).

The third stop light or top stop light, authorized in Europe since 1993, has been compulsory on all vehicles since 1999. This light should reduce multiple collisions by making the vehicle braking ahead more visible. The LED stop lights – developed by Valeo – come on 200 milliseconds quicker than the conventional incandescent lights. By giving the driver more time to react, the LED technology reduces braking distance: a gain of 5 meters at 90km/hour and 7.5 meters at 130km/hour.

Valeo Lighting Systems has also developed new technology aimed at differentiating the different car lights – an important element in vehicle styling. Its Velarc system is the first application in France of the discharge lamp technology (elliptical lights on the Renault Safrane). The light flow generated is twice that of a halogen lamp of the same size, but it consumes less energy and lasts four times longer. A discharge lamp is made up of a quartz bulb containing high-pressure Xenon, metallic salts and solid state halide. When the lamp is switched on, an electric arc is produced in the Xenon, evaporating the metallic salts and the halide, creating a maximal light flux. Extremely rapid ignition (around a second) is obtained by applying a high voltage using an electronic unit (ballast) developed by Valeo Electronics Branch. This unit, placed between the vehicle's electric circuitry and the lamp, generates a controlled voltage of 20,000 volts on ignition and an alternating voltage in a stabilized state. Compared to a 55/60 watt halogen lamp of the same size, a 35 watt discharge lamp creates double the flux (3,200 Lumens instead of 1,500). It also doubles the width of the field of view, improves lateral perception – important on winding roads. The discharge lamp also increases the minimum visibility distance to 100 meters (on headlights) without blinding oncoming traffic. In addition, the luminosity produced is evenly spread, reducing visual tiredness. Lastly, the discharge lamp is remarkable for its low energy consumption and long life (four times longer than an incandescent lamp).

Complex surface reflectors – such as the SC3 used on the Honda Civic in Japan – increase the quantity of light projected onto the road. Because the light is distributed better and more evenly, car designers are freed from many dimensional constraints. The new Baroptic lights and Expert lighting system have also helped. A SC light is composed of a light source, a protective shield, and a complex-surface reflector. Computers assist in the design of the reflector: 50,000 points define the mirror's surface. Each point is a facet which sends out light to a specific area. Depending on the type of application (headlight, fog light etc), the computer calculates the position of the points and defines the shape.

This new SC3 technology has given scope to far greater freedom of style:
- the light is diamond shaped,
- the mirror may be slanted up to 60° and still provide twice as much light as the classic parabolic version of the same size,
- the size of the light may be reduced without losing performance,
- the mirror may be perfectly smooth, or decoratively striped,
- the protective glass may be made of plastic – which is lighter and more malleable than glass. This is because SC technology spreads the heat produced more evenly. Another advantage of this is that in the event of an

accident, the light beam is unaffected and drivers can continue their route without any change in their own visibility or that of the oncoming traffic.

The technology used in Baroptic lights has led to greater scope in style, mainly because of the modular design and reduced volume concept (the volume gained leads to a more efficient use of space under the bonnet: thermic parts, transmission…). The "Expert" technology optimizes lighting whatever the weather, type of road or vehicle speed.

Innovations made by Valeo in lighting and signaling (Velarc, Baroptic, Expert) have reinforced the company's international development, particularly in the following programs (Figure 3):

- in the heavy goods sector with the Renault Premium or Isuzu 140,

- in the private cars sector with the GM Saturn, Ford Ka and Mondeo, Renault Espace and Scenic, Volkswagens (Golf IV), Fiat Palio, PSA 106, 607 and Saxo, Jaguar XK8, Ferrari Maranello, Nissan Primera, and the Suzuki Swift,

- in the "World Cars" program, including the new Opel Corsa Ford Fiesta and the Nissan Almera.

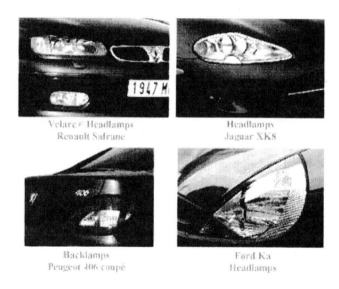

Figure 3. Valeo's technical innovation in lighting leads to greater scope in styles

2.5.2   Driving comfort improved with a new windshield-wiping system

Valeo's new system allies driving comfort and active safety: the wipers have a non-circular shape which increases visibility; new rubber materials improve both wiper resistance and the performance of the wiping system (wiping quality, aerodynamics, aesthetics, noise reduction, weight reduction of motorization mechanism). Improved style, better performance and longer product life will be obtained with the addition of electronics (rain sensors) and a new generation of materials for the arms/wipers unit (Figure 4).

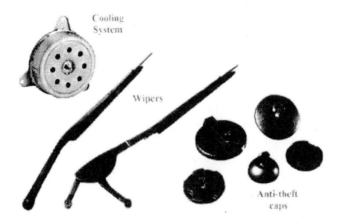

Figure 4. Wiping system

2.5.3 Development of electronics in control systems

Valeo has also developed software protection systems such as the immobilizer which, associated with a transponder key, or the latest generation of radio-frequency remote controls, guarantees the vehicle's inviolability and ease of use.

The opening/locking system called Sesame, developed by Valeo Security Systems, contains a microchip that can open the car door, adjust the driving seat and mirror, and even select a favorite radio station. The user may thus open the trunk, unlock car doors, and start the car – all without a traditional key. An electronic "identifier" – taken from transponder technology – is carried by the user, and this is detected by vehicle through induction. When the driver approaches the car a red light comes on, showing that the system has "recognized" them. The driver unlocks the car by simply using the door handle, the red light changes to green. If the user has their hands full, they can open the trunk with a mere movement of the hand.

Starting the car is just as easy: the driver needs only to place their hands on the steering wheel. A green light comes on on the dashboard, showing that recognition has taken place, the driver switches on and the car starts.

Valeo has been producing remote controls since 1983 and introduced the first generation of radio frequency controls in 1993 after the unification of frequencies in Europe at 434Mhz. Valeo produces around 10,000 remote controls a day. The ongoing process of technological development, along with recognized product, technical and industrial savoir-faire also meant that the company began to manufacture the fourth generation at the beginning of 1998.

Door handles and trunks have not only been designed with functionality and safety in mind, but also style. A combination of several different materials has been used (zamak, plastic...) depending on the identified function of each element: safety, mechanics, aesthetics, and ergonomics. The use of zamak to cover the handles has meant that each element may be customized (paint the same color as the bodywork, chrome). By associating several functions, the total number of components in the handle has also been reduced.

With the rapid expansion of the airbag market, Valeo has been developing live switches which link the airbag electrically and continuously to the steering wheel control functions (radio, cruise control etc.). This part is made up of a multitrack ribbon that rolls up and unrolls around a rotor connected to the steering wheel. Two of the ribbon tracks control the airbag, and in the future this will be increased to four with the introduction of the smart airbag. The traditional switch has a 3-meter long ribbon – which leads to a high cost and the problem of parasite noise (in spite of acoustic buffering). Valeo has innovated by incorporating this function into the commutator module, thus making better use of space, reducing cost and parasite noise. The new switch (with its differential rotor and 30 to 40 cm ribbon) proposed by Valeo cuts costs and has a highly acceptable level of noise in use (Figure 5).

Over the last few years, there has been a huge increase in the amount of information interesting the driver and passenger. This has to be made available to them on a single display for reasons of cost and space. This constraint means, however, that such a display may be optimally positioned in the top half of the central dashboard. Some automobile manufacturers have thus decided to combine this feature with others: the radio no longer displays itself – thus reducing the risk of theft. Such information is given instead by the time and external temperature display, the clock being automatically set by the RDS radio signal. The intelligence of this module serves not only to display data but also to process information selected from a data base made available through a data bus or conventional cable (a navigation aid system). Valeo developed this system in response to a customer need to optimize functionality and also display quality – particularly luminosity, regularity and contrast. In developing a lighting system and by using a choice of materials, this objective was reached.

Figure 5. Electronics at the service of comfort

Valeo is continuing its innovation policy with developments for a compact automatic gear-box calculator, intelligent wiper calculator, ballast for discharge lamps, electronic module for the engine cooling fan/motor systems and a control panel and regulator for the air-conditioning system.

2.6 Valeo's contribution to customer service

With a view to better servicing professional clients, Valeo proposes a range of elements and systems to cover the different maintenance and repair needs. The spare parts are kept in good condition thanks to special packaging, carefully studied to meet the needs of the profession. It provides instant product reference identification, ease of storage and optimal protection of the contents.

For wholesalers, automobile centers and specialized stores, the products are packed under the Valeo brand name using the well-recognized color green. For distribution to manufacturers, however, Valeo uses secondary packaging featuring the client's colors. This enables them to offer and guarantee original parts for a company like Renault, for example.

In conclusion, the Valeo case demonstrates the close partnership possibilities between an equipment supplier and an automobile manufacturer; in particular concerning assistance in product design, production management, after-sales service and tracking (traceability). This performance, clearly perceived on the technical level, is confirmed in the results of a multi-sector study described in Chapter 5.

3.   BRAND PORTFOLIO MANAGEMENT OF ZODIAC: BRANDS ORGANIZED BY SECTOR

3.1   History

In 1896, Maurice Mallet, an aeronautical engineer of the late 19th century, founded the aerodrome management company Mallet, Melandri and Pitray. In 1908, he created a dirigible balloon company specializing in the study, construction and commercialization of aircraft. In February 1909, after the launch of the first balloon, the brand name Zodiac was registered along with its logo showing a dirigible superimposed over the signs of the zodiac (Figure 6).

Figure 6. Logo of the Zodiac brand, registered in 1909 by the French Dirigible Balloon Company (Société Française des Ballons Dirigeables)

In 1911, the company – renamed Zodiac – diversified into monoplane and biplane manufacture. In 1934, a Zodiac engineer named Pierre Debroutelle had the idea of using material normally employed on dirigibles to build the first inflatable floater canoe: the inflatable boat was born. Because of its great practicality and high performance it had numerous applications in the military field, and also in the leisure sector. Doctor Bombard used this inflatable boat to cross the Atlantic Ocean in 1952 (just fishing and using the water from the rain and the ocean). The brand quickly became well known, liked, and trusted. The product was used in situations where the forces of nature had to be confronted – safety and performance were key factors. Allied with this was a pioneer spirit and innovative image.

Although for most people today, Zodiac is linked with inflatable boats (over a million boats sold worldwide) the company continues its aeronautical developments. In going back to its roots, the company is re-confirming its vocation of mastering air and water (Figure 7).

Figure 7. The new logo adopted in 1978 and the emblem of the 100th Anniversary of the company: symbol of continuity of the pioneering spirit combining the old logo (in the form of a dirigible) with the latest one (Z)

3.2   Activities of the Zodiac Group today

The group has a turnover of about 1 billion euros, 80% of which is generated in the foreign market. It employed 6,500 people and has three main branches of specialized activity:

• *Aeronautical equipment*: associating aeronautical activity targeted at constructors (civil and military aviation, helicopters, engines), and civil and armed services such as emergency evacuation systems, airbraking systems, de-icers, non-rigid fuel tanks, composite materials, super-insulators for satellites, scientific and weather balloons...

• *Airline equipment*: including activities concerning cabin equipment such as passenger seats, technical seats, modular systems, on-board sanitary systems for civil airline companies...

• *Marine-leisure*: oriented mainly to the non-specialist market (consumers), three divisions:

- marine: ranges of inflatable and semi-rigid boats,

- swimming pools: ranges of freestanding and sunken pools, spas, cleaning robots...,
- leisure: ranges of beach articles, inflatable, promotional and leisure items such as canoes and kayaks.

Zodiac and its different subsidiaries are world leaders in:

- *Aeronautical equipment*, world leader in emergency escape slides for civil aviation and floatation systems for safety-service helicopters (Air Cruisers, Aerazur), parachute systems (Aerazur, EFA, Parachutes de France, Pioneer), non-rigid fuel tanks (Amfuel, Superflexit, Aerazur, Plastiremo),
- *Airline equipment*, world leader in passenger seats for civil aircraft (Sicma Aero Seat, Weber Aircraft) and world leader in on-board sanitary systems (Mag Aerospace),
- *The marine-leisure sector*, world leader in inflatable boats (Zodiac, Bombard Jumbo), in inflatable water-sport items (Sevylor, Baracuda), free-standing pools (Debes and Wunder, B. Kern, Muskin, Europool) and pleasure-boat safety rafts (Zodiac, Bombard).

Almost two thirds of the group's activity concerns professional customers for whom Zodiac designs and commercializes different systems and aeronautical equipment. The internal and external growth strategy has enabled the group to widen their offer, making the best of technology synergies.

3.3   Brand policy

The group's brand policy is dictated by the renowned corporate brand Zodiac for the marine-leisure mass market branch. In this domain, the brand name Zodiac is visible, appearing directly on the products. In the other activity sectors of activity, oriented towards professionals and industry, the identity of the different subsidiaries is preserved, in conformity with company policy: brands are created independently and sign different productions. Nevertheless, the group's name is also mentioned (Malaval, 1998; Bénaroya, 1999).

This is the case of emergency slides used in the recent Airbus A319, A320 and A321 and Boeing B777 programs. They are manufactured both in the United States by Air Cruisers and in France by Aerazur (Figure 8).

Figure 8. Emergency Slides

This is equally true for airbraking systems such as those used in military and civil parachutes, engine braking, airdrops, ejector seats and also runway stop barriers. These systems are produced in Europe by Aerazur-Parachutes de France, and by Pioneer in the United States (Figure 9).

Figure 9. Example of a Zodiac parachute

In the airline equipment domain, Zodiac has been able to consolidate its position as world leader thanks to its association with the well-known brands of the subsidiaries Sicma Aero Seat in Europe and Weber Aircraft in the United States. Airline companies in this sector are constantly looking for ways to innovate and improve passenger comfort and service to differentiate and widen their offer. Seat dimensions, ergonomy, functionality (electric controls, head and foot rests, video, electronic games, telephones) become significant marketing sales points (Figure 10). The brands in the Zodiac group offer personalized passenger seats for tourist, business or first class as well as technical seats for the pilot and crew (in conformity with the new 16G norm which defines an impact resistance of 16 times the force of gravity).

Figure 10. Functional, ergonomic seats

Over and above the supply of the equipment itself, Zodiac offers solutions which help their clients to improve their technical performance. The gains in performance, safety, and comfort make their offer more attractive commercially. As world specialist in non-rigid composite materials, Zodiac is pursuing its program of developing new products and new technical solutions. It benefits from the synergy generated by its merger with specialized companies. Studies on technology and the utilization of high performance materials have enabled Zodiac to design products meeting the highest standards, both for the aeronautical and the marine-leisure branch. The company thus has a technological advantage in terms of design and creation of new complex materials and expert know-how in the use of aluminium in aeronautic products. Zodiac invests in CAD, robotics, new production techniques and processes (laser cutting, heat welding, molding, numeric machining, optimization of structure calculations, etc.). In this way, clients have access to the many technological advantages gained by the group in its different domains: nautical, space, civil and military aeronautics: Thermobandage (an industrial heat-assembly process), which uses a new-generation material Strongan Duotex made of a high-tech plastic-coated polyester support. Brand management within the Zodiac group operates on the following principles:

• Use of Zodiac as the corporate, federating brand:
- product brands: Sicma Aero Seat, Air Cruisers…
- process brands: Thermobandage, Strongan Duotex.

• Use of French and American brands mainly on the different respective markets.

4. THE INTEL CASE: FROM TECHNOLOGY TO ADVERTISING, A TRUE PARTNERSHIP

The Intel[1] brand illustrates an interesting example of customer company performance facilitation both from a technical and commercial viewpoint. This was achieved by the acquisition, over time, of a technological reputation mainly due to the different innovations during the brand's history.

4.1 History of the Intel brand

The company INTegrated Electronics (INTEL) was created in July 1968 in Mountain View, California, in the heart of Silicon Valley, by Gordon Moore and Bob Noyce (co-inventor of the integrated circuit), who were rapidly joined by Andrew Grove, the present day president. The objective of the new company was to exploit silicon microchip technology potential and launch semi-conductor computer memory onto the market.

In 1971, the Intel engineer Ted Hoff invented a product that proved decisive in the company's future industrial development: the microprocessor. It was the 4004 microprocessor which had 2,300 transistors and was capable of executing 60,000 operations per second – that is, it was equal in power to the first ENIAC computer (1946) with its 18,000 tubes, which took up a whole room and weighed 30 tons. About the size of a fingernail, the microprocessor is a silicon chip which serves as the brain of the computer. Intel's success was also due to the synergy of the microprocessor and the newly-invented EPROM (Erasable Programmable Read-Only Memory) – a permanent back-up memory allowing the OEM (Original Equipment Manufacturers) to stock microprocessor programs.

Other technological innovations were developed later by Intel: the RAM (Random Access Memory: live computer memory), the microcontroller (a type of industrial processor present in many equipment parts: ABS brakes, TV decoders, high speed trains, printers, photocopiers...). With miniaturization came improvements in performance, a reduction in energy consumption, heat production, an increase in power autonomy, and finally, a decrease in the cost of production of the microchip.

In 1982, IBM made the choice of integrating the Intel 8088 microprocessor into its first personal computer (PC). The notion of compatibility was born when other constructors quickly followed, adopting Intel (86 family) for their CPUs. During the 80's and the beginning of the 90's, various different models were developed: 8086,186, 286 then i386 and the 486[2]. The product strategy consisted of developing and launching a generation of chips available in a wide range (35 versions of the 486) to meet consumer needs. Then, before the competition could react and launch an equivalent product, Intel had brought out another, vastly superior new generation (Table 11).

Table 11. Some of Intel's main technological innovations

Generation	8086	8088	i286	i386	i486	Pentium	Pentium II
Start of research	1975	1976	1978	1982	1986	1989	1993
Launch	1978	1979	1982	1985	1989	1993	1997
Number of transistors	29,000	29,000	130,000	275,000	1.2 million	3.1 millions	7.5 millions
Speed in millions of instructions per second	0,29	0,29	1	5	20	100	500
Innovation	PC	PC	Data base	Graphic Interface (Windows)	Computer generated images	Voice recognition, financial analysis	Multimedia, sound and image processing

With the launch of the Pentium processor in 1993 (Figure 12), Intel followed its innovation policy illustrating Moore's Law: the performance of silicon chips doubles every two years[3].

Figure 12. The Intel Pentium processor with MMX media enhancement technology

Each new generation of microprocessor is more efficient, rapid and costs less that the previous generation (Figure 13). In 1997, the Pentium II was launched, to be followed by another code-named Merced.

Transistors per chip

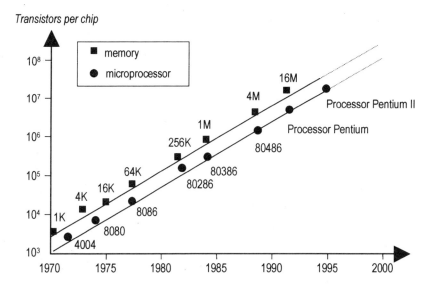

Figure 13. Moore's Law: every two years, the integration capacity of the silicon chip doubles

4.2   Intel today

Intel, with a staff of 65,000 is now the world leader in the processor sector: 84% of PCs use Intel, and turnover is about 30 billion dollars. Intel's success lies in its technological advance. AMD and Cyrix, its competitors, often produce quality clones but bring them onto the market two years later. Advanced Micro Devices (AMD) and Cyrix (brought out by National Semiconductors, leader in analogue products manufacture), have turnovers of 2.8 billion dollars and 265 million dollars respectively. The competition is hoping to reduce the development gap with Intel by bringing out the K6 (AMD), the M2 (Cyrix) and the C6 (IDT).

At the end of 1997, Intel reorganized its structure to accommodate the development of the lower-end product range computer market. Two divisions were set up: the Consumer Product Group – for the mass consumer market, and the Small Business and Networking Group – in charge of the small businesses market. In response to attacks by competitors on the basic PC sector, Intel launched the "Pentium Light" Pentium II processor in the second half of 1998. This light-weight presentation considerably reduced price (presentation without the Intel Pentium II characteristic black packaging, smaller than the classic Pentium II). Intel thus covers all market segments. With the Pentium II, the basis of the motherboard was changed.

Up until then, any square processor (Intel 486, Cyrix Media GX or AMD K6) could be used in Slot Socket 7. The Pentium II and its range, which are larger and rectangular, fit ad hoc into Slot Socket 1.

The Pentium II at 233 MHz, launched in January 1998, was the first 0.25 micron processor (code name Deschutes[4]). Compared to other processors of 0.35 microns, it represents a 40% gain of productivity and a cost benefit of 60 – 70%. Other Pentium processors at 350 then 450 MHz were launched from June 1998. The Pentium III at 1Gigahertz was launched during the year 2000.

4.3   Partners in technical improvement and innovation: an absolute necessity

The microprocessor industry drains capital: a factory cost a million dollars at the beginning of the 1970's, today it costs over 1.5 billion. Production complexity has increased with design and accuracy demands: over 300 stages are needed to produce a processor. Circuit engraving on the silicon necessitates greater precision. The first microprocessor was engraved using lines measuring 10 microns[5], Pentium used 0.35 then 0.25 microns. To illustrate this better, a hair has a thickness of 120 microns and an unrestrained human sneeze projects a million drops 45 times bigger than the circuits of the latest Intel processor. If one of these particles landed on the circuit, the effect would be as devastating as a tree falling on a high voltage cable. For this reason, the air in the factories must be particularly pure, almost 10,000 times purer than in an operating theater. In the most sensitive work areas, personnel wear white jumpsuits, special boots, mask, gloves, and apparatus to filter exhaled breath – all of which inspired the BunnyPeople Characters in the Intel advertising.

The computer industry (professional and non-professional PCs, work stations, multimedia, communication networks) uses 45% of the microprocessors produced (Figure 14). Constructors buy according to software and microchip compatibility. Other sectors concerned are non-professional electronics markets (television, videos…), on-board car electronics (braking system, ABS, airbag…), cordless telecommunication (flash memories). In the computer market, there is a close relationship between software and hardware: the operating system and the programs running it are directly linked to a given chip configuration. Clients working on a CISC (Complex Instructions Set Computer) cannot easily change, the software functioning under CISC will be lost and network communication with their own clients, sub-contractors and suppliers will be jeopardized.

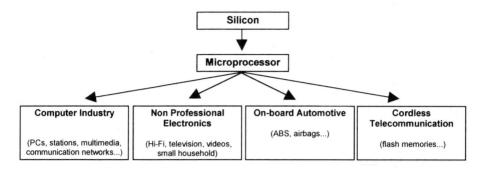

Figure 14. Simplified diagram of microprocessor user segments

Almost 90% of programs function with Microsoft-type systems; these are compatible only with CISC chips (Intel, AMD, National Semiconductors...). Because of high costs, chip manufacturers work either under CISC or RISC (Random Instructions Set Computer) architecture – the latter is less widely diffused because of cost and compatibility constraints (with Motorola, Digital, IBM, Hewlett Packard, Sun...). In the future, there will no doubt have to be a common base (partnership agreements between companies). The speed of product innovation imposes huge research and development costs on manufacturers. The constant increase in microprocessor sales means even greater investment in production facilities (factories, production tools...).

Intel has invested heavily in CISC technology with two groups of researchers: while the first group were launching the Pentium processor in 1993, the other had already began work on the Pentium Pro to be launched in 1995, two years ahead of the Pentium II launched in May 1997. Intel's aim is to supply its clients with a better product, for the same price as the previous generation; providing greater application possibilities.

An example of this is the MMX technology which has enabled Intel to improve the sound and image of software: this has meant that program developers – particularly of video games software – can create even more spectacular games. With the introduction of the CD-ROM and the development of DVD-ROM (Digital Versatile Disc), editors offering high technology, quality products obviously have the advantage. The futuristic motor racing game Pod launched by Ubi Soft has exceptional graphics and is more enjoyable to play. This was possible thanks to the innovative Pentium MMX technology which increased processing from 10 to 30% and improved image fluidity. Ubi Soft, created in 1986, is a French company specializing in the publishing, production and diffusion of interactive leisure products. It has over 1,500 people working for it, and a turnover of 135 million euros. After the worldwide success of its game Rayman (900,000 copies sold in two years and about 5 million sold total, the first game for use on the Sony Playstation), Ubi Soft developed Pod. It required 3 million euros investment to develop adequate systems to drive the game.

Intel's clients benefit from such new technology. Cooperation between Intel and Ubi Soft meant a joint promotional campaign for Pod and Pentium MMX (Pod was on display at the evening presenting the new multimedia processor). Over 5 million copies of Pod were sold (Figure 15). Similarly, the game Tonic Trouble – developed in 3D for real-time use – was the first optimized game for the Pentium II (1.1 million copies sold).

Figure 15. The complementarity of commercial and technological strategies between Intel and Ubi Soft

The brand's desire to contribute to improving client performance can be summarized in the 3 R's rule guiding the high technology sector: Research, Risk-taking and Responsiveness. Intel is constantly looking to improve the performance of its own products and those of its clients: 10 to 15% of turnover given over to research and development, risk-taking in new markets with new products or new partners, and high reactivity to market needs. In 1994, Intel was leader of CISC technology associated with Hewlett – Packard, specialist in RISC technology. Together they designed and produced a processor for the year 2000: the Merced. In doing this, Intel planned to penetrate the workstation market, and be more present on the non-professional electronics market – using its partner's RISC know-how.

As for Hewlett-Packard, it is already number one in computer networks and number two in workstations. Its strategy is to make deeper inroads into the PC manufacturer market, thus anticipating the growing competition between PCs and workstations. It is also strengthening its position relative to the IBM-Apple-Motorola alliance and their multi-purpose PowerPC processor.

In these two examples, Intel has developed complementary partnerships with its industrial clients. It has played the role of performance facilitator on a technical level, collaborating with others in the development and industrialization phase. Intel has facilitated commercial performance through the use of its logo Intel and slogan "Intel Inside", clearly visible on packaging bought by the final user. In this way, the client is reassured and the buying decision is made easier.

NOTES

1. Illustrations reproduced with the permission of Intel Corporation, © 1998 Intel Corporation, Pentium, MMX, BunnyPeople, the logos Intel and Intel Inside are registered trade marks of Intel Corporation.
2. See Chapter 3, The Characteristics of Business to Business Communication, 6- The Intel Communication Strategy.
3. Several computer specialists now put Moore's Law into question (every two years, the integration capacity of the silicon chip doubles) because upstream innovation is slowing down. Windows 98, is it not just an upgrade of Windows 95 rather that a technological innovation? Videoconferencing, DVD, voice recognition, digital photographs, digital video cameras and other digital equipment are not yet in the mass consumer sector because of their high cost.
4. Tradition goes that Intel christens its processors with a code name of a geographical location in the States.
5. 1 micron = 1 millionth of a meter.

REFERENCES

Bénaroya, Ch., (1999), "Under the signs of the zodiac: air and water control", *La Revue des Marques*, n°27, July.
Malaval, Ph., (1998), *Stratégie et Gestion de la Marque Industrielle*, Paris, Publi-Union.

Chapter 13

Equipment Goods Brands

Equipment goods and systems can be distinguished from intermediary goods by the fact that they stand alone: for the customer they are an independent entity. Normally they do not need to be built into another assembly. The equipment goods and systems category is much less homogeneous than the entering goods and intermediate equipment goods categories dealt with earlier. This is because in this large category there is both small equipment (individual protective equipment, office supplies, etc.) as well as very large equipment (supply of a transport aircraft or a freeway).

1. PURCHASEABILITY AND VISIBILITY OF EQUIPMENT GOODS BRANDS

Although they consist of finished goods, equipment goods are not normally purchaseable by the private customer, apart from material like goods vehicles, general office and IT accessories or hand tools. As can be seen from the table below (Table 1), we can distinguish the equipment goods which are non-purchaseable and non-usable from those which the consumer can use. By the very nature of their technical complexity and price, most equipment goods are not purchaseable by the general public.

The brand can be deliberately printed on the material, i.e. machine tools, in order to be seen by possible influencers (building sites, factory visits, vehicles). Whether consumers see finished equipment goods brands, depends however on two main factors: the possible access available to the final end user and the policy of the customer company and the supplier.

Table 1. Consumer access to equipment goods

	Categories	**Brand examples**
Purchaseable	• Office equipment • General office accessories • Small goods vehicles	• Post-It (3M) • Xerox • American Isuzu Commercial Vehicles
Non-purchaseable and non-usable by the private customer	• Trailer trucks • Mainframe computers • Individual protective equipment • Production tool • Packaging range	• Fruehauf, Fleetco, American Trailer Exchange, Anderson Manufacturing • Cray • Kimberly-Clark, WorkMaster Products, DuPont Protective Apparel • Case, Deere • Tetra Pak, Mead
Non-purchaseable but usable by the private customer	• Railway equipment • Planes	• Alstom, Siemens • Airbus, Boeing

As far as final end user access to equipment goods is concerned, it is possible to compare a delivery vehicle with a supercalculator or an office computer. The visibility of the vehicle is due to its frequent presence in the street, delivering to shops or houses. The very low visibility of the second, is derived from the fact that the end users do not usually have access to the IT department at the head office. A distinction must be made between the recurrent visibility of a transport vehicle and the one-off visibility of the public works contractor which only lasts for as long as the job in hand (Figure 2).

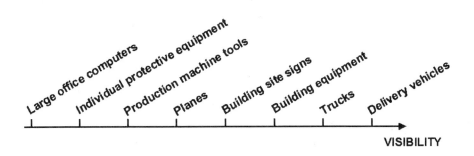

Figure 2. Examples of visibility levels by product category

The policy of the different players involved depends on the one hand on the dynamism of the supplier in displaying his name, and on the other on the acceptance of the customer. For example, even if the name of the public works contractor is visible for the duration of the roadwork, it certainly cannot be seen once the freeway has been delivered to the operating company (Table 3).

Table 3. The purchaseability and visibility of equipment goods brands

	Non visible to the private customer	Visible to the private customer
Non purchaseable, non usable by the private customer	• Cray computers • Xerox large office equipment	• Fruehauf trailer trucks • Building equipment Caterpillar
Non purchaseable, usable by the private customer	• Alstom subway • Highway infrastructures	• Airbus, Boeing planes • Volvo, Western Star Trucks buses

2.   DIFFERENT TYPES OF PERFORMANCE FACILITATORS

Generally, customer companies acquire equipment goods to increase their productivity and improve the manufacturing process and production quality. Equipment goods brands are therefore mainly evaluated as a function of their technical performance and capacity to improve that of the customer. There is a greater importance attached to technical criteria in the choice of equipment goods brands compared to the other categories of goods examined in previous chapters. Indeed, quite apart from the high cost, the purchase of equipment goods links the customer to the supplier brand for the life of the machinery and may also have repercussions on the actual organization of production.

Consequently, in the first place, equipment goods brands must contribute to improving customer productivity, directly in the factory for example. This is true for Tetra Pak in the packaging sector which offers machines with a higher operating rate and which are better adapted to the customer's activities. It could also apply to equipment, which reduces the number of manufacturing operations or simplifies the production process. Airbus in the aviation sector contributes to improving services offered by airline companies, thanks to the technical performance of its planes.

Equipment goods brands can also contribute indirectly to improving their customer's technical performance. Thus Fruehauf equips trucks with trailers specially designed to facilitate handling and loading/unloading. Other equipment such as Xerox copiers can contribute to simplifying certain administrative tasks and by so doing, improve the overall efficiency of the company. Similarly, the equipment could have a beneficial effect on the working conditions of the customer company's personnel, in turn improving productivity.

Grafted onto these contributions to customer technical performance, the equipment goods brands often offer commercial help. Latécoère, for example, not only design aeronautical equipment which fits perfectly into the production process, but also produce equipment designed to enrich the commercial offer of it's customers. The improvement in commercial performance of customers is therefore the result at the outset of greater technical efficiency and then subsequently, the possibility of diversifying the final offer to customers.

To illustrate the role of performance facilitator for equipment goods brands, "reference status" brands from industry will be used. Thus, Xerox, Fruehauf, and Latécoère will demonstrate the role of the performance facilitator on a technical level and Kimberly-Clark and Tetra Pak will provide examples at the technical and commercial level. A panoramic view of the brand in the aeronautics sector will be presented. Finally, Airbus Industrie provides an example of a brand, which facilitates technical performance above all but also the commercial performance of its customers.

3. XEROX: A "REFERENCE" BRAND IN DOCUMENT MANAGEMENT

In 1938, Chester Carlson made the first photocopy on ordinary paper using a process called xerography (from the Greek words xerox "dry" and graphein "to write") the rights of which were acquired in 1948 by the American company Haloïd. The latter, which took the name Xerox in 1961, has developed its document processing activities with for example the launch of color photocopiers in 1973, the first complete system for duplicating and finishing using a built-in computer in 1989 or the recto-verso DocuColor printer in 1996 (Figure 4).

THE
DOCUMENT
COMPANY
XEROX

Figure 4. Xerox logotype

Innovation has marked the history of the Xerox brand, to which can also be added apart from xerography, the electronic mouse, page-by-page laser printing, the invention of the Windows-based operating system and

WYSIWYG (What you see is what you get). Today, the Xerox group is present all over the world with almost 90,000 employees, and a total turnover of almost 20 billion euros.

3.1   Innovating for greater customer productivity

Technological innovation and research and development are at the heart of Xerox values, with famous research centers such as the PARC (Palo Alto Research Center) in the United States, the European Research Center in Grenoble (Centre de Recherche Européen de Grenoble) and the Welwyn Garden City Development Center in Great Britain. The solutions provided by the brand are born out of a commitment to improving the productivity of information processing in its customer companies. The optimization of the world of documents, from their creation to their management via make-up and circulation are the vocation of Xerox. There is in fact, a productivity goldmine for automatic and electronic information processing: almost 95% of all information is in the form of documents whose management and production can cost the company anything up to 8% of its turnover. In offices, 60% of time is spent working on documents.

Quite apart from their economic importance, these documents have a strategic dimension. They are not just a sheet of paper coming out of a photocopier or printer, or a picture on a screen, they are the embodiment of information, its accessibility, diffusion and decentralization. Clear, precise, readable and with the emphasis on the hierarchy and memorization of the information, documents are the main information medium and an irreplaceable tool in the decision-making process. By presenting useful information to the company in a pertinent, effective and persuasive fashion, the structure of a document highlights those ideas which are essential. Therefore any processing tools will be of paramount importance for the productivity and competitivity of a company.

For Xerox, it is a question of coming up with complete office automation solutions, which will allow companies and organizations to improve efficiency, running costs, and above all competitivity. To this end the company offers black and white or color electronic photocopiers and printers, fax machines, electronic document production systems, multifunction equipment and scanners. Such is the technological lead of Xerox that they can offer their customers, solutions which contribute to an increase in productivity and which take into account difficulties allied to the compatibility of IT systems and the different types of IT connections (networks, etc.).

3.2   A portfolio of equipment brands aimed at technical performance

Xerox chooses product names based on its corporate brand name for the different ranges it offers. Onto this name are added:

• A specific and significant designation (DocuPrint, DocuColor, Document Center etc.) which can if necessary have an alphanumeric reference added, indicating the technical characteristics such as the Xerox DocuPrint 180NPS which can deliver 180 A4 pages per minute (Figure 5).

• Number references which situate the equipment relative to the rest of the range and give the principal technical characteristics (number of pages reproduced per minute, etc.), such as the Xerox 5815 (15 color copies per minute).

Figure 5. The Xerox DocuPrint 180NPS: productivity and an image serving the customer

Xerox signs its products with its corporate brand name, which is visible on the front of photocopiers and equipment. The presence of the brand name on the product is a guarantee: by being perfectly identifiable, Xerox is totally committed to the customer company and end users. On large equipment, the presence of the Xerox brand is akin to having a name tag. High tech equipment such as this, renowned on the market for its high quality and innovation, can represent for the customer company visible proof of their own technical expertise in the service of their own customers. Using such equipment, they can demonstrate their professionalism and reinforce their image in terms of quality and productivity for their customers. In an effort to help customer companies optimize their equipment, Xerox has set up several procedures and links its offer to numerous services.

3.3   The presence of the brand extended to services

The main aim of Xerox, total customer satisfaction, comes second to the quality and efficiency of its services which offer a permanent guarantee for the performance and optimum profitability of the equipment. By so doing the brand has become one of the first in the world to have a total quality system, winning numerous trophies and awards for quality (European Quality Trophy, Deming Award, Malcolm Baldridge Award, etc.) and respect for the environment (World Environment Council). To the reliability of the equipment can be added the quality of the various services which make up the Xerox offer. These are especially effective due to their customer-based organization, made up of "Business Groups" and "Customer Business Units." All these actions have reinforced the rapidity, flexibility, reactivity and quality of the services offered. In this way, the brand has been able to offer as early as 1991, a service which was unique on the market: the Total Satisfaction Guarantee. This service allows for any customer who so wishes, to have his equipment replaced by an identical or equivalent machine (subject to having a Xerox maintenance contract).

Through the competence of its sales structure and that of its after-sales service technicians, the company is always on hand to intervene or offer help to its customers. Apart from the help line provided by the National Customer Support Center, Xerox offers equipment which has built in tele-diagnostic systems, capable of the early detection of signs of weakness or wear in essential parts and circuits, thus allowing a technician to intervene before a breakdown actually occurs. For example, in France, Xerox undertakes to react and, on average, be on the spot in two hours for all customers equipped with the Xerox Docutech system. In order to complete its own products and services, Xerox proposes solutions which are genuinely global by relying on specialized subsidiaries. The latter, by the clever use of "X" or the prefix "Xero" maintain a strong synergy with the Xerox brand.

• XES (Xerox Engineering Systems), specialized in engineering technical documents (plotters, industrial copiers, reproducing machines and digital hard copy systems),

• Xerobail specialized in the financing of office administration and IT solutions marketed by Xerox,

• XBS (Xerox Business Services), specialized in facilities management which means offering added value service provision in the sphere of document management (equipment, software, personnel, logistics, organization).

Only two subsidiaries do not incorporate the Xerox brand name:

• OTP specialized in the distribution of supplies and consumables,

• Servitique, specialized in multi-brand office and IT maintenance.

Together, these subsidiaries allow the Xerox brand to cover the field from equipment to customer services.

3.4   The presence of the brand on consumables

Xerox applies the same visibility policy it uses for machines to consumables. Thus the brand guarantees supplies such as packets of paper, floppy discs, rolls of fax paper, etc. The brand is present on the packaging of supplies and consumables, encouraging customer loyalty (Figure 6).

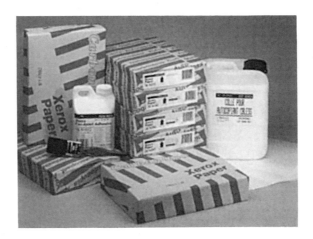

Figure 6. The Xerox brand extended to consumables

The brand signature testifies to a commitment to product and service quality. It reinforces its customer image. In order to maintain its renown and image in the eyes of a wide public, Xerox runs communication campaigns in the trade press, in popular magazines and in the mass-market media (e.g. the TV campaign for the Xerox Document Center). Through the diversity, quality and technological sophistication of its products and services, as well as its commitment to customer productivity, the Xerox brand is solidly associated by its customer companies with its signature "The Document Company". The visible presence of the Xerox brand from one end of the offer to the other, from equipment goods to services via consumables has allowed it to make a name for itself as: "Xerox, the document expert". And it is by facilitating and improving customer productivity that Xerox makes this position credible.

4.   FRUEHAUF: ROCK RUNNER, SPEED SLIDER… EVOCATIVE PRODUCT-BRANDS

4.1   Review of the group's history

Figure 7. Fruehauf logotype

In 1914 in Detroit, USA, a blacksmith Auguste Fruehauf designed and built a two-wheeled trailer that he fitted to the back of a Model T Ford: the trailer truck was born. The Fruehauf company was thus founded in 1918 (Figure 8). It was not until 1945 that the trailer truck concept appeared in France, initially with the signing of a trailer and trailer truck import and sales agreement.

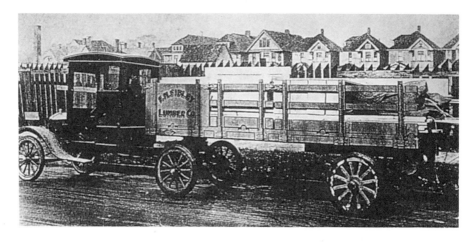

Figure 8. The first trailer truck in the world built in the Auguste Fruehauf works in 1914 for Frederick Sibley, coupled up to a Model " T " Ford Harry

The Fruehauf France company was founded in 1946 and developed in the 50's mainly by adapting trailer trucks to the needs of the French market. Between 1960 and 1970, Fruehauf France developed its position on the home market using a network of branch offices and sales outlets, while Fruehauf International developed in Europe. In an effort to avoid an inevitable takeover bid, the American group parted with its European subsidiary and in this way, Fruehauf became independent and French. Between 1970 and 1980, the firm consolidated by buying into the Benalu company, European leader in the construction of trailers and trailer trucks in aluminium.

In the eighties, the Fruehauf network became the Fruehauf Benalu network. A new visual identity was created, taking the form of a logo showing a Fruehauf and Benalu brand vehicle cornering (Figure 9).

Figure 9. Benalu logotype

In 1987, the Société Européenne de Semi-Remorques (SESR) was founded to coordinate Fruehauf's European trailer truck construction activities (Table 10).

Table 10. The distribution of the brands as a function of their different activities within the SESR group

ACTIVITIES	BRANDS
Industrial vehicle bodies	Blond Badouin
Design, manufacture and sales of trailers and trailer trucks	Fruehauf, Benalu, Trailor
Parts division	SMB

Since the end of the eighties, the group has launched new products and services, reorganized its export activity, and launched its Total Quality Project. Today, European leader in vehicle sales, Fruehauf and Benalu design and produce transport solutions covering all the needs of the market. The SESR group has almost 4,000 people working for it and has 15 industrial sites in 6 different countries.

4.2 Managing the portfolio of trailer truck product-brands

As far as product names are concerned, Fruehauf follows a European brand policy, in line with its status as the number one in Europe. The brands for trailers and trailer trucks are English sounding and correspond to a system of meaningful or evocative names, understandable in a large number of countries. For example, the brand name " Speed Slider Maxi " refers to a large volume, industrial transport trailer with side loading. Similarly, the trailer brand " Kombirail " is designed for mixed rail/road transport and associates the name and the specific vocation with the product.

The brands developed by Fruehauf are usually brand-ranges, combining in the same name and the same vocation, a set of homogenous equipment: Speed Slider, Euro Slider, Load Runner, Express Liner, Petro Tanker, Rock Runner (Figure 11).

Figure 11. Rock Runner: an example of a meaningful brand from Fruehauf

The brand names of the group's main ranges are characterized by their diverse origins (Table 12).

While Fruehauf was originally a family name, Benalu comes from the two words " benne " (truck) and " aluminium," recalling the original manufacturing speciality of the company.

The brand Trailor also comes from two words, " train " and " lorrain " (inhabitant of Lorraine), however today it evokes above all the English word " trailer".

Table 12. The portfolio of product-brands managed by Fruehauf

Brands	Characteristics
Speed Slider	Trailer with sliding roof and exclusive universal coupling device
Classic	87m^3 volume and 26 ton carrying capacity
Maxi	2.7 to 2.8m high side opening optimized with 1,100 truck tractors
Hyper volume	100m^3 volume and 2.9m high side opening for 950 truck tractors
Hyper charge	Up to 28 ton carrying capacity
On-vehicle jib crane	For 25 to 26 ton drums
Euro Slider	Polyvalent trailer with sliding roof, lateral, rear or roof loading
Classic	87m^3 volume and 26 ton carrying capacity
Maxi	2.7m high side opening optimized with 1,100 truck tractors
On-vehicle jib crane	For 25 to 26 ton drums
TIR liner	Polyvalent trailer with sliding roof, lateral, rear or roof loading, conforms to TIR international norms (high security customs seals...)
Express Liner	Logistics trailer combining max. volume, high carrying capacity and minimum maintenance costs
Parcel delivery	Designed for frequent loading bay visits, translucent roof for 24h activity
Maxi	Designed with anchorage points for rolls, retractable lifting tailgate
Fragile or	Giving 2.7m interior height (91m^3) with 1,100 truck tractor
delicate products	With built in pneumatic suspension, insulated roof, aeration devices, anti condensation system, TIR approval locking system
Load Runner	Trailer with skip for supplying bulk products to an open work site (gravel, sand, beetroots, demolition material, hot products such as " coated " ones): 26 ton carrying capacity, 19 to 24m^3 working volume
Rock Runner	Trailer with high elastic limit steel shell designed for heavy work e.g. rocks earthworks, demolition, large construction sites, freeways, TGV, etc. Up to 25 ton carrying capacity, 19m^3 working volume
Petro Tanker	Tanker trailer
Hot materials	Insulated design in stainless steel for transporting heavy fuel oils or bitumen
Gas distribution	Designed for transporting gas, petroleum products
Twin Liner	Trailer and carrier for high volume pallet transport
Twin Slider	Covered trailer and carrier for high volume pallet transport

The identity of the SESR group brands indicates their position as the specialist within their particular domain. In this way, Fruehauf is perceived positively over its whole range, for the strength and quality of its network and services as well as its standing as an international brand. Similarly, Benalu possesses a very good image within its speciality, where it is considered to be the European aluminium specialist, for transporting loose solids. In general, Fruehauf is considered to be the brand which started the idea of articulated trucks in Europe, and which has developed it using different, specialized bodywork. The Benalu brand will always be associated with the introduction of light alloys into the design of dump body trailer trucks.

These innovations confer on the two brands a pioneering and expert image, reinforced by the breadth of their experience, market knowledge and the wide range that they offer. By adopting a policy of visibility on their products, the Fruehauf and Benalu brands take on the role of a guarantee. The brands can be seen particularly on the rear, front and sides of trailers and trailer trucks. In addition, this visibility is combined with the use of a distinctive and personalized product design line which is easily recognizable. The visibility allows the brands to be easily identified and remembered particularly by transport professionals but also by most other road users. The vehicles are thus vectors for the brand image and become a support for communication.

Through having its signature on trailers and trailer trucks, Fruehauf is present over the whole road network used by the vehicles. This also allows professionals to benefit from a sort of " product demonstration." The frequent presence of the brand on fleets of vehicles belonging to leading transporters and professionals tends to reinforce Fruehauf's number one position. And the brand image can have an influence when it comes to buying. The supplier's durability, its financial solidity, and its reputation are all criteria taken into account at the moment of buying.

4.3 Fruehauf, a facilitator brand for technical and sales performance

What customers are really interested in from trailer and trailer truck constructors:

• The product itself in terms of strength, reliability, finish and homogeneity,

• Relations with the supplier in terms of technical presence, sales contacts, service capacity and respect of deadlines.

However, in spite of solutions, which give greater productivity and are more innovative, the price is often the one decisive factor in the final choice. Which is the reason why innovation and productivity are the two main axes of Fruehauf's strategy for improving their customer's competitivity. The two brands have the same vocation, that of making road transports more productive.

4.3.1   Performance facilitation at the technical level

Fruehauf and Benalu design, manufacture, and sell a complete range of "ready-to-use" trailers and trailer trucks which fulfill the needs of goods transport on the European market. Because of the diversity of types of transport, there are a number of market segments (Table 13).

Table 13. Product segmentation as a function of advantages sought

Product category	Market Share all brands	Products/Applications
Covered trailer trucks	37%	Sliding or hybrid blinds for transporting complete palleted loads very high freight , drum carrier
Trailers	13,5%	Trailers for complete loads (120m3, 38 europallets), for animals, loose material and milk collecting
Trailer trucks for vans	13%	Express cargo (87m3 carrying capacity) Transport of complete loads (33 europallets) Large volume transport (96m3 carrying capacity) Distribution (57 rolls)
Refrigerated trailer Trucks	9%	Transport at controlled temperatures (sea produce, fruit and vegetables, meat)
Trailer truck skips	9%	Transport of building supplies Transport of vegetables Transport of loose material (cereals, waste, old iron): steel skips (17 to 30m3), in aluminium (17 to 44m3) dump or moving floor
Tanker trailer trucks	7%	Transport of petroleum products (compartmented aluminium tanker Transport of hot materials (insulated stainless steel tank) Transport of dusts (aluminium dump silo, aluminium silo with outlet) Transport of chemicals (insulated stainless steel tank) Transport of foodstuffs (stainless steel tank) Transport of liquefied gas (steel tank)
Combination trailer Trucks	4%	Transport of shipping containers Rail / road transport

In-depth knowledge of their customers' activity, their economic constraints as well as any loading constraints allow Fruehauf to design new trailers and trailer trucks which fulfill needs and conform to the regulations. Activities such as earthworks, rock work or demolition require specific equipment, quite distinct from that used for transporting large volumes of vegetables or express cargo services for example.

In an effort to find possible improvements in terms of security (braking, surveillance), design or functions, partnerships have been set up with:

• Transporters and logistics specialists such as Danzas, Giraud, Dentressangle, Astre, etc.

• Truck specialists such as Renault, Volvo, DaimlerChrysler, etc.

• Shippers such as Usinor, Thyssen, etc.

One of Fruehauf's main objectives is to contribute to improving the loading and unloading time while at the same time getting the optimum carrying capacity. The vehicle turnaround time is thus improved which allows for more efficient customer logistics. For the design of their trailers and trailer trucks, Fruehauf and Benalu must therefore take all the following into account:

- Constraints because of regulations,
- Technical constraints associated with motor vehicle construction,
- The demands of shippers,
- Customer operating imperatives.

In all, numerous transport solutions have been set up by Fruehauf in order to:

- Facilitate side, rear or roof loading: removable bodywork, sliding blinds, fold-down side boards, sliding roofs, raise and lower devices for loading bays, quarter turn tensioners or reels for easy action, translucent roof for ease of cargo identification, rounded skip bodies and angled front part so that materials slide down easily, built in ladder for ease of access to bodywork, rapid rear unlock in case of partial unloads, etc.

- Pay particular attention to user personnel security: fold-down side boards with auto lock as freight pushes, foldaway, anti-slip ladder, sliding roof with built in cross piece for effective and rapid use, security seals and cables, anchoring straps, ABS braking, etc.

- Ensure the materials used have the longest life possible: heavy duty side board paint, obligatory fire extinguishers with waterproof casings made from weatherproof and recyclable materials, hardwood flooring, reinforced front part, struts with compensating shoes, rear protection for frequent loading bay visits, rising front axle to increase tyre life with lighter freight, flush rear lights for skip with protective grid, etc.

- Optimize the carrying capacity: flat floor, optimum side opening facility, etc.

- Make the vehicle more polyvalent: combination rail / road Kombirail®, conformity with anchorage requirements, roof insulation, anti-condensation system, universal couplings, etc.

- Reduce the minimum unladen weight: thinned chassis, use of aluminium wheels to increase tanker carrying capacity, etc.

Fruehauf, with its customers' requirements at heart and constantly searching for improvements, has developed the most complete range of trailer trucks, double trains and road trains in Europe.

4.3.2   Performance facilitation at the sales level

The two brands Fruehauf and Benalu are both determined to offer transport solutions which answer user needs and contribute to increasing road transport productivity (Figure 14), while at the same time respecting road user safety and the environment. Fruehauf and Benalu have complete control over the majority of their vehicles' basic components: axles, suspensions, chassis and bodywork. Right from the design stage, the two brands use reduced maintenance components (axles, suspensions) as well as hard wearing and reliable parts (bearings or electrical housings for example).

To ensure greater operating productivity for their transporter, as well as their own customers, Fruehauf designs highly reliable, long life equipment. Their industrial processes include shot-blasting, polyurethane lacquering and wax, cavity injection procedures.

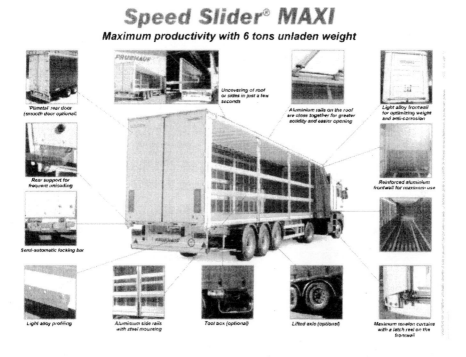

Figure 14. Fruehauf's contribution to customer productivity: Speed Slider to maximise loading/unloading speed

It is a case of designing equipment which is easy to use and set up, which corresponds to the requirements of modern logistics and is the right equipment at the right time (carrying capacity, empty weight, polyvalence, etc.). Also the vehicles must only require limited maintenance. Transporter professionals are looking to optimize the price per kilometer of a ton or cubic meter carried, in other words the carrying capacity transported. In addition, Fruehauf and Benalu seek to give their equipment the highest active and passive safety right from the design stages, by choice of materials, overall design study of the various elements, resistance tests, etc.

Thanks to this approach, Benalu obtained its ISO 9001 certificate in 1997 for:

• The design, manufacture and sale of trailers and trailer trucks,

• The repair, maintenance and sale of spare parts for Benalu brand vehicles.

Fruehauf and Benalu also make sure that their equipment offer is accompanied by a customer service and assistance structure close at hand. This relies heavily on what is now the number one assistance network in Europe consisting of 500 centers in 27 different countries along the main national and international roads. Here Fruehauf offer anything from advice to financing, from sales of new and used vehicles, maintenance, fitting and sales of original spare parts, after-sales service, to the provision of a 24 hour European assistance service called "Code Rouge." In this way Fruehauf stand out as being a partner brand at the commercial level, through their specialized knowledge of transporters and their activity, by their personalized way of answering needs thanks to their wide range, as well as by satisfying other demands (buying back used vehicles, expert appraisal, maintenance, financing).

In all, thanks to their commitment to customer productivity, the Fruehauf and Benalu brands are seen as partners in productivity or performance facilitators. Both brands contribute to safety in working conditions while at the same time facilitating the different loading and handling operations.

5.   LATÉCOÈRE: TECHNICAL PARTNERSHIP AND ITS OWN PRODUCTS

5.1   The rise of Latécoère

Founded in 1917 by Pierre-Georges Latécoère in Toulouse, the Société Industrielle d'Aviation Latécoère started by making warplanes such as the Salmson 2A2 or the Breguet XIV. At the end of the First World War, the company became involved in civil aviation with a special interest in extending aircraft range (Figure 15).

These efforts allowed Pierre-Georges Latécoère for example to make the first air crossing of the Pyrénées when he flew from Toulouse to Barcelona one and a half months after the armistice. In 1926, another project close to Pierre-Georges Latécoère's heart was achieved with the crossing between France and South America. In this way, the company designed and developed more than 83 aircraft study projects, made 33 prototypes (most of which were the largest of their era) and set up 11 series production aircraft for commercial airlines or military seaplanes for the Navy. Latécoère aircraft brought France 31 world records: in 1930 for example, Mermoz made the first seaplane crossing of the South Atlantic in a Latécoère Late 28.

Figure 15. Following World War I, the Latécoère France – Spain – Morocco line was born

In 1939, after having taken part in the French war effort and in the face of mounting clouds on the political horizon, the company gave up most of its factories. In this way it reduced its production potential and focused on activities which the enemy could not use. At the end of the Second World War, the company, which had in fact secretly continued its research, and hiding aircraft parts was in a position to offer the type Lionel de Marmier 75 ton Latécoère seaplane reinforcing its world lead in heavy lift aircraft.

5.2   Latécoère, technical performance facilitator brand

LATECOERE

Figure 16. Latécoère logotype

5.2.1   Latécoère, intermediate equipment supplier for manufacturers

With the restructuring of the French aircraft industry begun in 1950, the Latécoère company began to cooperate with various firms, by constructing tools and aircraft parts (Table 17).

Table 17. Examples of partnership projects made (1950 - 1970)

Activities and products	Materials and aircraft concerned
Prototype wings and pre-series equipped nose-sections, jet engine air intakes and outlets	Magister CM170
Prototype stabilizers	Potez 840
Most of the doors and hatches	MD315, SMB2, Mystère IV
Air intakes	Mirage III
Rear fuselage, doors, air brakes and intakes	Etendard IV M, Super Etendard
Rear parts of fuselage	Brèguet 941
Ailerons, flaps, numerous fuselage frames	Caravelle
Collaboration in the carrying out of various trials and construction of aircraft	Concorde
Presentation of studies carried out for the Aeronautical Technical Service, Army staff officers or the Navy	Late 640 and Late 256 (Escopette and Ecrevisse types) pulso-reactor experimental aircraft. Late 820 overseas support aircraft Late 839 military observation aircraft Late 703 amphibious colonial liaison aircraft

The accumulated know how and experience of the company had, for this period between 1950 and 1970, allowed it to become the specialist in environmental tests and mechanical trials and tests, as much for materials as for various structures (Table 18).

In the nineties, the company began to turn more towards the international scene, becoming the respected partner of the main international contractors such as Airbus, Boeing, McDonnell Douglas, and Dassault as well as participating in the main world aeronautical programs in the electrical-electronics field and on-board and ground equipment.

In 1998 the Latécoère company had developed a large amount of know how and acquired great experience in electronics (cabling and wiring looms, automatic testers, equipment systems and avionics, etc.) and composites (carbon fibers, Kevlar®, metal-metal bonding, etc.). It was one of the world leaders for human centrifuges for pilot training, astronaut and medical research.

Table 18. Examples of specific material developed by Latécoère (1950 -1970)

Activities and products	Names
Human centrifuges capable of accelerations of 15G with human subjects and up to 40G for equipment (45kg)	Latécoère 260
Centrifuges for experiments with rocket nose cones, simulating the surrounding atmosphere and able to give a mass of 2.5 tons an acceleration of 100G	Latécoère 265
Catapult + acceleration test installations: experiments with jet engines at take off, braking parachutes, arrester hooks, hydrodynamic research	Latécoère 768 + Latécoère 910
Vertical acceleration test machines	Latécoère 777
Landing gear tests	Latécoère 770
Weighing machines and strain gages for wind tunnels	
Electronically servo assisted valves for wind tunnels or simulation tanks	
Electronically servo assisted hydraulic actuators for static trials and aircraft endurance tests (Concorde)	Silat
Graded power (up to 1,400KW) automatically programmed climatic chambers for studying the behavior of rockets entering the atmosphere	
Studies and manufacture of missiles for the Navy	Malaface 258, Masalca, Malafon Z31
Study on a postal missile (not experimented with)	Latécoère 110

With a turnover of 160 million euros, the Latécoère company is now one of the leaders in:

• Studies and production of aeronautical structures and electronic assemblies: EADS (DASA + Aerospatiale-Matra + CASA), Dassault Aviation, Hispano-Suiza, Rohr, Boeing, Lockheed, Northrop Grumman, etc.

• Studies and production of satellite structures, on-board equipment and ground equipment for space activities: CNES, EADS, Alcatel Space, Matra Space, SEP, BAe, etc.

While it is often true that family names do not indicate any precise information but just recall the founder's name, the case of Latécoère is very different. In fact there are few family names as evocative as Latécoère. This word which recalls one of the most famous names in aviation, evokes memories of the beginnings of aviation and symbolizes the world of aircraft. This brand is thus known to the general public mainly because of its previous activities of designing and constructing aircraft. However, the skills of the company have evolved and the brand, whose image and renown are still well recognized by the general public, is today in fact known by professionals and the aeronautical world:

• For its expertise and design activities in the production of structures (fuselages),

• As well as for its complete, high tech equipment (centrifuges, etc.).

In fact, Latécoère is an intermediate and finished equipment supplier brand. The brand's objective is to contribute to its customers' success by enabling them to improve the performance of their products or processes. Thanks to a sustained effort in research and development and active collaboration with different partners, Latécoère has developed very high level equipment for:

• Aircraft structures: fuselage, wing and nacelle elements,

• Equipment and systems: looms and electrical assemblies, on-board equipment, human centrifuges, air combat restitution systems, ground equipment.

High aeronautical standards and requirements necessitate the design and production of high quality aircraft structures (Figure 19). Any contribution to the technical performance of constructor customers, necessarily involves the development of new solutions which allow a gain in assembly time or facilitate maintenance, but equally improve aircraft performance (weight, resistance, etc.). And this is how Latécoère has developed numerous technical partnerships, allowing it to design and offer high tech. and high performance equipment.

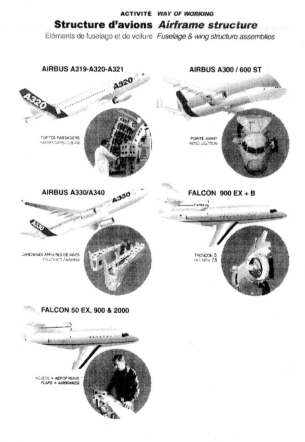

Figure 19. Some fuselage elements produced by Latécoère

The fuselage, wing or nacelle parts produced by Latécoère, mean participation in the following programs:
- Aircraft from the Airbus range A319, A320, A321, A330, A340,
- Military aircraft ATL2, Lockheed C130, Rafale,
- Business aircraft Falcon 50, Falcon 900, Falcon 2000,
- McDonnell Douglas aircraft MD 90 and MD 11,
- The Eurocopter helicopters.

As an equipment manufacturer of aircraft structures, the Latécoère brand is also associated with on-board equipment such as the software, limiting battery charging on the Airbus, pilot arming straps, the looms for the CFM 56 engines, the radio cables on the Falcon 2000 or the adapters for test programs. It is also present in ground equipment such as the cryogenic booms for Ariane 4 or the on-board/ground links for Ariane 5.

5.2.2 Latécoère, supplier of stand-alone equipment: centrifuges

Quite apart from the specialization in aircraft sub-assemblies for the main contractors, the brand also develops stand-alone equipment for sale to constructor customers as well as airline companies, like for example the training systems for air combat restitution (SEMAC) and in particular the human centrifuges.

In parallel with the development of aeronautics and aircraft performance, the pilots have been submitted to higher and higher G forces. Under high G loads, the pilot may lose consciousness as for example in air combat maneuvers. To deal with this risk and to preserve the plane and its pilot, it is necessary to train them in centrifuges capable of recreating G forces using specific systems simulating flight changes and accelerations. In the same way, medical research laboratories need human centrifuges to study the effects of high G forces, to determine their long-term consequences and develop means of protection against these effects.

The centrifuges developed by Latécoère are safe and reliable systems, which allow extreme tests to be carried out while at the same time permanently monitoring the pilot's well being. In this way pilots can train themselves to recognize and understand their resistance and physical reactions. In addition, the airline companies have a device for safety purposes and training which is capable of simulating the most difficult situations encountered by pilots (Figure 20).

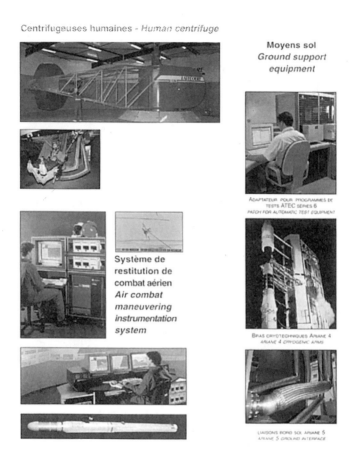

ACTIVITÉ *WAY OF WORKING*

Equipements & systèmes *Equipment & systems*

Centrifugeuses humaines - *Human centrifuge*

Moyens sol
Ground support
equipment

ADAPTATEUR POUR PROGRAMMES DE
TESTS ATEC SÉRIES 6
PATCH FOR AUTOMATIC TEST EQUIPMENT

Système de
restitution de
combat aérien
Air combat
maneuvering
instrumentation
system

BRAS CRYOTECHNIQUES ARIANE 4
ARIANE 4 CRYOGENIC ARMS

LIAISONS BORD SOL ARIANE 5
ARIANE 5 GROUND INTERFACE

Figure 20. Latécoère equipment

5.3   Sales performance facilitation

With a view to improving the performance of airline companies, Latécoère has developed a passenger video camera system, adaptable on Airbus as well as Boeing. This consists of on-board cameras called Landscape Video, which are designed to film, on board the aircraft and in real time, the landscape passing below. The passengers in this way "see" from their seat the journey unrolling and the various geographical features. This innovation from Latécoère helps the airlines to distinguish their offer and contributes to their own innovation. By offering views of the exterior to civil airline passengers using the " landscape video camera system " the company has a plus product. With this invention, Latécoère has shown that it is concerned with improving its customers' sales performance.

6. KIMBERLY CLARK: CONTRIBUTING TO CUSTOMER IMAGE

Figure 21. Kimberly-Clark logotype

Created in Neenah, Wisconsin, USA, in 1872, Kimberly Clark* company has a turnover of 14 billion euros and employs over 55,000 people in the world. In France, Kimberly Clark has been a familiar name to the general public since the 1960's thanks to famous brands such as Kleenex®, Kotex®, Scott® or Huggies®. In fact, the company set up in France in 1960 on the non-household market, initially as a joint venture with the paper manufacturer, Darblay, and its subsidiary, Sopalin. The development of their activity led Kimberly Clark to offer a range of bathroom products and industrial paper towels. This grew to include steel blue double thickness rolls, white rolls, nylon-reinforced super strong towels, precision towels, medical wipes for hospitals, etc. In the 1980's, the company regrouped its industrial activities into the Industries and Services Department for offices, industry, and the restaurant catering sector. New industrial products were launched such as Kimtex® towels, Kleenguard® protective clothing or the Workhorse▲ cloth range and Kimtuf▲ hand wipes.

In 1998, Kimberly-Clark, the European leader in the non-household market, was committed to supplying the best protection, cleaning, and care systems on the industrial products and sanitary hygiene market. This meant supplying systems to improve hygiene and better protect the individual, in bathrooms as well as in the workplace. Thus Kimberly Clark offered a complete range of systems such as:

• The Windows range of distributors of sanitary hygiene products, that are designed to go with bathrooms, guaranteeing continual hygiene and usage cost

---

* ® Registered Trademark *Kimberly-Clark, Kleenex, Kimwipes, Kimtex, Kleenguard*: Kimberly-Clark Corporation; *Scott, Scottex*: Kimberly-Clark Tissue Company
▲ Trademark *Workhorse, Kimtuf*: Kimberly-Clark Corporation
Windows, Wypall, Iko: Kimberly-Clark Tissue Company

control (folded or rolled hand towel distributors, liquid hand soap, toilet paper, perfume diffuser, toilet seat cover distributors),

• The range of high performance towel systems adapted to different users (systems for Workhorse▲ cloth, for Wypall▲ and Kimtex® towels, for Scott® Servi-Roll everyday towels or Kimwipes® heavy duty towels),

• The Kleenguard® protective clothing range, providing individual protection and comfort (against spraying from liquids, vapor from chemical products, dust, etc.),

• The Iko hand wash system range, for the protection, washing, and care of hands in industrial environments.

While product brands such as Scott®, Windows▲, Kleenex®, or Kleenguard® are already well known on the hygiene, protective clothing, and industrial towels markets, the Kimberly Clark corporate brand is less known in Europe. Thus in addition to introducing new systems, the company decided to run a European advertising campaign to promote its corporate brand. The campaign objectives were:

• To increase the penetration of products used uniquely in the non-household market,

• To rapidly increase the renown of the Kimberly-Clark brand,

• To establish Kimberly-Clark as a brand leader offering high performance solutions in the fields of sanitary hygiene and individual protection.

The campaign aimed to convince influencers in offices, the restaurant catering sector, and industry in general that Kimberly Clark solutions were superior to other systems on the market. The targets included the heads of general departments, buyers, production managers, maintenance people, and safety engineers. The goal was to strengthen the renown and image of Kimberly-Clark with directors and deciders. The concept of the campaign was to humoristically dramatize or exagerate situations, highlighting the imperfections and limitations of traditional systems.

At first, the main segments targeted were offices, hotels, the metallurgical industry, the chemical industry, and the restaurant sector. Before being launched, the campaign was tested in different European countries where it was well-received in terms of:

• Comprehension: sensitizing people to hygiene and protection issues, building an image as an innovative leader in a sector where traditionally products are not not highly differentiated,

• Adhesion and impact: the exaggerated situations were very well received thanks to the humoristic tone and the creative impact, lending Kimberly-Clark a warm and dynamic character.

Finally, the results of the study showed that through this campaign, Kimberly-Clark contributed significantly to the general growth of the market (Figure 22).

Are your old-fashioned work clothes
up to modern-day needs?

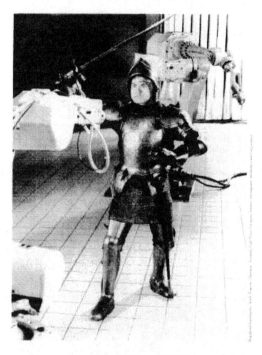

High protection solutions
for industrial workwear.

Kimberly-Clark offers tailor-made individual protection with comfort and style.
Kimberly-Clark has been awarded the CE mark in the Complex Category for its
protective coveralls CE 95 020. FOR MORE INFORMATION, CALL FREE 000 000 000.

Scott®, Trapsy®, Cleanweb®, Kimtex® and Kleenguard® are famous trademarks of Kimberly-Clark.

Figure 22. The Kimberly-Clark brand: improving productivity and working conditions

The media chosen was the trade press, a key media form for reaching buyers in industry, the restaurant sector, and services. Economic magazines and newspapers were also used to optimize the campaign with buyers, while reaching influencers and decision makers.

The press campaign was backed up by the impact of the television advertising, which accelerated the increasing awareness among the different targets. At least two of the three ads systematically appeared on the same commercial break in order to muscle the campaign efficiency. Globally, the communication campaign effectively strengthened the Kimberly-Clark brand by reinforcing its image as the leading hygiene specialist and a true partner to industry.

Above all, Kimberly-Clark improves the working conditions and life of its customers, as well as benefiting their own image. Personnel are happier working in a pleasant, well-cared for environment and wearing effective protective clothes adapted to their needs (Figure 23).

It only takes a few seconds
                        to destroy your company's image.

High image solutions
for everyday washroom problems.

Kimberly-Clark offers stylish systems for hand drying, toilet paper, hand cleansers, and air fresheners that impress users and provide home comfort.
FOR MORE INFORMATION, CALL FREE 000 000 000.

Scott, Towel, Windows, Kleenex are famous trademarks of Kimberly-Clark.

 **Kimberly-Clark**

Figure 23. Kimberly-Clark: a much higher commercial performance thanks to a better image

The way the premises of a company, in particular the bathrooms, are cared for is often a good reflection of the in-house atmosphere, and in any case, it projects a certain image of the company. Employee work clothes as well as the cleanliness of the environment can be positive factors for outsiders visiting the company premises. However if there is a careless attitude or poor hygiene, the image of the company as well as the comfort of staff will suffer. Thus, Kimberly-Clark products are more than just materials or equipment, they are attractive, efficient hygiene solutions with a double impact on both customers and personnel.

7. TETRA PAK BRAND: "MUCH MORE THAN THE PACKAGE"

Figure 24. Tetra Pak brand: a name, a logo and a tag-line

Tetra Pak was founded in 1951 in Sweden, to commercialize a new system of packaging, developed from research carried out in 1943 by Ruben Rausing. The brand takes its name from the shape of the package (taetrahedron formed by two perpendicular joints). Although the composition varies depending on the application and the type of product, Tetra Pak packages are essentially made from a polyethylene cardboard complex and for the aseptic packages, aluminium sheets. Following the acquisition in 1991 of Alfa Laval, a world supplier of materials and equipment for the food industry and other transformation-based industries, the group took the name of Tetra Laval.

7.1 Tetra Laval: a corporate brand

Tetra Laval group is present worldwide, with a turnover of close to 7 billion euros and 18,500 employees. It includes three autonomous industrial groups working in synergy, each with its own specialization:

- Tetra Pak, specialized in the development, production, and commercialization of complete processing, packaging, and distribution systems for liquid food products (milk, juice, fruit drinks, mineral waters, wine, etc.),
- Alfa Laval, specialized in the design, production, and commercialization of components and systems for production processes such as separators, heat exchangers, homogenizers, automated systems, and fluid transfer systems,

• Alfa Laval Agri, specialized in the supply of equipment and systems used in milk production and breeding of milk cows.

The three companies share a common visual identity, based on a logo, which recalls the tetrahedron shape of the original packages (Figure 25).

Figure 25. The logo

The logo includes an "alpha", referring to Alfa Laval. Representing 2/3 of the group's activity and a world leader in materials for the milk industry, Tetra Pak has become a reference status brand in the food-packaging sector as well as being widely recognized by the general public.

Tetra Pak's international slogan "More than a package" defines the territory of the brand which extends from the supply of machines and packing systems, to finished products, in other words, cardboard or plastic packages. In addition, this slogan expresses the idea that the brand is not just a supplier of packaging products and systems for different players in the food industry, rather it is a partner brand from a technical and commercial point of view.

Providing a complete range of processing and packing systems (machines, distribution equipment, complementary software services), Tetra Pak is a global supplier. This means Tetra Pak must have strong innovative capacity, provide a diverse range of products to meet specialized needs, and make a long-term commitment to customers.

7.2   Packaging product-brands: Tetra Pak, facilitating sales performance

Tetra Pak has a genuine policy of facilitating the sales performance of its customers. Starting with analyzing and forecasting the consumer habits of end customers, Tetra Pak better anticipates the needs of its industrial clients; in fact the goal of the brand and its customers is one and the same: satisfying consumers and gaining the confidence of distributors. Through feasibility studies and project support, the supplier brand works with its customers to make progress together.

Tetra Pak has carried out consumer research which shows that customers:

• Want a wide choice of tasty, sophisticated products made with respect for traditional methods,

• Pay close attention to the quality/price ratio,

• Like to feel informed, and consider numerous criteria when making choices including taste, user-friendliness, hygiene, and safety.

To answer these needs, Tetra Pak has developed different types of user-friendly packaging and opening systems (Figure 26). The range is constantly expanded with new more practical systems and multi-pack solutions which make transport from the store to the home easier. The Tetra Pak packaging range includes different families, whose brands generally have been created using the corporate brand "Tetra" to which are added specific, evocative names:

• *Tetra Classic*: the original tetrahedral packaging was followed by an aseptic version (Tetra Classic Aseptic) for packaging perishable goods that can be stored and distributed without refrigeration,

• *Tetra Brik*: the famous modular packaging, especially designed for "europalett loading", completed by an aseptic version (Tetra Brik Aseptic),

• *Tetra Rex*: the basic square packaging, used mainly for fresh products,

• *Tetra Top*: which meets the consumer demand for packaging that is easy to open, pour, and close,

• *Tetra Pouch*: the pillow shaped packaging made from a spool of multi-layer polyethylene film using the "form, fill, seal" process, providing fast filling and minimum product loss,

• *Tetra Prisma*: the latest packaging in the line has an attractive metallic surface with a large opening to allow drinking right from the package, and quick, easy pouring. It is an original alternative for products targeted at teenagers and kids.

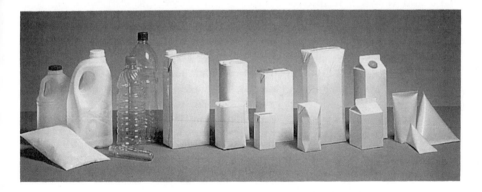

Figure 26. The Tetra Pak package range

The Tetra Brik package range consists of "TB" (Tetra Brik) and "TBA" (Tetra Brik Aseptic). TB packages are used for products with shorter preservation times such as pasteurized milk or freshly squeezed fruit juice, requiring distribution and storage that respects the cold chain. The principle of TBA packages is the following: the packaging material, delivered in compact spools, enters the filling machine where it is sterilized in a sealed aseptic container, then shaped into a tube and filled. This technique protects the product from any contamination. The packages formed are sealed at the level of the liquid, to prevent the entrance of air, which could damage the product in the package.

The two brand families can be produced in three different forms:

• Baseline: the Tetra Brik Baseline package conforms with international norms for loading pallets and is the most well known packing system in the world in a 200 ml, 250 ml, and 1,000 ml size,

• Slimline: the Tetra Brik Slimline package is so called for its slim, longer shape, which is easier to use and allows for better customer differentiation,

• Squareline: the Tetra Brik Squareline, in a square shape, is the most recent addition to the family.

A total of 17 different volumes are available, from the smallest 100ml TBA Baseline to the largest, 1,500 ml TBA Slim Recap. There are also different opening systems such as the pre-perforated, the straw, as well as flap systems such as PullTab, or the different cap systems: ScrewCap, ReCap and Unicap.

Although, its direct customers are industrial or professional, Tetra Pak has opted for a pull strategy, with the aim of developing demand downstream. That is why, in addition to advertising in the trade press, until 1996, Tetra Pak aimed its communication campaign, through television or magazines, at the general public. While this strengthens Tetra Pak's own image and renown, it also benefits its customers who can bank on this positive image in their own marketing campaigns. By familiarizing the general public with its packaging solutions, Tetra Pak's aim is to make its customers products more purchaseable. The sales arguments featured by Tetra Pak (optimal product protection, preservation of taste, protection of nutrients from air and light) enhance those developed by industrial clients for their own products.

One of the spearheads of Tetra Pak's communication strategy is its environmental policy. The aim of the brand is to provide "high quality, safe packaging systems for liquid food products at a low cost while respecting the environment".

This policy involves:

• Reduction at the source: the design of packaging systems using a minimum of natural resources and energy and producing a minimum of waste (package made from wood, a renewable resource, recyclability of polyethylene),

• The use of clean, cutting-edge printing and processing technologies for the manufacture of packaging materials (without chlorine gas processing, inks with no solvents, no heavy metals or toxic fumes, heating with natural gas, recycling of factory waste),

• Choosing suppliers who use the best, most environmentally friendly manufacturing technologies,

The company specifies that Tetra Pak products save energy and make the refrigeration of drinks unnecessary during storage. They also contribute to reducing atmospheric pollution by cutting down on transport costs:

• Before packaging: the delivery in rolls requires only two trucks to transport 1 million packages (versus 52 trucks for the same quantity of bottles),

• After packaging: there is a greater volume of the product transported (95% versus 65% for bottles), long storage without refrigeration.

The optimization of Tetra Pak packaging for energy purposes gives off as much energy with two tons of packaging as a ton of oil. The packages can be recycled using:

• Re-pulping, which consists in producing new paper by recuperating cardboard fibers,

• Conglomeration, using packaging to manufacture conglomerated panels (comparable to wood but thermoforming and water/fire resistant) for the furniture and building industry. This technique has resulted in the "Tectan®" brand, which refers to this specific process.

Tetra Pak's environmental policy brings to the brand and to the brands of its customers an added ecological dimension important for end consumers.

Tetra Pak also improves the products of its industrial customers by paying particular attention to the options for decorating packages. The graphic design of packaging is an essential element in product communication and an effective means of seducing end consumers. For example, there are three types of printing for Tetra Brik packaging: flexography (flexo-line, flexo-process), offset (photoprint), and helioengraving. The printing techniques (glossy, metallic…) optimize the image of the brands on the packaging.

Thus Tetra Pak improves the sales performance of its customers through:

• Providing information to final consumers on the advantages of Tetra Pak products,

• The excellent image and renown of Tetra Pak and its products,

• Working together on defining and optimizing the product offer, and providing consumer research.

While Tetra Pak is historically associated with cardboard packaging for liquid food products, in reality these are only one of the brand's many solutions including bottles or PET and EBM plastic bags, integrated processing and packaging lines, and separate processing units.

7.3   Tetra Pak, a processing and equipment brand: facilitating technical performance

The company's research and development laboratories have designed generations of materials that make production easier and faster, setting new profitability standards on the market, while preserving the essential qualities of products.

R&D at Tetra Pak is particularly geared to:
• The layer-extrusion technology,
• The design of integrated systems,
• Specialization in the agrifood industry and in-depth knowledge of the products processed and packaged by customers,
• Aseptic technology which preserves flavor and nutritive value, extending the preservation time of products without preservatives, additives, or refrigeration.

The R&D teams design new functions, machines, forms of packaging, opening systems, and new materials. For example, machines are equipped with systems for the simultaneous filling of two different products or two different volumes, new aseptization systems, sizes, etc.

These innovations have sometimes been the result of close collaboration between industrial customers and suppliers through common development projects and the sharing of know-how and technology. The partnerships involve thinking together about the present and future needs of consumers. Thus Tetra Pak invites its customers to take part in R&D teams for projects that do not necessarily meet the immediate needs of customers.

The company also involves its suppliers by relying on their specific expertise. The different partnerships and the company's own savoir-faire allow Tetra Pak to offer a vast range of solutions and production materials.

The only brand capable of designing and manufacturing complete processing, packaging, and distribution systems, Tetra Pak can be the unique supplier of its customers, thereby saving them time and money. Tetra Pak guarantees all of its systems. As a guarantee of quality, the company displays its brand visibly on the machines it commercializes.

The Tetra Pak brand and its logo appear clearly on the machine (Figure 27), whose "family name" is displayed on the control panels or units:
• "TBA" (Tetra Brik Aseptic) for the filling machines used for packaging of aseptic products,
• "TB" (Tetra Brik) for the machines used for the packaging of products that require refrigeration during distribution.

Figure 27. The TBA/19 Tetra Pak filling machine

The Tetra Pak range of machines and equipment includes processing and packaging systems. These integrated production lines allow customers to benefit from simple, effective, and inexpensive maintenance service, performed so as to limit down production time.

• The *processing systems* are designed for the manufacture of liquid food products such as milk, fruit juices, water, iced tea, soups, and sauces, as well as for the manufacture of cheese. The processing unit range includes Tetra Therm (direct heating by steam injection or indirect heating), Tetra Alex (homogenizer), and Tetra Spiraflo (heating by a tubular exchanger).

• *Filling and packaging systems* such as TBA/21, TBA/19, or TB/8 make it possible to package liquid food in a variety of formats. The TBA/21 for example is the most recent system integrating the latest technology in aseptic packaging: automatic control of the operation of the machine, the sterility parameters, and the cleaning procedure, automatic connection of paper, storing of 2 spools, etc. Volume kits can be added to the basic machine to meet the specific manufacturing needs of certain customers. In addition to its advanced automation, this equipment offers high capacity production as well as considerable flexibility in adapting to different volumes and shapes (8,000 packages an hour for the 125 to 330 ml format and 7,000 packages an hour for the 355 to 1,136 ml). This flexibility of use is particularly noticeable when changing from one volume kit to another, which only requires 2-3 hours of work by two technicians depending on the configuration of the bottom of the packages.

The TBA/19, for 100 to 300 ml boxes, is a compact, high yield machine (7,500 packages an hour) offering different opening systems and other options. The TB/8 is a packaging machine, which uses the ultra-sound soddering technique, with a potential yield of 6,000 packages an hour for 500 and 1,000 ml formats. A recent Tetra Pak innovation is Tetra Nova Aseptic, an aseptic filling machine for 2 liter cartons which does not use hydrogen peroxide for disinfection, as the package is delivered flat and sterilized. It accomplishes the filling process in aseptic conditions using an original technique (Table 28).

Table 28. Brand management at the Tetra-Laval group

Performance type	Targets	Categories concerned	Main brands
Sales performance facilitator	Consumer market	• Packages • Closing systems	Tetra Classic Tetra Brik (Baseline, Slimline, Square Line) Tetra Rex Tetra Top Tetra Pouch Tetra Prisma ScrewCap, ReCap, UniCap
Technical performance facilitator	Industry	• Machines • Production process	TB: TB8... TBA: TBA/19, TBA/21 Tetra Nova Aseptic Tetra Therm Tetra Alex Tetra Spiraflo "Tectan ® " (recycling)

The Tetra Pak machine range allows its customers to increase productivity in accordance with the company philosophy that "a package must save more than it costs". Thanks to its commitment to improving technical and sales performance, Tetra Pak manufactures, sells, installs, and maintains complete equipment, preparation lines, and machines (Tetra Pak Maintenance System, ProTimer...). By training operating staff (on-site training or in training centers, self-learning CD-ROM's, etc.) and helping to set up equipment, Tetra Pak facilitates its customers technical performance right from the upstream phase of production. The different services offered by Tetra Pak (market studies, assistance in planning and distribution, assistance with designing the decoration of packaging, etc.) make it a genuine partner brand on both a commercial and technical level.

8.   AIRBUS: " SETTING THE STANDARDS "

The Airbus Industrie consortium was created in 1970 as an economic interest group (GIE) to relaunch the European aeronautics industry. In just thirty years, Airbus Industrie, the aeronautics subsidiary of EADS (DASA + Aerospatiale-Matra + CASA), has become the number two aircraft builder in the world; with its large family of success stories such as the A300, A310, A320, A330, and A340, among others, Airbus Industrie has truly re-energized the world market (Figure 29).

⊚*AIRBUS INDUSTRIE*

Figure 29. The Airbus logotype

8.1   The Airbus brand policy

The meaningful brand "Air-Bus" designates the product itself as well as the group that designs it. Airbus thus plays the role of both product-brand and corporate brand. Literally "a bus for the air", the brand has the advantage of being immediately understandable in English speaking countries. The initial aim of the company was to design, manufacture, and sell a 300 seat aircraft. This project provided the name for the first aircraft, the Airbus A300, upon which the brand policy was built. The programs that followed were given names based on the Airbus corporate name and the first name of the first A300 aircraft. Thus the Airbus portfolio includes Airbus 310, Airbus A319, Airbus A320, Airbus A321, Airbus A330, and the Airbus A340. The name of each Airbus in the range varies depending on the technical characteristics and the chosen options (long or shortened models, etc.) such as the Airbus A310-300, Airbus A330-200 or the Airbus A340-600, etc.

The Airbus brand is often highly visible on the aircraft and can be seen for example on the rear fuselage or on the front door. Even inside the planes, passengers are aware of the brand, which is featured on the safety instructions and mentioned in the pilot's welcome speech.

The Airbus brand is synonymous with the aeronautics industry and high technology. It is perceived as an innovative and reliable brand that habitually shakes up the sector. Airbus also symbolizes the European capacity to design, mobilize, and win. Accordingly, for the 25th anniversary of the first flight of the A300 on 28th October 1972, Airbus launched a worldwide media campaign addressing the general public and highlighting its role in the construction of the European Community. Furthermore, the campaign recalled the brand's solid contribution, through its competitive innovations, to the modernization of the worldwide aeronautics industry (Figure 30).

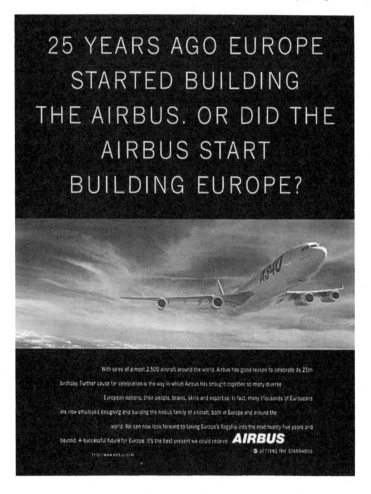

Figure 30. Airbus highlights the synergy between the building of Airbus by Europe and its own contribution to building Europe

The campaign was launched:

• In different European newspapers such as the *Sunday Times* in Great Britain, *Le Monde* and *Le Figaro* in France, *Die Welt* and *Focus* in Germany, *Corriere Della Sera* in Italy, *El País* in Spain, *De Standaard* and *Le Soir* in Belgium,

• In more international magazines such as *The Economist WW*, *AWSJ*, *Feer*, *Newsweek*, *Fortune* and *Asiaweek*.

On a more regular basis, Airbus's communication policy is based essentially on product communication oriented to professionals in the aeronautics industry. Airbus communicates mainly in technical journals or in specialized aeronautics magazines such as *Aviation Week, Flight International, Airline Business, Air Transport World*, or *Air & Cosmos*.

The aim is to reach populations that are not directly targeted by the sales department, but who are influential in making decisions in airline companies and governmental bodies (Figure 31).

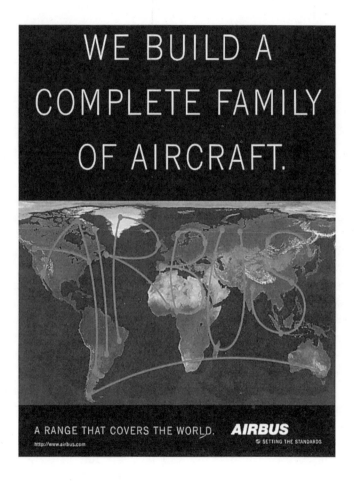

Figure 31. An example of Airbus brand corporate communication: the Airbus "signature" is obtained from different destinations in the world

Airbus brand policy also targets a wider public including private individuals and political decision makers. In addition to advertisements in national daily newspapers or in general economic magazines, Airbus uses press relations. For new orders or the signing of new contracts, the media generally features the expected positive effects on the European economy in terms of activities, employment, or the trade balance.

In general, television is little used by aeronautical builders. However, Airbus launched a major campaign on CNN with ads featuring the inside of the four-engine Airbus A340. A humorous tone was deliberately chosen, targeting the passenger in the middle. In this way, Airbus has tried to raise the passenger comfort standards of long distance flights in North America by recommending a new arrangement of seats in the cabin.

8.2   Airbus: facilitating performance

Faced with solidly entrenched competition, Airbus, right from the beginning, developed original and innovative aeronautics programs. The result? In less than 30 years Airbus has gained control of half of the world civil aviation market. Today most of the world's major airlines are Airbus customers. The strength of the brand lies in its capacity to innovate and listen to customers. Thus the aircraft are designed in consultation with customer companies so as to define the expected cost, comfort, and performance requirements.

Taking into consideration customer expectations at the earliest stages, Airbus continually strives for new, better solutions (A3XX for instance). For Airbus, the goal is to establish the new market standards, as the brand slogan specifies "Setting the Standards". The fact that today Airbus offers the most cutting edge range of aircraft in the world is testimony to the brand's genuine commitment to customers.

Airbus's contributes to its customers' performance in many ways. First, there is the homogenous design of the cockpits, facilitating pilot training and making it easy to change from one aircraft in the range to another. Aircraft maintenance is facilitated thanks to the ergonomic design of equipment, and of course cost reduction, better knowledge of parts, and maintenance operations, etc. From a technical point of view, Airbus seeks to optimize aircraft performance and reliability, thereby reducing costs from stopovers, or holdups due to technical reasons.

For example, the Airbus A340 can take off full in difficult weather conditions. This makes it possible to avoid reducing the freight transported by the aircraft, which can achieve its flight even in temperatures above 40°C on the ground, as is the case in Pakistan for example. This argument was featured in a 1997 campaign in which the Airbus A340 was presented as the highest performing aircraft "under the sun", in both a literal and figurative sense (Figure 32).

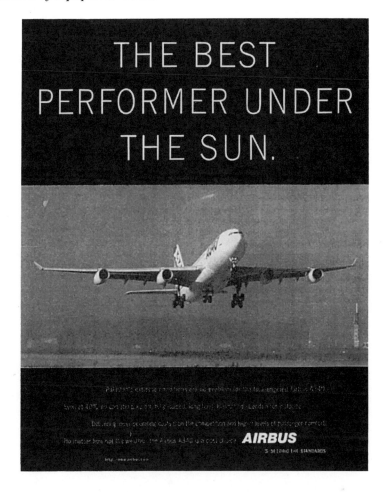

Figure 32. Airbus, technical performance serving airline companies and passengers

By improving technical performance, Airbus seeks to better satisfy the airlines and their passengers. For example, the long distance range of the A340 eliminates long, costly, and annoying stopovers and leaves passengers feeling less tired at the end of their journey. In this way, Airbus helps the airline companies to improve their service and thus their sales performance.

Airbus has carried out a number of studies on the lines used by its customers or on passenger satisfaction. The companies have specific and up-to-date information on their market and can improve their service. In addition to these marketing tools, the very image of the Airbus brand can reinforce that of customer companies by serving as a guarantee. The brand projects positive associations such as comfort, reliability, quality service, innovation, etc.

For example, Biman company in Bangladesh used the Airbus brand in its own communication campaign in *Far Eastern Economic Review*, insisting on the quality and interior comfort of the A310-300 making the flight particularly pleasant. This use of the Airbus brand is totally coherent with the Biman slogan, "Your home in the air" (Figure 33).

Biman's all-new Airbus 310-300 offers a
wide choice of entertainment. 4 channel touch-screen
video in Executive Class, 12 channel seat audio choice
and an airshow system.

You are invited to fly this lovely new Airbus.
A refreshingly quiet cabin.
A decidedly enjoyable flight.

Fly Biman – Your home in the air

Figure 33. Airbus: a guarantee brand facilitating the sales performance of Biman

The Airbus brand and in particular the A310-300 were also used by the airline Austria, in its communication policy. In its press campaign, the Asian company, Dragonair features the modernity of its fleet made up of A330's and A320's integrating the highest level of service and technology.

Singapore Airlines, in its communication campaign, highlights its service presenting the A340 with all of its advantages (non-stop range, comfort, etc.). In a campaign targeting travel agencies, Air Lanka presented itself in 1994 as the first Asian airline to offer the comfort of the "most modern commercial aircraft in the world", the A340. The Spanish company Iberia and the British company Virgin Atlantic have also featured the Airbus A340 in their campaigns as a guarantee of quality and service: the technological advancement of Airbus ensures safer and more comfortable long distance flights.

Through its innovative policy and its commitment, Airbus has become a brand that significantly improves the performance of its customers both on a technical and commercial level.

Chapter 14

Business to Business Service Brands

1.   THE MAIN CHARACTERISTICS OF PROFESSIONAL SERVICES

Professional services are all the services on the market which aimed at companies:

• Furniture, goods and equipment rental for companies: rental of cars and industrial vehicles, building equipment (cranes, cement-mixers, scaffolding, etc.), office and IT equipment (word processors, photocopiers and scanners, computers and peripherals, telephone equipment, software license fees), farming machinery (tractors, combine harvesters, etc.), transport and freight equipment (freight cars, containers, ships, planes, etc.), machines and equipment (machine tools, boring and exploratory equipment, telecommunication and electronic equipment, measuring instruments, etc.),

• IT and telecommunications services: consulting, design of programs, data processing, technical assistance, maintenance, system integration, network management, etc.,

• Legal services: counseling and representation (for civil, penal or administrative matters or for work or business disputes), counseling and assistance (for patents and royalties), drawing up and recording of acts (statutes, trust deeds, etc.),

• Assessment and consulting professions concerning the supply to companies of tools for help with financial and economic decision making, e.g. for accounting (book-keeping, audits, etc.), market research and opinion polls, economic and financial studies, management consulting,

- Architectural and engineering activities associated with building construction, infrastructures, industrial installations e.g. architects, surveyors and quantity surveyors, professional engineers,
- Advertising and communication professions including the management of advertising media (central merchandising and advertising space administration), publicity agencies and groups, agencies specialized in direct marketing, telemarketing, motivation agencies, design-communication, brand creation agencies, etc.,
- Personnel selection and sub-contracting activities, e.g. temporary work or industrial cleaning companies (interior premises, sterile rooms, sensitive sites, industrial and commercial buildings, transport such as buses, trains, planes, subway, etc.),
- Other services for companies: building rental, security and surveillance (goods and personnel security), press and publicity dispatch, mass mailing, organization of fairs and salons, business travel agencies, collection of commercial receivables, various services linked to office work, secretarial work, translation, publishing, industrial design, etc., photographic studios.

Most of the characteristics associated with the marketing of services to the private customer can be found in the professional service sector:

- *Immateriality and intangibility* of services: before it has been actually carried out, the nature of the industrial service can indeed be difficult for customers to visualize. In view of this intangibility, customers feel that they are taking a greater risk. In addition, they are rarely in a position to accurately assess the technical value of the service rendered. To diminish this risk, they look for concrete elements to go by; service companies therefore put the accent on customer references and previous experience. They also try to make their service more tangible, by linking it up to visible elements and materials such as having the staff uniform in the colors of the company and with the company logo, or by having the brand visible on the material necessary for the service and also on any documents, e.g. the initial estimates as well as the concluding reports;
- *Variability*: a service, unlike a product, is difficult to standardize. Service activities are characterized by a strong human element both on the part of the customer and the service provider. Nevertheless, in order to guarantee their customer a certain standard of service, the companies concerned develop quality control and invest in procedures aimed at quantifying the different phases of their services.
- *Perishability and non-stockability*: although demand very often fluctuates and is difficult to predict, services cannot be stocked which makes them difficult to manage; it is a particularly perilous procedure when large investments mean high fixed costs as in the case of an airline company.

• *Indivisibility*: when a service is provided, the customer judges an entity. The absence or negative perception of one of the elements, automatically downgrades the overall evaluation.

It must be emphasized that services are often very closely linked to industrial products in the sense that they can constitute a follow-on or follow-up, e.g. after sales service (maintenance, repairs, etc.). More generally, services play their part either directly (rental of equipment, temporary work, etc.), or indirectly (marketing advice, transport services etc.) in the production of industrial goods. The service itself can carry a tangible element in its wake; the menu in the cafeteria, regular functioning of a machine tool, presentation of training documents, etc. Industrial services are therefore made up of a combination of tangible and intangible elements.

2.   THE PURCHASEABILITY AND VISIBILITY OF PROFESSIONAL SERVICE BRANDS

Also in the professional services category, there are "mixed services", which concern both companies and private customers. Thus some of these services are used by households, e.g. legal services, lawyers, car rentals. In the same way, companies often use services mainly aimed at the private customer such as health or laundry services, etc. General public travel agents, such as Club Med, have also developed a business travel service, aimed at companies (conducting sales team seminars, conferences, congresses, etc.) thus becoming a business to business service brand.

As regards professional brands, certain services such as banking or insurance can be bought by the general public via specially adapted offers. The general public's access to professional service brands is in this way wider than for the equipment goods brands, intermediate equipment products or entering goods (Table 1).

Owing to their dual targets of professional and private customers, "mixed" professional service brands have been forced early on to run communication campaigns aimed at the general public. Cases in point are bank and insurance company campaigns or those of temp agencies like Adecco, VediorBis or Manpower (see below the example of the main temporary work service brands). The renown of "mixed" professional service companies in the eyes of the general public is thus much greater than that of entering goods or equipment goods companies whose accessibility to private customers is much more recent. It is easier for companies offering industrial goods and complementary services under the corporate brand name to opt for mass market communication, and this allows them to increase the renown of their brand over the whole portfolio of activities covering different populations. The awareness of strictly professional service brands (ie business to business service brands) in the eyes of the general public is comparable to that obtained by entering goods and equipment goods.

Table 1. End-customer access to professional services

	Category	Brands
Purchaseable	• Leasing companies • Telecommunications • Documents, mail and express parcels • Removal transport, movers • Delivery, chartering	• Rentway, TradeLease... • AT&T, Bell South, France Telecom... • TNT, Dynamex, U-Ship, Skypack, Advanced Courier Services... • Home Moving & Storage, Alpha Moving & Storage, Steinway Moving, The Right Move, Super Movers Inc., We Haul, American Red Ball, Action Express Moving... • DHL, UPS, Fedex, Brink's...
Not purchaseable by the private customer	• Goods transport • Cleaning • Facilities management • Temporary workers • Management and administration consulting • Maintenance • Rental companies	• Golden Eagle, Intermodal Transportation Services... • Industrial Cleaning Services International, International Service System... • EDS, Grosvenor Service... • Adecco, VediorBis, Manpower... • Andersen Consulting, ADLittle, PriceWaterhouseCoopers... • Air Repair, Aircraft Service International... • United Rentals, Utility Equipment Leasing Group, Downs Equipment Rental...
Not purchaseable but useable by the private customer	• Catering • Data banks	• Sodexho Alliance, Compass-Eurest... • Kompass, Europages, Bottin, Dun & Bradstreet...

The "mixing" potential of professional service brands only explains a part of their high level of visibility vis-à-vis the private customer. In fact, the non-material nature of the service in itself, leads service companies to set up a visibility strategy designed to give their service tangibility and thus make the customer feel safer. The fundamental nature of services makes the visibility criteria, used up to now to study business to business brands, quite ambiguous: the service itself is not visible either to customer companies or private customers. Thus services can be classified according to the visibility of their brands rather than the services themselves. Only tangible elements allow services to become "visible" for customer companies and perhaps private customers. What is at stake with visibility is customer loyalty: once the service has been carried out, and in the absence of any visibility, the brand is no longer "physically" present in the customer company and in fact risks being forgotten. By putting its brand on building site compressors for example, Hertz, one leader for rental of industrial equipment, "materializes" the rental of equipment by linking it to its brand. The industrial customer "sees" the service provided and the general public around the building site can identify the rental brand. In the same way, by putting its brand on the work clothes of its employees and on its vehicles, Industrial Cleaning Services International makes its service visible not only directly to the customer company, but also to the private individuals who see the vehicles parked in the road (Figure 2).

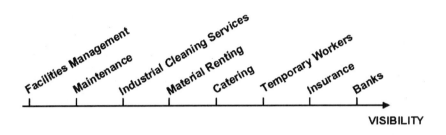

Figure 2. Examples of visibility levels of some professional services for the general public customer

The different vectors of communication play a particularly important role in the visibility of industrial service brands. Compass-Eurest or Sodexho napkins are a reminder of their catering services, the automatic International Service Systems brand hand-dryers recall their cleaning and hygiene service and the gold and brown UPS vehicles indicate a transport service. Different publicity gifts (calendars, scratch pads, pens, etc.), can also be a useful support in that the service brand has more long-term visibility. In order to "display" the service, the brands surround themselves with tangible elements such as slogans describing the activity, or visible brands on the products used to provide the service, etc. The visibility of the service brand to internal and external business targets allows the services to be made more tangible and thus increase their impact.

The different communication media are aimed at two main targets: businesses and private customers. For businesses it is necessary to distinguish on the one hand the decision-makers and the buyers and, on the other the company employees along with their visitors. Certain services such as management consulting are aimed mainly and "structurally" at the decision-makers and the buyers without the employees or the visitors having any real possibility of seeing the service being carried out. The consultants could walk about inside the company with briefcases or documents carrying their company brand, but their service and their brand are not really visible to the personnel and even less to private customers. Similarly, banking service brands are generally inconspicuous in the workplace, except to a few people from the accounting and finance department.

As with entering and equipment goods brands the trend is more and more for business to business service brands to advertise themselves to the general public. Good examples are the press and TV campaigns run by Andersen Consulting or Kompass. Sponsoring cultural (Sodexho Alliance and the World Youth Days) and sporting events (UPS and the Nagano Olympic Games; Compass-Eurest and the soccer matches on Canal + TV channel...) is another line of communication taken by business to business service brands in order to develop their renown and visibility in the eyes of the general public.

However, for a large number of industrial service brands, communicating with the general public is a delicate affair in that their services are abstract and complex (technical maintenance services, specialized training, etc.). Service brands with names which have a literal meaning such as Chronopost or Manpower have a considerable advantage since they allow more resources to be directed at developing the image and the renown and less on explaining and describing the activity. This cuts both ways, because by having brands which are too meaningful and descriptive, service companies will have greater difficulty diversifying away from the original activity.

Therefore business to business service brands require a solid and coherent identity built up over time, from which their credibility and legitimacy can develop. In this way they are drawn into adopting visibility strategies akin to those used by brands from other categories of goods.

Above and beyond their brand, they must really " demonstrate " the value of their service. In fact it is not just a question of fulfilling the function expected by the customer (cleaning, workforce, catering, etc.), but rather of providing the service the most closely adapted to the needs and activities of that customer company (frequency and urgency of cleaning, services under sterile conditions; selection, training and management of temporary personnel; diversity and dietary content of catering menus, flexible working hours, etc.). When they buy services, customer companies are motivated by the expectation of a superior quality service and by an optimization of the in-house activity. Therefore professional service companies have no choice but to become veritable partners of customer companies by helping them to improve their functioning.

3. A CLOSER LOOK AT TEMPORARY WORK SERVICE COMPANIES

For the general public, one of the most familiar professional services is without a doubt temporary work. This has a specific status in that the direct customers are companies looking for temporary workers. Private individuals can be "producers" in this service by putting themselves forward as candidates for the jobs offered. In a way, temporary work can be thought of as a "mixed service", because although it addresses companies in the main, it also needs the private individual, without whom the service would be impossible.

It is therefore not surprising, in view of this, to find that over the last few years, temporary work service brands have developed mass-media advertising campaigns, e.g. Manpower on TV. These actions, with an eye to promoting the brands, have been reinforced by buy-outs and mergers, which have modified their positions within the sector. Thus in 1996, Adia and Ecco merged, giving rise to Adecco which became the world leader in human resources. Similarly, VediorBis arose from Bis, Elan and Vedior. In the wake of this, the new companies, Adecco and VediorBis have launched large poster and TV advertising campaigns to promote their new brands.

Adecco have continued in the same vein as before, using the private Adecco aerobatics team stressing the values of perfectionism, competence, taking responsibilities and having a team spirit, speed, precision and reliability (Figure 3).

Figure 3. The Adecco logo

VediorBis have not linked their brand advertising to that of their founding companies (Figure 4). Rather the campaign is centered around presenting the human richness of temporary staff.

Figure 4. The VediorBis logo

This concentration within one sector allows the companies to be more present on the international scene and in this way ensure that their customers get a service covering all the different occupations over a much wider activity zone. Temporary work service companies are not in the business of "supplying workers" but rather of becoming partners in their customers' development. Their role is one of discovering, accompanying and drawing together human potential. They have developed a high quality know-how (ISO 9002) in terms of helping to define profiles, recruiting, and evaluating skills. For example, VediorBis offer their customers a range of software "Temp'Pro" designed to improve the quality and productivity of the management of temporary, trainee and term contract personnel, by means of made-to-measure spreadsheets and tables. Adecco has developed a recruitment method called "Xpert" which allows detection of skills required for the particular post and precise identification of the candidate's skills.

Finally Manpower has put together a whole range of selection tools, from Ultraskill which tests secretarial skills over a large range of computer programs, to Linguaskill which measures the linguistic level of a candidate, Comptaskill for accounting, Ultradex for production personnel, Ultrapro for maintenance, electrical, transport, etc (Figure 5).

MANPOWER

Figure 5. The Manpower logo

The temporary work companies are thus seeking to accompany their customer companies in their quest for higher productivity and profitability, regardless of size or activity sector. They have set up structures specialized by occupation, such as the service sector, building, industry, transport, food and agriculture, pharmaceutics and chemistry, IT, accountancy, insurance, catering and hotels, etc. In the nuclear sector, due to the inherent risks, whether to staff or the environment, a Cefri certificate must be obtained for sub-contractors, training organizations and temporary employment firms in order for them to be able to work on nuclear power sites. Thus, Manpower and Adecco for example have set up a specific quality assurance process covering recruitment, medicals, risk prevention training, individual exposure monitoring, and relations with the customer company. Once they have obtained the Cefri certification, they can channel personnel onto nuclear power sites safe in the knowledge that they conform to all the security regulations.

4. PROFESSIONAL SERVICE BRANDS: FACILITATING PERFORMANCE

Business to business service brands can be thought of as brands which contribute to the improvement of the functioning of customer companies in terms of productivity, then in terms of image, and finally in terms of in-house climate. The customer companies decide to seek help from professional service companies not only for one particular need of the moment, but also for the other advantages that they offer. Service providers often play a multiple role. For example, by renting production equipment, which is perfectly adapted to working conditions, the customer company will benefit from improved in-house functioning in terms of productivity. But at the same time, the company which has supplied the new equipment must also train the operators and in this way the customer company profits indirectly from an improvement in in-house training which in turn can translate into an improved in-house climate.

In a completely different domain, a bank such as Paribas, one of the three top world banks for financing international trade, accompanies its customers in their business dealings. In fact, Paribas has developed its banking services by adopting original and personalized solutions. In its corporate ads, Paribas puts the accent on imaginative customer service, using the slogan: "The worth of a bank is the worth of its ideas". Similarly, companies which rent high-tech equipment (software, computers, IT systems, etc.) such as ECS, Eqip or Continental leasing allow their customer companies to benefit from state-of-the-art equipment and improved budgetary flexibility.

Service brands can contribute to an improvement in their customers' productivity while at the same time helping their teams to work under more favorable conditions (hygiene, acoustic, thermal, etc.). Eurest, a subsidiary of the Compass group is a good example of a performance facilitator and of a service brand directed towards improving the functioning of customer companies. To this end Eurest takes care of catering management allowing customers to economize on costs in this area. The influence of Eurest extends beyond merely supplying a meal; rather it sets up a complete service from initial supplies through logistics, not to mention providing varied, high quality, nutritive meals. It is no longer a question of giving a meal to the employees of a company, but rather an agreeable moment spent with guests, offering them numerous and varied menus. More than just serving a meal, it becomes a question of respecting customs, traditional recipes, and the eating habits of the particular region in question. In addition to respecting tastes and habits, there is also thoughtfulness and listening, adding a touch of warmth to the occasion. The employees of the customer company are in a more positive professional climate, conscious of the efforts made by management and by Eurest to satisfy them. The brand, which is present on the napkins, is visible to the personnel; the slogan is: "We make your difference, our difference". More than meals, Eurest offers personalized company catering, reflecting the image and profile of the customer companies.

Moreover, services supplied by service brands can reinforce the image of the customer company relative to their own customers and partners. This is the case for Industrial Cleaning Services International, which takes care of cleaning premises and vehicles or Grosvenor Service who cover working clothes. In a similar way, DHL state that " We keep your promises" in terms of delivery delays, while the "Time masters" Chronopost, ensure rapid and punctual deliveries, allowing their customers to honor their engagements. The image of the customer company through the eyes of their own customers is enhanced by the quality of the service supplied. And it is this quality which is most often stressed by service companies, who have recently started to adhere to the ISO certification, initially developed for industrial companies.

The different ways in which business to business service brands facilitate performance can be illustrated using detailed examples. Andersen Consulting and EDS are a case in point, particularly in the productivity and management area. The case of Microsoft illustrates the facilitator role at a technical (productivity) and commercial (image and sales) level.

5. ANDERSEN CONSULTING: THE ART OF KNOWING HOW TO ORCHESTRATE TALENTS

Andersen Consulting, the world leader in management consulting and information technology, has a turnover of 9 billion euros with around 65,000 consultants and staff. As a professional services company, its vocation is to help companies and administrations successfully undertake in-depth transformation in order to increase their performance.

To increase the value of companies through the quality of their products and services, Andersen Consulting has designed an excellent methodology called " Business Integration ", based on the following elements:

• *Strategic vision*, which means translating ideas into high performance results: an excellent strategy is useless if it cannot be carried out in an excellent fashion,

• *Reconfiguration of processes*: excellent processes are intangible values, which can give a real competitive edge,

• *Mobilization of teams*: by helping to define strategy, teams are more motivated to reach project goals,

• *Technology* can be used to acquire a strategic advantage: technology is a lever for transformation to give market superiority.

At Andersen Consulting, the integration of these ideas becomes " The art of creating value for its customers". This "art" relies on a capacity to integrate skills by manipulating the most appropriate levers, while at the same time taking into account the particular characteristics of the company and the sector in which it operates. Indeed, this is one of the reasons why almost 10% of the turnover goes into training consultants, developing methods and know-how, staying in tune with the latest technological developments and creating new solutions. Andersen Consulting forges links with its customers as well as with other leading industrial companies. This has been the case with their "loyalty-partnership" with Havas Advertising in France, or in the E-business domain with Advance Bank, CSTAR, Cambridge Child Care, Nbtel, Deutsch Telekom Electronic Invoice. Taken together, these actions allow Andersen Consulting to develop along with their clients their combined experience and know-how.

Andersen Consulting's expertise supplies the raw material for their corporate advertising campaign. Thus, one of their sequences – Museum – shows a pictorial representation of four musicians with widely differing styles playing together in perfect harmony.

The storyboard of this advert expresses this "art of giving value" whose success depends upon complementarity and synergy between various skills (Figure 6).

Andersen Consulting has used this metaphorical representation to characterize and explain its profession: "Business Integration". This involves mobilizing and "orchestrating" those fundamental resources which are the skills of the company in terms of strategy, processes, behavior for change and technology, by focusing them on a common objective: improving the performance of the company.

**Are you sure all of your company's talented
individuals are working in perfect harmony ?**

ANDERSEN
CONSULTING

Figure 6. Andersen Consulting: the art of knowing how to orchestrate talents

It is in this way that Andersen Consulting defines its actions aimed at helping customers to better satisfy their market. Its presence all over the world allows it to offer a global service regardless of where the customer company is located and with the required functional and sectorial experts. All of this explains why it carries out assignments for 18 out of the top 20 groups in the world and for two thirds of the top hundred.

6.   EDS: A SERVICE BRAND DIRECTED AT CUSTOMER PRODUCTIVITY

Founded in the United States by Ross Perot, Electronic Data System (EDS) is today the world number one for services based on information technology and communication. The EDS brand, created from the initials of the company name has been used right from the start (Figure 7).

Figure 7. The EDS logo

Although originally in English, the three letters EDS are a worldwide brand, with no translation necessary. The company is present in 45 countries and includes more than 130,000 people worldwide; EDS serves over 9,000 customers and had a turnover of more than 19 billion euros.

6.1   EDS activities

With the buyout of A.T. Kearney in 1995, EDS has reinforced its management consulting services even more. With a workforce of almost 2,000, the company is at present one of the leaders on the French market in information services, particularly concerning facilities management, integration and management of IT systems.

The organization of EDS, which was certified as an ISO 9001 service company in 1996, reflects it's customers' activity sectors, in order to be in phase with them and better understand the challenges they face. In this way, specific solutions adapted to each activity sector can be produced, e.g. EDS Epsydre is a service dealing with water management solutions and EDS Esquif for management of health insurance.

Organization within EDS is based on skills crossover: there is a horizontal relationship between each division in order to communicate innovations and solutions put into place as much as possible and facilitate their transposition. There is a sort of benchmarking allowing the best-in-class solution to be applied.

6.2   The brand's commitment to customer performance

The whole company is angled towards developing customer performance in terms of information management. But beyond this, it helps to improve their commercial performance and improves staff productivity.

To do this, working within the organization outlined above, EDS has developed skill hubs concerning:

• *Services linked to information systems and technologies*: This covers the design and development of specific IT systems, system maintenance and the migration towards new system architectures. There is also system integration with the development of interfaces, the company's different systems and the setting up of software packages (SAP, Baan, Oracle Applications, etc.). Finally, EDS sets up facilities management, taking complete charge of customer's IT systems management even going to the point of sometimes taking on some of its customer's staff (resource management, network administration and management, etc.). For example it is in this area of activity that year 2000 update projects have been dealt with,

- *Process management*: EDS offers to optimize the management and/or integration of certain procedures which are run badly by the customer who is specialized elsewhere (consumer service, purchasing, etc.),

- *Management consulting*, using the skills developed by A.T.Kearney in particular. This consists of providing consulting on strategy, operations (sales, logistics, etc.) or technological issues (new applications, etc.). It is designed to improve customer performance within their strategic objectives,

- *Internet and the E-markets*: EDS sets up Internet/Intranet/Extranet sites, teleservice systems, on-line catalogues, E-message services, on-line services destined for high-input general public use, etc.,

- *CoSourcing*: this concept, which was invented and registered by EDS, is a new way of working between supplier (EDS) and customer, going beyond IT. It means building up a genuine partnership " to find together the source of " the best possible performance, by establishing specific economic and financial objectives and appropriate means. The contractual undertaking by EDS is to do everything required such that the customer attains his objectives, sharing the risks and linking remuneration in part to the results obtained.

Apart from the technology in itself, EDS therefore offers its skills, know-how and experience to reduce the customer's management costs, to accelerate the launch of new products (management of information, stocks, logistics, sales, etc.) and to reinforce the links between its customers and their own customers and suppliers.

EDS's communication policy focuses on presenting itself not as a traditional business to business service supplier, but as a component in the success of its customers: "Our undertaking: to enhance your productivity". The brand, associated with its facilities management specialty, publicizes its different know-how and in particular its services connected with the Internet and e-business. And it was on the innovative theme of CoSourcing that EDS launched a worldwide publicity campaign in 1996, with TV commercials in France on the news-TV LCI, and pages in newspapers such as Le Monde or Les Echos, showing examples of CoSourcing. In the IT sector, this concept has in fact been so successful that it is now commonplace. CoSourcing has therefore developed the renown of EDS which benefits from its image as a leader and precursor.

The message of the EDS brand is to display its vocation of helping customers to develop competitive advantages within their markets, by setting up IT systems which correspond in the best possible way to the demands of their economic activities and organization. EDS's first commitment is to produce a tangible impact on its customers' performance. Advertising is based mainly on results obtained and principal accomplishments. Thus EDS in 1994 announced that following the signing of a contract with Xerox, it was henceforward linked to its customer's performance. Solid partnerships with prestigious customers are the best sort of publicity.

The identity of the brand as a performance facilitator is recalled in all EDS advertising material whether in press communiques, media publicity, interviews with directors, sales handouts or in the various public events in which the company participates (sponsorship of the Barcelona Olympic Games, the Soccer World Cup in France, etc.). The EDS staff, well aware of the message developed by the brand also act as spokesmen, giving a coherent image.

EDS sponsorship is not financial support, but direct implication in the event, participating in the organization by offering its services and skills in information technology. This type of sponsorship, a shop-window of achievements, fits perfectly with the EDS communication policy. For example, during the Football (soccer) World Cup in France, EDS was selected as the IT official supplier. The result was that about a hundred persons, working full-time for three years took charge of the overall management of the project, from the development of a ticketing service, to the establishment of a system for transmitting the results, not to mention the accreditation of 50,000 VIP's and journalists and the development and updating of the "France 98" website.

7.   MICROSOFT: " HOW FAR WILL YOU GO? "

Founded on 4 April 1975 by William H. Gates and Paul G. Allen, Microsoft® development was based on the creation of office software (e.g. Works, Multiplan, and then Word and Excel, Office 97) and operating systems (Ms-Dos, Windows 95, Windows 98, Windows NT, etc.). With a staff of more than 30,000 and a turnover of almost 16 billion euros (for almost $158 billion share capital market value), Microsoft® is today the world leader for the supply of computer (PC) software[1] (Figure 8).

Figure 8. The Microsoft[R] logo

7.1   Microsoft[R]: an institution and a brand of products

The brand name Microsoft[R] was derived from the words micro, as in microcomputer, and soft as in software. Thus the Microsoft brand encapsulates the material and non-material connotations of this product category. At the outset, Microsoft[R] was a product-brand (Ms-Dos: Microsoft[R] Disk Operating System; Ms-Works: Microsoft[R] Works) ensuring the coherence between the brand, its image, and its position such that the product on offer to the customer was clearer. Since that time, with all the diversification that has taken place in new markets, Microsoft[R] has become a signature-brand. It groups together products which each have their own brand and undertakings, all backed by the corporate brand.

This strategy has allowed the brand to evolve, including categories of products which are further and further away from the initial one, all of which enhances and enriches the signature-brand. However care must be taken so that the signature brand does not lose its special nature and that its image is not diluted by too many new product categories. This is the reason why Microsoft[R] cultivates its identity very strongly. To this end, Microsoft[R] conducts a rigorous, coherent corporate communication policy in the trade and popular press and on TV. These actions designed to strengthen its image and renown, reinforce and support its visibility strategy.

It is a question of developing the visibility of the Microsoft[R] brand by bringing it to the fore:

• At the very heart of the product, by having the brand displayed permanently on the screen,

• On the product (Figure 9), on the packaging and the computers, indicated by decals such as " Designed for Microsoft Windows 98 " on PC's,

• All around the product by being highlighted in press or TV campaigns.

Figure 9. Examples of Microsoft® product brands: Windows NT Server, Exchange Server, and Windows 95

The corporate slogan for Microsoft® in France, "How far will you go?" [2] (Jusqu'où irez-vous?), expresses the readiness of the brand to accompany its customers regardless of their objective. This invitation to experiment with all the possibilities offered by IT, neatly sums up the innovative character of the company and its confidence in the future. Bill Gates, the founder, embodies company values as being a "computer genius" with a capacity to innovate, market vision and a permanent commitment to improving performance.

The rigorous management of Microsoft® allows advertising campaigns for the product-brands to be launched, all backed by the corporate brand (Table 10).

Table 10. The management of product brands by Microsoft®

Signature brand	Product brands	Product	Advertising slogan
Microsoft®	Windows	Operating system	" Start doing. "
Microsoft®	Office	Office software	" Get your work done easier and faster. "
Microsoft®	Project	Project management software	" Planning your next project won't be a project in itself. "
Microsoft®	Publisher	Publishing software	" Let you get creative right away. "
Microsoft®	Encarta	Interactive encyclopedia	" As close as you can get to being there. "
Microsoft®	Internet Explorer	Internet navigation software	" Get connected. "

7.2 Microsoft®: a brand serving customer performance

Microsoft® offers different products designed to satisfy the fast evolving needs of its customers:

• The Windows NT operating system destined for network providers and high level workstations, or Windows 95 and Windows 98, which are easy to use and increase productivity by integrating the latest technological developments (3D, video, sound, Internet, etc.),

• Network administration software such as BackOffice, which helps network controllers and developers to manage the channeling of data (applications, providers for a customer/provider environment),

• Development software tools for facilitating the creation of IT solutions,

• Office software whose applications are destined for the Windows environment and also for that of Apple Macintosh (Microsoft® Office),

• Internet software,

• Software for the general public.

Looking at the Microsoft® offer, it would seem that it is an entering goods brand. However, Microsoft® is not just a software supplier but also a service provider, especially for IT consulting.

Microsoft® Consulting Services (MCS) help businesses and service companies for example, to design and produce IT solutions using Microsoft® technology. This service is called corporate Microsoft® in order to benefit from brand awareness. Product Support Services (PSS) is Microsoft®'s technical assistance service or hot line. Several levels of service are offered, from the " Standard support " which gives free telephone assistance for 30 days concerning languages and development software and 90 days for operating systems and other software, up to " First Global Service " which is personalized and accessible 24 hours a day, 7 days a week. Between these two there is an incident support for occasional needs or supplementary support.

Microsoft® aims just as much at the individual user as at small, medium and large organizations. Computer manufacturers such as HP, Compaq or Toshiba are known as OEM's (Original Equipment Manufacturers) who integrate Microsoft® technology and products. In France, business to business customers have taken on a strategic importance for Microsoft® with:

• 2,8 million small (SORG) and medium (MORG) organizations,

• Large organizations (LORG).

While Microsoft office software is very well known to the general public, products for companies find themselves in a much more bitterly contested sector (Novell, Lotus, Borland, Sun, Oracle, etc.). And this is one of the reasons why Microsoft® has launched its "Specialized Solutions Partners" program. This consists of collaboration between IT professionals (added value retailers, Service Companies in IT engineering, editors, providers, consultants, developers, system integrators, retailers, etc.) and Microsoft® in order to develop IT solutions and services which are the most adapted to the user's needs. These partners, selected because of their skills, all have official approval:

• "Microsoft® Partner Solutions First" for large service and consulting companies,

• "Microsoft® Partner Solutions Approved Technical Training Center" for private training organizations,

• "Microsoft® Partner Solutions Approved Support Center" for support and technical assistance companies.

The Microsoft® brand can therefore be found in the partners' guarantees, thus prolonging the visibility of the service brand. These partners are independent businesses capable of helping companies to set up IT solutions which correspond to their needs. They provide numerous services such as consultation, training, development, and personalized solutions. Microsoft® supports its partners by:

• Marketing operations aimed at promoting and publicizing the solutions that have been put in place: presence in the official Microsoft® partners catalog on the Microsoft® website, on the Microsoft® stands at trade fairs, publication of customer references in the Microsoft® Solutions magazine,

• The bestowing of the "Microsoft® Solutions Partner logo" allowing them to strengthen their market visibility.

Microsoft® also makes available its technical support along with a kit which contains a large amount of technical, marketing and commercial information, necessary for setting up IT solutions. In passing, Microsoft® products can be used internally by partners with preferential conditions, and special tariffs are available for the acquisition of all complementary products. Quite apart from commercial development, the technical partnership allows Microsoft® and the various other participants to enrich their database with:

• The collection of information which could lead to a project,

• The development of new solutions and their transposition to other projects,

• The acquisition of new references.

A technical performance facilitator for its customers by helping with innovation and design, Microsoft® is also a commercial performance facilitator via the brand's marketing and sales support of the brand.

More than just a software supplier, Microsoft® is thus a genuine service provider enabling customers and partners to improve their own particular operations. The offer aims to make customers' IT systems as efficient as possible in order to improve their productivity. This policy has contributed to making the Microsoft® brand the second in America in terms of capital value, just behind General Electric.

NOTES

1. Microsoft® is a registered trademark of Microsoft Corporation.
2. See Chapter 9, The Logotype and the Visual Identity Code, 3- Slogans and Brand Signatures.

Chapter 15

Industrial Distributor Brands

Industrial brands can be analyzed in terms of the status of the supplier company, which can be either a producer or distributor of products or services. Today, just like in the consumer sector, the distributor brand concept has taken off in business to business.

Industrial distributor brands (IDB), which are a relatively recent development, can be found in the three business to business categories analyzed earlier: entering goods, equipment goods and professional services.

To fully grasp the different markets concerned by the distributor brand in the business to business context, two main areas need to be distinguished:

• The supply of industrial distributor brand goods or products to professionals, following the example of the consumer market where distributor brands have been developed by the big retailers,

• The industrial supply of finished products stamped with the brand of the retail distributor.

Analyzing these two scenarios will help to clarify the relationship between the industrial brand and its environment.

1.   THE SUPPLY OF INDUSTRIAL DISTRIBUTOR BRANDED PRODUCTS

The "industrial trader" or "industrial distributor", can deal in products or equipment with a highly variable degree of technological sophistication and size (dimensions, volume, financial cost...).

The brand used by the distributor can be non-visible or visible to the end user (Figure 1). The second case is closest to the classical meaning of distributor brand as defined by the consumer sector.

• When the brand of the distributor is visible, it has complete control over the transaction. The distributor is responsible for the quality of the goods supplied and not just the quality of the delivery service or the logistics. When the distributor actually puts his own brand on the product, he is really substituting his own identity and thus capacity to influence for that of the supplier.

• When the distributor brand is not visible, the distributor must back up the supplier's marketing strategy. In this case, the distributor relies on the promises and arguments developed by his chosen suppliers.

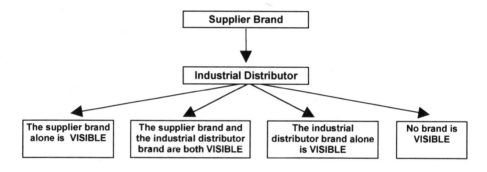

Figure 1. The supplier brand and the industrial distributor brand: the different relational and visibility levels

1.1   Entering goods

For entering goods, distributors usually do not substitute their own brand for that of the manufacturing supplier. A good example is one European leader in electronic components distribution, Tekelec, who supply products under their original well known brand names (IBM, Siemens, Toshiba, STMicroelectronics, etc).

Tekelec, which has been ISO 9002 certified for the quality of its logistics and services, has developed its know-how around service provision to industry:

• In terms of logistics, punctuality and delivery times of between 12 and 48 hours,

• In terms of technological watch, playing the role of scout, startup capacity and as a distributor of innovative, technologically advanced products.

Tekelec has in particular become the number one distributor in Europe for Intel microprocessors, handling the brand since its inception.

Rexel, a subsidiary of the Pinault-Printemps-Redoute group (PPR group: Pinault, Guilbert, FNAC, Conforama, Redcats, Gucci, Yves Saint-Laurent...), is the world leader for the distribution of low-voltage electrical equipment, necessary in particular for the installation and use of electricity in residential and industrial buildings. With a workforce of almost 17,000, the company had a turnover of more than 5.2 billion euros and is present throughout a large network of sales outlets in Europe, Brazil, and the United States. Under the brand names of its suppliers, Rexel distributes a diverse range of more than 100,000 general and specialized products to a professional customer base made up of electricians, electrical installation companies, industrial and service sector companies, public organizations, and retailers. The deliberate non-standardization of its products and services is also reflected in how it manages its own Rexel brand. The Rexel group was built up by the federation, around common commercial objectives and strategies, of a group of small and medium-sized businesses having very different profiles, customers and markets. This decentralized culture allowed the subsidiaries to retain their identity, their trade name and also a large part of the initiative, while still benefiting from the group know-how.

The distributor brand is generally non-visible even when it concerns lower risk technology products such as in the building sector for example. The large European building material distributors such as Pinault, Point P, Gedimat or Bigmat have decided to rely mainly on their supplier brands such as Lafarge for cement and plaster, Saint-Gobain for glazing, Guiraud and Gelis for bricks, Feder and PPB for beams and pre-stressed floors...

Pinault, specialist in the distribution of wood and building materials, uses its own brand for its complementary product ranges. The Pinault brand gives its name to whole families of products such as wood treatment products, polyurethane foams, ranges of glues and sealers as well as small hardware products. For these ranges, the Pinault brand is the only one visible to the buyer whether he be a professional (self-employed, large company employee...) or a do-it-yourself enthusiast (Figure 2).

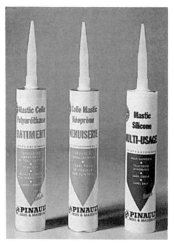

Figure 2. An example of complementary products: the Pinault building chemicals range

A second example is the building materials Point P trade name (a subsidiary of Saint Gobain) which uses the brand "Les Exclusifs" (*The Exclusive*) on a varied range of products including tiles, parquet and laminated flooring. "Les Exclusifs" results from a Point P selection policy of products offered by industrial suppliers. The concept behind the "Les Exclusifs" distributor brand, corresponds in fact to the distributor's expertise at selecting product ranges on offer as a function of the end customer's expectations and the evolution of materials. By selecting and featuring these chosen products, the volume of sales for the trade name are increased. This then allows Point P to make a more competitive offer thanks to the gains made on the purchase price. What should be noted is that unlike Pinault, neither the corporate brand Point P, nor its logo appears on the product. "Les Exclusifs" is the only brand visible. In the building sector, most of the distributor brands are not visible to the buyers, who thus rely on the marketing of the main manufacturer brands.

1.2   Equipment goods

As for equipment goods, distributor brand visibility is much more an issue for the goods than for heavy ones.

Actually the heavy goods category (large trucks, machine equipment, robots...) is not concerned because usually it involves direct transactions between the manufacturers and the industrial customers without an intermediate distributor. This is true for the Tetra Pak packaging product line, blowing machines for the production of PET plastic packing from the world leader Sidel, and Mannesmann machine tools, among others. On the other hand, for light goods (small power tools, small air compressor...) as a whole, distributor brand visibility is a major problem.

In the small and medium size industrial handling equipment sector the distributor Manutan uses two types of branding: the manufacturer's brand or its own distributor brand, Manutan. This distributor, whose originality stems from opting as early as 1966 for mail order catalogue sales, has become number one in this activity by offering a complete range of products from handling/lifting, storage equipment to products for the workshop, general equipment or office supplies (1,000 page catalogue with 40,000 references).

Manutan puts its logo onto material as varied as elevating platforms, pallet trucks, folding cranes, or straps for which it has, in passing, developed a specific brand, Manufix. However, overall, within the same ranges, Manutan mainly offers material from manufacturers such as Demag, Palair, Stahl, Tiger, Bosch, Dremel, Stanley, 3M, Esselte...

It should be noted that certain importing-wholesalers and dealers in machine tools or specific equipment, sometimes also put their own brand onto machines and equipment bought from manufacturers. Certain production companies do some distribution on the side, to complete the ranges that they sell, using sundry equipment or accessories bought from other suppliers, placed under their own brand.

Nonetheless, the manufacturers big brand names are generally kept as such by the distributors because of their inherent sales interest or because of conditions imposed by the suppliers. Globally, the distributor brands, which are visible by the end customer –the user –, seem to be mainly reserved for low involvement products, those which are more commonplace or which can be used by professionals but also by the general public. Raja company which has developed a policy of distributor brands by product category is a case in point: Rajabag for bin bags, Rajabook for sending individually packaged books, Rajabox for packing individual packets, Rajalist to hold the accompanying documents for packages, Rajabulle and Rajamousse for packing...

The same distributor brand policies are also used for office supplies (Buro+...) or in medical and dental sundries. Most medical equipment distributors for example, rely on the established brands of the manufacturers. For example in the domain of disinfection and sterilization of instruments this is true of Bodedex, Corsolex, Bomix, Korsolin, Bacillol from Beiersdorf or in the domain of dressings, with the brands Askina, Tegasorb, Medipore, Micropore, Transpore, and Tegaderm, all from 3M.

1.3   Services

In principle, services do not lend themselves to distributor brand strategies, because service suppliers "deliver" to their professional customers with no intermediaries. However an analogy can be found with distributor brands when the brand of the service provider is substituted for that of the equipment manufacturer. In this case, the service company stamps its brand on the tangible elements of its service. Elis, a company in the supply and maintenance of linen and working clothes, is an example. This European leader puts its brand onto the different accessories offered by the service, from the one-wipe hand towel dispensers down to the plastic sacks to take the cleaned clothes and the delivery vans decorated with the Elis logo and the "Le propre en action" (Cleaning action) tagline.

Similarly, service companies in the company catering market, sign the various accessories and sundries which are part of what they provide. This is true of table napkins and individually wrapped sugar lumps under the brand Sodexho Alliance or Compass-Eurest, rather than the manufacturer's brand.

On the industrial goods rental market, hire firms use their own brand, which thus masks the equipment manufacturer's brand. This is true for United Rentals, Utility Equipment Leasing Group, Downs Equipment Rental... with building site equipment, lifting equipment, Hertz or Europcar for goods and industrial vehicles.

2.   THE INDUSTRIAL SUPPLY OF FINISHED PRODUCTS OR ENTERING GOODS FOR CONSUMER GOODS DISTRIBUTORS

Distributor brands can be analyzed from yet another angle: the relationship between an industrial company and the brand of a consumer goods distributor. There are three possibilities (Figure 3):

• Finished products stamped with the consumer goods distributor brand,

• Entering goods incorporated into finished products stamped with retail distributor brands,

• Hidden-brand finished goods.

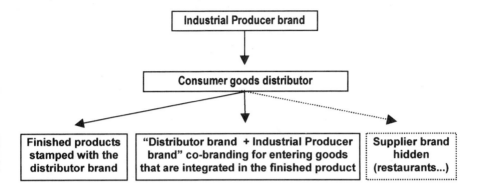

Figure 3. The industrial manufacturer brand and the distributor brand strategies

2.1 Finished products stamped with the consumer goods distributor brand

Producing goods which are then branded with the distributor brand can be a part of business to business marketing. This is because the manufacturer has no direct contact with the end consumer. The distributor, with his brand visible on the packaging acts as a screen, since the consumer does not know the identity of the manufacturer, sometimes even believing that it is the distributor himself. The supply of such a product starts off with setting out the specification requirements, most often defined by the distributor's very own marketing department. These specifications are then presented to the store managers and the regional directors in order for them to put forward a sales volume commitment (Figure 4).

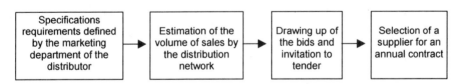

Figure 4. The distributor brand: the stages in the selection process for an industrial manufacturer

After these forecasts have been approved at the national level, the distributor can then put the project out to tender with the different suppliers of the sector concerned, sending out the specification requirements and also the quantities envisaged for the period under discussion. Manufacturing contracts are usually for a period of one year, sometimes two. This means that a contract might not be renewed the following year: which is what happens each time another manufacturer offers a lower selling price.

The development of distributor brands in Europe has two main consequences for manufacturers:

• The first consequence is negative and in a nutshell is the vulnerability of the customer portfolio. All too often, small businesses allow a particular purchasing group to progressively predominate in their turnover; this is particularly true where the company verges on a mono product profile. The production company has therefore almost no room for maneuver vis-à-vis the distributors and the future can be very uncertain if there is a fall in prices for international reasons.

• The second consequence is positive. A company can make a successful start-up thanks to supplying distributor product brands. In fact, because of the end customers demand for the distributor brand, the production company can access a large volume of sales. In the factory this translates into getting competitive cost prices and making additional investments. Under these conditions, the company can thus establish a strategy, which includes the development of its own brand.

Cantalou is an example of a small family business, which has become a European leader for chocolate bars. With most of its activity in supplying the main European brands, Cantalou has, over the last few years, relaunched its own Cémoi brand. Similarly, Rouleau Guichard has followed the same strategy in the under garments sector by supplying in particular, Tex product brand for Carrefour, Tissaïa for Leclerc...

2.2 Entering goods incorporated into finished products stamped with retail distributor brands

In the competition between manufacturer brands and distributor brands, the former have developed more sophisticated products in response to consumer expectations. With this in mind, partnerships have been formed between manufacturers who "integrate" the finished product and entering goods manufacturers who "incorporate" it, which make the promise and the plus-product possible. Take the example of a hiking boots manufacturer such as Aigle who accepts a partnership offered by Gore-Tex$^{®}$. Thanks to the membrane incorporated, the boot is waterproof while at the same time allowing perspiration to pass out.

At this level the manufacturing brand (Aigle) comes out on top because it has repositioned itself relative to the distributor brand (such as Decathlon). To make up the lost ground, the distributor brand will ask the entering goods manufacturer for a similar partnership which will thus be established between the two manufacturers of finished products and entering products on behalf of the distributor brand. The latter will in this way be legitimized in the eyes of the consumer thanks to the juxtaposition of the famous entering goods brand. For this particular competitive situation, the Décathlon brand associated with the Gore-Tex® brand is a good example.

The new trend is for distributors like Décathlon to develop their own second brand, this time for the components of the finished product, which thus imitates the co-branding technique used by manufacturers. The table below summarizes the five stages corresponding to the progressive takeover of the brand concept by the distributor, from the simple brand to the brand tandem via co-branding (Table 5).

Table 5. The different stages of development of the distributor brand in relation to the manufacturer brand

Phase	Product	Brand(s)	Stages
1	Sports shoes	Aigle	Setting up a classical brand positioning i.e independent.
2	Sports shoes, hiking, more complex shoes *(use of materials such as membranes...)*	Aigle + Gore-Tex	Setting up of a more complex positioning developed with the supplier via *co-branding*
3	Sports shoes	Décathlon	Distributor describes itself as an " integrator "
4	Sports shoes *E.g..: Hiking +use of complex materials (membranes)*	Décathlon + Gore-Tex	Distributor brand is legitimized by the presence of the supplier brand with its technical renown
5	Sports shoes *E.g..: Hiking +use of complex materials (membranes))*	Décathlon + new membrane distributor brand (1998)	Appropriation of both " brand " stages - integrator - supplier

2.3 Hidden-brand finished goods

Hidden brands refer to branded finished products sold to professionals, who are not distributors, and who do not necessarily want to reveal the brand to their customers. In general these finished products are specially designed for professionals, such as for example, cleaning products like Johnson or Henkel or coffee produced by Douwe-Egberts.

Unlike with distributor brands, manufacturers control the specifications. Nevertheless, this case is still close to distributor brands because the manufacturer is not identified by the end consumer. For example a restaurant owner often prefers the supplier brand to be hidden from clientele, who are meant to think that the meal is entirely "home-made".

This chapter has presented an overview of how industrial suppliers can be linked to distributor brand strategies. This relationship could involve a new product destined for the general public with a finished product supply or the supply of goods to be incorporated into the end product. Or it could more particularly involve goods for a company, whether entering goods, for example in the building sector, or light investment goods in the office supplies sector, handling or industrial packing. Although it is only a recent concept, it is safe to say that the industrial distributor brand will tend to develop by osmosis with the evolution of the consumer goods market.

Conclusion

Most of the many books that have been written about branding focus on consumer products and luxury goods. This book demonstrates that business to business branding is fast developing at the very time when the brand concept would seem to be endangered by its own success through trivialization, especially for everyday household products.

The development of industrial marketing coincides with increasing advertising budgets for business to business brands and ever more sophisticated brand policies, involving the juxtaposition of product brands and corporate brands. In addition, more and more often the process of creating brands is being handled by professionals specialized in finding the most effective names that can be easily pronounced and memorized, and which are evocative in a wide range of geographic areas. This trend is even more recent in business to business services.

Careful study of business to business buying, increasingly handled by an informal buying center rather than a structured buying department, has revealed professional buyers' main expectations from brands. Differentiation, positioning, and capitalization are essential just like in the consumer market, while the irrational dimensions of choosing brands are of only minor importance in the industrial context. However, these are combined with the need for risk reduction and performance facilitation. Contrary to general thinking, the brand plays a role in the purchasing process at the level of the buying center, in particular for important transactions. It has been demonstrated that this influence is even more important for new purchases, when many people are usually involved in the decision, and the stakes are high. To win over a new customer, or to keep regular customers loyal, brands must use all the different channels for reaching each of the in-house targets, from the customer's marketing department to production. The aim is to create in-house support in the buying department. Through their different roles, business to business brands have come to be seen as performance facilitators.

The supplier brand can be perceived as a performance facilitator:

• From a technical point of view by: making innovation possible, improving productivity and quality control, and providing maintenance,

• From a sales point of view by: helping to define and customize the product, or participating in communication campaigns such as co-branding with the customer's brand to improve sales,

• From an operational point of view by: improving productivity or the in-house climate to image building (for example as projected by personnel).

On an operational level supplier brands can be classified; this can be very useful in that it allows the supplier to correct the perceived drawbacks that can be associated with each type of performance facilitation. For example, a partnership that is seen as particularly strong from a technical point of view can make the customer afraid of becoming dependent. Without completely eliminating this fear, the supplier can develop information and training measures to make sure that the customer is confident in his technical independence, while ensuring his loyalty.

In the same way, when the partnership is perceived as strong from a sales point of view, this can give rise to fears that the supplier will raise prices. In this case the supplier brand needs to develop a strategy for facilitating innovation and differentiation right from the design stage, for example.

In addition, three new concepts have been suggested: "printability", "visibility", and "purchaseability"; these help to better understand the brand strategies used by business to business companies. With this in mind five separate brand categories have been defined:

• Entering goods brands,
• Intermediary equipment goods brands,
• Equipment goods brands,
• Business to business service brands,
• Industrial distributor brands.

Depending on the case, a visibility or a purchaseability strategy can be developed to create final demand for the product or service proposed. The visibility of the supplier brand to the end customer must be accompanied by the appropriate communication policy.

This visibility is an extremely important factor in the customer-supplier relationship; yet today there are still great differences in how it is handled depending on the sector of activity. Visibility is more accepted when there is little risk of the end product becoming banal. In the building sector, the presence of high performance supplier brands is seen above all as an advantage, especially in terms of differentiation. This is also true of the textiles and clothing industry where the increasing numbers of supplier brands have developed extensive communication campaigns. However, in the automotive sector, until now, manufacturers have been extremely slow to accept supplier brand visibility, fearing a decrease in differentiation perceived by end customers; this is also true in the packaging sector, particularly for food.

With the growing need for former sub-contractors to assert their own visibility, their brands now require a much more coherent policy, starting with choosing appropriate brands, whether corporate or product brands. This coherence also means defining and respecting a clear visual identity code, as well as ensuring brand protection. With globalization, the international dimension of branding must also be considered, even for small and medium sized firms initially operating in only one country. However, there is no ready-made solution as far as choosing between going global or maintaining local brands.

Today, whatever the activity sector, equipment goods, business to business services or entering goods, products are becoming increasingly sophisticated and complex. This phenomenon has put an even greater premium on demonstrating the reliability and legitimacy of the supplier of the product or service to the end customer; as such, the guarantee that a renowned supplier can provide is extremely valuable. This has given rise to the development of numerous technical and sales partnerships between different players in the same branch. Co-branding is the most striking example of this, when the customer company accepts the visibility of his supplier. In other cases, the customer can require tracking, so as to identify the manufacturer, place, and exact date of production. Analyzing these trends has highlighted the growing importance of branding in business to business, a fact confirmed by the positive reactions of the companies contacted for the writing of this book. And it would seem that business to business branding can only continue to grow in the years to come.

Bibliography

BOOKS

Aaker, D. A. et Lendrevie J., (1994), *Le management du capital de la marque*, Paris, Dalloz.

Aaker, D.A., (1991), *Managing Brand Equity : Capitalizing on the Value of a Brand Name*, New York, Free Press.

Abelson, R .P., (1968), *Theories of Cognitive Consistency : A Source Book*, Chicago : Rand McNally, Raf.

Andrews, D.C et Andrews, W.D., (1993), *Business Communication*, 2ème édition, New York, Macmillan.

Andrieu, O. et Lafont, D., (1995), *Internet et l'entreprise*, Paris, Eyrolles.

Arnold, D., (1992), *The Handbook of Brand Management*, Century Business, Londres, The Economist Books.

Assael, H., (1987), *Consumer Behavior and Marketing Action*, 5ème édition, Londres, International Thomson Business Press.

Barthes, R., (1985), *L'aventure sémiologique*, Paris, Le Seuil.

Bateson, J., (1995), *Managing Services Marketing. Text and Readings*, 3ème Éd., Orlando, Fla., The Dryden Press.

Baudrillard, J., (1974), *La société de consommation*, Paris, Gallimard.

Bauhain-Roux, D., (1992), *Gestion du design et management d'entreprise*, Paris, Éditions Chotard et Associés.

Beaudoin, J-P., (1995), *Conduire l'image de l'entreprise*, Paris, Liaisons.

Beltram, A. et Ruffat, M., (1991), *Culture d'entreprise et histoire,* Paris, Éditions d'Organisation.

Benard, A. et Fontan, A-L., (1994), *La gestion des risques dans l'entreprise : management de l'incertitude*, Paris, Éditions d'Organisation.

Bennett, P. D. (1988), Dictionary of Marketing Terms, Chicago, *American Marketing Association*.

Benoun, M. et Héliès-Hassid, M.L., (1995), *Distribution, Acteurs et Stratégies*, 2ème édition., Paris, Economica.

Beon, P., (1995), *Comment développer la communication interne ?*, Paris, Nathan.

Bernstein, D., (1984), *Company Image and Reality, A Critique of Corporate Communication*, New York, Holt., Rinehart and Winston.

Bienveniste, F. et Piquet, S., (1988), *Pratique du Parrainage*, Paris, Vuibert

Blanc, F., (1988), *Marketing Industriel*, Paris, Vuibert.

Boneu, F., (1990), *L'entreprise communicante : Démarches et méthodes de la communication interne*, Paris, Éditions Liaisons.

Bonoma, T.V., Zaltman G. et Johnston W.J., (1977), *Industrial Buying Behavior*, Cambridge, Marketing Science Institute.

Botton, M. et Grunow-Jannin M., (1992), *Créer et protéger ses marques*, Paris, Lamy / Les Echos.

Botton, M., et Cegarra, J-J., (1990), *Le nom de marque*, Paris, McGraw-Hill.

Bromley, D.B., (1993), *Reputation, Image and Impression Management*, New York, John Wiley & Sons.

Brun, M. et Rasquinet, Ph., (1996), *L'identité visuelle de l'entreprise au-delà du logo*, Paris, Éditions d'Organisation

Caron, F., (1981), *Histoire économique de la France, XIXème et XXème siècles*, Paris, Armand Colin.

Cauzard, D., Perret J. et Ronin, Y. (1989), *Images de marques / Marques d'images*, Paris, Ramsay.

Chapman, E.A., (1987), *Exhibit Marketing: A Survival Guide for Managers*, New York, McGraw-Hill.

Chase, C. et Barasch K., (1977), *Marketing Problem Solver*, New York, Chilton Books.

Chernatony, L. (de) et McDonald, M., (1992), *Creating Powerful Brands*, Londres, Butterworth-Heinemann.

Chetochine, G., (1993), *Le management stratégique de la distribution*, Paris, InterÉditions.

Cintas, Y. et Dupuis, E., (1990), *Communiquer avec la presse*, Paris, Éditions d'Organisation.

Clouet, P., (1989), *Les achats : un outil du management*, Paris, Éditions d'Organisation.

Colla, E. et Dupuis, M., (1997), *Le défi mondial du bas prix*, Paris, Publi-Union.

Comte, A., (1844), *Le discours sur l'esprit positif*.

Corey, E.R., (1976), *Industrial Marketing, Cases and Concepts*, 2ème édition, Englewood Cliffs, N.J., Prentice-Hall.

Cowell, D., (1984), *The Marketing of Services*, Londres, William Heinemann.

Cox, D.F., (1967), *The Influence of Cognitive Needs and Styles in Information Handling in Making Product Evaluation*, Boston, Harvard University.

Darmon, R-Y., (1998), *La vente, De la persuasion à la négociation commerciale*, Paris, Éditions EMS.

Dauzat, Dubois et Mitterand, (1971), *Dictionnaire étymologique*, Paris, Larousse.

Daviet, J-P., (1988), *Un destin international, la Compagnie de Saint-Gobain de 1830 à 1939*, Paris, Éditions des Archives Contemporaines.

Dayan, A., (1994), *Marketing industriel*, Paris, 3ème édition, Vuibert.

De Maricourt, R., *et al.*, (1997), *Marketing Européen*, Paris, Publi-Union.

De Narbonne, A., (1993), *La communication d'entreprise, Conception et pratique*, 2ème édition, Paris, Eyrolles.

Décaudin, J-M., (1995), *La communication marketing, Concepts, techniques stratégies*, Paris, Economica, Collection Gestion

Delorme, C., (1991), *Le logo*, Paris, Éditions d'Organisation.

Detrie, P et Meslin-Broyez C., (1995), *La communication interne au service du management*, Paris, Éditions d'Organisation.

Dimitriadis, S., (1994), *Le management de la marque, vecteur de croissance*, Paris, Éditions d'Organisation.

Dordor, X., (1993), *La presse pro : mieux la connaître pour mieux l'utiliser*, Paris, Dunod.

Doyle, P., (1994), *Marketing Management and Strategy*, Hemel Hempstead, Prentice Hall.

Dubois, B., (1994), *Comprendre le consommateur*, 2ème édition, Paris, Dalloz.

Dubois, P-L. et Jolibert, A., (1992), *Le marketing, fondements et pratique*, 2ème édition, Paris, Economica, Collection Gestion.

Dussart, C., (1983), *Comportement du consommateur et Stratégie de marketing*, Montréal, McGraw-Hill.

Éditions Francis Lefebvre, (1994), Création, valorisation, protection : dossiers pratiques, Levallois Perret.

Eiglier, P., et Langeard, E., (1988), *Servuction, Le marketing des services*, Paris, McGraw-Hill.

Encyclopédie de Gestion, (1997), Paris, Economica.

Engel, J.F., Blackwell R.D. et Kollat, D.T., (1978), *Consumer Behavior*, 3ème édition, Orlando, Fla., The Dryden Press.

England, W.B. et Leenders M.R., (1975), *Purchasing and Materials Management*, Homewood, Ill., Richard D. Irwin.

Farnel, F., (1994), *Le lobbying : stratégies et techniques d'intervention*, Paris, Éditions d'Organisation.

Filser, M., (1994), *Le comportement du consommateur*, Paris, Dalloz, Collection Précis de Gestion.

Floch, J-M., (1995), *Identité visuelle*, Paris, PUF.

Ford, D., (1997), *Understanding Business Markets: Interactions, Relationships and Networks*, 2ème édition, The International Marketing and Purchasing Group (IMP), Londres, The Dryden Press.

Futrell, C., (1993), *Fundamentals of Selling*, Homewood, Ill., Richard D. Irwin, 4ème édition.

Galey, B.C., (1997), *De mémoire de marques*, Paris, Tallandier.

Garbett, Th. (1981), *Corporate Advertising : the What, the Why and the How*, New York, McGraw-Hill.

Gauchet, Y., (1996), *Achat Industriel, Stratégie et Marketing*, Paris, Publi-Union.

Grunow-Jannin, M. et Botton, M., (1992), *Créer et protéger ses marques*, Paris, Lamy/Les Echos.

Hague, P. et Jackson P., (1994), *The Power of Industrial Brands*, Londres, McGraw-Hill.

Hamon, M., (1988), *Du soleil à la terre, Une histoire de Saint-Gobain*, Paris, Jean-Claude Lattès.

Hanlon, A., (1977), *Creative Selling Through Trade Shows*, New York, Hawthorn Books.

Hardy, K.G. et Grath A.J., (1988), *Marketing Channel Management, Strategic Planning and Tactics*, Glenview, Ill., Scott, Foresman and Co.

Hart, N.A., (1995), *Strategic Public Relations*, New York, Macmillan.

Hassel, C.V., (1990), *Le marketing industriel européen*, Paris, Éditions d'Organisation.

Hebert, N., (1987), *L'entreprise et son image, La publicité institutionnelle : pourquoi, comment ?*, Paris, Dunod.

Hermel, L. et Scholasch, A., (1996), *Le marketing industriel*, Paris, Economica, Gestion Poche.

Heude, R.P., (1988), *L'image de marque*, Paris, Eyrolles.

Howard, J.A. et Sheth, J., (1969), *The Theory of Buyer Behavior*, New York, John Wiley & Sons.

Hutt, M.D et Speh T.W., (1995), *Business Marketing Management, A Strategic View of Industrial and Organizational Markets*, 5ème édition, Orlando, Fla., The Dryden Press.

IMP Group, (1982), *International Marketing and Purchasing of Industrial Goods : An Interaction Approach*, New York, Editor Hakan.

Iteanu, O., (1996), *Internet et le droit : aspects juridiques du commerce électronique*, Paris, Eyrolles.

Johnston, W.J., (1981), *Patterns in Industrial Buying Behavior*, New York, Praeger.

Kapferer, J-N. et Laurent G., (1992), *La sensibilité aux marques*, Paris, Éditions d'Organisation.

Kapferer, J-N. et Thoenig J-C., (1989), *La marque : nouveaux enjeux, nouvelles perspectives*, Paris, McGraw-Hill.

Kapferer, J-N., (1995), *La marque, capital de l'entreprise*, 2ème édition, Paris, Éditions d'Organisation.

Keegan, De Leersnyder, (1994), *Marketing sans frontières*, Paris, InterÉditions.

Keegan, W.J., (1995), *Global Marketing Management*, Englewoods Cliffs, N.J., Prentice-Hall,

Kotler, P. et Dubois B., (1997), *Marketing Management*, 9ème édition, Paris, Publi-Union.

Lambin, J-J., (1986), *Le marketing stratégique*, Paris, McGraw-Hill.

Laurent, F., (1991), *Valoriser votre communication :média planning, presse et climats de lecture*, Paris, Éditions d'Organisation.

Le Men, Y., (1990), *Pratique du marketing direct*, Paris, Dunod.

Lebahar, J-C., (1994), *Le design industriel, sémiologie de la séduction et code de la matière*, Paris, Parenthèses.

Leenders, M. R. et Blenkhorn, D. L., (1988), *Reverse Marketing, The New Buyer Relationship*, New York, Free Press.

Lehu, J-M., (1997), *Praximarket, Les 1000 mots-clés pour maîtriser le marketing*, Paris, Jean-Pierre de Monza.

Lendrevie, J. et Lindon, D., (1997), *Mercator*, 5ème édition, Paris, Dalloz.

Levitt, Th., (1965), *Industrial Purchasing Behavior, A Study of Communication Effects*, Boston, Harvard University.

Libaert, T., (1992), *La communication verte : l'écologie au service de l'entreprise*, Paris, Liaisons.

Lindon, D., (1991), *Le marketing*, Paris, Nathan.

Longatte, J., (1993), *Marketing industriel : de la stratégie à l'opérationnel*, Paris, Eska.

Macrae, Ch., (1992), *World Class Brands*, Reading, MA, Addison-Wesley Publishing.

Mahin, P.W., (1991), *Business to Business Marketing*, Needham Heights, Allyn and Bacon.

Malaval, Ph., (1996), *Marketing Business to Business*, Paris, Publi-Union.

Malaval, Ph., (1998), *Stratégie et Gestion de la Marque Industrielle*, Paris, Publi-Union.

Malaval, Ph., (1999), *L'essentiel du Marketing Business to Business*, Paris, Publi-Union.

Malaval, Ph., (2000), *Marketing, facteur de développement*, Paris, L'Harmattan.

Marion, G., (1989), *Les images de l'entreprise*, Paris, Éditions d'Organisation.

Martin, C., (1990), *Le comportement du consommateur*, Paris, Dalloz.

Martin, S. et Védrine, J-P., (1993), *Marketing, Les concepts-clés*, Paris, Éditions d'Organisation Université.

Michel, D., Salle, R. et Valla, J-P., (1996), *Marketing industriel, stratégies et mise en œuvre*, Paris, Economica, Collection Gestion.

Millier, P., (1993), *Le marketing des produits high-tech*, Paris, Éditions d'Organisation.

Morgan, G., (1989), *Images de l'organisation*, Paris, Eska.

Morrill, J.E., (1971), *How Advertising Works in Today's Market Place : The Morrill Study*, New York, McGraw-Hill.

Mucchielli, R., (1972), *Opinions et changement d'opinion*, Paris, ESF.

Murphy, J.M., (1990), *Brand Strategy*, Cambridge, Director Books.

Nemarq, A., (1981), *Comment attaquer les marchés internationaux de biens d'équipement*, Paris, Masson.

Nicosia, F.M., (1966), *Consumer Decision Processes*, Englewood Cliffs, NJ, Prentice Hall.

Olins, W., (1991), *Identité d'entreprise : pour rendre la stratégie d'entreprise visible*, Paris, InterÉditions.

Osborn, A., (1971), *L'imagination constructive*, Paris, Dunod.

Pache, G., (1994), *La logistique : enjeux stratégiques*, Paris, Vuibert.

Parkinson, S.T. et Baker, M.J., (1986), *Organizational Buying Behavior*, Londres, The Macmillan Press.

Patti, C.H. et Frazer C.F., (1989), *Advertising A Decision-Making Approach*, Chicago, The Dryden Press.

Péninou, G., (1972), *Intelligence de la publicité*, Paris, Robert Laffont.

Perrotin, R. et Heusschen, P., (1995), *Acheter avec profit*, 2ème édition, Paris, Éditions d'Organisation.

Perrotin, R. et Louberu, J-M., (1996), *Nouvelles stratégies d'achat : sous-traitance, coopération, partenariat ?*, Paris, Éditions d'Organisation.

Perrotin, R., (1995), *Le marketing achats*, 3ème édition, Paris, Éditions d'Organisation.

Petrov, J., (1993), *Comportement du consommateur et marketing*, Sainte-Foy, Éditions de l'Université Laval.

Pras, B. et Tarondeau, J-C., (1981), *Comportement de l'acheteur*, Paris, Sirey, Collection Administration des Entreprises.

Quarante, D., (1994), *Éléments de design industriel*, Paris, Polytechnica.

Reeder, R. R., Brierty, E. G. et Reeder, B. H., (1991), *Industrial Marketing, Analysis, Planning and Control*, 2ème édition, Englewood Cliffs, N.J, Prentice Hall.

Rège, P., (1989), *À vos marques*, Lausanne, Fabre.

Regouby, R., (1988), *La communication globale, Comment construire le capital image de l'entreprise*, Paris, Éditions d'Organisation.

Ries A. et Trout, J., (1986), *Le positionnement*, Paris, McGraw-Hill.

Robinson, P.J., Faris, C.W., et Wind Y., (1967), *Industrial Buying and Creative Marketing*, Boston, Allyn and Bacon, Inc.

Ronin, Y., Perret J. et Cauzard, D., (1993), *Le livre des marques*, Paris, Éditions du May.

Room, A. (1982), *Dictionnary of Trade Name Origins*, Londres, Routledge & Kegan P.Plc.

Runyon, K.E. et Stewart D., (1987), *Consumer Behavior*, 3ème édition, Columbus, Ohio, Merrill Publishing Company.

Salle, R. et Silvestre, H., (1992), *Vendre à l'industrie : approche stratégique de la relation business to business*, Paris, Liaisons.

Saporta, B., (1989), *Marketing Industriel*, Eyrolles.

Schulman D., (1991), *Le design industriel*, Paris, PUF.

Schwebig, P., (1988), *Les communications de l'entreprise : au-delà de l'image*, Paris, McGraw-Hill.

Semprini, A., (1992), *Le marketing de la marque, Approche sémiotique*, Paris, Liaisons.

Semprini, A., (1995), *La marque*, Paris, PUF, Que sais-je ?, n°2982.

Sherlock, (1992), *Le marketing business to business*, Paris, Dunod.

Siquier, P., (1990), *La communication business to business*, Paris, Dunod.

Szapiro, G., (1988), *Les 10 principes de la communication industrielle*, Paris, Éditions d'Organisation.

Szapiro, G., (1998), *Communication business to business, Les 7 pyramides de la réussite*, Paris, Éditions d'Organisation.

Tarondeau, J-C., (1978), *L'acte d'achat et la politique d'approvisionnement*, Paris, Éditions d'Organisation.

Thil, E. et Barroux, C., (1983), *Un pavé dans la marque*, Paris, Flammarion, Collection Enjeux pour Demain.

Union des Annonceurs et Piquet, S., (1985), *Sponsoring et mécénat*, Paris, Vuibert.

Vernhet, A., (1991), *La Graufesenque, céramiques gallo-romaines*, Éditions Du Beffroi.

Veys, P., (1991), *Le secteur tertiaire*, Paris, Vuibert.

Viardot, É., (1992), *Le marketing de la high-tech*, Paris, Publi-Union.

Villemus, P., (1996), *La fin des marques ?, Vers un retour au produit*, Paris, Éditions d'Organisation.

Watin-Augouard, J., (1997), *Le Dictionnaire des marques*, Paris, JV&DS-Sediac.

Watkins, T., (1986), *The Economics of the Brand*, Londres, McGraw-Hill.

Webster, F.E. et Wind Y., (1972), *Organizational Buying Behavior*, Englewood Cliffs, N.J., Prentice-Hall.

Webster, F.E., (1979), *Industrial Marketing Strategy*, New York, John Wiley & Sons.

Westphalen, M-H., (1989), *Communicator*, Paris, Dunod.

Williamson, O.E., (1975), *Markets and Hierarchies*, New York, Free Press.

Williamson, O.E., (1985), *The Economic Institutions of Capitalism-Firms, Markets, Relational Contracting*, New York, Free Press.

Wind, Y., (1982), *Product Policy : Concepts, Methods and Strategy*, Reading Mass, Addison-Wesley.

Woodside, A.et Vyas N., (1984), *Industrial Purchasing Strategies*, New York, Lexington Books.

Zeyl, A. et Dayan, A., (1995), *Force de vente : Direction, organisation, gestion*, Paris, Éditions d'Organisation.

SPECIALIZED JOURNALS AND TRADE PRESS

Actes de l'AFM (Association Française de Marketing)

Adetem

Advances in Consumer Research

Advertising Age

British Journal of Management

Business Marketing

Business Weeks

California Management Review

Communication CB News

Courrier International

Décisions Marketing

Documentation Française (La)

Échos (Les)

Encyclopédie du Marketing

Enjeux Les Échos

Essentiel du Management (L')

European Business

European Journal of Marketing

European Journal of Purchasing and Supply Management

European Management Review

Exhibitor

Expansion (L')

Expression d'Entreprise (L')
Figaro Économie (Le)
Financial Times
Génie Industriel
Gestion 2000
Harvard Business Review
Harvard L'Expansion
Industrial Marketing
Industrial Marketing Management
Industrial Relations Journal
Industry Week
Institut du Commerce et de la Consommation
International Business Review
International Journal of Advertising
International Journal of Purchasing and Materials
  Management
International Journal of Research in Marketing
International Marketing Review
Journal du Négociant (Le)
Journal of Advertising
Journal of Advertising Research
Journal of Business and Industrial Marketing
Journal of Business Research
Journal of Business to Business Marketing
Journal of Communication
Journal of Consumer Marketing
Journal of Consumer Research
Journal of International Marketing
Journal of Marketing
Journal of Marketing Communications
Journal of Marketing Research
Journal of Personal Selling and Sales Management
Journal of Product and Brand Management
Journal of Product Innovation Management
Journal of Professional Services Marketing
Journal of Purchasing
Journal of Purchasing and Materials Management

Journal of Quality Management
Journal of Strategic Marketing
Libre Service Actualités
Logistiques Magazine
Management Decision
Management International Review
Management Review
Marketing Magazine
Marketing Management
Marketing Mix / Marketing Vente
Marketing News
Marketing Research
Marketing Science
Médias
Monde (Le)
Moniteur (Le)
Personnel Psychology
Point (Le)
Points de Vente
Qualitique
Recherche et Applications en Marketing
Research in International Marketing
Research in Marketing
Revue de Marques (La)
Revue des Acheteurs
Revue Française de Gestion
Revue Française du Marketing
Revue Internationale de l'Achat
Sales and Marketing Management
Small Business Report
Stratégies
The Total Quality Review
Trade Show Bureau
Usine Nouvelle (L')
Vie Française (La)
Wall Street Journal

Subject Index

Index of Brands and Companies